Objectives and Methods

for

Secondary Teaching

WALTER D. PIERCE

MICHAEL A. LORBER

Illinois State University

PRENTICE-HALL, INC., *Englewood Cliffs, New Jersey* 07632

Library of Congress Cataloging in Publication Data

PIERCE, WALTER D (date)
  Objectives and methods for secondary teaching.

  Includes bibliographies and index.
  1. High school teaching.   I. Lorber, Michael A.,
(date) joint author.   II. Title.
LB1737.A3P55   373.1'1'02   76-26662
ISBN 0-13-628958-4

To our wives, Pam and Ellen,
whose patience is infinite

©1977 by Prentice-Hall, Inc.,
Englewood Cliffs, New Jersey 07632

Printed in the United States of America

10   9   8   7   6   5   4   3   2   1

PRENTICE-HALL INTERNATIONAL, INC., *London*
PRENTICE-HALL OF AUSTRALIA PTY. LIMITED, *Sydney*
PRENTICE-HALL OF CANADA, LTD., *Toronto*
PRENTICE-HALL OF INDIA PRIVATE LIMITED, *New Delhi*
PRENTICE-HALL OF JAPAN, INC., *Tokyo*
PRENTICE-HALL OF SOUTHEAST ASIA PTE. LTD., *Singapore*
WHITEHALL BOOKS LIMITED, *Wellington, New Zealand*

Contents

Preface

Many educators have come to realize that a potential solution to several pervasive needs in education today can be found in competency-based education. In their attempts to make the transition from the traditional approaches commonly used in teacher education to those used in competency-based education, teacher educators and students often find themselves attempting to use a basic secondary-education methods text that emphasizes the teaching *process* with a supplementary paperback that focuses on the teaching *product*.

This text is designed to include the elements commonly found in secondary methods texts, but it is written with an internal consistency that agrees with and actively incorporates fundamental principles espoused by the competency-based education movement. It therefore includes such things as sample precise instructional objectives for the users of this book at the beginning of each chapter (other objectives can be built by the reader as his or her needs dictate), model self-instructional packages, and a basic schematic model for understanding competency-based education as it influences the practicing teacher. In addition, practical matters, such as the teacher's role in discipline and an approach to continuous self-improvement, are included, with emphasis on aspects relating to competency-based education.

Another unique feature of this book is a new approach to classifying objectives in the affective domain, which is useful in a practical approach because it assists in solving the teacher's often-felt dilemma when dealing with affective domain objectives. The relationship between the cognitive domain and affective domain is discussed in a way so as to make affective domain objectives more useful.

This book was made possible through the assistance of many people. Specifically, we wish to thank Dr. Charles Gray for his efforts with the affective domain chapter; Dr. Leo Eastman, who foresaw the development of competency-based education and proceeded in that direction early in the movement; and Dr. Albert Upton, whose patience in explaining what should be obvious is limitless. Finally, we thank the Professional Sequence staff at Illinois State University for their many ideas and contributions.

W.D.P. / M.A.L.

1

A Theoretical Foundation For Instruction

Among the most intriguing questions confronting the educator bent upon improvement is where to start. One could focus first on the processes within the classroom and the transactions between pupil and teacher, or on the rationale behind any particular educational endeavor. After careful consideration of various starting points, however, it becomes apparent that the components of any logical instructional process are intwined and inseparable. Hence, one starting point that makes good sense is to attempt to conceptualize a complete process initially and subsequently to examine its parts in relation to the whole.

The procedure most often used in this regard is to focus initial and continued attention on the activities involved in teaching-learning situations. Concern about instructional activities not only dominates most texts dealing with education, it frequently dominates everyday discussions among teachers. It is not uncommon, for example, for students to hear one teacher ask another, "What are you doing in class today?" The question seems perfectly appropriate to students because when they get home and their parents inquire about school, their parents are likely to approach the matter in exactly the same way, i.e.; "What did you do in school today?"

A more appropriate question, however, would be, "What will your students be able to do after instruction that they were unable to do prior to instruction?" But this question is not usually addressed. Many students and teachers seem to accept the idea that activities such as talking about the economy or going on a field trip are of prime importance in and of themselves. The fact that they are vehicles by which skills and information are acquired is usually overlooked. This is not to say that instructional activities are not important; a major portion of this book is devoted to helping teachers improve learning activities. What is even more important, however, is understanding how to select particular activities and how the activities can be made into an effective instructional program. This understanding can be facilitated by an exploration of a theoretical foundation for instruction, and it is the function of this chapter to provide an overview of the theoretical model discussed in the remaining chapters of this text.

OBJECTIVES

The student will:

1. When given a blank schematic of the Logical Instructional Model, label each stage in writing and without error. (Knowledge)
2. Explain orally the function of each stage of the Logical Instructional Model and its relationship to the other stages. (Comprehension)
3. Observe a one-hour lesson and specify, in writing, which stages of the Logical Instructional Model were manifested in the lesson and which specific activities support those assessments. (Analysis)
4. Design a unique schematic that depicts the educational process and defend the logic of the model by explaining, in less than three pages, the interrelationships of its stages. (Synthesis)

FOUR-STAGE MODELS OF INSTRUCTION

In recent years a number of educators have developed models of instruction that consist of four basic elements: (1) preparation of precise instructional objectives: (2) preassessment of students to determine their abilities relative to the objectives: (3) instructional activities to insure achievement of the objectives: and (4) evaluation to determine whether students are able to achieve the objectives.

In 1970 Popham and Baker in *Systematic Instruction,*[1] and Kibler, Barker, and Miles, in *Behavioral Objectives and Instruction,*[2] depicted these

---

[1] James Popham and Eva Baker, *Systematic Instruction* (Englewood Cliffs, N.J.: Prentice-Hall, 1970), pp. 13 and 18.

[2] Robert J. Kibler, Larry L. Barker, and David T. Miles, *Behavioral Objectives and Instruction* (Boston: Allyn & Bacon, 1970), p.3.

four stages in schematic diagrams. Popham and Baker used the diagram in Figure 1 to show the model and its self-correcting features.

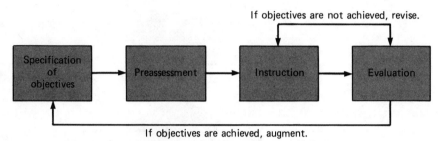

FIGURE 1   A Goal-referenced Instructional Model with Courses of Action
Dictated by Evaluation of Results

The diagram by Kibler, Barker, and Miles is very similar. Using the title "General Model of Instruction" and somewhat different labels, they included a "Feedback Loop" to examine the first three stages when such an examination was indicated by the results of the evaluation. The "General Model of Instruction" is diagrammed in Figure 2.

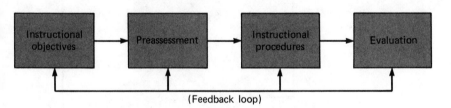

FIGURE 2   A General Model of Instruction

As basic and revealing as they are, both schematics leave a number of questions unanswered. Both, for example, imply that instruction must follow preassessment. This ignores those instances in which preassessment indicates that students already possess the competencies sought. In the model diagrammed in Figure 1 it is assumed that if the objectives are not achieved the fault lies in the instruction. Although this point is taken up in accompanying materials, the model itself could be interpreted as not considering those instances in which students enter the class without the beginning competencies necessary for success. The model diagrammed in Figure 2 carries a number of implications in the "Feedback Loop," but if students are unable to achieve the objectives no specific course of action is implied other than a general reassessment of each and every stage of the model. A more precise and detailed model might be even more helpful.

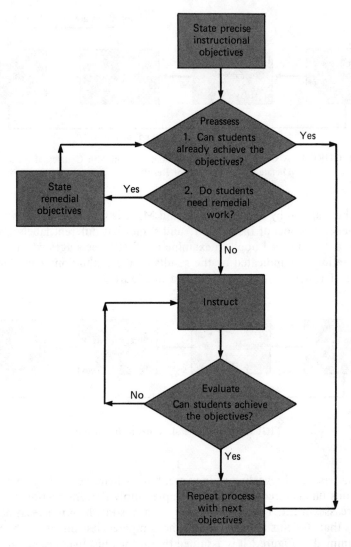

FIGURE 3   The Logical Instructional Model

A LOGICAL INSTRUCTIONAL MODEL (LIM)

The Logical Instructional Model, diagrammed in Figure 3, builds upon the excellent work already done by Popham and Baker, and by Kibler, Barker, and Miles. It is an attempt to diagram schematically a theoretical foundation for the instructional process that is more complete and more self-explanatory than preceding models. The remainder of this chapter is devoted to providing an overview of this model, and the following chapters are largely devoted to building the understandings and skills necessary to making the model a viable and sound basis for instruction.

State Precise Instructional Objectives

Although it may sound like a contradiction in terms, the place to begin planning an instructional procedure is with the instructional results. The first and most important point to be considered is *what students should be able to do after instruction*. Making this decision is the single most complex and difficult step in planning for instruction.

In every community there are political, sociological, psychological, practical, and subject-matter considerations that must be taken into account when curricula are being built and objectives decided upon. What individual teachers must do is sort out the various factors, classify them into a priority (or pressure) order, and use them to assist in the selection or writing of precise instructional objectives that will satisfy students, parents, administrators, boards of education, and themselves. This is no simple task, especially considering that most teachers have had little, if any, formal training in the writing of precise instructional objectives.

School systems throughout the country are going about the task of acquiring precise instructional objectives in a variety of ways. Some, for example, are purchasing compilations of objectives and asking their teachers to choose and alter objectives rather than write them originally. Other school systems are asking teachers to write objectives for their own classes, while still others are organizing teachers according to subject matter or grade levels and asking them to write objectives on a collective basis.

Below are specific, but typical, kinds of questions teachers must ask themselves as they begin to focus on their objectives.

1. Will the objectives assist in satisfying student needs?
2. Can the students attain the objectives?
3. Are the objectives worthy of attainment?
4. Do the objectives lead to a series of increasingly more important objectives?
5. Are the objectives compatible with the overall goals of the community and school?
6. Are the objectives relevant and reflective of social and cultural realities?
7. Are the necessary human, physical, and financial resources available?
8. Have ideas for objectives been considered from sources such as students and parents?

In addition to being able to justify the inclusion of each objective, the teacher must phrase each so that it conveys the exact instructional intent. At the very least, each objective should specify exactly what each student is to be able to do at the end of the instruction, and how well he or she must do it. In addition, most objectives will need some clarification of the exact conditions under which the specific competency will be demonstrated.

Obviously the stating of precise instructional objectives is a thought-provoking and time-consuming task, but since every other part of the instructional process depends directly on the objectives, they are all-important. If the objectives are poor the rest of the instructional process is likely to be poor also, but if the objectives are well stated, include an observable behavior, and are measurable, then the instructional process is more likely to be equally strong.

Preassess

Once the precise instructional objectives have been explained to the students, the teacher's next step should be to preassess students' abilities. Since the teacher is seeking to compare the abilities students possess prior to instruction with those they will need in order to demonstrate the specified competencies, the preassessment often consists of an equivalent form of the final evaluation instrument. Properly conducted preassessments can yield a great deal of valuable information, but they primarily provide data related to two specific questions.

The first question is: "Do students already possess the specified competencies?" In some instances it might happen that students already possess the skills and /or information necessary to demonstrate the stated competencies. In these cases it would be pointless to proceed with the planned instruction because it is not needed and would only bore the students. Once the determination is made that students can, in fact, perform as required, they may immediately move to new objectives.

The second question is: "Do students need remedial work?" In some instances preassessment might reveal that students lack the basic skills and /or information they need to begin working toward achievement of the stated objectives. The objectives, for example, might call for students to utilize the multiplication tables, but this skill might not be among the students' current abilities. In these cases the teacher has no logical alternative but to state remedial objectives that will provide students with the background necessary for further progress, and to go through the instructional model with these alternate objectives as the starting point. Students are then more likely to profit from instruction relating to the original objectives.

It is unfortunate when students need remediation because less time is then available for work toward the original objectives. In most cases, however, students will have the background necessary for further instruction and the teacher may need to provide only a brief review of background material. It is obviously crucial to determine, as accurately as possible, if students do need remediation.

The facts preassessing reveals about students may indicate that a teacher must go back and provide instruction other than that for which he or she is specifically responsible, or that the teacher must skip over instruction that has been carefully and painstakingly planned. This may explain why many teachers simply do not preassess their students; which, in turn, may account for a good deal of the frustration and boredom of which many students complain.

Instruct

By and large, teachers are paid to instruct students. The skill with which instruction is carried out depends largely on the abilities of the teacher, but there are innumerable procedures for improving instruction. Some procedures concern themselves with specific kinds of instructional activities and ways of making them more interesting and therefore more effective. Other procedures focus on basic principles of learning. In this text, specific activities and principles are both explored, and it is at the risk of redundancy (but with the hope that if they are reviewed they may be seen in a new perspective) that a few basic principles are included here. Other collections of such principles can be found in a wide variety of sources from Kibler, Barker, and Miles,[3] to the Wisconsin State Department of Public Instruction.[4]

1. *Students differ in ability and rate of learning just as they differ in more observable characteristics such as height, weight, and appearance.* Not only must teachers be aware of such differences, they must make each student aware of his or her own learning characteristics.

Teachers need to help individual students overcome their weaknesses and increase their self-esteem by emphasizing their strengths. Because the weaknesses are so obvious and easy to pinpoint, many times teachers forget about the need to emphasize strengths, and they are thus less successful than they might be. Students will not respond as fully if they feel their weaknesses will continually be exposed. Provisions for fast learners to remain interested and occupied with enrichment material, and for slow learners to obtain the help they need to continue learning are necessary, although sometimes difficult to achieve in every classroom.

[3]Kibler, Barker, and Miles, *Behavioral Objectives,* pp. 7-9.
[4]See "Learning Principles, Wisconsin State Department of Public Instruction" in Leonard Clark, ed., *Strategies and Tactics in Secondary School Teaching* (Toronto: Macmillan, 1968), pp. 100-107.

2. *Principles of retention and practice govern learning.* There are certain psychological principles that, when properly applied, can assist students in the acquisition and use of information.

- a. Retention of information is increased if the information has meaning to the student.
- b. When teaching principles and abstractions for later application, the teacher can increase students' retention by using examples and illustrations.
- c. After an initial teacher presentation, the acts of the students are more important than the acts of the teacher. The most obvious way for a student to acquire a particular skill is to practice it.
- d. A number of short practice sessions distributed over a longer period of time generally results in better retention of the information or skill than a few long practice sessions grouped closely together.

3. *Prior to beginning instruction teachers should determine which skills students must acquire in order to achieve the objectives.* Assuming students have the prerequisite skills, the links between the skills to be acquired and those already acquired need to be clearly established in order to assure students that their abilities are steadily being increased, expanded, and strengthened. If students perceive the instruction as leading to goals they consider valid and important, they will participate actively in the activities and facilitate their own learning.

4. *Lack of student desire to learn (motivation) insures instructional failure.* It is generally accepted that *intrinsic* motivation (a desire to learn that comes from within the student) is far superior to *extrinsic* motivation (a desire to learn that is generated by external pressure—either positive or negative). When a student arrives at a class without a built-in desire to learn, however, it becomes the responsibility of the teacher to foster such a desire in the student. The following are some points teachers should keep in mind concerning motivation.

- a. If a student perceives the learning as fulfilling a need, he or she is more likely to be interested in engaging in that learning.
- b. If students are permitted to help select objectives and activities they tend to be more committed to the achievement of the objectives and the success of the activities.
- c. If a student can see visible progress toward a goal (positive feedback), motivation can be initiated and maintained.
- d. The influence of peers and their attitudes toward learning can have tremendous influence of the success of the instruction. Trying to motivate a single student without considering the attitudes of his or her friends may be futile.
- e. Competition can be an effective source of motivation if the student sees a chance to win, but either winning or losing too frequently reduces the effectiveness of competition.

f. When teachers use many extrinsic rewards to build motivation, they must be alert to the problem of students working for the rewards rather than to achieve the instructional objectives. The ends can become muddled.

5. *The proper organization of information into a knowledge structure will facilitate learning.* Most people have had at least one or two teachers who knew a great deal about their subject matter but who were not effective teachers. It is likely that many of these teachers' problems stemmed from their inability to organize their information into a pattern that made sense to their students. The arrangement of information into a hierarchical form, such as from simple concepts to complex ones, makes the information more digestible for students and speeds learning.

6. *Students will achieve competencies more quickly if models of the desired skills or products are supplied early in the instructional process.*

The skills of the classroom teacher are the keys to increasing learning. Chapter 6 of this book is designed to assist teachers in increasing their skills in a variety of instructional procedures. These skills can be learned, and their acquisition is important to all teachers.

Evaluate

The purpose of instruction is to help students acquire the knowledge and skills they need to achieve the specified competencies. It makes sense, then, to follow instruction with evaluation. There are, however, a number of more specific reasons to evaluate the progress of students. One reason to evaluate, for example, is to help teachers determine the effectiveness of particular instructional activities. If students are unable to demonstrate achievement of specified objectives after engaging in what the teacher thought would be helpful instructional activities, those activities obviously did not meet the teacher's expectations. The students' performance will provide the kind of data the teacher will need to justify modifying or eliminating that particular activity.

Evaluations are also used as part of the basis for the making of long-range plans by students and parents. The results of teacher-made tests and a wide variety of standardized tests are usually taken into consideration whenever students begin thinking about going to college or getting a job, and these forms of evaluation frequently have great influence on the final decision.

The single most important reason to engage in the evaluation of students' progress is, of course, to determine whether each student can demonstrate certain competencies. To make this determination, teachers have traditionally relied heavily on paper and pencil tests such as objective and essay tests. With the increased interest in precise instructional objectives, however, teachers are finding that there are other means of evaluating students' accomplishments that reflect instructional intents better. Today instead of having students demonstrate competence solely by passing tests, more and more teachers are writing objectives that call on students to demonstrate alternate skills more akin to those needed in life outside of the school setting.

If, at the evaluation stage, students cannot achieve the specified objectives, there should be little need for the teacher to reassess each stage of the entire instructional procedure, since the Logical Instructional Model provides specific checks as each stage is encountered. If students cannot achieve the objectives at this point, the problem most likely resides in the instruction stage. It could be that the instructional procedures were inadequate or that insufficient time was expended, but in any event the problem should be solvable with additional, and perhaps alternate kinds of, instruction. It would not be appropriate at this point to blame the objective or the preassessment for the students' inability to demonstrate the specified competency.

With practice, the steps described in the Logical Instructional Model will result in student achievement of specified objectives and may be repeated with successive sets of objectives.

EXTENT OF USE OF THE LOGICAL INSTRUCTIONAL MODEL

This discussion of the Logical Instructional Model and the place of precise instructional objectives within that model should not lead the reader to presume that the model or precise instructional objectives are meant to be all-inclusive. Teachers are hired to help students learn and there are many learning experiences that help students learn but that do not lend themselves to implementation via the LIM or to definition in precise terms. It would be foolish to advocate the elimination of all such activities and to rely solely upon the LIM. Instead, it is suggested that prospective teachers view the LIM and the use of precise instructional objectives as a means of establishing the framework of an instructional program. The objectives that are stated and discussed with students are those that are most basic and most essential to a particular course of study. Other objectives will certainly be achieved by students along the way, but the crucial ones will have been specified in very precise terms.

The same line of reasoning pertains to utilization of the LIM. The LIM is a workable and efficient approach to instruction, but it is not necessarily the best approach to use in every single instance of instruction. There will be many times when common sense dictates some instructional approach other than the LIM, and in such instances deviation from the model is quite appropriate. By and large teachers will find that everyday instruction will proceed more smoothly if the steps in the LIM are followed, but some circumstances may require different steps and, provided they are effective in helping students learn, they can, and should, augment the systematic process inherent in the model.

SUMMARY

This chapter has presented three instructional models, all based on the same general principles. The last model, the Logical Instructional Model, is more detailed than its predecessors and is examined most fully.

The first step of the Logical Instructional Model is to state precise instructional objectives. The purpose of these objectives is to specify, in terms that are both observable and measurable, those minimal things students will be able to do after instruction.

The second step of the LIM is to preassess students' abilities with respect to the abilities required for achievement of the objectives. Two specific questions are answered via the preassessment and two specific courses of action delineated. The first question is whether or not students can already achieve the objectives. In some cases students may already possess the needed skills and/or information and have no need of further instruction. In these cases the students can simply move on to the next objectives. The second question is whether or not remediation is needed. In a few instances students may not have acquired the beginning competencies required for successful progress. In these cases the teacher must write remedial objectives and provide the necessary background.

The next step in the LIM is the providing of needed instruction. The purpose of the instruction is to enable students to achieve the stated objectives.

The last step in the LIM is to evaluate. Here the teacher engages in evaluations for a number of reasons, the most important of which is to determine whether students have achieved the stated objectives. If they have, the next step is to repeat the process with a new set of objectives. If they have not achieved the objective, the problem will have been narrowed to the instruction stage and the teacher can determine what additional instruction is necessary.

The chapter has presented a model of an instructional procedure. The subsequent chapters will explore some of the reasons that prompted its development and expand upon each stage of the model.

SELECTED READINGS

DAVIES, IVOR, *Competency Based Learning: Technology, Management and Design*. New York: McGraw Hill, 1973.

KIBLER, ROBERT J., DONALD J. CEGOLA, LARRY L. BARKER, and DAVID T. MILES. *Objectives for Instruction and Evaluation*, Boston: Allyn & Bacon, 1974.

MAGER, ROBERT R., and J. McCANN, *Learner-Controlled Instruction*. Palo Alto, Calif.: Varian Associates, 1961.

POPHAM, JAMES, and EVA BAKER, *Systematic Instruction*. Englewood Cliffs, N.J.: Prentice-Hall, 1970.

2

Objectives, Aims, Purposes, Goals

what are we really after?

One of the most important steps in a viable teaching-learning process is the specification of instructional objectives. For some time educators have been concerned with the formulation of instructional objectives, but consensus has still not been reached as to the form or content of such objectives. One need only look at the objectives written in different secondary schools in order to confirm a lack of consensus concerning goals. The ever-increasing range of courses, services, and activities housed in public schools is testimony that disagreement about the specific objectives of the public schools is widespread.

This chapter will trace the development of educational "goals" through the years and examine a number of the more important attempts by educators to establish goals. This background information is intended to help prospective teachers understand how and why the objectives stated by many typical schools came into being. This understanding, in turn, sheds light on the process by which these objectives may be improved.

OBJECTIVES:

The student will:

1. Write the names of at least three committees that have structured aims for secondary schools. (Knowledge)
2. Explain in his or her own words the central themes that the three cited committees utilized in their construction of aims. (Comprehension)
3. Distinguish, and describe in a paper of no more than three pages, at least two similarities and two differences between each of three sets of aims for the American secondary school. (Analysis)
4. Design, organize, and write a set of at least four aims for the American secondary school, giving rationales for each aim included, and organize these rationales into a series of criteria for judging secondary-school aims. (Synthesis)
5. When presented with a set of secondary school aims, apply his or her own criteria to the given aims, judge them as worthy or unworthy, and provide a rationale for each judgment. (Evaluation)

EDUCATIONAL GOALS

Early Educational Goals

During prehistoric times it can be assumed that education consisted of the young imitating their elders. Even if man had wanted to attempt formal education, there would have been little need to specify the goal of this instruction because it was obvious: survival. The penalty for failure to learn one's "lessons" could be early death.

Formal education itself probably began at the point in time when the division of labor made it possible for some individuals to engage in activities other than hunting, fishing, and gathering. It is likely that with the rise of a priest class and the training of future priests, formal education experienced its genesis.

During the Egyptian period the priest class managed whatever formal education existed (mostly the training of more priests and scribes), and the general population had little to gain from the goals of that education. For the vast majority of youngsters during ancient Egyptian times, education involved an informal apprenticeship process. Parents could apprentice a son with the "educational goal" in mind that the son would become a skilled workman. If this goal was not achieved, it is likely that parents soon stopped sending their sons to that particular master. Girls were taught homemaking skills in their homes but were not included in the "formal" education afforded the boys.

The parallel between popular interest in educational goals and popular participation in education can be illustrated in the case of the Hebrews. The Hebrews had a religious commitment to education in that each boy was to be taught the *Torah* (the five books of Moses). All Hebrew men were expected to help see that the goal was achieved and the rabbis (teachers) were elevated to the highest social position in recognition of their efforts in this direction.

Greek and Roman education represented a different approach. If one could not afford a tutor for one's child, there were little chance for formal education in either ancient Greece or ancient Rome. Education among the aristocracy was of high caliber, but there was little interest in goals for education because education itself became the goal. No formal education for practical skills was necessary in aristocratic education because all manual work was done by the lower classes. In this environment, the study of music, mathematics, and rhetoric flourished, but there was no worry as to whether or not what was being learned was of immediate and practical value; this was simply not a point of concern.

During the Middle Ages the dichotomy between education for the aristocracy and education for the masses grew. Sons of wealthy families spent their time learning about grammar, rhetoric, and dialectic (the trivium), and arithmetic, geometry, astronomy, and music (the quadrivium). These subjects became the seven liberal arts, and their pursuit, by way of formal education, was limited to "gentlemen." As for the masses a formal apprenticeship program came into existence during the Middle Ages and attention to educational "goals" was manifested in the working of the law of supply and demand: The better a skilled craftsman was at achieving the goal of training other capable craftsmen, the more business he received.

The operation of early universities was also geared to the law of supply and demand with respect to goals. The compensation of teachers at these institutions depended upon the schools' ability to achieve goals deemed important by enough students to support the teachers financially. Precise goals became relevant during the nineteenth century when mass education began to take hold and, even more important, when people began to support education with public funds.

Today's Needs

When formal education involved a small percentage of the total population, there was little problem with its concern for matters that had little or no practical value. If scholars wanted to debate the question of how many fairies could dance on the head of a pin, it was completely acceptable; the work of the world would still get done. Today's world is rather different. Since the founding of the first public secondary school in Boston in 1821, the

United States has had publicly-supported secondary schools, and a high percentage of our current teenage population attends these schools. In this kind of situation, the broadening of mental horizons by the study of academic subjects is not sufficient. Taxpayers are demanding that high school graduates acquire marketable skills so they will not become burdens on society. Schools are being forced to assume not only their traditional roles, but also the roles once assumed by parents, craftsmen, and guilds. Furthermore, since the masses are now paying for this educational process, they want to know what they are getting for their money. They want educators to state their goals so that it can be seen whether or not those goals are being accomplished. The movement associated with this thrust is often referred to as *accountability*.

Looking at education in the past, it can be seen that one rather consistent, if nebulous, goal has been to pass down the cultural heritage. A look at mankind's attempts to avoid continually rediscovering the wheel leads one to the conclusion that people wanted their children to benefit from their experiences, to avoid making the same mistakes, and to have better life overall than they themselves had. There is, however, a basic dilemma built into this goal or hope, and the problem is now one of our most serious.

If the fact is accepted that the intellectual abilities, physical skills, and value structures of preceding generations form the substance of what the younger generation is to be taught, the implication must also be accepted that each generation attempts to make its successor as nearly like itself as possible. Proponents of this view might diagram the function of formal schooling as in Figure 4.

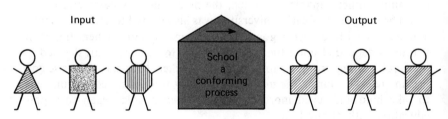

Input   Output

School
a
conforming
process

FIGURE 4

A shining example of the impact of this goal is the study of American history, which is mandated by almost all states in the Union. This particular course has traditionally been a curricular inclusion because many Americans have felt that youngsters should have a knowledge and appreciation of their country's past. If all students could learn similar things, they might all thus end up with similar attitudes.

The problem with this view of the school process is that as each succeeding generation learns of its past, it tends to reject much of what its predecessors held near and dear. Looking again at the requirement that all students study American history, it can be seen that although the original goal was to make Americans more alike in their knowledge and appreciation of their past, things are not working out quite as expected. Today students learn that while Washington championed freedom, he also kept slaves; that only some of the colonists supported the Revolution, while others were outright Tories, and still others were relatively neutral; that many Americans treated the Indians and the Mexicans rather shabbily; and that industralists were somewhat less than fair to their workers during the late 1800s and early 1900s. Each generation of graduating students is quite different as a result of formal schooling. Schools do change people, for better or for worse, but a more accurate diagram of formal schooling might well look like Figure 5.

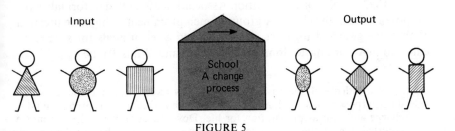

FIGURE 5

Two incompatible views of the function of education, one formal and one informal, are inherent in the foregoing. If the emphasis of education is to be on making people more alike, then goals for this end can be formulated and taxpayers can see if the goals are being accomplished. If the emphasis of education is to be on individuality, then goals for this end can be formulated and taxpayers can judge if these goals are being accomplished. Unfortunately, society has not taken a firm stand on what it wants its schools to do. In the United States, with a population of over 220 million, there are nearly as many different views of just what schools should be accomplishing. In an attempt to alienate no one, educators have avoided stating goals that can be closely scrutinized. This, in turn, has opened the door to charges of doing the wrong thing, and, conversely, of not doing anything at all. What attempts have been made to state educational goals? How did secondary education arrive at its present position?

ATTEMPTS TO DEVELOP AIMS

The change in the purposes of secondary education over the past two hundred years has been enormous. Education has moved from the colonial period, in which a selected few fortunates attended the *Latin Grammar School* solely in order to gain entry into a colonial college, to today's mammoth network of comprehensive and specialized secondary schools that covers the entire nation. These schools are designed to serve the entire U.S. adolescent population and they attempt to teach everything from how to drive a car and change a diaper to modern calculus. They are accused of not doing enough (why else was Russia first in space and not the United States?) and of doing too much (as in sex education).

Have people tried to define the purposes of the American secondary school throughout its history? The answer is yes, but with varying degrees of skill and success. Some of the efforts are described below.

The Committee of Ten

In 1893 the National Education Association attempted to formalize the purpose of the high school. A group of men prominent in higher education at the time gathered together and formalized a set of goals for secondary education. According to John S. Brubacher and Willis Rudy[1]

> They wrestled with the basic problem of how to articulate the college with a dual-purpose high school, a high school which had to serve as preparation for college and also as preparation for life. Down to 1893, when the committee reported, the prestige of the college preparatory function had predominated, enabling the colleges to dictate the high school curriculum. After the report of the committee, however, the high school came to enjoy a more independent position.

Four of the specific recommendations are cited as examples of the Committee of Ten's efforts:

1. That all pupils should pursue a given subject in the same way and to the same extent as long as they study it at all.
2. That every subject studied should cultivate the pupil's powers of observation, memory, expression, and reasoning.
3. That the function of the high schools should be to prepare pupils for the duties of life as well as to prepare them for college.
4. That colleges and scientific schools should accept any one of the courses of study as preparation for admission.[2]

[1]John S. Brubacher and Willis Rudy, *Higher Education in Transition* (New York and Evanston, Ill.: Harper & Row, 1958), pp. 241-242.
[2]*Report of the United States Commissioner of Education*, vol. 2, parts III and IV, 1892-1893, pp. 1474-75.

The Committee on College Entrance Requirements

In 1899 the Committee on College Entrance Requirements of the National Education Association reiterated a triple function of the secondary school:

1. Preparation for life.
2. Preparation of teachers for the common schools.
3. Preparation for college.[3]

That they additionally attempted to paint a more congenial educational picture by stating that programs should be flexible, have a variety of electives, and take into account the students' abilities, points up the NEA's growing concern for, and influence over, the conditions of learning.

The Commission on the Reorganization of Secondary Education

By 1913 the Commission on the Reorganization of Secondary Education, appointed by the NEA, recommended what was to become probably the most famous statement of the purposes of the high school. Labeled the "Seven Cardinal Principles of Secondary Education," these aims were memorized by countless numbers of prospective teachers as part of their preservice training. In a recent informal study[4] conducted and replicated six times, with separate groups of thirty to forty prospective teachers who attempted to construct their own set of aims for the high school, at least six of the original seven principles were *still* on those groups' final lists of worthwhile aims for today's youngsters. A summarized version of the "Seven Cardinal Principles" follows:[5]

1. *Health.* Good health habits need to be taught and encouraged by the school. The community and school should cooperate in fulfilling the health needs of all youngsters and adults.
2. *Command of Fundamental Processes.* The secondary school should accept a responsibility for continuing to teach and polish the basic tools of learning,

---

[3]*National Education Association Proceedings* (Washington D.C.: National Education Association, 1899), pp. 635-36.

[4]Walter D. Pierce, unpublished informal study of broad goal setting by college students, Illinois State University, 1972.

[5]*Cardinal Principles of Education*, United States Bureau of Education Bulletin no. 35 (1918), 5-10.

such as arithmetical computation, reading, and writing, that were begun in the elementary school.

3. *Worthy Home Membership.* Students' understanding of the inter-relationships of the family in order for the give-and-take to be a healthy, happy affair, should be advocated by the school. Proper adjustment as a family member will lead to proper acceptance of responsibility as a family leader in later life.

4. *Vocation.* The secondary school should develop an attitude in students that will lead to an appreciation for all vocations. The basic skills of a variety of vocations should be made available to students who have the need and /or desire for them.

5. *Citizenship.* A basic commitment to proper citizenship on the part of students needs to be fostered and strengthened during the adolescent years. The secondary school needs to assume this responsibility not only in the social sciences, where one would ordinarily assume it would be handled, but in all subjects.

6. *Proper Use of Leisure Time.* The student should be provided opportunities while in secondary school to expand the available possibilities for leisure time. The commission felt that leisure time properly used would enrich the total personality.

7. *Ethical Character.* The secondary school should organize its activities and personal relationships to reflect good ethical character, both to serve as an exemplar and to involve the student in a series of activities that will provide opportunities to make ethically correct decisions.

The Seven Cardinal Principles were an attempt by a group of educators to use the needs of society and the individual as a basis for describing what secondary schools should accomplish. Other attempts were subsequently made to identify the central goals of schooling, and a few of the most noteworthy are described below. Depending upon the prevailing issues of the particular time and place, the statements made by these groups show slight changes in emphasis and style. They are therefore best looked at in terms of the social situation in which they were articulated.

The American Youth Commission

By 1937 the country was deep in the Depression, and educators were looking at education in terms of how it could help students get and hold jobs. The principle of vocational preparation became predominant: "American youth need opportunity for economic independence. They need information on how to prepare for, find, and hold a satisfying job."[6]

---

[6]H. R. Douglass, *Secondary Education for Youth in Modern America* (Washington, D.C.: American Council on Education, 1937), p. 137.

The Educational Policies Commission

In 1938 the Educational Policies Commission set forth a series of goals arranged in four major divisions with subsections concerning "the educated man." The four main divisions included: (1) self-realization; (2) human relationships; (3) economic efficiency; and (4) civic responsibility. A typical goal format under the civic responsibility subsection was: "The educated person respects the law."[7]

The National Association of Secondary School Principals

After World War II a shift in priorities increased the emphasis on science. John S. Brubacher[8] credits Herbert Spencer with a large portion of the responsibility for this shift because of an essay of Spencer's that drew wide attention entitled "What Knowledge Is of Most Worth." Spencer's opinion was that in spite of the commonly held position that those things taught in the liberal studies are the most worthwhile, the priority should actually be on the practical, and he felt the knowledge of most practical worth was science. It is certain that the wartime development of radar, sonar, rockets, and atomic bombs did nothing to undermine this popular opinion.

In 1947, the National Association of Secondary School Principals delineated the "Imperative Needs of Youth." These goals repeated in essence the Seven Cardinal Principles, and added statements on appreciating aesthetics, becoming an intelligent consumer, and understanding the methods and influence of science. The thrust of the list of goals changed from a "command of fundamental processes," to an emphasis on rationality, clear expression of thoughts, and reading and listening with understanding.[9]

The Educational Policies Commission

In 1961 the Educational Policies Commission again set forth a series of goals for secondary schools. These goals, once again, caused a reassessment and restructuring of secondary schools. Without completely abandoning the

---

[7]Educational Policies Commission, *The Purpose of Education in American Democracy* (Washington D.C.: National Education Association, 1938), pp. 50, 72, 90, and 108.

[8]John S. Brubacher, *A History of the Problems of Education* (New York: McGraw-Hill, 1947), p. 16.

[9]*The Imperative Needs of Youth of Secondary School Age*, National Association of Secondary School Principals Bulletin no. 31, (March, 1947).

ideas embodied in the preceding statements of goals, the Educational Policies Commission emphasized the idea that the primary objective of education should be to improve the rational powers of students. The specific aims included in the older lists were reexamined in light of the goal of creating the rational person.[10]

THE EFFECT OF BROAD AIMS

When one sits back and contemplates the energy and effort expended to produce the above lists of aims, two specific questions come to mind: Of what value are these lists of broad aims, and what forces really influence the schools?

It is immediately obvious that in order for school goals to have effect, the goals must *reach the student*, which means it is ultimately up to the individual teacher to implement the goals. Does the publishing of these lists affect the teacher in the classroom? Probably not as much as one would like. Teachers, by and large, tend to teach not only the *way* they themselves were taught, but also *what* they themselves were taught. The rewording of a broad aim by a new commission in Washington will not necessarily bring about a major change in a tenth-grade English class in Skokie, Illinois.

What really influences a typical secondary school then? The most obvious answer is that when someone in a *position of power* perceives a needed change, he or she then goes about making it happen. A few hypothetical examples follow:

1. The PTA president thinks sex education is needed and influences a community action group to push for the adoption of a course. Pressure is exerted through appropriate channels until a course is adopted by the board.
2. In a new suburb the superintendent is able to get a bond issue passed for a new high school after several failures by promising the voters open classrooms and a modified schedule.
3. The Russians beat the United States in launching the first satellite. The schools are blamed for not teaching scientific know-how. Congress approves funds for improving the teaching of science, math, and foreign languages, and thousands of teachers are given additional training in these areas.
4. The black majority in a suburb of a large city picket and petition until courses in black studies are offered.

All of these situations can produce changes that influence the lives of students—perhaps profoundly; and yet, none of them is based directly on an

[10]*The Central Purpose of American Education* (Washington, D.C.: National Education Association, 1961).

overview of the broad aims described in any of the official lists surveyed above.

How does a math teacher go about, in his or her regular teaching capacity, emphasizing good health? Surely there are incidental moments of reinforcement, and he or she can function as an exemplar, but the goal of good health would be viewed by most teachers as one for another subject area such as physical education or home economics. If it is the case then that each broad aim will be taken care of by specific subject-matter areas, what subject will emphasize ethical character? Where will the children who are not going to take home economics learn about worthy family membership?

The problem is obvious: If broad aims are to be implemented, they must be translated into programs at the local level with specificity and vigor. Consider the following "Educational Philosophy," which was prepared for an accreditation visit by the staff at Downey Senior High School in Downey, California.[11]

> communicate (read, write, listen, speak, view) with precision and discrimination.
>
> understand the methods and applications of science (observe, experiment, record, analyze, predict) and the implications of scientific facts concerning the world of man.
>
> develop mathematic skills for practical operations and subsequent training.
>
> have historical perspective to understand the rights and duties in a democratic society and to be able to assume these responsibilities.
>
> develop the foundation skills and information that enable individuals to pursue successfully a trade or a profession either immediately or after further training.
>
> know how to purchase goods and services intelligently, with a proper understanding of our economic system.
>
> appreciate the significance of the family as the important unit of our society.
>
> develop and maintain good health.
>
> become aware of, and conform to, accepted moral values.
>
> appreciate the values of the arts, including literature, music and fine arts.
>
> use leisure time in constructive and socially desirable activities.
>
> make a realistic evaluation of their interests, aptitudes, and achievements.

These aims are worthwhile. They are commendable, and typical of broad goals used by thousands of high schools across the country. However, it is possible, and desirable, to effect a translation of such goals into precise objectives that will give specific directions for the accomplishment of those objectives. Why is this translation so seldom made? One can only surmise on the basis of an analysis of what is actually happening.

---

[11]*Accreditation Report from Downey Senior High School*, Downey Unified School District, Downey, Calif. (February, 1969), Appendix 4-1.

Education in America is built on a foundation of federal interest, state responsibility, and local control. When a prominent group such as the NEA or one of its subgroups voices a set of objectives for secondary schools, it is assumed by most local educators that these "experts" have researched the problem and speak from a position of knowledge. This knowledge, however, comes from the pooling of a variety of ideas, and the objectives thus generated are, of necessity, general guidelines suitable for use by almost all secondary schools in the United States. It has not been the intention of any of the national groups to prescribe instructional objectives for any particular school district because these groups are well aware of the wide variety of needs that exist. But because schools were not forced by law to have precise objectives or to rigorously monitor students' progress, they ignored this crucial responsibility altogether. They acted as though freedom to act responsibly was freedom to not act at all.

As a consequence of neglecting to focus on precise educational *outcomes*, schools have tended to justify their existence by focusing on the *process* by which students are educated. This focus of attention has often caused a misdirection in efforts to educate. Teachers, for example, are evaluated in terms of a series of political considerations, which include items such as "personal characteristics" and "maintenance of a neat classroom." Thus the emphasis is on the behavior of the teacher and how well he or she measures up to the conceptual model of the ideal teacher that the evaluator has in mind. Tragically, however, there are few evaluation forms with a section dealing with the *amount of learning* that is taking place as demonstrated by specific acts of the students. All too frequently no one asks, "What are students achieving?" The most important aspect of teaching—increasing the knowledge and skills of students—is usually neglected. Just as it does not make much sense for a law firm to employ a lawyer who persists in losing cases, it does not make much sense for schools to employ teachers who consistently fail to help students learn. Educators must be able to tell the taxpayers what the schools are *really* after and demonstrate to them that they *can* achieve their goals. Taxpayers demand accountability.

Schools continually receive broadly stated goals from national and state organizations. To be workable in any given classroom, however, these goals need to be reworded into precisely stated objectives. Unfortunately, many schools try to make minor wording changes instead of the major changes actually needed and thus end up with nebulous goals that make competence assessment all but impossible. If school administrators evaluate teachers solely on the basis of process considerations, ignoring product considerations (i.e., student growth), public education may lose the support of the taxpayers. Taxpayers want to know what they are getting for their money, and schools must be prepared to tell them. Parents may soon be asking teachers, "How do you *know* that my Johnny is developing an ethical character?" and "What *specific* things can my Mary do now that you have taught her about worthy home membership?"

What are the implications? The changes coming about now in education will continue and accelerate. When teachers pass each other in the hall, the kind of question they ask each other will become, "What will your students be able to do after today's instruction?" rather than the now-common question, "What are you going to be doing with your kids today?" While the second question may be more sociable, it avoids the real issue. Educators must define their purposes, goals, aims, objectives, and ends specifically and be able to tell the taxpayer what the students can accomplish as a result of schooling.

The teaching skills to be presented later in this book focus on those that are useful tools for enhancing learning. There is one tool, however, that is so basic and so useful that the following two chapters are devoted exclusively to its use. That tool is the precise instructional objective.

SUMMARY

Public education's penchant for failing to state any goals but very general ones grows out of the history of education, stretching back to prehistoric times when formal goals were unneeded. There seems to be a direct relationship between popular interest in educational goals and popular participation in education. Throughout biblical, Greek, Roman, medieval, and colonial times, when only a relatively few individuals received a formal education, the public was not concerned as to what the goals were because they were not directly involved.

In the course of the development of mass education, overall goals underwent a significant change. Instead of focusing only on matters of the mind, as more and more people began going to school, schools also began to focus on more practical matters. In addition, as education came to be publicly supported, the need for formal statement of goals became more acute. Educators now must decide, for example, if education is attempting to make students more like or more unlike each other. The goals educators espouse have to reflect their decision and must satisfy the people paying the bills.

In the United States a number of attempts (from the Committee of Ten in 1893, through the development of the Seven Cardinal Principles in 1913, to the Educational Policies Commission in 1961) have been made to formalize goals for secondary schools, but these broad goals were, necessarily, not specific enough to assist directly in the creation of proper educational experiences. The vacuum left by the failure of educators to specify their goals has been filled by people in positions of power who have perceived needs and wrought changes in particular schools. This trend has been obscured by educators who focus attention on the process of education rather than upon its outcomes.

Education cannot continue to avoid its responsibility to state precise goals. Hard economic facts of life mandate that educators be able to specify educational objectives so that their accomplishment is observable. Precision in generating educational objectives has become imperative.

SELECTED READINGS

BAKER, EVA L., and W. JAMES POPHAM, *Expanding Dimensions of Instructional Objectives*. Englewood Cliffs, N.J.: Prentice-Hall, 1973.

BINDER, FREDERICK M., *Education in the History of Western Civilization*. Toronto: Macmillan, 1970.

BRUBACHER, JOHN S., and WILLIS RUDY, *Higher Education In Transition*. New York: McGraw-Hill, 1947.

EBY, FREDERICK, and CHARLES FLINN ARROWGOOD, *The Development of Modern Education: In Theory, Organization and Practice*. 2nd ed. Englewood Cliffs, N.J.: Prentice-Hall, 1952.

GREIR, COLIN, *The Great School Legend*. New York: Viking Press, 1972.

KATZ, MICHAEL B., *The Irony of Early School Reform*. Cambridge, Mass.: Harvard University Press, 1968.

MEYER, ADOLPHE E., *An Educational History of the American People*, 2nd ed. New York: McGraw-Hill, 1967.

RIPPA, S. ALEXANDER, *Education in a Free Society: An American History*, New York: David McKay, 1967.

SILBERMAN, CHARLES E., *Crisis in the Classroom, The Remaking of American Education*. New York: Random House, 1970.

TYACK, DAVID B., ed., *Turning Points in American Educational History*. Waltham, Mass.: Blainsdell, 1967.

3

Writing and Using Precise Cognitive Instructional Objectives

Anyone who talks with educators today or who reads current educational journals cannot help but be aware of the increasing use of precise instructional objectives; they have become part of a continuing expansion of competency-based education programs and are crucial to increased efforts aimed at achieving accountability among educators. Many school systems throughout the country are providing (either by choice or by legislative fiat) in-service education for their teachers to prepare them to write and use precise instructional objectives. This in-service work is often followed by workshops during which teachers are expected to begin writing precise instructional objectives for their courses. Personnel directors in many districts are actively seeking teacher candidates who can demonstrate their ability to write and use precise instructional objectives, and more and more teacher preparation institutions are providing both undergraduate and graduate courses that include the study and use of precise instructional objectives.

With this increased interest, it behooves the prospective teacher to venture into a classroom (or a job interview) only after acquiring the basic skills of writing and implementing precise instructional objectives. This chapter is intended to help the reader develop the skills necessary to write and modify such objectives.

OBJECTIVES

The student will:

1. List, in writing, all six levels of the cognitive domain in Bloom's *Taxonomy of Educational Objectives.*[1] (Knowledge)
2. Describe, in writing, the cognitive activity called for at each level of the cognitive domain, in terms that agree with those espoused by Bloom. (Comprehension)
3. When given ten instructional objectives, label at least eight as: (1) Lacking an observable behavior; (2) Lacking a minimum acceptable standard; (3) Both 1 and 2; or (4) Acceptable. (Analysis)
4. Write at least three precise instructional objectives each of which contains an observable terminal behavior, conditions, and a minimum acceptable standard, and that show the development of a specific skill or ability through three levels of the cognitive domain. (Synthesis)
5. When presenting objectives for an instructional situation to students, judge whether suggestions advanced by the students about the objectives are appropriate or inappropriate for that situation and give a rationale for each judgment. (Evaluation)

GENERATING OBJECTIVES

Gathering The Content Base

Once written and distributed, precise instructional objectives are available for critical examination by a wide variety of people. Therefore, the wise teacher will make it a point to consider a number of factors when writing the objectives, among which are the needs and desires of the students, the teacher's own academic strengths, the expectations of the school and community, and the limitations imposed both by state requirements and by the nature of the subject itself.

A good way for teachers to begin the process of writing precise instructional objectives is to write down the particular skills and content they feel could logically be a part of their proposed course and would be of most help to students once they leave the class. Particular attention should be paid to including skill and information areas that would be of real help to students in their day-to-day affairs. For example, it makes little difference if a person can or cannot list the first ten presidents of the United States (except on a quiz show), but being able to describe the division of powers in the federal

[1] Benjamin S. Bloom, ed., *Taxonomy of Educational Objectives, Handbook I: Cognitive Domain.* (New York: David McKay, 1956).

government may help a person to understand the antagonism that often exists between the legislative and executive branches, and thus to explain the governmental problems that are so confusing and frustrating to one who lacks such knowledge.

After writing down their own ideas, teachers may obtain other ideas by scanning current texts in their subject area, reading through curriculum guides and resource units, and talking with other teachers, administrators, and parents. It is also helpful to pursue compilations of precise instructional objectives (see Appendix A).

Having compiled what is likely to be a rather lengthy list, the teacher is ready to begin converting the original list into a set of precise instructional objectives. The teacher should not be alarmed if there is little student contribution at this point. The most valid student input will come after the initial work. The steps described here would take place prior to the first class and would provide the teacher with a basic list of essential objectives to which student suggestions could be added.

THE PARTS OF COGNITIVE AND PSYCHOMOTOR OBJECTIVES

Observable Behavior

The first step in transforming the "raw material" into precise instructional objectives is to specify an observable terminal behavior for each objective. An observable terminal behavior describes, in terms of activities that a person can actually see and measure, exactly *what a student will be expected to do at the end of instruction.* Experience has shown that terms such as "define in writing," "underline," and "diagram" are more effective in describing expected behaviors than are terms such as "know," "learn," and "understand." The latter terms are not directly observable and can be interpreted in a number of ways. Consider the following examples:

1. The student will know the difference between prose and poetry.
2. The student will define, in writing, the terms *prose* and *poetry* and illustrate each definition with the name of an example.

Since the word "know" in the first objective represents a behavior that is not directly observable, the student cannot determine how the teacher expects the knowledge to be demonstrated, and neither the teacher nor the student can ascertain when, or if, the objective is finally achieved. If no observable behavior is stated, the objective is useless in terms of telling students exactly what is expected of them: It does not convey instructional intent.

The second objective contains an observable behavior: "define in writing." Since the teacher and students can now describe how achievement of the objective is to be demonstrated, it becomes easier to plan instruction that will help students acquire the necessary skills, easier for students to focus their efforts on achieving the specified skills, and easier for both students and teacher to determine when, in fact, the objective *is* achieved.

It should be noted that words such as "know," "learn," "understand," "grasp," and "discern" do not necessarily have to be avoided when writing precise instructional objectives. If it is felt that such words are necessary to convey instructional intent, the teacher may use them but should be sure to include an explanation of how the implied behavior is to be demonstrated. Consider, for example, the following objective.

> The student will demonstrate an understanding of prose and poetry by writing the definitions of these terms and illustrating each definition with the title of an appropriate example.

This objective contains an observable terminal behavior, but it is unnecessarily wordy. In many instances teachers will find that words such as "learn" and "understand" are superfluous and do not assist in clarifying the instructional intent. The fewer words used to convey the instructional intent clearly, the less chance there is for misinterpretation.

Some terms, such as "identify," "differentiate," and "solve," are less ambiguous than such terms as "know" and "learn," and yet they describe purely mental activities—activities that go on in the student's head—and are therefore not directly observable. In order to make these terms less ambiguous, teachers must again be sure to specify a means by which the activities can be observed: "identify in writing," "differentiate by recording on a checklist," or "record on paper the step-by-step procedure." By indicating to students what specific activity will be required to demonstrate the competence overtly, teachers not only sharpen the mental picture students have of what is expected of them, but they also tend to reduce anxiety. The expected behavior is now clear.

Sometimes it makes sense to have students demonstrate a competence orally. While this kind of competence demonstration has its place, there are disadvantages that must be kept in mind. If an objective requires a student to "state orally" certain specifics, the reliability of the competence demonstration is compromised if other students hear the recitation. It would be illogical, for example, to write an objective that stated, "The student will state orally the three measures of central tendency," unless provisions were made for each student to demonstrate the competence privately. If the competence were demonstrated in a classroom setting, the teacher would be unable to differentiate between those students who actually understood the material and those who were merely parroting what they heard others say.

Since it is likely that a large number of the objectives will be demonstrated in writing, it may be advantageous to state at the beginning of the list of objectives that all objectives will be demonstrated in writing unless otherwise specified. This procedure will eliminate the need to include the words "in writing" in virtually every objective.

Conditions

Once the observable terminal behavior is decided upon, the teacher is in a position to add any special limitations or freedoms that will exist when the behavior is demonstrated. Conditions frequently refer to time limits or to the use of aids or special equipment, but they can refer to whatever factors are considered important to the demonstration of the terminal behavior. A physical education teacher, for example, might consider it important to specify "using a regulation baseball" in an objective concerning the hitting of line drives, in order to avoid any question as to whether a baseball or a softball is to be used. Again, the function of conditions is to clarify further the student's mental picture of the constraints or other conditions that will affect the demonstration of the specified competence. Consider the following objectives.

The student will:

1. Describe, in writing, at least two possible advantages associated with the use of precise instructional objectives.
2. Using only notes, describe, in a paper of no more than two pages, at least two possible advantages and two possible disadvantages associated with the use of precise instructional objectives.

The first objective contains an observable terminal behavior (describe, in writing), but the students do not know if they will be expected to memorize the required information or if they can simply open a text and copy what they need. In the second objective doubts are removed. The condition that notes may be used is clearly stated and there is little room for misunderstanding. Likewise, the specification of length (in a paper of no more than two pages), gives students an even more complete description of constraints.

While statements of conditions are usually quite helptul and are sometimes absolutely necessary in order to avoid misunderstandings, some care must be taken in their use. Preconditions such as "after a lecture" or "after reading chapter ten" usually weaken an objective because they limit the sources from which a student may draw information in formulating responses. Certainly it would not be a teacher's intention to penalize a student for having acquired information or skills outside the class, and yet conditions such as those just mentioned imply such a penalization. If, on the other hand, the limitation is crucial to the objective for some specific reason, such preconditions must be included.

There are few instances in which the prerequisites for an objective need be included in the objective itself. Generally speaking, a precise instructional objective need not concern itself with how a student acquired the knowledge or skill to demonstrate a particular competence. The manner in which a student prepares for eventual demonstration of a competence falls within the realm of teaching-learning activities. At this point in formulating objectives, the main concern is not determining how the student will become proficient enough to demonstrate the competence; it is specifying the competence itself with as much clarity as possible.

Another point to remember is that it makes little sense to attempt to state all conditions for all objectives. For example, the condition "with no aids" will probably be common to many objectives. To include the words "with no aids" in each and every objective, however, would be both repetitive and distracting. A more logical solution would be to state the conditions common to most objectives at the beginning of the list of objectives, and to discuss the general nature of these conditions with students prior to instruction.

As a general rule teachers should state conditions whenever there is a possibility that doubts or misunderstandings may arise. If there are any doubts as to whether conditions are needed in a particular objective, be safe and include them. Keep in mind that if no conditions are specified in the objective, adding constraints at the time the competence is to be demonstrated may result in strong student resentment.

Minimum Acceptable Standard

The last element included in a complete precise instructional objective is a minimum acceptable standard of performance. The teacher must decide how well each of the observable behaviors must be demonstrated in order for it to be deemed acceptable.

Given the kind of behavior called for in the objective, the minimum acceptable standard can be stated in quantitative terms, qualitative terms, or both. As the name suggests, quantitative terms specify amounts or numbers and qualitative terms specify particular points or aspects that are sought. The following are examples of objectives using quantitative and/or qualitative minimum acceptable standards.

The student will:

1. Given four sets of symptoms, diagnose, in writing, the correct disease in *at least three* of the cases.

2. Write *at least ten* precise instructional objectives, each of which contains *an observable terminal behavior, conditions,* and *a minimum acceptable standard.*
3. Explain, in writing, the proper use of the wood lathe including: (a) *the procedure for mounting material;* (b) *the proximity of the rest block to the material;* (c) *the speed of the chuck;* (d) *the proper use of tool bit;* and (e) *safety precautions.*

The first objective utilizes only a quantitative standard (at least three). The second example combines a quantitative standard (at least ten) with a qualitative standard (contains an observable terminal behavior, conditions, and a minimum acceptable standard). The third contains a qualitative standard that describes the minimum elements necessary in a student explanation (points a-e).

A common misconception concerning minimum acceptable standards is that the specification of allowable time or lengths of answers is, by itself, sufficient to clarify what is expected as a minimally acceptable performance. Generally these are conditions, not minimum acceptable standards. Consider the following objectives:

The student will:

1. Describe, in a paper of not more than two pages, the results of World War II.
2. Type at least two letters in one class period.

In the first objective students could argue that they should receive credit for achieving the objective for writing simply: "The Allies won." This answer would meet the condition "in a paper of not more than two pages," but it confuses conditions with minimum standards because the teacher failed to include a minimum standard. According to the second objective the student could turn in two messy, error-filled pages at the end of the period and be upset if they were not accepted. In neither objective did the quantitative limitations convey the true minimum standards. The teacher did not state the complete instructional intention.

If, however, time or length is a consideration for achievement, then it can be a minimum standard. For instance, in the objective "The student will be able to run the 100-yard dash in 13 seconds," time is certainly the minimum acceptable standard. Similarly, a teacher who is teaching how to summarize can include "in less than one page" as part of a minimum standard.

Qualitative standards present a more involved problem for those writing objectives, for they often imply subjective judgments, and it becomes difficult to describe the particular attributes or characteristics that must be included in the terminal behavior demonstration if that demonstration is to be declared acceptable. For example, the objectives stated above are improved as additional qualitative standards are added.

The student will:

1. Describe, in a paper of no more than two pages, the results of World War II in terms of at least two economic developments in France and Germany.
2. Within one class period, type a one-page personal letter and a one-page business letter, using the block style, with no typographical errors.

As rewritten, the objectives begin to communicate instructional intent more clearly and minimize the chances for misunderstandings. As more standards are added, the picture of the desired end product will become more and more clear in the mind of the student. To try to include every possible point, however, would make the objective so cumbersome that it would be virtually useless.

For instance, in attempting to establish qualitative standards for either of the two objectives above, the teacher will undoubtedly consider many factors such as logical organization, completeness, relevancy, neatness, spelling and punctuation errors, and other considerations that are either too common or too vague to specify. Common kinds of standards as well as common kinds of terminal behaviors and common kinds of conditions can be stated at the beginning of a list of objectives, thus eliminating the obligation of stating them for each objective.

Of course, the task of specifying standards for logical organization, completeness, relevancy, or other similarly nebulous factors is admittedly difficult; in fact, in some instances it may even be impossible. While it is desirable to communicate clearly to the student exactly what will be sought in the response or skill demonstration, at the same time it is necessary to keep the objective to a reasonable length. In the objective concerning the results of World War II, for example, the parameter "in terms of at least two economic developments in France and Germany" gives the student a clearer picture of how he or she is to orient the answer. Adding the words, "See the handout for further minimum standards" would allow the teacher to describe further minimum standards without loading down the objective with material that might detract from readability and interest.

The fact that all possible qualitative standards are not included in each objective should not be taken as an abdication of the teacher's right or professional obligation to make judgments concerning overall quality, and this point should be made clear to students. Teachers should simply acknowledge the fact that many instructional objectives deal with complex concepts or human behaviors and that the objectives are therefore attempts to convey, as far as possible, the true instructional intent by specifying as many pertinent parameters as makes good sense. If teachers want students to refer to particular ideas, points, or aspects when demonstrating a competence, they should identify those points in the objective, but terms such as "main ideas," "most important points," and "major aspects" should be used with the understanding that the teacher is willing to accept the student's opinion regarding these matters. If teachers are not precise in describing terminal behaviors or minimal acceptable standards, they should not hold the students accountable for the consequences of misinterpretation.

Review

In review, the first step in writing objectives is the decision as to what the teacher really wants students to do after instruction. He or she must consider not only the needs and desires of the students but also his or her own subject-matter strengths and weaknesses, the expectations of the school and community, and relevant state regulations. The teacher seeks ideas for objectives from current texts, other teachers, administrators, parents, curriculum guides, resource units, and compilations of existing objectives.

After acquiring all this "raw material," it must be refined and converted into a series of precise instructional objectives by phrasing each idea so it specifies a particular behavior to be overtly demonstrated, describes the pertinent conditions that will exist at the time the behavior is demonstrated, and clearly states a minimum acceptable standard of performance. In short, the teacher must convey to students, as clearly as possible, exactly what they will be expected to do after instruction.

PRACTICE IN WORKING WITH OBJECTIVES

Practice Exercise 1: Characteristics of Objectives

Many of the following objectives are stated in unacceptable form. Use the following rating scale to pinpoint the weakness(es) in each objective, rewrite the objective in acceptable form, and check your responses with those furnished. An objective may be rated using more than one response.

(*Note*: It can logically be argued that if an objective contains no observable behavior, then there is no way for it to contain a minimum standard. This is because if it is impossible to observe *what* the student is going to be able to do, then it is impossible to determine *how well* he or she has to do it. For purposes of this excercise, however, proceed on the basis that some objectives *intend* to contain minimum standards even though the observable behavior is not properly defined.)

Rating Scale:

1. Lacks an observable behavior
2. Lacks a minimum acceptable standard
3. Lacks conditions
4. Contains all three necessary elements

The student will:

1. Know the democratic principles upon which our country is founded.
2. Be an alert and an aware citizen.
3. Know the names of both U.S. senators from his or her home state.
4. Demonstrate comprehension of selected accounting practices by completing accounting forms selected by the teacher without error.
5. Prescribe appropriate medication for a surgery patient.
6. Take an active role in society.
7. Demonstrate typing skill by typing two letters in class, using block style, without errors.
8. Write a proper personal letter.
9. Understand the plight of the poor people in our country.
10. List orally the three branches of our federal government in class.
11. List orally the strengths and weaknesses of the United Nations.
12. Understand two steps in the committee process.
13. Appreciate the benefits of competency-based instruction.
14. Sincerely believe in just one reason to participate on a committee.
15. Demonstrate a comprehension of behavioral objectives by achieving a score of at least 80 percent on a forced choice test dealing with behavioral objectives.

Rating Scale Answers:

1. 1, 2, 3
2. 1, 2, 3
3. 1, 3 ("Both" is a quantitative minimum standard.)
4. 4
5. 2, 3 ("Appropriate" does not describe a precise minimum standard.)
6. 1, 2, 3
7. 4
8. 2, 3 ("Proper" does not prescribe a precise minimum standard.)
9. 1, 2, 3
10. 4 ("All" is implied as a minimum standard because of the number "three.")
11. 2, 3 (How many strengths and weaknesses?)
12. 1, 3
13. 1, 2, 3
14. 1, 3
15. 4

The following objectives are examples of rewrites based on the original, and contain an observable behavior, minimum standard, and conditions. It is expected, of course, that rewrites may vary considerably from these models:

The student will:

1. Write, in class, all requirements for election and lengths of term for U.S. congressmen.
2. Select a current legislative issue; write a one-page letter to his or her congressman expressing his or her views on that issue; and give at least two reasons for those views in the letter.
3. Write the names of both U.S. senators from his or her home state.
4. Given the necessary ledger and journal entries, complete a balance sheet with no errors.
5. Given a hypothetical description of a surgery situation, prescribe the medication necessary.
6. After reading the details in the local paper, write a letter to the editor of the local paper expressing his or her views on a current local problem containing at least two rationales for those views.
7. (No changes needed).
8. Write a one-page personal letter containing at least a heading, saluation, body, and closing, without grammatical error.
9. State orally at least three factors inhibiting the elimination of poverty within our country.
10. (No changes needed.)
11. List, in writing, with no aids and within thirty minutes, at least two strengths and two weaknesses of the United Nations.
12. Describe, in writing, at least two steps in the committee process.
13. Describe, in writing, at least three benefits of competency-based instruction.
14. Describe orally to the class at least one reason to participate on a committee.
15. (No change needed.)

Self-Test: Rewriting Poorly Stated Objectives

Rewrite each of the following objectives so that they contain an observable behavior, minimum standard and conditions.

1. The student will develop good instructional objectives.

2. The student will know why behavioral objectives are important.

Checking the Rewritten Objectives

1. Look at the rewritten objective. Ask yourself the question, Does this objective tell me what the student is going to be able to do after the lesson that I can observe? If it does, then the objective includes an *observable behavior.*

   In objective 1 above, the word "develop" is imprecise. A person could develop objectives in his or her head but that would be unobservable. It would be better to say "develop and write," "orally state," or just "write."

   In objective 2, the word "know" is not observable. Observable behavior could be "orally state," "explain," "describe in writing," or "demonstrate understanding by taking a test."

2. Second, ask yourself if the rewritten objectives answer the question, "How well does the student have to demonstrate the observable behavior?" If your objective answers this question, then the objective has a *minimum standard.* In objective 1 "good" does not give us a minimum standard.

3. Third, ask yourself if the rewritten objective answers the question, "Under what circumstances will the student demonstrate the observable behavior?" If the objective answers this question, then it has the necessary condition or conditions.

Possible Rewrites

The student will:

1. The student will write, without aids and within ten minutes, two behavioral objectives each of which contains an observable terminal behavior, any necessary conditions, and a minimum acceptable standard.
2. The student will orally state in class at least two reasons for the wide acceptance of behavioral objectives by educators.

Self-Test: Characteristics of Objectives

Use the following rating scale to pinpoint the weakness(es), if any, in each of the following objectives:

Rating Scale:

1. Lacks an observable behavior
2. Lacks a minimum acceptable standard
3. Lacks conditions
4. The objective is acceptable

The student will:

1. Write a critical reaction to *Moby Dick.*
2. When asked by the teacher, state orally the names of two wartime presidents.

3. Recite the Pledge of Allegiance with no errors.
4. Demonstrate a knowledge of proper tool use by selecting a saw with which to cut plywood.
5. Understand quadratic equations well enough to solve, on paper, any three that are given, without the use of aids and within thirty minutes.
6. Demonstrate easy mathematical skills with at least 80 percent accuracy.
7. Understand fully the terms volt, ohm, and alternating current.
8. Demonstrate good physical condition, in part, by running the mile in less than six minutes.
9. Translate written French into written English.
10. Be proud to be an American 85 percent of the time.

Answers to Self-Test on Characteristics of Objectives

1. 2, 3
2. 4
3. 4
4. 2, 3
5. 4
6. 1, 3
7. 1, 3
8. 4
9. 2, 3
10. 1

CLASSIFICATION OF OBJECTIVES

The charge is often leveled at the school teacher that he or she is teaching at, and testing at, too low an intellectual level.[2] One procedure to insure that students do have an opportunity to develop all their skills is to classify precise instructional objectives into some scheme that makes their analysis possible.

One of the most popular classification schemes was the one developed in 1956 by a small group of researchers working under the direction of Benjamin Bloom. The classification scheme developed included three "domains": the *cognitive* domain, the *affective* domain, and the *psychomotor* domain. The *cognitive* domain concerns itself with the acquisition and manipulation of factual information and is the primary focus of this chapter. The *affective* domain concerns itself with such things as emotions, traits, attitudes, reactions, values, and moral judgments (see chapter 4) and the *psychomotor* domain concerns itself with the development of physiological skills.

---

[2]Walter Pierce and Howard Getz, "Relationships Among Teaching, Cognitive Levels, Testing and IQ," *Illinois School Research*, 6, no. 2. (Winter 1973), pp. 27-31.

By placing objectives into appropriate domains and appropriate levels within those domains it becomes possible for teachers to determine if too many objectives are focusing on two few skills and it then becomes possible for teachers to modify those objectives to insure that a wider range of skill development is provided for.

The Levels Within the Cognitive Domain

The first publication to come out of the group working with Bloom was entitled *Taxonomy of Educational Objectives—Handbook I: Cognitive Domain.*[3] It is in this publication that the cognitive domain is described and the levels within it explored in detail.

When working with the cognitive domain it is important to remember that the hierarchy of levels is an artificial division of intellectual skills. Although the taxonomy is one of the most popular classification schemes available, there may be instances when it is difficult to determine at exactly which level a particular objective should be placed. This difficulty may be caused, in part, by the fact that there is frequently some overlap between levels and in part by the fact that the levels are an attempt to arrange skills in a hierarchy. The possibility of some haziness in classification does not seriously lessen the usefulness of the taxonomy. The vast majority of objectives will fit logically into one or another of the levels.

The cognitive domain is divided into six major levels, and each of these major levels is divided into sublevels. This exploration of the cognitive domain will primarily be restricted to the six major levels, but if teachers desire to explore any of the levels in greater depth the use of Bloom's handbook is recommended. The following discussion is intended to give teachers enough skill to make initial classifications of objectives for the purposes mentioned above. Studying the material that follows and practicing the excercises will enable a teacher to examine and even defend his or her objectives as to the variety of intellectual levels they include.

Knowledge. The first, and lowest, level of the cognitive domain is knowledge. At this level the student is expected merely to recall information he or she has been exposed to or to recognize information presented. The main skill emphasized by objectives written at this level is simple remembering. Listed below are some examples of objectives written at the knowledge level.

The student will:

1. List, in writing and from memory, the first ten presidents of the United States.
2. Given an outline map of the United States, write the name of each state in the appropriate place.

[3]Bloom, *Taxonomy of Educational Objectives.*

3. Given a list of twenty people, underline all the names of famous mathematicians.

Comprehension. The second level of the cognitive domain is comprehension. It is the view of many educators that it is this level that is most emphasized in today's schools. If this view is correct, our level of emphasis is disappointing because the comprehension level is low in the hierarchy of intellectual skills. This level indicates that the student not only can recall information but also is familiar with the meaning of the information to the extent of being able to make some use of it.

Bloom includes three kinds of intellectual skills in the comprehension level. The first of these is translation, the ability to make a one-for-one conversion from one form or language to another. The second skill is interpretation, which is the ability to generalize or paraphrase information, and the third skill is extrapolation, which is the ability to go a little beyond the information given and make predictions based on the information presented. Examples of observable behaviors reflecting each of these skills are shown below.

The student will:

1. Given a mathematical formula, restate it orally in sentence form so that the restatement is mathematically correct.
2. Given a paper written by a French politician, paraphrase it in written English and include at least four of the five points in the original paper.
3. Given a graph showing traffic fatalities per thousand miles of travel for U.S. drivers over the past five years, estimate orally the number of traffic fatalities per thousand miles of travel for U.S. drivers for the subsequent year if the trend depicted in the graph were to continue.

Application The third level of the cognitive domain is application. Application is essentially the act of applying some abstraction to a new or unique concrete example, without prompting. Bloom describes the distinction between the levels of comprehension and application thus: "A demonstration of 'Comprehension' shows that the student *can* use the abstraction when its use is specified. A demonstration of 'Application' shows that he *will* use it correctly, given an appropriate situation in which no mode of solution is specified."[4] It is useful to think of the student understanding a principle or rule at the comprehension level, and then using that principle or rule in a practical situation at the application level. Examples of objectives written at the application level are shown below.

The student will:

1. Given the principles necessary to construct a do-loop, use them to build a do-loop in FORTRAN that works when run on a computer.

[4]Ibid., p. 120.

2. Given the dimensions of a room and the cost of paint, calculate and write down how much paint will be needed and what it will cost.

✗ 3. Given a five-step procedural scheme for menu preparation, follow the steps to prepare a written menu for twelve consecutive meals.

Analysis   The fourth level of the cognitive domain is analysis. At this level students should be able to break an idea into its constituent elements or internal organizational principles, and to perceive relationships among those elements or principles, within one "whole," or between several "wholes." Analysis, in its fundamental form, is seeing similarities and differences between things. Examples of skills included in the analysis level are shown in the objectives listed below.

The student will:

1. Given a series of rock samples, sort them into four categories of his or her own choosing.
2. Given a series of precise instructional objectives, cross out all words in each objective that are superfluous in terms of observable behavior, conditions, or minimum acceptable standards.
3. Given six advertisements, label each as to which advertising technique is predominant.

Synthesis   The fifth level of the cognitive domain is synthesis. Synthesis means the creation of something new from previously existing elements or principles. The levels of the cognitive domain are cumulative, and this cumulative aspect becomes evident when a student is asked to create, from the knowledge and skills previously acquired, something that is new and unique (at least to the student). Certainly the student needs to have mastered material in the area at the preceding levels before he or she can be successful at the synthesis level. Even then, developing something that is unique is not often an easy task. Some objectives written at the synthesis level are shown below.

The student will:

1. Originate and deliver an extemporaneous three-minute speech on a given topic that contains an attention-getter, body, summary, and close.
2. Prepare a written itinerary that will enable him or her to visit at least three nonadjacent countries on a budget of five hundred dollars.
3. Given appropriate data concerning school drop-outs, generate and write out a hypothesis that would reflect the factors given and that could be tested empirically.

Evaluation   The last, and highest, level of the cognitive domain is evaluation. Evaluation means the formation of a judgment and the substantiation or justification of that judgment by reference to facts, examples, or specific criteria. Evaluation, then, means considerably more than simply saying that this is better than that. The judgment must be made on the basis of specific criteria. Examples of objectives written at the evaluation level are shown below.

The student will:

1. Given ten precise instructional objectives for a hypothetical learning situation, judge which one would be best and support the choice by stating at least four reasons for it in a paper of no more than one page.
2. Given a description of a room and a variety of pieces of furniture, select furnishings for the room and provide a written rationale for the choices, indicating how and why they "go together."
3. Take either a pro or con position concerning mandatory school attendance and defend the position by citing specific facts or examples in a paper of no more than two pages.

If teachers have a rational and workable classification system for their objectives, they can label each of their objectives with an appropriate level. Teachers should not be surprised to find many (maybe even too many) objectives written at the lower levels. If they do, or if any level is too heavily represented, modification of objectives is in order so students will be assured of the opportunity to develop a variety of intellectual skills.

PRACTICE IN CLASSIFYING OBJECTIVES IN THE COGNITIVE DOMAIN

Practice Exercise 2: The Domains

Classify each objective below as belonging to the cognitive (c), affective (a), or psychomotor (p) domain.

The student will:

___ 1. Explain, in writing, which of two possible solutions to the problem of social unrest is most likely to eliminate the problem.
___ 2. Recite the Emancipation Proclamation from memory with no more than two errors.
___ 3. Thread a movie projector so that, when the projector is turned on, the film will not flicker.
___ 4. Show increased interest in band music by attending eight out of the ten concerts offered during the year.
___ 5. Given thirty quadratic equations, solve correctly, on paper, at least 80 percent of them.
___ 6. Demonstrate concern for the democratic principles of free enterprise by stating these concerns orally.

____ 7. Show a growing interest in art by participating extensively in discussions about art forms.

____ 8. Transfer bacteria from a culture to a petri dish in a manner that produces properly spread colonies and no contamination.

____ 9. Write an original short story that has appropriate sentence structure and organization and that meets the requirements of heightened action.

____ 10. Given a series of paintings, explain, in writing, which one is best, and why.

Answers to Practice Exercise 2

1. C	5. C	8. P
2. C	6. A	9. C
3. P	7. A	10. C
4. A		

Practice Exercise 3: Cognitive Levels

Classify each objective into its level within the cognitive domain. Check your responses against the answers provided. Resolve any discrepancies by further study, analysis, and/or consultation with your instructor and/or peers. Always classify the objectives at the highest level implied.

Levels of the Cognitive Domain

1. Knowledge   4. Analysis
2. Comprehension   5. Synthesis
3. Application   6. Evaluation

Each student will:

____ 1. Given three garments of varying prices, choose the garment considered to be the best buy, and give three written reasons for the decision based on the construction of the garment.

____ 2. List, in writing, at least five factors that led up to the Spanish-American War.

____ 3. Given a new list of possible reasons for World War I and World War II, classify them, in writing, under World War I or World War II with no errors.

____ 4. State, in writing, four common ingredients in pastry.

____ 5. Given the necessary material, compare, in writing, the state welfare program in Illinois to that in California on at least five points.

____ 6. Explain, in writing, using at least five examples, why many blacks moved to the North at the end of the Civil War.

____ 7. Given comprehensive material on the waste of natural resources, write an original legislative bill calling for conservation of natural resources.

____ 8. Given necessary materials, develop a unique written ten-year plan for the economic development of a hypothetical country.

___ 9. Given a written quiz on ceramics and explain in ten minutes three ways of hand-building a pot.

___ 10. Given sculptures done by peers, choose one he or she judges to be best, and defend that choice by citing, in writing, at least three points of superiority in the selected piece.

___ 11. Given the names of two Cubist painters, contrast and compare the styles of each painter in a one-page paper citing at least four similarities and three differences.

___ 12. Solve 90 percent of the two-digit multiplication problems on a written math test.

___ 13. Using the volume and concentration formula, calculate and write down how much one gram of N HCL will have to be diluted to prepare 500 ml of .5N solution.

___ 14. Given a list of tasks that must be done during an eight-hour period, create a written work plan that organizes the tasks so that the time will be used efficiently to complete them.

___ 15. Use Roberts' Rules of Order to conduct a class election without any violations of procedure.

Answers to Practice Exercise 3

1. 6	6. 2	11. 4
2. 1	7. 5	12. 3
3. 4	8. 5	13. 3
4. 1	9. 2	14. 5
5. 4	10. 6	15. 3

TESTING OBJECTIVES FOR CLARITY

Once teachers have ascertained that their objectives are technically correct and provide for student development at a variety of cognitive levels, they should test to see if they communicate the instructional intent clearly. On occasion teachers will become so involved in the instructional process that the *means* to the ends are communicated to students as objectives, rather than the ends themselves. Phrases such as "will read" and "will attend" are almost sure giveaways that the objective is more a learning activity than an objective. Teachers should remember that objectives do not specify how information or skills will be acquired, only the ultimate behavior sought.

Mager[5] suggests that one way to test the clarity of a precise instructional objective is for the writer to consider whether or not another competent person could, on the basis of the written objective(s), differentiate

[5]Robert F. Mager, *Preparing Instructional Objectives* (Palo Alto, Calif.: Fearson Publishers, 1962), p. 52.

between students who can and those who cannot demonstrate the competence described, with the same degree of precision as could the writer of the objectives.

Another way a teacher may test objectives for clarity is to ask someone else (a co-worker, a friend, or student) to read each objective and discern what he thinks he would have to do to demonstrate the competence. If the reader's interpretation differs from the writer's, or if the writer finds himself saying, "what I really meant was . . . ," the misleading objective(s) should be rewritten. This second method is particularly useful if students are used as readers, since they will be more representative of the potential "consumers" than anyone else. It may be, for example, that the level of reading difficulty of the objectives is inappropriate for the potential users. If a fellow teacher reads the objectives this factor may pass unnoticed; if students read the objectives they will be quick to point out that they simply cannot understand what was written and intended.

For the purpose of clarity, when presenting objectives to students for large units of instruction, it is best to reveal those objectives that describe the ultimate instructional intent rather than the enabling objectives. Consider the following:

The student will:

1. Write the definitions of the terms *fact* and *opinion*.
2. When given a series of statements, label, in writing, those that are facts and those that are opinions.
3. When given a newspaper editorial, underline all statements of opinion and explain, in writing, why those statements are opinion.

Of these three objectives, the last best describes the terminal objective. The first two objectives may serve as objectives for individual lesson plans, but the last one more accurately reflects the ultimate instructional intent of the teacher. The teacher may well choose to include only the last objective on a list of course objectives given to students. The connection between the first two objectives and the final objective could, and should, be pointed out to students at the time those objectives are used in particular lessons, but the crucial terminal behavior is expressed in the last objective.

The Use of Precise Instructional Objectives

It is the teacher's task, as the subject-matter specialist, to prepare the basic competencies with which students will deal. Subsequently, it is possible to provide for student participation by handing out the list of objectives, discussing them with students, and asking for suggested additions, deletions, or modifications. It should be impressed upon students that the success of their year or semester will depend, to a large degree, on their involvement in the education process. If they have ideas for things they would like to explore within the framework of the subject area,the teacher may assist them in stating and clarifying those ideas. The teacher's function, as a person with a responsibility for student development, will be to evaluate the ideas contributed and, to the extent possible, include them in the list of objectives following the same procedures followed when the original objectives were written. Everyone in the class should clarify any questions he or she has concerning the objectives and should understand that it is toward the accomplishment of these goals that all instruction will be aimed. The teachers should point out how particular teaching-learning activities contribute to the eventual achievement of one or another of the agreed-upon objectives.

After putting considerable effort into a set of objectives, some teachers may be reluctant to make changes in them. However, if the teaching-learning situation changes dramatically (the schools are closed for a month during the winter due to a fire, a war is declared, or even something less momentous such as a spontaneous class-wide interest in a strike occurs) it may become crucial to reassess and modify the original objectives.

SUMMARY

There is little doubt that the use of precise instructional objectives can be a useful tool in modern education. Since the number of school systems requiring teachers to learn to write and use precise instructional objectives is increasing, and since more and more recruiters are looking for teacher candidates who already possess these skills, prospective and practicing teachers need to become familiar with both the writing and use of such objectives.

The first step in writing precise instructional objectives is to determine exactly what it is students should be able to do after instruction. As a base for building objectives, teachers may turn to their own academic backgrounds, current texts, the needs and desires of their potential students, the expectations of the school and community, other teachers, administrators, resource units, curriculum guides, and compilations of existing instructional objectives.

The second step in the writing process is to rephrase each of the ideas so that it communicates instructional intent clearly; i.e., it specifies an observable terminal behavior, conditions under which that behavior will be demonstrated, and a minimum acceptable standard of performance.

The third step is to classify each of the objectives so one can determine which intellectual skills will be emphasized. One very useful classification scheme has been developed by Bloom et al.[6] Bloom divides the thinking skills into a hierachy of six levels: (1) knowledge—simple recall of informa-

---

[6]Bloom, *Taxonomy of Educational Objectives.*

tion; (2) comprehension—understanding information and being able to translate it, interpret it, and extrapolate from it; (3) application—being able to apply information to new or unique situations without prompting; (4) analysis—being able to break a "whole" into its constituent elements and/or perceive relationships among elements; (5) synthesis—being able to create a "whole" that is unique at least to the creator; and (6) evaluation— being able to make a value judgment and justify it with reference to specific facts and examples, or with reference to given criteria. If it is discovered after categorizing the objectives that too much emphasis is being given to one or two intellectual skills, or that some skills have been given insufficient attention, the list of objectives should be adjusted to remedy the situation.

After the objectives have been classified and any inconsistencies eliminated, the teacher should test the objectives for clarity. Procedures for such tests include asking students to read the objectives and report what they think they would have to do to demonstrate competence. If the objectives are not clear to members of this sample population they should be rewritten.

The fifth step involves obtaining input from the students themselves. It is the teacher's task to evaluate student contributions and add appropriate objectives to the original list (or to delete or modify the objectives).

Finally, teachers will want to make sure each student has a clear perception of each objective. As the class engages in various teaching-learning activities, the teachers will point out how those activities will help students achieve the agreed-upon objectives.

SELECTED READINGS

ARMSTRONG, ROBERT J., TERRY D. CORNELL, ROBERT E. KRANER, and E. WAYNE ROBERSON, *The Development and Evaluation of Behavioral Objectives*. Worthington, Ohio: Charles A. Jones, 1970.

BAKER, EVA, *Defining Content for Objectives*. Los Angeles: Vincet Associates, 1968.

BLOOM, BENJAMIN S., ed., *Taxonomy of Educational Objectives, Handbook I: Cognitive Domain*. New York: David McKay, 1956.

CLARK, D. CECIL, *Using Instructional Objectives in Teaching*. Glenview, Ill.: Scott, Foresman, 1972.

EISNER, E. W., *Instructional and Expressive Objectives: Their Formulation and Use in Curriculum*, AERA Monograph Series. Chicago: Rand McNally, 1969.

GRONLUND, NORMAN E., *Stating Behavioral Objectives for Classroom Instruction*. Toronto: Macmillan, 1970.

HARMES, H. M., *Behavioral Analysis of Learning Objectives*. West Palm Beach, Fla: Harmes, 1969.

KAPFER, MIRIAM B., ed., *Behavioral Objectives in Curriculum Development.* Englewood Cliffs, N.J.: Educational Technology, 1971.

KYRSPIN, WILLIAM J., and JOHN F. FELDHUSEN, *Writing Behavioral Objectives.* Minneapolis, Minn.: Burgess, 1974.

McASHAN, H. H., *Writing Behavioral Objectives: A New Approach.* New York: Harper & Row, 1970.

POPHAM, W.J., and E. BAKER, *Establishing Instructional Goals.* Englewood Cliffs, N.J.: Prentice-Hall, 1969.

TANNER, DANIEL, *Using Behavioral Objectives in the Classroom.* New York: Macmillan, 1972.

4

Writing and Using Objectives in the Affective Domain

Although there is some disagreement among educators concerning the inclusion of the affective domain in the curriculum, one thing stands out clearly: emotions, attitudes, feelings, values, and morals exist, and profoundly affect all human endeavors. The values and feelings of students are shaped daily by activities in which they engage in school. Much of this shaping is incidental, and as such is not scrutinized carefully as to its influence on students. Given that affective behaviors do occur in the classroom daily, teachers are increasingly attempting to identify elements of this domain and to improve student understanding and achievement of selected affective domain objectives.

OBJECTIVES

The student will:

1. Be able to recall facts about affective domain objectives as demonstrated by correctly answering 80 percent of a series of questions based on procedures

for writing objectives in the affective domain. (Knowledge—Comprehension)

2. Given a series of affective domain objectives, be able to classify each into levels within the Pierce-Gray classification scheme. (Analysis)

3. Given a hypothetical situation describing a classroom and learning experience, be able to design at least three affective domain objectives for that situation that do not violate principles described in this chapter. (Application)

4. Show an increased appreciation of objectives in the affective domain as demonstrated by an increase in the percent of positive statements written in response to the open-ended sentence "Affective domain objectives are _____" in a pre- and post-test design. (Conforming)

5. Demonstrate that he or she feels affective domain objectives are important by voluntarily increasing the quantity of affective objectives he or she includes when writing objectives for an actual or hypothetical high school course and by supplying logical reasons why they were included. (Validating)

PROS AND CONS OF AFFECTIVE DOMAIN OBJECTIVES

Various criticisms have been made of attempts to use precise education objectives when working with the affective domain. A few of these need examination before an approach to the problems of learning to write good affective domain objectives is begun.

1. *The educator can never be sure that a behavior he or she is accepting as evidence of an affective domain change represents the affect he or she was attempting to change.* This position is sometimes true, but often not. If a teacher is working with a student who constantly loses his temper in an effort to try to help the student attain more self-control, the student could very well exhibit behaviors that the teacher could recognize and accept as demonstrating an increase in self-control. That is, if the student simply loses his temper less, the teacher can observe this easily by his conduct. In attempting to increase tolerance in youngsters who demonstrate elements of bigotry, accepting a decrease in the number of times minorities are referred to derogatorily by those students is appropriate behavioral evidence of an effort on their part to conform to a more generally accepted societal behavior.

2. *If teachers share affective domain objectives with students, their students may just "fake" the hoped-for behaviors in order to please.* This statement about affective domain objectives simply emphasizes the point that sometimes it is wise to share affective objectives and sometimes it is not.

If the teacher has students who do not care for school and who show their disregard by being discourteous to staff and fellow students, not to share an intention to attempt to change that attitude and behavior makes no sense. When a student interrupts consistently, there is nothing wrong with pointing out that he or she should be more courteous and not interrupt. Perhaps the student will stop interrupting but not really "mean" the change in behavior; however, not letting the student know of the teacher's displeasure would only aggravate the situation. This kind of affective objective should be shared.

If students saw an objective such as the following before answering questionnaires dealing with their feelings about mathematics, the questionnaires would be invalidated: "Students will gain an appreciation of mathematics as it is used outside of the classroom, to be demonstrated by answers on pre- and post-treatment open-ended questionnaires dealing with students' feelings about mathematics. Answers on the follow-up questionnaire will include more positive statements about mathematics." Students might well respond in a way they think would please the teacher rather than as they feel. Responses in this case should be anonymous, and the teacher should use the instrument for his or her own benefit to see if there was indeed an overall increase in appreciation among the entire class.

3. *Affective domain objectives are hard to write.* Most of the problems teachers have with writing affective domain objectives are attributable to muddled thinking. Confusion exists about individual affective domain objectives versus the ones written for all students in a class, and also about which behaviors are good for assessing the components of an affective objective. If the reader completes this chapter and practices writing affective objectives, he or she will be well along the road toward clearing up such confusion and being able to write and use the basic types of affective domain objectives.

4. *Affective objectives do not lend themselves to decisions concerning promotion, retention, or grading.* When the time comes to assign a grade to a student, it is expected that this grade will reflect academic standing rather than "sociability" or attitudinal standing. These latter aspects of human growth may be reported separately but do not have a place in determining academic grades.

5. *It is virtually impossible to select affects such as attitudes and values that everyone agrees are "proper."* Certainly the affective objectives sought by the teacher must be in tune with those sought by society in general but the question is, What comprises the societal position? Value fads must, of course, be avoided, but the question of which values to work toward requires careful thought. Certainly a value such as "It is better to tell the truth than to lie" is one that is almost universally accepted, even though moral dilemmas may be generated by logical arguments that rationalize the essential "goodness" of a particular white lie.

The initial affective objective writing skills presented and practiced in this chapter are designed for those objectives with which few, if any, arguments can be made as to worth. They are based on a presumption that education and self-improvement are accepted by society as being worthwhile.

INDIVIDUAL AFFECTIVE OBJECTIVES
VERSUS GROUP AFFECTIVE OBJECTIVES

Much of the confusion about writing affective domain objectives is eliminated when the teacher realizes that these objectives fall into two categories: objectives written for individual students and objectives written for all students in a class.

When an experienced teacher looks about a busy classroom, each student may well represent a different challenge in the affective domain. One student may be self-conscious, and the teacher hopes to help him become more self-assured. A second student may dislike the subject, and the teacher hopes to build some interest before the semester is over. Perhaps a third student is often discourteous, and the teacher hopes to make her aware of other peoples' rights, and so on. The teacher, in effect, has individual objectives in mind.

The affective problems just described warrant individual affective alterations, and these desired alterations require the construction of individual objectives. The teacher may build objectives in each case using a set of components different from those used when constructing cognitive, psychomotor, or group affective objectives.

On the other hand, there are many affective objectives that the instructor will wish each student in the class to attain. For instance, if a class were to study the problems of the American Indian and Indian reservations, the teacher would want the students to appreciate the need for all American citizens to support actions taken to rectify instances of inequality. In this instance the affective objective for the group may contain specific behaviors as precise as those found in individual affective objectives, cognitive objectives, or psychomotor objectives.

PARTS OF AFFECTIVE OBJECTIVES
FOR INDIVIDUALS

There are two essential elements that *must* be included in a "basic" affective objective:[1] the first element is the specific affect that warrants change; the second is the behavior or set of behaviors that the teacher will accept as evidence that the student is attempting to change his or her behavior and, also, the affect.

---

[1]"Basic" here refers to the three lower levels in the Pierce-Gray Classification of Affective Objectives covered later in this chapter.

For example, suppose the teacher would like to help a student become less self-conscious. A behavior reflecting the student's self-consciousness is a lack of participation in class discussion. Without specifying the procedure the teacher will use to help the student at this point, an objective may be formulated for the individual that would read, "The student will indicate more self-assurance during the course of the semester as exhibited by increased participation in discussions."

Because the teacher is dealing with an individual, it may not be necessary to structure a specific numerical criterion as a minimum acceptable standard. For this student the teacher may be satisfied if there is a shift from zero participation to an occasional instance of participation. For other students this objective may make little sense. In fact, the teacher may have students whom he or she wishes to inhibit because they dominate discussions without realizing they are interfering with the participation of others. In this case an objective could be constructed that would read, "The student will show more sensitivity to the rights of others as demonstrated by a decrease in dominance of class participation time." In this objective the affect is "show more sensitivity to the rights of others," and the observable behavior is "a decrease in dominance of class participation time."

In many instances a teacher will become aware of individual objectives for students and be able to share these objectives with parents. Often parents and teachers can work together. For instance, if a student is discourteous to others, and if both parents and teacher are attempting to help the student appreciate the feelings of others, desired results may be obtained more rapidly; the teacher and the parents can identify cooperatively a wide range of behavioral instances that would indicate student growth toward the goal.

Once the affective objective is pinpointed, movement toward the objective can be identified more easily, progress charted, and often satisfactory results obtained.

PARTS OF "BASIC" GROUP AFFECTIVE OBJECTIVES

Basic affective objectives for all students (group objectives) are made up of several parts, and the teacher needs to be concerned about the quality of those parts. The accepted procedures for assembling good affective domain objectives for groups have been synthesized concisely by Blaine Nelson Lee and David Merrill:[2]

1. A high-probability student approach behavior that is observable by the teacher will be described.

[2]Blaine Lee and David Merrill, *Writing Complete Affective Objectives: A Short Course* (Belmont, Calif.: Wadsworth Inc., 1972), p. 7.

2. Realistic criteria that can be used to assess a pattern of approach will be specified.
3. A free-choice, no-cue situation in which the approach behavior may occur will be described.
4. The attitude to be demonstrated will be described.

Observable Behaviors for Affective Objectives

In many situations, teachers can link behaviors to affects with reasonable assurance that the behaviors reflect the identified affect. For instance, when a student brings artifacts from home to the history class voluntarily and participates in discussions often and enthusiastically, the teacher can be reasonably sure that this behavior represents some interest in history. When a student's behavior exhibits characteristics that identify him or her with a specific affect, the behavior is labeled *approach behavior*. No one would conclude that the student who brought artifacts to a history class was exhibiting an approach behavior that indicated interest in mathematics.

Of course it is possible that the artifact was brought to class because of another less obvious reason—to impress the teacher or parents or earn a higher grade, but the formulation of "basic" affective objectives does not necessarily include probing to determine the precise reason for a behavior. Such a determination is a part of objectives written for "rationalized" affective objectives, which are those constructed for the three higher levels in the Pierce-Gray classification for affective objectives, covered later in this chapter. At this point the teacher may use a variety of more general affects (i.e., show interest, appreciate, approve of, accept, acclaim, support, enjoy), to indicate a student's attempts to arrange his or her behavior to harmonize with that generally accepted as positive by the participants in the educational environment.

On the other hand, a student known to have historical artifacts at home who refuses to bring them to school and is inattentive or disruptive during discussions of history can be thought of as exhibiting the opposite of an approach behavior. Such a behavior is labeled *avoidance behavior*. Avoidance behaviors can also be used to indicate affects.

Often the teacher will detect students who exhibit neither avoidance nor approach behaviors; those for example, who will upon request bring in an artifact but exhibit neither enthusiasm or rejection in a discussion of it. Such a behavior is labeled *neutral behavior*. As the teacher builds basic affective domain objectives, he or she will find approach behaviors most useful, avoidance behaviors of some use, and neutral behaviors of least use. Therefore, most of the examples given in this chapter concern approach behaviors.

Many behaviors can be identified as approach behaviors, but if, upon reflection it becomes obvious that a particular behavior would be unlikely to occur, then it would be of little use in an objective. It would be foolish to anticipate that a high percentage of students in a beginning art class would indicate their increased interest in art by voluntarily completing an oil painting at home in their spare time. On the other hand, after giving students unstructured time in the art room, the teacher might expect a reasonable percentage of students to engage in some artistic endeavor. When the behavior has a good chance of being exhibited by students, it can be labeled as *high-probability behavior.*

When selecting. affective objectives for groups, the high-probability behavior is most useful. There is little sense in structuring affective objectives for groups when there is little chance that the behaviors will occur. Similarly, there is no point in building affective objectives for groups that call for behaviors that cannot be observed by the instructor. On occasion, when working with a parent, the teacher may be able to accept evidence from the parent about a behavior that the teacher could not actually see for himself or herself, but the teacher is most confident if the behavior is directly observable.

Suppose in a homemaking class the teacher was trying to help students appreciate the importance of a well-rounded diet.

The initial affective objective might read, "The student will exhibit an understanding of a nutritious diet by making at least one selection from each of the four basic food groups as he or she goes through the school cafeteria lines at lunch." This objective is within the realm of observability, but is troublesome to validate. However, if the teacher *did* choose to station herself inconspicuously near the line and record such behavior, the observation would be classified as *direct* because it was observed by the teacher. If the behavior were reported to the teacher it would be classified as *indirect.*

Conditions for Affective Objectives

When writing affective objectives, the teacher is first of all interested in specifying conditions. Three important conditions are to be considered.

Condition 1: More Than One Possible Approach   The first condition specified for a basic affective objective is that the student be able to choose among approaches or responses. For example, the student may choose between approaches one and two (going to the art museum or going to the science fair), or between an approach and a position of neutrality (going to the art museum or not going). The intention of the instructor may well specify the structuring of the conditions and behaviors.

Condition 2: No Teacher Coercion   The second condition that one specifies in order to write an affective objective is that the teacher make no attempt to influence the behavioral choice of the student. One must remember that teacher influence need not be as overt as the reward of grades or other obvious attempts to extrinsically motivate. The teacher may just offer verbal or nonverbal cues that can have a pronounced influence on behavior.

The description of conditions should include circumstances in which either the students do not know their behavior is being used as evidence of affective changes, or if they do know, they are confident that they may behave naturally without fear that a particular choice could influence their position in the school's reward system.

This condition often seems to be the most difficult to build into basic affective objectives with assurance. When the teacher is in contact with the students, and therefore in a position to make direct observations, the fact of his or her presence will influence the behavior of the students: "If students think they are being evaluated, they tend to respond the way they feel teachers expect them to respond."[3] Hence, indirect measures often provide more assuring evidence of student growth.

Condition 3: Reasonableness   Even when the first two conditions are met in the basic affective objective, it must have the quality of being reasonable. When dealing with the affective domain, the teacher must use the behavior exhibited by the student as evidence that some affect is being demonstrated. If the conditions surrounding that behavior have been structured by the teacher in such a way as to inhibit responses one way or another, then the behavior is rendered valueless. The teacher must make the conditions surrounding the behavior well within the possibility of expectation, and therefore reasonable.

Criteria for Affective Objectives

In many instances it would not be realistic to assume that when a basic affective objective contains an approach behavior, even under ideal conditions, all students in a class will exhibit that set of behaviors. If the instructor is interested in structuring standards to judge the effectiveness of his or her attempts at affective changes, then the criterion level that is important in the basic affective group objective is the *group* criterion level. An example of such a basic affective objective class criterion level would be, "When given the opportunity to participate in an informal discussion with a visiting lecturer, *at least two-thirds of the class* will engage in such discussions as an indication of their interest in the topic."

If, on the other hand, the teacher is interested in a minimum indication by each student, then a *student criterion level* may be included. An example of a student criterion level might be, "As an indication that the student feels that speech development is important, he or she will voluntarily do at least two of the following: (a) attend a special help session, (b) analyze the speech

---

[3]Ibid., p. 48.

of a major political figure, (c) volunteer to give an extra speech to the class."
It is also possible to use degree of involvement by counting the number of
times the behavior is repeated, for instance the number of times the student
participates in discussion.

As with cognitive objectives, there may be instances where the teacher
relies on the *quality* of the behavior to indicate the amount of affective
change. For instance, in the case of a boy in physical education class, the
degree of interest in physical activity could be measured by the number of
times the student failed to dress (student criterion level), or it could be
evaluated in terms of the effort he expended while participating. The
qualities of minimum participation must then be described. This procedure
can often be aided through the use of a checklist. Questions such as, "Does
the student make an effort to catch difficult fly balls?" or "Does the student
run with full speed on the base paths?" may assist in determining the quality
of the effort.

For another example of a qualitative criterion, suppose two students
could engage in the approach behavior of joining and attending the science
club, and both could enter projects at the science fair. If one of the students
spends more time on an elaborate science project while the other student's
project is much less involved, the quality of the project may be considered as
a sound basis for the statement that one student is more involved than the
other in science.

The Complete Group Affective Objective

The four basic parts to an affective objective for all students, then, are
(1) the *affect*; (2) an *approach behavior* the teacher will accept as evidence
that the affect has been modified and that has a high probability of being exhibited; (3) the *conditions under which the behavior will be exhibited, including
alternatives, student free choice, and reasonableness;* and (4) *a criterion level*
that either tells the percent of the class that will exhibit the behavior (class
criterion level), gives the number and/or kinds of activities the students will
engage in, or describes the qualities desired in the behavior (student
criterion level).

Lee and Merrill[4] give the following example of such an objective:

Example: High School Biology Class

Behavior: Coming to class early. (High probability approach behavior;
directly observable)

Conditions: Teacher does not ask students to come early, but has room open
so that they may; does not reward those who come early, but has biology

---

[4]Ibid., p. 87.

books available for students to browse through. (Alternatives; no-cue, free-choice testing situation)

Criterion: One-third of the students will come early each day throughout the semester and 90 percent of the students will come early at least once. (Number; pattern; realistic)

Attitude: Interest in biology

The above objective contains all the necessary elements. Perhaps when written as a single objective, the affect would go first, so that the objective would read something like, "As a demonstration of interest in biology, one-third of the students will come to biology early each day and 90 percent of the students will come early at least once voluntarily, without teacher reward, to browse through available books."

PRACTICE IN WRITING BASIC AFFECTIVE DOMAIN OBJECTIVES

Exercise 1: Individual Basic Affective Domain Objectives

In each of the following situations write a basic affective domain objective for an individual that contains an affect and an observable behavior that you would accept as evidence of a change in the affective domain of the student.

1. Tom exhibits his lack of courtesy by interrupting, grabbing objects from other children, and never saying "thank you" or "please."

2. Mary says she can't stand blacks and demonstrates her feelings by making derogatory remarks about blacks in discussions.

3. Harriet sees little value in going to school and rarely turns in assignments.

4. Frank says he hates (your subject) in general, and your remedial class in particular.

5. Joe is extremely self-conscious and unsure of himself.

6. Ruth has grown up in an environment where time is of little importance. She is often late to school.

Sample Answers for Basic Affective Domain Exercise 1

Your answers may, of course, not agree completely with these sample answers. The crucial thing is to determine that your objective contains a reasonable observable approach behavior, and that the behavior can be linked with the affective domain area with which you wish to work.

1. When confronted with social situations during the semester, Tom will show more respect for others as demonstrated by an increase in his saying "thank you" and "please," and a decrease in instances of his grabbing objects from other children.
2. Mary will change her attitude during the semester as evidenced by a decrease in negative verbalizations about blacks and an increase in instances of inclusion of blacks in school social situations in which she is involved.
3. Harriet will begin to see the importance of school as shown by the submission of more and better assignments over a period of time.
4. Frank's negative attitude about (my subject) and (my class) will decline during the school year. This will be indicated by either (1) an increase in voluntary positive statements about the subject, (2) a decrease in negative statements about the subject, (3) an increase in the quantity and/or quality of work submitted.
5. More occasions of participation in class discussion and committee work will be accepted as evidence that Joe is becoming more self-assured.
6. As punctuality becomes an observable trait exhibited more often by Ruth, it will be assumed that being on time is a value she is adopting.

Exercise 2: Group Basic Affective Domain Objectives

In each of the following situations, fill in the blanks beside the four elements in a group basic affective objective, and then use these answers as a basis for generating a complete objective in the space that follows. A sample of an appropriate objective for each situation follows the exercise. A sample using these steps follows.

Sample Situation   You teach art in a community made up primarily of factory workers. The parents and students in the community are accustomed to attending to more practical considerations and there is a widespread neglect of an appreciation of artistic endeavors.

Affect Needing Attention: [Students need to build a feeling that art can become an important addition to their lives.]

Behavior: [Participating in a submission of student artwork for a rotating art display. (High-probability approach behavior; directly observable)]

Conditions: [Art teacher does not give credit in class for artwork selected to be on display, but arranges for a continual revolving art display in a prominent location on campus. Artwork in all media is included at a variety of quality levels. (Alternatives prôvided; free-choice situation)]

Criteria: [Art teacher hopes that at least 80 percent of the art students will ask that at least one of their art products will be put on display before the end of the course, and that at least 25 percent of the students will ask more than two times. (Specific quantity; realistic)]

Complete Objective: [Given a free-choice, no-cue opportunity to put their artwork on display in the art display case, 80 percent of the art students will volunteer at least once and 25 percent of the students will volunteer at least three times as evidence of their increased feeling that art can become an important addition to their life.]

Situation 1: Boys' P.E. You are a seventh-grade boys' physical education teacher. The elementary school district that sends its students to your school de-emphasizes physical fitness. Additionally, there are few organized community team sports such as Little League baseball available for youngsters. As a consequence there is a noticeable lack of interest in P.E. Part of your job is to increase student interest in their own physical development and sports.

Affect Needing Attention:

Behavior:

Conditions:

Criterion:

Complete objective:

Situation 2: English and Social Studies   As a CORE teacher of English
and social studies in a rural community, you notice a general compliance
about doing assignments on the part of almost all your students. The class is
generally apathetic about social studies, however, with little genuine interest
in the subject. Since most of the students ride the bus to and from school,
there is little chance to use before- or after-school situations to assess any
increase in the interest you feel is necessary.

Affect Needing Attention:

Behavior:

Conditions:

Criterion:

Complete Objective:

Situation 3: Mathematics   In the school district in which you teach,
there is a requirement for graduation that each student pass at least one
course in mathematics before graduation. You teach a senior math class for
those seniors who have not met this requirement. You have discovered a
general pattern among the students: They can do well enough after the class
has worked on a given topic, for a period of time, but when a new topic is
introduced, their initial reaction is to moan and groan.

Affect Needing Attention:

Behavior:

Conditions:

Criterion:

Complete Objective:

Sample Answers for Basic Affective Domain Exercise 2

Situation 1: Boy's P.E. (page 61)

Affect Needing Attention: [Interest in physical skill development and sports.]

Behavior: [Staying after school or arriving early to school to participate in organized sports as part of a team or group. (High-probability approach behavior; directly observable)]

Conditions: [Teacher organizes a wide variety of sports activities and games, and introduces unused equipment, advertising its availability. No credit is given in regular P.E. for such participation. (Variety of alternatives for participation; free-choice situation)]

Criterion: [At least 25 percent of the students will participate by staying after school or arriving early to engage in the activities made available each day. Before the end of the school year it is hoped that all students who are physically able will have participated more than one time. (Realistic and precise)]

Complete Objective: [An increase in interest in physical skill development and sports will be evidenced among the students as demonstrated by participation of at least 25 percent of the students before or after school in team or group sports activities each day and participation of all physically able students at least once during the school year.]

Situation 2: English and Social studies (page 62)

Affect Needing Attention: [Interest of students in social studies.]

Behavior: [Voluntary selection of social studies material during "free reading periods." (Observable, high-probability approach behavior)]

Conditions: [The teacher sets aside part of a period each week for "free reading." In the back of the room the teacher makes available a wide range of reading materials including many selections that are oriented toward social studies. During free reading periods students are allowed to bring their own books or browse through and select materials from the class library. (No-cue, free-choice situation with alternatives)]

Criterion: [The teacher hopes that by the end of the semester at least 20 percent of the students will be reading materials during the free reading period that have a social studies orientation and that at least 80 percent will have read such material before the end of the semester.]

Complete Objective: [Given an opportunity to read a variety of materials during a scheduled free reading period, at least 20 percent of the students will choose material with a social studies orientation to read during any specific free reading period by the end of the semester, and at least 80 percent of the students will read such materials at least once. This behavior will be used as evidence that there is an increasing interest in social studies on the part of students.]

Situation 3: Mathematics (p. 62)

Affect Needing Attention: [Initial reaction to newly introduced topics.]

Behavior: [Less verbalization of displeasure and more positive verbalization when a topic is introduced. (High probability; directly observable)]

Conditions: [Teacher does not tell the class of his or her displeasure at negative student reactions to new topics. No reward for positive reactions is given. (No-cue situation with free choice and an alternative)]

Criterion: [After noting the average amount of time used by students in negative reactions to the introduction of new topics, the teacher anticipates that the length of class time spent in verbalizing negative reactions will gradually be diminished until no negative verbalizations or only positive verbalization will be in evidence by the end of the course. (Directly observable; quantifiable; realistic)]

Complete Objective: [When new topics are being introduced, class time spent on student negative reaction to the topic will gradually diminish until no negative verbalizations will be in evidence by the end of the semester.]

Now that you have practiced writing affective objectives for groups, you can see that your answers may have varied considerably from the models that have been provided. Further practice is provided without models. If you follow the procedure outlined in your practice, you should be able to generate effective basic affective objectives for groups. You may wish to validate your efforts by asking your instructor or peers to criticize your work.

Situation 4: Foreign language   You are a foreign-language teacher who realizes that even though there are out-of-class opportunities to practice the

foreign language you teach, few students are interested to the point of pursuing voluntary practice opportunities.

Affect Needing Attention:

Behavior:

Conditions:

Criterion:

Complete Objective:

Situation 5: Student government   You are an activities director in a large surburban high school. Unfortunately, apathy has grown about student government. You wish to increase interest and thereby participation in student government. (Caution: the *techniques* by which you are going to increase the interest are not part of the objective.)

Affect Needing Attention:

Behavior:

Conditions:

Criterion:

Complete Objective:

Situation 6: Industrial Arts   You are an industrial arts teacher in a high school in the suburbs in which there is a high percentage of upper-middle-class professionals. Most students are college bound. Not only is enrollment down, but the students who do enroll apply themselves minimally to the work.

Affect Needing Attention:

Behavior:

Conditions:

Criterion:

Complete Objective:

CLASSIFYING AFFECTIVE DOMAIN OBJECTIVES TO AID TEACHING

In the cognitive domain, the classification of objectives serves several useful purposes. First and foremost it provides a logical arrangement of intellectual skills so that the teacher can insure that a variety of such skills are practiced. This primary need makes such a classification extremely worthwhile, and teachers who use it actively have an helpful tool available for assistance when making decisions about a variety of objectives. The sample cognitive objectives at the beginning of each chapter in this volume have been arranged to use such a taxonomic classification.

Teachers will find the following affective classification scheme similarly useful in helping students identify affects and deal with these affects with increasing degrees of cognition. The intent is to reduce instances of unthinking responses and to increase instances in which students will make decisions involving values on the basis of serious thought. That is, the teacher assists students with affects identified at a particular level to move to an affective level that involves contemplation.

Pierce-Gray Classification of Affective Objectives

It would be possible to classify affective objectives using several different sorting factors. For instance, if the criterion chosen were the degree of permanence of the affect in the individual, "love" would be classified higher than "interest," for the greater the degree of permanence, the higher the classification on the scale. Intensity would be another possible sorting factor. But after an examination of various possibilities for a viable sorting factor that yields a high degree of usefulness to the teacher, it is apparent that the *degree of cognition in the affect* holds the highest promise for usefulness.

There are six levels in this classification model. The reader will note that the word "level" has been used to differentiate the categories, and is a helpful convenience in conceptualizing the classification scheme. Whether an increase in cognition actually moves the individual "up" in levels is a moot point. Higher levels, here, simply mean that more cognition is necessary.

The practice excercises up to this point have been designed to allow the reader an opportunity to acquire the skills necessary to write acceptable basic affective objectives: the ones that are found at the lower three levels in this classification. At the higher three levels, the teacher's intent changes to an examination of values and of reasons for values held. This change allows the degree of cognition to increase to the point at which the affective objective may take a form more similar to that for cognitive objectives, as practiced in chapter 3.

Level I: Emoting   The term *emoting* describes a lack or minimum of cognitive input. Words that imply this level are those that indicate the individual is unable to verbalize about the situation; the affect is too strong to allow reason. To an observer, the reason for the emotional behaviors are obscured. The emotion is apparently irrational. Some of the common terms that represent examples of emoting are euphoria, guilt, depression, kleptomania, rage, and hysteria. At the emoting level are classified many of the more severe student psychological problems encountered in classrooms. It is beyond the scope of this book to examine these at length. In the day-to-day routine of teaching, the instructor may encounter nonrepetitive emotional displays; these are usually considered to be within a "normal" range. If, however, the behavior is repeated, then the teacher must judge whether the behavior has a detrimental effect on the class and whether the student needs professional help.

Objectives at this level will almost always be formulated for individuals. It is important to reinforce at this point that if an emotional behavior is reoccurring, the teacher may well need to seek the assistance of specialists. Following are sample affective objectives that are written at this level.

The student will:

1. Begin to overcome her acute self-consciousness as demonstrated by her occasional participation in class discussions.

2. Exhibit an increase in self-control as shown by his ability to decrease the instances of temper displays occurring in the classroom.

Level II: Reacting   When the teacher can identify the stimulus that is initiating the affective response, the response is labeled "reacting." Reacting behaviors are predictable. At the time the individual reacts, there is no cognitive decision made as to what form the reaction will take, but the teacher can identify its probable cause. Reactions are usually of relatively short duration. Words often used to identify this level are disgust, embarrassment, joy, anger, dislike, nostalgia, jealousy, and shame.

With some reactions, students will often find it difficult to think about their affect during and following their occurrence. Other reactions are open to misinterpretation, and the student will exhibit a reluctance to engage in conversation about them. For instance, immediately after seeing someone accidently slipping on an icy step, most observers will attempt to ignore the situation, realizing that any discussion will only intensify the embarrassment the individual feels. There are some reactions, however, that allow the individual to engage in discussion soon after their occurrence. To the individual these reactions are usually socially and personally acceptable, for instance, moments of nostalgia. Finally, there are reactions in which the cause is easily accepted and the reaction is even pleasurable. These reactions are often used by teachers to assist in motivating students.

At this level teachers may construct affective objectives both for individuals because of their specific reactions or for the class as a whole. Samples of objectives written at this level might be:

The student will:

1. Overcome initial embarrassment and withdrawal characteristics when class discussion of sexual behavior takes place during the health unit, as exhibited by increased participation over the course of the semester.
2. Demonstrate an increase in neutral or positive verbal reactions and a decrease in negative reactions when math problems that involve metrics are introduced in class.

Level III: Conforming   At this level is classified the majority of commonly written affective objectives. Whenever educators describe an affective situation with an implied attribute of worth that students should adopt, they are operating at the conformity level. This is in line with the historical function of school, which has been to pass on those values held to be important or even crucial to the growth of society from generation to generation.[5]

When an individual *could* begin to supply a reason for his or her responses to encountered ideas, notions, or situations, he or she is operating

[5]See chapter 2.

at the conforming level. However, at this level the reasons, if given at all, are given with little examination as to their worth. The student is able to identify a reason he or she thinks is within the realm of acceptability and adapts it to the situation. The affective response, therefore, has not been qualified. For example, a student may have grown up in a tightly-knit family that holds family loyalty above most other values. When asked why he feels this stance is important he may respond that "the family that sticks together will survive all crises situations," simply because he has heard it said often.

Students may vary within the conforming level; some must reflect momentarily to supply a handy rationale for their affective response, others can furnish a rationale immediately because of previous use. In most situations the student exhibiting behaviors that can be linked to affects deemed worthwhile are not questioned as to their rationales. If the teacher does make such inquiry, then a process has begun that has as its primary purpose movement to the three higher levels in this classification.

The objectives submitted in the practice exercises for group-based affective objectives are classified at this level. Other examples follow:

1. Student appreciation for the importance of making wise consumer purchases will increase as demonstrated by the participation of at least 90 percent of the class during the semester in discussions of personal experiences in making choices after comparative shopping. No credit will be given for such participation.

2. Students will demonstrate an increased willingness to engage in cultural self-improvement by voluntarily attending at least two of the following events: (1) an art lecture; (2) a symphony; (3) a museum tour; or (4) a ballet performance.

3. The student will indicate a greater interest in subject matter by showing an increase in the number of homework assignments turned in on time.

Level IV: Validating (Processing Values)   Ultimately, the student begins to examine the rationales behind his or her attitudes and consciously examines them for their worth. Thus, those values held and the reasons for those values are analyzed and accepted or rejected on their intrinsic merit, rather than on a superficial basis.

Early in this process the student quite often tentatively accepts and rejects rationales for values, examining and comparing them to other rationales and values he or she already holds. Thus, the student begins to build a pool of validated values along with the examined rationale that justifies their inclusion. Particular values become defendable by the student.

The teacher may determine through discussion if the student is operating at the validation level. By asking for rationales, the teacher can assist the student in the validation process. If, for instance, the teacher inquires why the student wants to run for student body secretary and receives the answer, "Because I want to become a professional secretary when I get out of school," the act of running and serving as student body secretary may be validated as to whether it will, in fact, assist the student in attaining the goal.

The values held, and their rationales, may be circular at this level. For instance, a student may feel that being able to join honor societies is important because membership provides opportunities to meet more people who may become friends. He or she likes having friends because he or she feels it will make him or her more popular, which is desirable because it will allow the opportunity to participate in honor societies. In these instances a value adopted becomes the rationale for another value at the same level.

Objectives at this level may take the form of cognitive objectives. They must simply and explicitly state the validation of the rationale that the student has determined. For example:

1. When asked to explain why he thinks his assisting in a drama production is important, the student will be able to give a reason or reasons that are logical for his circumstances.
2. When confronted with an opportunity to visit New York City for a week, the student will be able to defend the importance to her or him of staying at home by supplying at least two valid rationales.
3. The student will be able to explain why she spends most of her homework time working on mathematics.

Level V: Integrating (Integrating Values)   In everyday life, the individual encounters situations that assist him or her in beginning to integrate the various values he or she has adopted. Because choices must be made between values, an internal hierarchy of importance begins to develop, and the relationships between these values becomes apparent and consistent.

The individual begins to be able to respond in terms of values organized as to their relative worth to him or herself, and in particular situations the individual can identify the relative importance of a particular value and explain why it is more or less important than related values. A philosophical position has begun to emerge.

When assisting students in developing an integrated system of values, teachers can help by insuring that whenever values are given as rationales for other values, students learn to break out of the circular patterns described earlier. That is, the value submitted as the rationale should be a longer-term value, or a more important value for the individual. If, for instance, instead of giving the reasons mentioned above, the individual believes the reason for joining honor societies is to improve social skills, and if that individual wishes to improve social skills because such skills are necessary to his or her occupational goals, then the individual has begun to integrate values.

For any individual, a complete compartmentalization and total value hierarchy may be impossible. But for most ordinary decisions, the structuring of such an integrated system allows common everyday decisions to be made against this rationalized background. At the next level, the individual examines these judgments.

Samples of affective objectives written at this level might include the following:

1. When discussing reasons for his commitment to scuba diving, the student will be able to supply rationales that indicate that scuba diving provides experiences that have various long-term benefits.
2. In response to inquiry, the student will be able to consistently provide rationales for her involvement in service activities that indicate a concern for society rather than just herself.

Level VI: Value Judging   When placed in a position of rendering a value judgment, the individual is influenced by varying degrees of cognition and his or her value hierarchy. If the situation involves more than one value at a particular level in this hierarchy, this conflict may cause more problems in rendering a value judgment than when it does not. For instance, the question of whether or not a student thinks a particular poem is beautiful may be answered with more ease than a question regarding the morality of abortion.

It is also possible for the student, at this point, to become disenchanted with the criteria (integrated values) that he or she has used to render such judgments. When such a disenchantment occurs he or she may well return to the level of integrating values and examine and revise values and their rationales.

For purposes of teaching, objectives at this level are often written purposely to set up a value conflict. The teacher then works to assist students in resolving that conflict. During this process, not only is the value conflict resolved but the student is offered an opportunity to validate his or her values by examining their rationales, and also to integrate them according to their importance.

Samples of objectives that present value conflicts at this level follow:

1. When presented with the alternatives of cheating on an exam in order to get into college or failing the exam but maintaining moral integrity, the student will be able (a) to render a decision, and (b) to explain rationales for that decision that are logically or empirically sound.
2. After observing a friend who has done her many favors engaged in an act of blatant theft, the student will be able to resolve the conflict between peer loyalty and belief in justice by describing valid reasons for her judgment and action.

A Model of the Relationships Between
the Cognitive and Affective Domains

A representation of the merging of the affective and cognitive domains is presented in Figure 6.

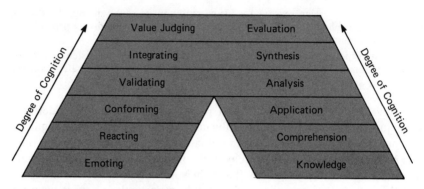

FIGURE 6　The Relationships Between Bloom's Cognitive Taxonomy and the Affective Domain

The schematic is not meant to imply that there is a completely analogous relationship between the domains at each level of the diagram, but there are a number of similarities, and the more one investigates these, and the more one's understanding of both domains increases, the more one is struck by these similarities.

Level I: Emoting—Knowledge　In the cognitive classification scheme, the student at the knowledge level is dealing with the primary operation of *remembering content.* In the affective domain, the student at the emotion level works with the fundamental operation of dealing with *involuntary emotions.* In both the affective and cognitive domains the intellect initiates efforts to expand upon these initial operations. In the cognitive domain the data remembered are manipulated with more and more sophistication. In the affective domain the individual uses increasing amounts of intellect to control and use the affect for positive purposes.

Level II: Reacting—Comprehension　When working in the cognitive domain, a person at the comprehension level is able to attach more and more meaning to content and facts. An individual can explain concepts in his or her own words or change ideas from one form to another. At the reacting level in the affective domain a similar phenomenon takes place in relation to emotional responses. They are interpretable and begin to have meaning. Discussions of such reactions become possible.

Level III: Conforming—Application   At the application level, in the cognitive domain the individual uses rules, procedures, or methods and applies them in order to complete tasks. He or she does not question their use or attempt to change or formulate new principles. Whatever was given as convenient to his or her purpose is utilized with minimum hesitation. In the affective domain at Level III the student uses or applies handy rationales to explain previously adopted attitudes. This is done with little thought as to the real worth of the rationales. The individual is satisfied if the immediately available rationales seem to be effective.

Level IV: Validating—Analysis   The element common to the usual processes identified as being analytical (i.e., classifying, deducing, inducing, comparing, and contrasting) is the ability of the individual to discern similarities and differences between things. "Right" answers are determined by the individual in the cognitive area of ideas and concepts through the use of analytical skills in problem solving.

Although not aware of the process, a person functions similarly at the validating level. He or she begins to view previously unquestioned values and rationales with an inquiring eye. the similarities and differences between values and rationales begin to become apparent, and inconsistencies emerge that may be obviously untenable. He or she may deduce that a value held is acceptable, whereas the rationale was superficial but replaceable by one that is viable.

Level V: Integrating—Synthesis   The synthesis level in the cognitive domain implies the development of a unique product by the student. Concepts, principles, and ideas are blended in ways that are new for the individual. In the affective domain the individual begins to put values and their rationales into his or her own individualized hierarchy. This hierarchy is, of necessity, unique to the individual.

Level VI: Value Judging—Evaluation   The value judging level is an area that has received more empirical scrutiny than many other affective components. In this area a person makes moral judgments as well as highly cognitive evaluations. In both cases an opinion is rendered. It is difficult to discern in many cases whether someone is rendering a judgment that is based upon his or her value hierarchy or is able to assess the relative worth of factual or empirical evidence to reach an opinion. When the criterion for making the judgment is primarily the assessment of facts, it is labeled "evaluation"; when the criterion is primarily based on the value hierarchy, it is labeled "value judging." In most situations a blend of both will have influenced the judgment.

The Pierce-Gray Classification
and Approaches To Value Education

The Pierce-Gray Classification of Affective Objectives has been designed so that it will not be in conflict with notions of value clarification[6] or efforts to assist students in their development of moral reasoning.[7] Both approaches depend upon motivating students to examine their rationales for values held, to validate and integrate values and rationales, and to make value judgments based on value criteria. Extended discussions of these approaches is beyond the scope of this book, and the reader is referred to and encouraged to investigate the selected readings at the end of this chapter for further study in this area.

Formal Assessment of Affective Objectives
For Groups

In addition to using the wide range of behaviors exhibited by students in the usual school circumstances to assess affects, it is also possible to construct formal evaluation instruments. These formal evaluations of student affects use some type of paper and pencil evaluation in which the student responds to one or a series of questions or open-ended situations. They may be teacher-constructed or ready-made instruments.

The following situation is an example of a formal, teacher-constructed group assessment of a specific affective change. A teacher has discovered that many of her students display evidence of prejudice toward Mexican-Americans. In order to assess any teacher-inspired change in this affect, the teacher needs to preassess student attitudes. Students are asked to respond in an open-ended way to a short story about a racial situation involving Anglo-Americans and Chicanos. The teacher computes the percentage of positive statements, negative statements, and neutral statements the students made. The teacher then utilizes teaching and environmental procedures designed to lead to an increase in student understanding of the deprivation and frustrations of Mexican-Americans. After teaching such a unit, the teacher asks students again to respond formally to the situation. The percentage of positive and negative statements may then be rechecked. By using such a procedure, teachers can determine if their efforts have desired effects.

[6]Louis E. Raths, Merrill Harmin, and Sidney B. Simon, *Values and Teaching* (Columbus, Ohio: Charles E. Merrill, 1966).

[7]Lawrence Kohlberg, "Stage and Sequence: The Cognitive Development Approach to Socialization," in D. A. Goblin, ed., *Handbook of Socialization Theory and Research* (Chicago: Rand McNally, 1969.)

There are also formal instruments available for measuring changes in the affective domain. One of the pioneer efforts in this regard is *Attitude Toward School*, a collection of affective objectives and instruments from the Instructional Objective Exchange. The following excerpt from the Introduction of the collection serves to clarify its development.[8]

> In January 1970, representatives of Title III programs in approximately forty states gathered for a meeting in Washington, D.C., to discuss the availability of objectives and measuring devices which might be used for their educational needs assessments and evaluations, particularly in the affective domain. Representatives of the Instructional Objectives Exhange joined with those educators on that occasion to indicate that after approximately eighteen months of nationwide searching, only a few affective objectives and measures had been located by the Exchange. It became apparent that if rapid progress toward development of affective objectives and measures was to be made, some individual or agency would systematically have to undertake the development work.
>
> The Title III representatives decided to pool certain of their financial resources and cooperatively support a development project by the Instructional Objectives Exchange. The assignment was to produce objectives and measures which might be employed for educational needs assessment and educational evaluation in specific affective areas. After considerable discussion regarding the affective dimensions most in need of assessment, two high priority affective areas were identified, namely, the learner's (1) attitude toward school and (2) self-concept. The Instructional Objectives Exchange was commissioned to develop a number of objectives in these two fields (at several age/grade levels) and to make these available, not only to the Title III projects but to other educators in need of such measures.

The primary purpose of this material, then, is to measure the effects of attitude toward school and self-concepts. Many of the measuring devices are inferential, self-report measures in which the real objective is concealed from the respondent. Other techniques are labeled observational indicators.

An example of an inferential item in which the student responds to a hypothetical situation follows.

> It is assumed that from the alternatives a student selects in these hypothetical situations, his attitude toward the social structure and climate of his own school may be inferred.[9]
>
> School is out for the day and Dick and Jane are leaving. A long camera shot shows the principal standing near the door talking to a couple of students as the other students come out of the building.
>
> (a) He is standing there to watch for rule breakers.
> (b) He usually comes out of his office at this time to meet kids who want to talk informally.
> (c) He is waiting there to greet a visiting member of the school board.[10]

[8]*Attitude Toward School* K—12, Instructional Objectives Exchange, P.O. Box 24095, Los Angeles, 1971, pp. 2-3.
[9]Ibid., p. 82.
[10]Ibid., p. 86.

It can be seen from the item that inferences about a student's perception of his or her school and the student's affects that pertain to school could be measured. It is certainly not beyond the capability of teachers with specific instructional interests in the affective domain to construct items that would check group affective shifts as a result of instruction.

SUMMARY

Controversy continues over the school's specific role within the affective domain, but the existence of the affective domain as a pervasive influence in schools cannot be denied. Thus criticisms and responses to those criticisms have been presented to familiarize the student with problems associated with objectives for the affective domain.

The teacher who intends to deal in the affective domain needs proficiency in the construction of affective domain objectives for both individuals and groups. Each type of objective has a different use and different components in the construction of its parts.

When classifying objectives into taxonomic categories, it seems most useful to classify according to the degree of cognition involved. This helps the teacher to direct activities more clearly and assist students to cope with their emotions and reactions and examine their values and the rationales for their values.

Through the use of the higher levels of the affective domain, the teacher can effectively organize to improve the ability of students to work with value judgments. It is also possible to assess the value positions of students through the use of formal instruments.

SELECTED READINGS

HUDDAN, EUGENE E., *Evolving Instruction*. New York: Macmillan 1970.

KLAUSMEIER, HERBERT J., and CHESTER W. HARRIS, eds., *Analysis of Concept Learning*. New York: Academic Press, 1966.

KOHLBERG, LAWRENCE "Stage and Sequence: The Cognitive Development Approach to Socialization," in D. A. Goslin, ed., *Handbook of Socialization Theory and Research*. Chicago: Rand McNally, 1969. A good basic presentation of the Kohlberg theory.

_____, "The Child as a Moral Philosopher," *Psychology Today*, September 1968. A view of the young child from the standpoint of Kohlberg's ideas about the development of moral judgment.

KOHLBERG, LAWRENCE, and C. GILLIAGAN, "The Adolescent as a Philosopher," *Daedalus*, 1971. A view of the adolescent from the standpoint of Kohlberg's ideas about the development of moral judgment.

KOHLBERG, LAWRENCE and E. TURIEL., eds., *Moral Development*. New York: Holt, Rinehart and Winston. Presently available only in prepublication form. Appears to be a comprehensive survey of research undertakings in the area of moral development. Includes material on the most recent adaptations and revision of Kohlberg's theory.

KRATHWOHL, DAVID R., BENJAMIN S. BLOOM, and BERTRAN B. MASIA, *Taxonomy of Educational Objectives—The Classification of Educational Goals*, Handbook II: Affective Domain. New York: David McKay, 1964.

LEE, BLAINE, and DAVID MERRILL, *Writing Complete Affective Objectives: A Short Course*. Belmont, Calif.: Wadsworth, 1972.

LICKONA, THOMAS *Discussion Guide: A Strategy for Teaching Values*. Pleasantville, N.Y.: Guidance Associates, 1972. A teacher guide for an elementary school program that utilizes the ideas developed by Lawrence Kohlberg and his associates.

LOCKWOOD, ALAN, *Moral Reasoning*. Middletown, Conn.: American Education, 1972. A pamphlet that is a part of the Harvard Social Studies Project. The publication is designed for secondary school students and presents a number of ideas about moral reasoning, including those of Lawrence Kohlberg.

PORTER, N., and N. TAYLOR, *A Handbook for Assessing Moral Reasoning*. Cambridge, Mass.: Moral Education and Research Foundation, 1974. A handbook designed for teachers and researchers interested in developing procedures for measuring individuals with respect to level or stage of moral reasoning attained.

Social Education, 39, no. 1 (January 1975). The entire issue is devoted to articles dealing with the teaching of moral reasoning at both the elementary and secondary levels.

RATHS, LOUIS E., MERRILL HARMIN, and SIDNEY B. SIMON, *Values and Teaching*. Columbus, Ohio: Charles E. Merrill, 1966.

5

Preassessment

the great time saver.

It is unfortunate that many teachers consider the time-consuming task of assessing the status of their students at the outset of instruction as burdensome. The time may be rationalized, however, if it is realized that accurately preassessing students can avoid the hours of frustration that often occur when teachers are unaware that a task prerequisite to a particular learning skill was not mastered by students.

In its strictest sense, preassessment within the Logical Instructional Model is an attempt to pinpoint the student's exact developmental status with regard to a specific instructional objective. Besides this precise definition, however, there is the total assessment of the student that may be taken into account as the teacher plans learning activities. This chapter, therefore, is divided into two parts. The first part discusses the nature of the adolescent and attempts to familiarize the prospective teacher with certain psychological principles that characterize high school students. It leads the preservice teacher toward the ultimate skills of general psychological student assessment. The second part of the chapter deals with more formal techniques of assessment of pupils in relation to the specific objectives.

OBJECTIVES

The student will:

1. Write from memory four sources of data useful in an assessment of the psychological position of the student. (Knowledge)

2. Explain in his or her own words, what is meant by the terms *partial independence* and *adolescent culmination*, and give an example of each. (Comprehension)

3. When given a sample cumulative record of a hypothetical student, locate and pull out eight assigned items commonly found in cumulative records. (Comprehension; Application)

4. When given two sample cumulative records of hypothetical pupils, identify and specify in writing six similarities and six differences in the two students' backgrounds that could be utilized in psychological preassessments of the two students. (Analysis)

5. When given a behavioral objective for a secondary school course in the preservice teacher's major field, describe in writing a preassessment procedure for that objective that would determine each student's status in relation to that objective. (Synthesis)

6. When given a total design for a unit of instruction that follows the Logical Instructional Model, evaluate the preassessment section of that unit and determine if in his or her opinion it is satisfactory or unsatisfactory, giving at least four reasons for his or her decision in less than four pages. (Evaluation)

UNDERSTANDING THE ADOLESCENT: PSYCHOLOGICAL PREASSESSMENT

There are many personal attributes that assist teachers when working to improve their teaching. One that is extremely helpful to quality teachers is a sincere respect for people. Complete competence as an instructor involves liking and enjoying pupils, while at the same time being able to ascertain their relative place in the growth pattern. If these two aspects of teaching can be blended with a realistic assessment of student learning skills, then the production of high-success-probability learning experiences is attainable.

A component helpful in cultivating the attributes of respect and enjoyment of students is the ability to understand the basic influences in their lives. Every student and every class is unique, but there are certain general characteristics that are useful as guiding principles.

Adolescence

The term "adolescence" brings to mind stereotyped images, but it is our best description of a traumatic period in the life of a growing, learning, human being. What is the adolescent circumstance? The average entering age for the intermediate school is about twelve years old. Most twelve-year-olds are considered to be, and behave as, children; yet six years later an eighteen-year-old has completed secondary school and has acquired most of the characteristics of adulthood. He or she can vote, fight in wars, marry and raise children, and in many states legally purchase and consume alcohol. What of those years of transition? Most of the time the adolescent lived in a state of "betweenness." He or she was too old to be considered and treated as a child, and too young to be considered an adult. A period of rapid growth and the trauma of sexual development with all the concomitant problems of adjustment was experienced, for better or worse.

A peculiar dichotomy emerges during adolescence: a preoccupation with "I" that results in a self-centeredness that overpowers reason, accompanied by serious self-doubts. Peer approval becomes a pervasive urge. At the same time, there is a push and pull toward and away from the adult world. Adult parent-teacher approval seems necessary, yet adolescents feel they have "copped out" on goals of self-reliance if this approval smacks of dependence. At the same time this period of trauma is going on, the adolescent is surrounded by the "teen" culture. This culture leads to fads of dress and social behaviors that are often viewed with shock by elders.

Adolescents are the way they are because of the varying sociological influences that surround them. The range of allowable behaviors that the adolescent exhibits must be broad enough so that the perplexities of growth can be successfully solved, and narrow enough so that law breaking and antisocial behaviors are inhibited. At the same time, good models of the adult world must be available and commonly accepted values of society exhibited and understood by all. These circumstances add up to no small order for teachers, parents, and school.

Needs of the Adolescent

Teachers are usually aware that people have certain basic needs that must be fulfilled in order for them to survive. These needs encompass both the physical realm and the psychological realm. Today, fortunately, the majority of students' physical needs have been satisfied; however, educators often ignore physical needs because it is easy to assume that all students have satisfied these needs. Alcorn, Kinder, and Schunert[1] have compiled some statistics that open one's eyes to the problem.

> High school teachers instruct approximately 150 to 200 students each day. Research-based estimates indicate that in an average group of that number:
>
> 1. Five to ten will have speech defects requiring attention if therapy has not been provided in the elementary school.

[1]Marvin D. Alcorn, James S. Kinder, and Jim R. Schunart, *Better Teaching in Secondary Schools* (New York: Holt, Rinehart and Winston, 1970), p. 21.

2. Three to six are afflicted with hearing loss enough to require medical attention.
3. Twenty to fifty require corrective lenses to achieve "normal" vision.
4. Ten to fifteen suffer from known allergies, such as eczema, asthma, hay fever, and hives.
5. One to ten have epilepsy, diabetes, or cardiac disability.

And this is not to mention the students who come to school hungry, not necessarily because there was no food in the house but because home conditions were such that the food was never prepared or eaten.

The teacher is not expected to be able to identify instantly all cases of physical deficiencies, but teachers do vary in their sensitivity. In an investigation of a case of a high school student's poor vision, it was discovered that two teachers out of six had recognized the problem in the youngster and had adjusted seating arrangements to put her close to the chalkboard. In one class she was close to the front by "the luck of the draw," and in her other two classroom-oriented subjects she was in the back or middle. And this case was not difficult to spot because the student's glasses were referred to as being like the "bottoms of coke bottles." How many difficult-to-spot cases go undetected?

The psychological needs of the adolescent are just as important as the physical needs, but even more difficult to spot. Many teachers have found it useful to combine the many views of needs into one category: self-concept. There are widely differing definitions for the term *self-concept*, but they generally focus upon how the person views himself, i.e., well liked versus not well liked, attractive versus unattractive, able versus unable. The actions of people are governed, to one extent or another, by their self-concepts, and many acts people engage in are directly aimed at trying to improve self-concepts. In school, when a student cannot engage in "acceptable" acts to acquire praise, success, recognition, or even a sense of accomplishment, he may well turn to "unacceptable" acts and become a "discipline problem." It must be remembered that students usually prefer to engage in "acceptable" acts since such acts tend to produce more widely valued positive feedback, but if these actions are beyond the capability of the students or scorned by those whose opinion they value, other, less acceptable actions *will* be taken. An important part of your role as a teacher will be to help all students, the able and the not so able, to find acceptable ways to build and continually improve a favorable self-concept.

Many sociologists have pointed out that an obvious place for fulfillment of the satisfaction of needs has been the family, but with the loosening of this unit in our society has come an increasing pressure on other institutions to accept more responsibility for insuring such satisfaction. Regardless of many educators' reservations, the fulfillment of needs is now becoming a task for both home and school. But at the same time the adolescent attempts to satisfy felt needs, he or she is preparing to move to adulthood and this growth of independence can conflict with need satisfaction.

The preparation for the end of adolescence begins even before puberty, but it is at the end of adolescence that the student becomes increasingly able to free himself or herself from perceived adult constraints. He or she may first be treated as an independent person by an employer, a Sunday school director, a traffic guard, or often a teacher.

To generalize the proper position for the teacher, the work of Stone and Church is quoted: ". . . in addition to providing a rational society for him to grow up to, adults can best help the adolescent into adulthood by treating him, at least in public, as much as possible as an adult without, however, throwing him so completely on his own that he is overwhelmed by anxiety."[2] Any adult who has continuous contacts with adolescents is fortunate if he or she does not have difficulty maintaining a consistent attitude. Because of the transition process, it is difficult to render adult treatment to an adolescent during periods in which the youngster undergoes a temporary reversion to immature behavior. On the other hand, an obvious inconsistency on the part of the adult leads to adolescent resentment.

Crucial to the adolescent's development is a proper relationship between the adolescent and his or her parents. The time period from childhood to adulthood is a series of experiments in which both parent and child begin to tolerate periods of severance. But this severance always happens with the unspoken mutual understanding that it is temporary. When adolescence is nearing culmination, the attitudes of the youngster and parents must be refocused so that there is greater respect for each other as worthy individuals in society, free of debts to each other, but willing to assist each other, individual to individual.

The risks involved at this time of life are great. Few, if any, families experience a smooth transition in this time of "partial independence." The maturing youngster often involves himself or herself in activities that seem exciting and adult-like, without benefit of parental approval. In most cases the level of involvement in these activities will allow the adolescent to feel that he or she has lived a moment of independent, adult-like existence without risking too much. Depending upon the background and situation, this risk taking varies tremendously from individual to individual. For instance, the smoking of a cigarette at a slumber party may seem extremely daring to a protected, middle-class, suburban high school girl. For another girl, an unapproved absence from home over a weekend may be necessary for the same effect. A particular combination of geographical location, ethnic background, and peer relations may stretch the gap between the parent's definition of tolerable exercises in partial independence and the student's definition beyond immediate reconciliation. At various times teachers must adopt a stance that renders as much assistance as possible to students

[2]L. Joseph Stone and Joseph Church, *Childhood and Adolescence—A Psychology of the Growing Person*, 2nd ed., (New York: Random House, 1968), p. 498.

when they have crossed the boundary of parent acceptability. Student behavior in school during these periods of personal trauma may be erratic, and can best be handled if the teacher realizes what psychological and sociological phenomena surround the adolescent during this period.

As rational people with an educational commitment to the processes of analysis as a means of learning and solving problems, teachers will often inspire discussions of issues that youngsters feel are pertinent to them. Because the youngster is involved in the arguments being presented, he or she may perceive them from a position several degrees away from the teacher's position. For example, when a discussion in social science class on the role of the family unit is raging hot and heavy, the student taking a rather negative view of the family unit's value may be speaking from a position tempered by his doubts about the relationship between his own father and mother.

SOURCES OF INFORMATION IN ASSESSING STUDENTS

Some teachers excuse themselves from doing any kind of assessment of their students with such comments as, "Oh, I don't want to prejudge him," or "Everyone starts with a clean slate in my class." However, students are not the same and their records can assist in indicating their status in relation to many objectives. If teachers are not going to use the data that has been gathered, then there has been a considerable waste of time and effort. An analogy could be made to the physician who does not use medical records in his or her diagnosis because he or she does not wish to prejudice a medical judgment. Such a procedure would be considered unthinkable.

Cumulative Records

Every school system seems to have its own record-keeping system. In larger schools, the cumulative records of students are usually kept in the counseling office. In smaller schools, they may be in the principal's office. Often they are in the hands of the elementary teacher or, at the secondary level, in the hands of the homeroom teacher.

The cumulative records of any student may include any or all of the following:

1. The academic grades received throughout the educational career.
2. Intelligence scores at various grade levels (usually including the tests taken).
3. Achievement scores in various subjects at different grade levels.
4. Vocational preference tests results.
5. Aptitude test scores.

6. Anecdotal records by teachers, principals, counselors, coaches, or other staff members.

7. Records of conferences held about, or with, the student between any of the staff, perhaps including parents.

8. Doctors' records of physical examinations, illnesses, and sometimes attendance records.

9. Self-portraits and autobiographies.

10. Copies of letters from or to the school about the student.

11. Helpful comments by teachers about successful techniques to assist in teaching the student.

12. Records of transcripts or other information sent to or received from other schools.

13. Records of police inquiries or information released to prospective employers or responses to other legal inquiries.

Record-Keeping Ethics   There are two main problems connected with the maintenance of records, especially since the use of computers is making it possible to collect and store large amounts of information and retrieve it more and more rapidly.[3] The first question is, What kinds of information about pupils should be maintained in schools? This question has an obvious answer: only that data should be kept that is pertinent to the learning situation. However, the school has accepted more and more responsibility for the development of not only the intellectual aspects of the personality, but also the emotional growth of the individual. In this context, the rationale for collecting any bits of information that could help students make personal adjustments is supplied. The terminal point in collecting information has yet to be defined.

A second question that needs attention is, Who should have access to this information? Present school law in various states differs somewhat on this point, but it is generally the case that only the student, his or her parents or legal guardians, and school personnel have access to confidential records, and after the student is eighteen, even parents must have their child's permission.

With recent federal legislation that allows parents of pupils less than eighteen years old legal access to such records, and pupils over eighteen personal access when they formally request it, some schools are formulating new policies that restrict the information that may be accumulated. The full ramifications of the legislation have not yet been felt, but it appears that parents and students may demand removal of anecdotal records they perceive as being negative, and that such demands must be complied with.

Teachers must exhibit the highest degree of professionalism when dealing with school records. This means the teacher is charged with the respon-

[3]V. S. Teitelborum, "School Records Can Be An Invasion of Privacy, " *Today's Education*, 60, no. 5 (May 1971), 43-45.

sibility of gathering all information available, applying high evaluative skills to analyze it, and then using that information for diagnostic purposes. At the same time, however, such information must be treated as private. This delicate use of professional judgment is more difficult than one would suppose.

The Student as a Source

Besides access to the records available in the office, an equally important source for information about students is the students themselves. At the beginning of the school year, asking students to respond to questionnaires or open-ended sentences can tangibly help the teacher assess the status of his or her pupils. Samples of categories of inquiry that are important to the teacher in assessment are the following:

1. Students' perception of their previous background in the subject.
2. The types of classroom activities they think they like best.
3. What their perceptions are of benefits they will receive from the class.
4. Whether they think they will like or dislike the subject.
5. What their study-area situation is at home.

As long as the information obtained is defensible in terms of the educational process, the teacher should encounter little friction. Be cautious, however, about a question such as, "Do you have a set of reference encyclopedias at home?" It seems to be an acceptable question educationally, but if its purpose is to gather the names of prospective customers for a part-time sales venture, it becomes highly unethical.[4]

Strategies for Blending Psychological Preassessment and Instruction

Many teachers who make a conscientious effort to gather information about their students from cumulative records and student self-reporting devices fall short when it comes to the actual use of this information in planning for instruction. There has been a general "impression" of the student planted in the brain of the teacher, and it may alter teaching behavior at times, but not in any formalized fashion.

Better educationally is the use of a strategy for data gathering and review that logically leads the teacher to decisions regarding the types of ac-

[4]Teachers can be held legally responsible for statements and comments they make about students. It would be extremely unwise, for example, to write (or say) that "Johnny steals" or that "Johnny seems to have homosexual tendencies." Cumulative records can be helpful, but they *can* be misleading. Anecdotes, opinions, and similar "soft" data must not be taken as gospel. Students' opinions, attitudes, and feelings change rapidly during adolescence, and "soft" data may easily be outdated and no longer applicable.

tivities and teacher reactions that will maximize learning and psychological growth.

To illustrate, the following procedure has been effective for some teachers. At the outset of the term, the teacher constructs a five- by eight-inch index card for each student. This card has categories for each type of information that relates logically to the particular subject being taught. The cumulative folders are perused and helpful data transfered to the card.

As the term begins, further information is added from student self-reporting devices, parents, counselors, and other staff who can supply information. At predetermined times (perhaps at three-week intervals) the cards are formally reviewed, but the teacher does not stop there. On each card a section labeled "Suggested Strategies" is entered. In this section the teacher attempts to devise ideas for instruction that may help the particular student.

For example, suppose in filling out cards the teacher finds a student with two evident needs. Entries in the cumulative folder and input from staff and the teacher's own observations identify a problem in the affective domain and a strength in the cognitive domain. The student is self-conscious and has a tendency to isolate herself, but at the same time she exhibits a strength in the writing of papers. The teacher makes the notation "Attempt to have student share her quality papers with the class" on the card and looks for such opportunities.

The essential ingredient is the change from an intuitive approach to a formalized one. The formalized approach does take some time, but the results generated from its use make the effort more than worthwhile.

PREASSESSMENT PROCEDURES FOR SPECIFIC INSTRUCTIONAL OBJECTIVES

After preassessment of the relative psychological status of the student, the teacher is ready to check the student's abilities in relation to specific objectives. Teachers may find themselves in one of several positions when it comes to the objectives of the course or courses they teach. In some they may have the flexibility to adjust their objectives after preassessment; that is, in extreme cases an objective decided on may be abandoned completely after preassessment because it has been found to be inappropriate. A better approach would be to specify whatever remedial objectives and activities were necessary to provide the background needed for success. This raises the question of how much "catch-up" a teacher can engage students in without totally ignoring mandates to prepare them for entry into subsequent courses.

In many situations the teacher will, in fact, have restricted freedom to abandon objectives or to add remedial objectives even though it would be logical to do so. In the foreign language and mathematics programs in many schools, the teacher is committed to bringing the students to a certain point so that they may proceed to the next course. In these instances, preassessment does not necessarily lead to the abandonment of the terminal behavior but rather to adjustments in en-route objectives in order to reach the terminal objective in the most expedient way. It is in such situations that the need for a self-paced, competency-based approach to education is most obvious.

Cognitive domain objectives can be classified into several categories for preassessment purposes. First, many objectives lend themselves to formal preassessment procedures that can be checked with paper and pencil tests. It is obvious that the teacher must make sure that the students understand some basic areas of information before higher-level objectives are attempted in which that information is manipulated. When the objective is of a higher order, the preassessment may be a search-and-find mission to uncover a set of data that will serve as the vehicle for practicing some particular analytical skill. In this case, the teacher can choose a content topic that the preassessment has shown is already familiar to the members of the class, and spend the time on organizing, classifying, comparing, or in other ways intellectually analyzing and manipulating the data.

Of course, there are many instances where the objective for a class is the simple acquisition of a body of knowledge. Here the pre-test may be a sampling of the same types of items that will be found on the final test. It may also be in situations such as this that the teacher will be preassessing only at the beginning of a course in order to determine the initial entry points for the class members because the nature of the subject makes it highly unlikely that any students can already demonstrate competency of the terminal objective.

Other types of objectives do not imply an evaluation through the use of paper and pencil tests. This leads to a basic principle to follow when dealing with preassessment: Approach any preassessment in the most direct, expedient way. There is no need to conceal or be overly subtle about preassessment. If the terminal behavior is that the student be able to discern fact from opinion in editorials, the teacher should make his or her preassessment a sample of that skill. Leading a discussion about a television editorial seen in class and attempting to assess each student's ability in this skill from their responses is inefficient and unnecessary.

If the behavior being preassessed is a skill that cannot be measured through paper and pencil tests, then the teacher must work to structure the classroom activities in such a way as to check each student's ability without "losing" the rest of the class. If, for instance, the skill being preassessed is the ability to give a five-minute extemporaneous speech, it would be possible in a thirty-student class to inhibit completely students' intrinsic motivation through a string of poorly done five-minute speeches that would last for three or four days. Preassessment intended to group students for emphasis of specific content and practice is obviously in order, but a procedure must be developed to preassess skills that is not wasteful.

Another approach may be necessary for preassessment of objectives that utilize psychomotor skills. An art instructor may preassess and determine that a student possesses the necessary prerequisite skills to produce a unique piece of jewelry. Some of these prerequisites will already be known because of their use in prior projects. Preassessment in this case may be as simple as asking the student whether or not he or she is familiar with the operation of a new tool necessary to construct a new project. If the new tool is such that a safety factor is involved, preassessment may of necessity be much more formal.

Another preassessment situation may allow the teacher to choose paper and pencil procedures or to use alternatives. When dealing with higher-order cognitive objectives, many may be stated in a way that allows for paper and pencil tests for preassessment, and teachers may wish to use such tests. In some instances, preassessment through the use of paper and pencil tests is possible even though the terminal behavior is not stated in a way that implies a paper and pencil evaluation. For instance, if a terminal behavior in a general business class is written as "The student will be able to compare three products in a grocery store for price and quality and choose the best buy," a preassessment might describe the situation hypothetically and the students' responses would still give the instructor reliable information as to the areas of instruction that need emphasis. Conversely, the teacher may be able to determine, through a series of direct questions, the relative student ability for an objective that will ultimately be evaluated through a paper and pencil test.

Student Reaction to Preassessment Tests

It is unfortunate but true that many students have been tested to the point of psychological reaction by the time they are in high school. The mere fact that there is going to be a test may be cause for alarm for some students. For this reason, when the preassessment involves a paper and pencil test, the teacher may face a mild dilemma. To avoid trauma, the students should be told that the preassessment instrument will not count on their grades. This announcement, in turn, may cause some students not to make the serious effort necessary if the teacher is to assess properly the position of class members in relation to the objective. That extrinsic motivation can have a significant effect on raw scores has been convincingly shown in such studies as that of Farr, Trunman, and Blanton in which "junior high school students in a control group, when the time between pre- and posttesting was only one week, gained an average of 10.2 raw score points on the *Nelson Reading Test* even though no specific instruction in reading intervened." However, an equivalent experimental group's average gain was significantly higher with the only difference being extrinsic motivation in the form of prizes at the time of the post test.[5]

Neither telling students that a pretest will count on grades nor using rewards such as transistor radios and candy bars (as Farr et al. did) seems to be an appropriate procedure for preassessment testing. It behooves the teacher, then, to create a healthy climate for preassessment, and to encourage effort on the part of students on the basis of the ultimate saving of their time and effort by providing information that allows the teacher to develop superior learning activities on the basis of information gathered.

After a pretest has been administered it is often tempting to use the results of that test as a teaching tool. Students are usually interested in·how well they did on any test they take, and going over items may be the only further "teaching" some students who scored well need in order to achieve the objective. This procedure, however, makes it necessary for the teacher to produce a larger item pool if the final evaluation of the objective is based upon the same items or type of items. Suppose, for instance, in a remedial eighth-grade English class the teacher wanted students to be able to identify incomplete sentences when presented with a series of complete and incomplete sentences. If the preassessment items are later used as part of instruction, then different items must be constructed for the final evaluation because rather than learning the characteristics of incomplete and complete sentences, many students may be able to recall the specific items and their answers without understanding the concepts. Thus, the final evaluation would be changed from an application (or even analysis) level skill to a knowledge level skill.

How Much Preassessment at One Time?

As Popham and Baker[6] point out: "Another pretesting consideration is whether the student will come to feel frustrated if he scores poorly on the test. This is a factor to consider, and may suggest that pretesting be conducted in small pieces rather than in one overwhelming course covering session."

There are several reasons for avoiding very large preassessment sessions. One is the frustration that some students may feel if they know nothing about the material at all. At worst they will not only be agitated

[5]Roger Fan, J. Tunman, and B. Elget, "How to Make a Pile in Performance Contracting," *Phi Delta Kappan*, 53, no. 6, (February 1972) 367-69.
[6]James Popham and Eva Baker, *Systematic Instruction* (Englewood Cliffs, N.J.: Prentice-Hall, 1970), p. 74.

during the test itself, but they may also build a resistance to learning the material. Another reason for preassessing for the upcoming objectives as they are approached is that there will be some student change. A preassessment for many objectives at the beginning of a course may no longer be valid several weeks later. Students who have since learned prerequisite tasks through classroom instruction may now see relationships that need not be emphasized, while a preassessment given too early may indicate that they do need emphasis.

A third reason for spacing preassessment has been alluded to previously. It is often easier to get a serious effort from a student on a short instrument than on one that is attempting to preassess many things. The problem of maintaining interest and motivation exists when students know that the score will not count if their grade enters the picture. If manageable, some of this problem may be alleviated by allowing students who score well on the preassessment instrument to be classed as having "proficiency" and moved out of the objective and on to another area.

It sometimes happens that the preassessment will reveal that students are already able to demonstrate the bulk of the terminal behaviors sought. This situation may be painful for the teacher because many preplanned lessons may have to be put aside and new ones generated. The extra effort will be well worth the trouble, however, since any other course of action will result in boredom for many of the students.

SUMMARY

This chapter includes a description of two basic types of preassessment important in attempts to maximize pupil learning. The first is the psychological status of the student, and the second is the intellectual position in relation to a specific objective.

Every human has basic needs, and at the age of adolescence these needs are crucial and powerful. They involve both the physical and emotional realms and drive the adolescent to test his or her independence against a dependence upon family, teachers, and other adults.

In order to adjust the classroom to the needs of the students, the teacher must gather data from an assortment of sources. The professional teacher handles this data in such a way as to make an accurate diagnosis of the status and needs of the student, and always treats the data in a confidential manner. A basic attitude the teacher should develop is that the adolescent needs to be supported as he or she struggles to gain full independence in a partially independent setting. As much as possible the adolescent needs to be treated like an adult.

After preassessment of the psychological status of the adolescent, the teacher preassesses the students' intellectual position in relation to objectives. After preassessment, teachers may or may not adjust their adopted behavioral objectives or their learning activities.

There are a variety of preassessment procedures, both formal and informal, available to the teacher. Each has advantages and disadvantages in relation to the type of objective adopted. In addition to the selection of the proper procedure for preassessment, the teacher must also be aware of the possibility of varying reactions to preassessment instruments on the part of the students.

SELECTED READINGS

ALCORN, MARVIN S., JAMES S. KINDER, and JIM R. SCHUNART, *Better Teaching in Secondary Schools*. New York: Holt, Rinehart and Winston, 1970.

COMBS, ARTHUR W., *Perceiving, Behaving, Becoming: A New Focus for Education*. Association for Supervision and Curriculum Development, a department of the National Education Association, 1201 Sixteenth Street N.W., Washington 6, D.C., 1962.

DeCOCO, JOHN P., *The Psychology of Learning and Instruction: Educational Psychology*. Englewood Cliffs, N.J.: Prentice-Hall, 1968.

GAGNE, ROBERT M., ed., *Learning and Individual Differences*. Columbus, Ohio: Charles E. Merrill, 1967.

HOOVER, KENNETH H., *Learning and Teaching in the Secondary School*, 2nd ed. Boston: Allyn & Bacon, 1968.

INLOW, GAIL M., *Maturity in High School Teaching*, 2nd ed. Englewood Cliffs, N.J.: Prentice-Hall, 1970.

MOULY, GEORGE J., *Psychology for Effective Teaching*, 2nd ed. New York: Holt, Rinehart and Winston, 1968.

POPHAM, JAMES, and EVA BAKER, *Systematic Instruction*. Englewood Cliffs, N.J.: Prentice-Hall, 1970.

STONE, L. JOSEPH, and JOSEPH CHURCH, *Childhood and Adolescence—A Psychology of the Growing Person*, 2nd ed. New York: Random House, 1968.

6

Selecting
Instructional Procedures

There are two basic principles underlying the discussion of instructional procedures in this chapter. The first principle is that the vast majority of instructional procedures should be carefully planned. While it is true that extemporaneous experiences are occasionally both enjoyable and valuable, it is more often the case that they are simply time-fillers resulting from inadequate planning. Since time is a valuable commodity to both teachers and students, the careful planning of instructional experiences can maximize the effective utilization of class time by minimizing essentially nonproductive activities.

Among the factors to be considered when planning instructional procedures are: (1) the particular instructional objectives to be achieved; (2) the time available; (3) the materials available; (4) the background of the students; and (5) the size and physical arrangement of the group of students.

The second principle is that instructional experiences should be varied. A steady diet of any one approach, no matter how successful it may have been originally, will ultimately pale with continued use. Interest can best be stimulated and maintained if change in instructional procedures is frequent and meaningful. Using a variety of procedures will facilitate the achievement of specified objectives. The variety of terminal behaviors stipulated in almost any list of instructional objectives can be viewed as a mandate for a variety of instructional experiences. This analysis is deliberate since there is a tendency for teachers to find an approach that seems to work well and then to become afraid of change. They become unsure about alternatives and unwilling to attempt anything new. A lack of teacher enthusiasm results from seldom attempting or experiencing a new pattern and students detect this lack of enthusiasm and react similarly. On the other hand, if a teacher becomes enthusiastic and interested in "doing something different," students will tend to reflect that excitement or interest. Just as variety in instructional experiences can help maintain the interest, vitality, and morale of the students, it can do the same for the teacher.

OBJECTIVES

The student will:

1. When given, on a multiple-choice test, a series of instructional objectives and/or situations and a series of instructional procedures, match the most appropriate experience with the objective or situation in at least 80 percent of the cases. (Application; Analysis)
2. When shown a film, videotape recording, or demonstration of any instructional procedure discussed in this chapter describe, in less than two pages, at least one strong point and one weak point in its use and prescribe corrective measures (if any) that are necessary. (Analysis; Evaluation)
3. Write two precise instructional objectives (one reflecting lower-level cognitive skills and the other higher-level cognitive skills) and develop, in less than two pages, at least a two-point rationale supporting his or her choice of particular instructional procedures most likely to help students achieve the stated objectives. (Synthesis; Evaluation)

TYPES OF INSTRUCTIONAL EXPERIENCES

Formal and Informal Lectures

Lectures at the secondary level have fallen into some disrepute, simply because there have been too many lectures that were poorly done by too many teachers. A good lecture—one that is well planned and delivered smoothly and with conviction—can be an exciting learning experience and will be perceived as such by students. The line between such a lecture and an artistic performance is very fine indeed, and the extensive use of lectures must be reserved for the teacher with the personality and ability to do such work. It is possible for almost any teacher to plan and orchestrate a lecture that is cohesive and polished and that will capture the interest of all but the most reluctant student. The time spent in planning such a lecture, however, precludes all but an occasional use of this experience by most teachers.

Rather than striving for the perfect "formal" lecture, that is, a lecture in which students do little except listen to a virtuoso performance, it behooves most teachers to concentrate on identifying those points, skills, and procedures that will enable them to deliver an "informal" lecture. That is, one that provides for student participation rather than passive student reception. This approach has the advantage of being well within the capabilities of most teachers, insures student interest, and is thus more universally useful. From this point on, the term *lecture* refers to the informal lecture unless otherwise stipulated.

Uses of Lectures   Lectures are appropriately used: (1) to quickly and concisely present to students a great deal of new and integrated information; (2) to clarify relationships among general points or between specific causes and effects; (3) to explain procedures; and (4) to summarize information. It is reasonable to ask why teachers should not simply use handouts to convey this information to students, since most students can read and comprehend at a rate of about two hundred fifty words per minute whereas most can listen and comprehend at a rate of only one hundred fifty words per minute. In many situations in which lectures are used, a handout *would* be as appropriate or even more appropriate; however, there are other situations, particularly those in which teachers may wish to add emphasis by inflecting their voices or to make instant modifications on the basis of student reactions, in which lectures are clearly an appropriate instructional experience. Additionally, the informal lecture allows for spontaneous student response and questions, and thus points can be clarified as they are raised by the students. Obviously, this is not usually possible during a reading.

Planning Lectures   There are a number of appropriate lecture-planning procedures. Perhaps the most common is to construct a word or phrase outline. As the first step in this process, the teacher describes the specific instructional objective students will be able to achieve after listening to, and participating in, the lecture.

The kinds of objectives for which lectures are most appropriate are generally those at the lower cognitive levels. For example:

Each student will:

1. Explain in writing six causes of the first World War I.
2. Write, in his or her own words, the definition of ethnocentrism and illustrate it with at least two examples.

The objectives are appropriate to lectures since their terminal behaviors are not time-consuming (and thus do not infringe on the time available for the lecture) and do not require much, if any, student practice. With such objectives, students can be expected to demonstrate successfully the desired behavior simply by virtue of having been exposed to the information.

The objective will serve as the standard against which all prospective constituent elements of the lecture will be compared. Those elements that clearly contribute to student achievement of the objective will find their way into the word or phrase outline while those that contribute little or nothing will be discarded. This procedure assures cohesiveness in the lecture and facilitates evaluation of the lecture's effectiveness. The outline may consist of short sentences, phrases, or even single words. Many teachers have found they can lecture most effectively if they reduce their notes to a minimum. Voluminous notes, either in the form of lengthy outlines on sheets of paper or many brief items on index cards, tend to inhibit the lecturer rather than help. Faced with very detailed notes, many beginning teachers tend to refer to the notes more often than necessary, simply because they are there. In some cases the referrals become so frequent that the lecturer is, in effect, reading the notes. Additionally, voluminous notes tend to tie the lecturer to the podium, increase the probability of losing one's place, and decrease the opportunities the lecturer has to look at the audience while speaking. Extensive notes, in most cases, simply do not add to the smoothness and polish of a final delivery.

The lecture outline should serve to spark the speaker's memory, not as a source of new information. The outline contains the key phrases, facts, figures, names, dates, etc., that are at the heart of the material, and helps the teacher organize the material into logical blocks and to subdivide these blocks into manageable sizes to facilitate student learning. When giving an initial lecture, teachers may find it helpful to make notes concerning the approximate length of time each part of the lecture should take.

Another part of planning concerns checking the content for its suitability for the student's level. It is easy to make notes without realizing that the students may not be familiar with certain terms, especially those that are technical or complex. If such terms are used in the outline they should be starred or otherwise noted to remind the teacher to define and explain them.

During the planning of lectures, teachers should consider the use of appropriate instructional aids. Almost any lecture will hold student attention longer when the lecturer includes pictures, maps, graphs, cartoons, or similar aids. The time to consider the use of such aids is when the lecture is being planned, and appropriate steps in ordering should be taken early.

There are two parties in an informal lecture: the students, and the lecturer. Teachers who use this learning mode can often increase their effectiveness by working with students to insure that common-sense note-taking procedures are used. For example, teachers can instruct students that

1. Each set of lecture notes should start on a separate page and carry the date and title of the lecture (as well as the lecturer's name if a guest is presenting the lecture).
2. A consistent outline format should be used, such as the following:
   I. Major Topic (The Purpose of Outlining)
      A. Subheading (Logical Organization of Content)
         1. Explanations (Sequential Steps: Causes and Effects, etc.)
            a. Further explanations
3. Notes tend to be more useful if the student attempts to write down only major ideas and points, rather than trying to copy the lecture word-for-word.
4. They should look for techniques such as the restating, rephrasing, and listing of points on the board or overhead projector as clues that these are major points.
5. Contextual clues such as "There are *three* main facts here . . ." are often used at the beginning of a series of points and can facilitate the outlining of the information.
6. The development of a personal shorthand system for abbreviating frequently used words and phrases can save considerable time.
7. There are advantages to writing neatly enough that recopying the notes is not necessary. Students can read and study neatly written notes in less time than it takes to recopy them. Some students, however, find that the act of recopying or rephasing notes assists in learning.
8. Space may be allowed, as the notes are being taken, to add personal thoughts, comments, questions, and reactions later.

Delivering the Lecture   After considerable effort to prepare material properly for a lecture, teachers may find that the students will deem the mode ineffective because of delivery or style. Lectures, as with any other instructional procedure, are enhanced by the stimulation of student interest *at the very beginning*. Student interest and student involvement are closely tied. Useful techniques for establishing motivation include: asking a question or posing a pertinent problem and eliciting student responses; asking students to respond to a graphic situation, picture, or quotation; asking a student to recount briefly personal experiences relevant to the lecture material; or revealing related startling facts. This initial interest arousement is enhanced by involving students as directly as possible and should "tune them in" to what the lecture is about. There is some evidence that teachers who can initiate lessons well can elicit more learning than teachers who do not concentrate on the initial stages of a presentation.[1]

[1] Robert F. Schuck, "The Effect of Set Induction Upon Pupil Achievement, Retention and Assessment of Effective Teaching in a Unit on Respiration in the BSCS Curricula," *Educational Leadership Research Supplement*, 2, no. 5 (May 1969), pp. 785-93.

Language usage can also contribute to, or detact from, the effectiveness of a lecture. Using language of appropriate complexity and formality is an art worth practicing. If new words are to be introduced, clear definitions should be made so that students will understand their meanings in the context in which they are used. Language complexity early in the lecture will cause students to "tune out" because they feel the lecture is going to be "over their heads," making it difficult to recapture their interest.

Good lecturers will often explain to students how the lecture is organized (cause-effect relationships, chronological order, easy-to-difficult, concrete-to-abstract, rule-example-rule, etc.). This helps students orient their thinking and organize their notes.

The effectiveness of lecturers is increased by visually reinforcing verbal information. If students *see* important facts, figures, names, and dates, as well as *hear* them, the probability of their being remembered increases. Furthermore, varying the stimulus can, in itself, be a device helpful in refocusing the attention of students whose interest may be wavering. Among the most common kinds of visual aids are prepared posters, chalkboards, overhead projectors, and opaque projectors. These devices are easy to use and provide sufficient latitude for creative utilization.

The ways in which lecturers use their voices also influences effectiveness. Voice inflections, for example, can place emphasis on particular points and can dramatize quotations and asides. By varying the pitch and volume of the voice, lecturers add the variety necessary to capture the interest of the students. Rate, too, is important. Although most people can listen and comprehend from about 125 to 150 words per minute, a lecture is intended to instruct, and to do so properly, the rate at which the lecture is delivered should be slower, from 110 to 130 words per minute. The rate of delivery depends on the purpose and complexity of the material. In the case of most lectures, teachers should allow time for students to listen to what is being said, comprehend what they hear, and relate new information to what is already known. This last step cannot be done when the material is complex or if it is delivered at too fast a rate.

Teachers *can* improve their own lecture delivery techniques. By taping segments of their own speech and dividing the number of words spoken by the number of minutes elapsed, the words per minute can be calculated. It will also become apparent if there is a tendency to vary delivery rate. If there is a tendency to mispronounce particular words, to use personal pronouns, or insert phrases such as "you know" or "uh," listening to recorded lectures will make it immediately apparent. Teachers simply do not realize their own idiosyncracies until they listen to themselves and analyze what they hear.

Just as the use of formal visual aids adds to the interest of a lecture, the physical movements of the lecturer can also. Appropriate hand and arm movements can help punctuate sentences and emphasize important points. Moving from behind the desk or podium and walking about can provide visual stimulation, but all of these movements must stop short of being distracting. The use of a videotape recorder to detect and correct inappropriate physical movements can be revealing and beneficial.

The use of numerous and relevant examples has been shown to facilitate student understanding of content. Generous use of examples, nonexamples, analogies, and illustrations will help keep student interest high and produce more learning.

When students are actively involved, their interest is higher and the teacher can assess responses for students' understanding. Student participation is best encouraged by careful planning. Procedures found helpful to many teachers include preparing sets of key questions to be asked at appropriate places in the lecture. The experienced teacher makes maximum use of nonverbal clues and student behaviors that indicate confusion. The use of students in the class to reiterate points by answering questions will often clarify important points for students who are still struggling with a new idea.

A good lecture concludes with a summary and review of the main points. While such a summarization and review can be done verbally, it may be helpful to students if the lecturer makes use of visual aids. The visual reinforcement helps emphasize important points, and it gives students a chance to double-check notes, fill in points they may have missed, and correct errors.

In summary, although the lecture is in some disrepute, it is one of the most often used instructional procedures. Lectures have the advantages of enabling teachers to present to students a large body of information in a relatively short period of time, and they are relatively easy to direct and control.

Some possible disadvantages of lectures are that they can encourage passive, rather than active, student participation; that they may not provide much of the student-teacher interaction needed for proper evaluation of the instructional process; that they can foster unquestioning acceptance of presented material; that they may not capitalize on student curiosity or creativity; and that they tend to center more on the content than on what the student is to do with the content.

Questioning

The judicious use of questions can be the basis for valuable instructional experiences. Questions can be used to find out how well students understand a particular block of information; to shift student attention from one point to another; to increase retention of important points by isolating and emphasizing them; and to point students in the right direction before starting assignments. Perhaps their most valuable use, however, is to elicit high-order thinking on the part of students as questions are asked that call for analysis, synthesis, and evaluation skills, and to provide practice for students in formulating and orally communicating specific answers to specific questions.

The following four principles have been found to be helpful in increasing the effectiveness of questions:

1. *State the question clearly and precisely.* A question such as "What about the Confederate Army during the Civil War?" for example, leaves the student little direction in his answer. Better questions might be "What types of supply problems did the Confederate Army have?" or "Was the leadership of the Confederate Army as well trained as the leadership of the Union Army?" It is unfair to insist upon or expect a precise answer to an imprecisely worded question.

2. *Pause after asking the question.* When teachers ask questions in a classroom, it is desirable for all students, not just those called upon, to profit from the questions. A pause after a question is asked, increases the probability that all students will think about the answer. The pause allows students the time needed to formulate good-quality answers.

3. *Call upon students at random.* Since it is desirable for all students to think about the questions, teachers should not follow any pattern when calling on students. Any pattern, whether it is a seating arrangement, an alphabetical arrangement, or any other kind of sequence, has the effect of reducing attention on the part of those students who feel they will not be called upon.

4. *Provide immediate feedback to students.* Teachers should indicate the appropriateness of student answers. If an answer is not wholly correct, one should try to use the part that is correct, or state the question to which the given answer would have been appropriate. If students are assured that their responses have value, active participation will continue.

Questioning is, by its very nature, threatening to some students. There will always be students who cannot answer a particular question and who will thus feel embarrassed. Although this problem is inherent in the questioning experience and can cause the alienation of particular students, teachers can do much to minimize its effects. They can develop the skills of providing verbal and nonverbal clues to students who seem to be having difficulty, and of encouraging elaboration of partially correct answers. It is reasonable to expect teachers to be able to develop questioning techniques that will not humiliate a student who provides an incorrect answer.

Categorization of Questions   The nature of questions may be varied to insure differing types of responses from students. One convenient way of categorizing questions to see the frequency of a particular type is to compare them to the taxonomic divisions of the cognitive domain. The following examples may be helpful in placing questions into appropriate categories and are also indicative of the types of objectives for which this procedure is appropriate:

1. *Knowledge (or simple recall)*. "What are the three basic parts of a precise instructional objective?"
2. *Comprehension (or understanding)*. "What is meant by the term *in loco parentis*?"
3. *Application (or using information)*. "Traveling at 55 miles per hour, how long would it take to get from New York to Los Angeles?"
4. *Analysis (or pulling an idea apart)*. "What words or phrases does the author of this article use that cause the article to be biased?"
5. *Synthesis (putting together something new)*. "How would you have improved upon Germany's strategy during the Battle of Britain?"
6. *Evaluation (or making and defending a judgment)*. "Who do you think our best president was, and why?"

Another way to categorize questions is according to their essential function.

1. *First-Order Questions.* A first-order question may be defined as any question that has served its purpose as soon as an acceptable answer is given. Any of the six categories of questions described earlier can be considered first-order questions if their answers are clear-cut and if no further elaboration is elicited or desired.
2. *Probing Questions.* A probing question is asked to encourage students to go beyond their initial responses to explain themselves further. An example of the use of a probing style might be, "Good, you're right so far, now can you give us an illustration . . . ?" By asking students to provide examples, illustrations, rationales, etc., teachers can frequently determine the depth of students' understanding of material more accurately than by using first-order questions alone. A follow-up probing question often begins with "why."
3. *Open-Ended Questions.* An open-ended question has no definite right or wrong answer. A question such as "What do you think about the probability of extraterrestial life forms?" is asked to encourage students to go beyond the recollection or explanation or previously acquired information and to hypothesize, project, and infer. Such questions are particularly well suited to the initiation of discussions.
4. *Convergent Questions.* Convergent questions are arranged in a series and designed to "converge" on a particular point or idea. For example, questions such as, "Are there fewer or more farmers now than twenty years ago?" and "How do farm subsidies affect consumer prices?" could be used to help students focus attention on the issue of government farm subsidies. Convergent questions may be used to induce a principle or deduce an answer.

5. *Divergent Questions.* Divergent questions, as the name implies, are asked in order to draw a student's attention away from one point and allow it creative freedom to settle on a different but related point. Divergent questions are particularly useful in inspiring student discovery of analogous situations. "What present-day parallels do we have, if any, to the Athenian agora?" is an example of an analysis-level question being used to stimulate divergent thinking.

Encouraging students to ask questions is a skill that can be manifested in numerous ways. Teachers can assist students in phrasing questions and make it clear they feel questions indicate a willingness to learn, not ignorance, on the part of students. They can respond to students' questions thoroughly, courteously, and in a friendly manner and indicate the importance of students' questions by comments such as "That was a good question because . . ."

Discussions

Discussions, in one form or another, are among the most commonly used instructional experiences. A discussion differs from usual conversation in that the intent and content of discussions are more carefully delineated and structured. Conversations that occur spontaneously are usually not intended to achieve specific objectives and are therefore essentially random. Instructional discussions have a specific purpose and direction. Their function is to help students acquire the information and skills necessary to achieve specific objectives. Typical of objectives calling for one or another kind of discussion are the following:

The student will:

1. Describe, in writing, the contents of a survival kit to be taken into the mountains by hikers planning a two-week camping trip.
2. Describe orally either a strength or a weakness in a given political system and explain why it is a strength or a weakness.

The skills and information necessary to achieve these two objectives can be acquired by students in a number of ways; however, the discussion is one logical learning procedure. For example, using a discussion to give students practice in analyzing the components of survival kits in general will directly contribute to their ability to compile such components into a kit for any given situation later. The second objective can be achieved directly using the discussion since each student can be given the opportunity to participate and hence demonstrate the required behavior.

General Discussions   The least specific of the discussion types is the general discussion. The purpose of general discussion is to give students practice in on-the-spot thinking, clear oral expression, and posing and responding to questions. Such discussions are also useful for assessing the diversification of views and exploring ideas.

As with any discussion, the teacher's initial step is to gather together and make available to students appropriate background information, materials, and sources. The success of a discussion as an instructional experience depends upon the degree to which students are informed and prepared. Without background in the topic students will be unlikely to make good contributions to a discussion. Proper procedure often leads to the recording of key questions for use in stimulating or changing the direction of the discussion. By using key questions, discussions can be guided along those lines most likely to contribute to student achievement of the instructional objectives.

Since one of the aims in discussions is to encourage student-to-student communication, it can be helpful to arrange desks or chairs in such a way that students can comfortably see each other. Circular, semicircular, or horseshoe arrangements are useful. Some teachers seem to be reluctant to join such an arrangement, but if the teacher remains apart from the students there is a tendency for the discussion pattern to go from student to teacher to student rather than from student to student.

It can be useful to agree, with students, on certain discussion ground rules. Some of these ground rules may be that contributions will be impersonal; that ideas, not the people who suggest them, will be the focus of the discussion; and that common social courtesies will be observed. If there are consistent violations of the rules, students may wish to establish a process for helping their peers who are lax in proper participation procedures.

It is common for teachers unconsciously to allow one or two students to monopolize the discussions. This problem can be avoided by asking for the comments and opinions of those students who do not volunteer to participate, but care should be taken not to force such participation. If students feel threatened, their participation will decrease rather than increase. Asking for opinions rather than for specific facts is a good way to encourage participation without posing a threat.

The problem of digression often emerges in general discussions. Some digressions that lead away from the objective may deal with information that has meaning and relevance for the students. It is up to the teacher to decide whether the digression is important enough in its own right to allow it to continue.

Guided or Directed Discussions   A directed discussion is appropriate if students are to be guided through a series of questions to the discovery of some principle, formula, relationship, or other specific preselected result. In guided discussions students are given practice in inductive or deductive, step-by-step thinking, and since the thinking is convergent, the net result is to lead the students toward a common revelation of a major principle or conclusion.

There is some danger in using directed discussions because the teacher will have determined what the students are to discover. If students become too frustrated in the chain of logic leading to the discovery, they may react with the attitude, "Why didn't you just say so in the first place?" and the value of the experience will be lost. Many teachers who use this technique feel that using it for only ten- or fifteen-minute blocks of time works best. Once the conclusion is reached or the principle is discovered, a shift to another instructional experience to utilize that conclusion or principle logically follows. It has also been found helpful to begin guided discussions with a statement such as "There is an underlying point here . . ." or "Let's see if we can reach a conclusion concerning . . ." Statements such as these help set the stage for the guided discussion and minimize the possibility of students seeing the experience as guesswork.

An analogy might be made between a guided discussion and a programmed text. In each case the most likely student responses to questions must be anticipated and appropriate questions (or instruction) planned. Both are designed to provide reinforcement to the student for correct answers and are built around a series of sequential steps. The important difference is that in a guided discussion the teacher very closely monitors the interaction and can modify the remaining questions to capitalize on some unexpected student response.

If used cogently, guided discussions can provide an additional rich instructional experience. Students enjoy discovering and solving, and once they have found a principle, they remember it longer than if it is simply explained to them.

Reflective Discussions   Reflective discussions are used to assist students in developing analytical skills, arriving at alternative explanations, finding solutions to selected problems, and classifying ideas into major categories. These skills relate directly to objectives at the higher cognitive levels (i.e., analysis, synthesis, and evaluation). A typical objective for a reflective discussion might be, "Students will explain orally how some aspect of daily life would differ if we lived under a socialistic government."

When using reflective discussions teachers define a particular problem relative to the instructional objective. Then a series of open-ended questions are devised to encourage a variety of possible responses. Additional specific questions will spontaneously be generated and asked during the discussion.

To help maximize the benefit from reflective discussions, teachers often delegate one student to list the identified main points of each response on the chalkboard. To supplement this listing the teacher then elicits from the class appropriate headings for clusters of responses that have points in common. In this way students are given practice in classifying ideas and in analysis skills, a basis is provided for predicting and hypothesizing solutions to the original problem.

Unlike guided discussions, which can often be conducted at a rapid rate since the teacher has prior knowledge of the result, reflective discussions should be conducted at a relatively slow pace and include periods of silence. Time must be allowed for students to consider alternate possibilities and to think about the ramifications of those possibilities. Many teachers complain that the slowness of reflective discussions is a serious drawback and that the discussions take time that can be used in more valuable ways. Other teachers feel the "thinking" time required is one of the strongest attributes of reflective discussions and use the discussions frequently. In deciding how often to use them, the teacher must weigh these factors and balance time used against the opportunities for divergent responses, large-scale student participation, practice in classification, and reflection.

Inquiry Discussions and the Scientific Method Inquiry discussions are used to provide students with opportunities to use an analytical approach for reasoning and acquire new information with a minimum of help from the teacher. In inquiry discussions students practice critical thinking, gathering and analyzing data, and drawing conclusions on the basis of evidence rather than intuition.

It is vital that students have access to appropriate resources (books, maps, instruments, graphs, etc.) if inquiry discussions are to be worthwhile. Such materials are most effectively used if they are available in the classroom itself, but if this is not practical, they could be placed on reserve in the school library or in other central locations.

Inquiry discussion is often used in conjunction with what is called the *scientific method.* The steps of the scientific method are usually stated in a form such as the following:

1. Identify the problem.
2. Formulate a hypothesis (a probable solution or explanation).
3. Gather, evaluate, and categorize available data.
4. Reach some conclusion (either reject or support the hypothesis) on the basis of the evidence acquired.
5. Take some action appropriate to the results (write a letter to an appropriate party concerning the implications of the conclusions, let other interested parties know of the results, etc.) so that students will be reinforced for their efforts.

When used as part of the scientific method, most inquiry discussions will be but one part of an overall scheme including several types of instructional experiences. An inquiry discussion will prove valuable at each of the five phases of the scientific method, but using the method itself could occupy a widely varying amount of class time. To facilitate utilization of this method, the teacher can establish a timetable with the class, assuring that the investigation will move along smoothly and will conclude by a certain date. Time is allowed for consolidation sessions during which progress to date can be evaluated and future plans refined.

When used as a single-period experience, an inquiry discussion follows the same scientific method used in longer-term investigations, but the data-gathering process is abbreviated, with all information coming directly from the students (usually based on their experience and their assigned reading). To keep this process from deteriorating, the teacher must be alert for incorrect, incomplete, or misleading student input. When misinformation is detected, teachers often are able to use the instance to generate students' interest in finding out more from sources at hand or from sources available for an out-of-class venture. For purposes of inquiry discussions it is usually inappropriate for the teacher to act as a major source of information. The teacher's role is that of resource person—one who helps point students to the sources of information—rather than a supplier of data. This is in contrast to guided discussions in which teachers not only provide information but also direct students to predetermined outcomes.

For example, assume that a teacher adopted the objective, "Each student will describe, in writing, at least five sources of information needed by a modern world leader in order to function effectively." This objective might be partially achieved by providing students practice in determining what kinds of information the president of the United States needs and how that information is, or might be, acquired. This session lends itself to an inquiry discussion. For example, the following steps could be followed:

1. *Identify the problem.* As a beginning point the teacher could ask students how they think the president gets information relevant to decisions he makes. This line of questioning usually results in a number of ideas, but the need to pinpoint more specifically the kind of information being discussed will almost certainly emerge. The type of information available from newspapers, for example, is different from that available from top-secret dispatches. Once the problem is restated precisely, the second step can be taken.

2. *Formulate a hypothesis.* Through the use of questions some probable hypothesis can be structured. The teacher does not leave an impression that all possibilities are equally valid, thus precluding the need for further analysis. All ideas concerning a hypothesis may be accepted, but the class should decide on a limited number for further investigation.

3. *Gather, evaluate, and categorize available data.* It is at this point that inquiry discussions may prove difficult to complete within a single class period. Ideally, students would search out all types of data and subject them to a detailed analysis. If only a single class period is to be used, the teacher must make extensive use of questions and clues and must encourage students to analyze their own answers. By questioning, sufficient data can often be acquired and analyzed. If sufficient data are not acquired after questioning,

data-gathering teams may be necessary and analysis postponed for a subsequent time.

4. *Reach some conclusion.* Once the data are gathered and analyzed, the class is ready to reach a conclusion. The acquired facts are related to the original hypothesis. Properly handled, the facts should support or reject the hypothesis. In the process, students will have acquired practice in the skill of applying the scientific method to a problem and they will have engaged in analytical thought.

5. *Take some action.* A logical application of the practice just engaged in would be to have students demonstrate the lesson's objective by casting it in a hypothetical situation. (For example: The student is now the president of the United States. How will he organize his information-gathering "machine" and of what will it consist?)

If, when an inquiry discussion is initiated, students realize they do not have sufficient information to reach intelligent conclusions, intervening plans for obtaining additional data emerge. Once the data have been acquired, the class reviews the initial steps and proceeds through the remaining steps. For those teachers who utilize the scientific method inquiry approach, acquisition of the data is as important as producing the result.

Exploratory Discussions   Exploratory discussions have almost as unstructured a framework as general discussions, but there are some important differences. Exploratory discussions are intended to enable students to discuss controversial issues (such as premarital sex, use of illegal drugs, abortion) without fear of censure. Such discussions help make students aware of the other students' views and can thus help them become more tolerant of differing notions.

When exploratory discussions are conducted, teachers must define the topic clearly with the understanding that there will be no negative criticism of other student views during the discussion. That does not preclude disagreement and alternative views, but if a tone of ridicule emerges, students will become reluctant to voice further opinions thus defeating the purpose of the discussion. While the later scrutinizing of a general class feeling is not threatening to individuals and can cause little harm, the scrutinizing of a particular student's opinion or comment may cause negative attention to be focused on him or her and may thus cause a psychological reaction.

One of the problems of exploratory discussions is that they are often explorations into the affective domain, and a precise definition of what was gained by students is difficult. Students may feel that little was accomplished. To minimize these difficulties, teachers can synthesize the various contributions and use them as a basis for further instructional experiences that are more precisely defined. There may be few concrete accomplishments directly attributable to an exploratory discussion, but there may be many students who are enlightened by the variety of opinions held by their peers and who are thus given new insights.

Exploratory discussions may also be used in conjunction with a resource person knowledgeable in the area to be studied. The function of such a person would be to present new ideas and opinions to which students could respond.

Evaluation of Discussions Discussions are time-consuming instructional procedures in relation to content gained by students, especially in comparison to experiences such as reading assignments or lectures. The advantage most forms of discussion have over information-gathering procedures, however, is that they capitalize upon student curiosity and creativity, encourage participation, and allow for development of higher-level thought processes.

Discussions, like all instructional procedures, must be evaluated to determine effectiveness. The best way to judge a discussion is to determine if students can achieve the instructional objective for which the discussion was chosen as the learning activity.

Practicing teachers find it useful to note which students do or do not contribute to discussions and what types of contributions are made by individuals, for comparison with evaluation results. It is sometimes found, for instance, that even though students did not participate vocally in a discussion, they were mentally involved and developed analytical skills. Nonparticipation may indicate that the student needs special, individualized help, but it may also mean these students are simply thinking about what is being said. By comparing evaluation results to patterns of participation it may be possible to determine which students need the maximum amount of encouragement to participate, since participation, in their case, aids learning.

The quality of students' responses is a valid indicator of the effectiveness of discussions. When students make comments indicative of muddled thinking or misconceptions the teacher is alerted to a need to clear up the confusing points or misconceptions. On occasion, however, students make such comments purely for effect—to impress their peers or to elicit special attention from the teacher. If it becomes clear that a student is engaging in "artificial" participation, attempting to take care of the problem during the ongoing discussion is likely to produce denials or challenges by the concerned student and should be avoided. A private conference is usually more fruitful.

Effective evaluation of discussions takes thought, but the potential for improvement makes the effort worthwhile. The more discussions are used and evaluated, the more polished the teacher will become in their use. By providing for student demonstrations of instructional objectives, and by keeping track of participation, teachers can polish their ability in this instructional procedure.

Brainstorming

Brainstorming is an instructional procedure similar in many ways to an exploratory discussion. Brainstorming is used to generate a wide variety of creative ideas concerning a problem in a short period of time.

To conduct a brainstorming session, the teacher acts as a facilitator. The facilitator's primary responsibility is to see that proper procedures are followed. Brainstorming uses relatively few, but crucial, rules. After the problem is identified, the facilitator explains that the point of the brainstorming session is to acquire as many creative ideas as possible. Everyone is encouraged to contribute any idea regardless of how "far out" it may seem. The facilitator makes it clear that no idea or contribution is to be discussed, evaluated, or criticized during the brainstorming session, and that each idea suggested will be added to a written list of ideas that will be compiled.

The effectiveness of a brainstorming session depends on rapid pace, short duration, and close adherence to the rule that no idea or contribution during the brainstorming is to be discussed. At the end of the session the class will have a number of suggestions written down relating to the central topic. The facilitator then helps the class divide the ideas into general categories and move into an exploratory discussion in which the various ideas are discussed. If such discussion is allowed to interrupt the brainstorming session itself, the necessary freewheeling atmosphere is inhibited.

One common use for brainstorming sessions is to acquire seed material for more complex tasks, such as synthesizing. Thus, a teacher might use a brainstorming session to help students generate ideas with which to build a rationale for or against suggested governmental legislation.

Demonstrations

Demonstrations have the unique advantage of enabling students to observe the demonstrator engaged in a learning task rather than simply talking about it. A correctly conducted demonstration, whether of some laboratory procedure, physical skill, or other action, is often a stimulating instructional experience because it demonstrates a living model. A typical objective calling for a demonstration might be, "Each student will apply an arm splint, which meets Red Cross requirements, to a 'subject' within three minutes."

To make demonstrations effective, teachers must often break down entire processes into component parts and decide what aspect of the skill, process, or procedure will be demonstrated in the time available. This is necessary because most demonstrations are a part of a larger task that cannot be demonstrated in its entirety during usual school time allotments. For instance, one demonstration in home economics may include the selection of a dessert, say, a cake, and include the exact choice of type of cake, possible substitutions of ingredients, proper blending procedures, and possible pitfalls. Including baking time and frosting may not be possible in the usual time allotment.

Having decided what can adequately be demonstrated within the time allowed, the teacher then proceeds to plan the component parts of the demonstration. Depending upon the nature of the demonstration, initial steps may include an overview description of the skill, process, or procedure. If machinery or equipment of any kind is to be used, the safety aspects are stressed. An outline of main points is often written on the chalkboard for quick reference, or students may be given handouts containing this information. Very detailed descriptions are often not necessary because students are able to understand terms, labels, and relationships easily as they view the demonstration.

During planning for the actual demonstration, the teacher will need to test all the equipment to be used to be sure it functions properly. Before the demonstration is conducted, the environment is arranged so that all students can see what is happening. If small instruments or fine manipulations are called for, schools so equipped often use a closed-circuit television camera or videotape equipment. Many classrooms in which large numbers of demonstrations take place are equipped with overhead mirrors above demonstration tables. Effective demonstrations blend a teacher's verbal skills with accompanying psychomotor skills. Gifted demonstrators are able to use the full range of questioning skills, drawing students' attention to crucial steps and to the way in which various steps are carried out. Exaggerated movements are to be avoided since they might confuse or mislead students as they attempt to practice the movements later.

Demonstrations that can be followed by immediate student practice appear to be of maximum effectiveness. If it is not possible to provide for immediate practice, a review is necessary before delayed practice is begun. If no student practice is available, it may be possible that an alternative experience would be as effective as a fully prepared demonstration. If the length or complexity of the demonstration prohibits immediate practice, it may be possible to divide the demonstration into two parts. The biggest asset of a demonstration is its ability to guide and precede students' actual involvement in a similar experience.

When the demonstration involves valuable or potentially dangerous material or equipment, teachers must weigh carefully the dangers and benefits involved. If material or equipment is too dangerous or too valuable, it may be wise to choose a different procedure. Students are in school to learn, but not in an environment where they take unnecessary risk.

As students practice the skill or procedure, the teacher provides individual corrective feedback and encourages students to assess their own performances. Good teaching demands, of course, that allowances be made for individual differences that may make a difference in the way instructions are carried out. For example, if the instructions begin, "Using your right hand . . . ," left-handed students may find such a movement awkward. In addition, allowance must be made for deviation among students' approaches. All students do not exhibit the same techniques in practice, and for some students certain procedures may come easily. If a particular student's idiosyncracy is deemed detrimental to later performance, however, it warrants early correction.

One effective way to conclude a demonstration is to conduct a short questioning session covering specific procedures, terms, labels, and cause-effect relationships. If the practice of the demonstrated skill or procedure is to result in some product (as opposed to resulting in the improvement of some process), examples of satisfactory and unsatisfactory products should be made available so students can compare and contrast their own products with the models. Opportunities for creative responses in the product's development should be encouraged as long as established standards are maintained.

Modified (or "British-Style") Debates

Formal debates have some drawbacks for classroom use because of the limited number of students who can actively participate. By using a modified debate, however, some of this weakness can be minimized. Modified debates can be used to present both sides of a controversial issue (either as new information or as a review); to stimulate thinking; to encourage voluntary student participation; and to bring an entire class into a debate.

To use a modified debate procedure, the class first identifies a problem. Small teams (of three or four students) are selected to research and present each side of the problem. After the teams have acquired their data, the actual debate is conducted.

To begin the debate, a speaker from each side makes a formal presentation of about five minutes in length. A second speaker from each side then has an opportunity for rebuttal, again with a time limit of about five minutes. The rest of the class will now have been exposed to new ideas and information. The moderator then encourages questions and comments from the rest of the students. These questions and comments can be directed to a particular team or team member, or to a previous contributor. Care is taken to see that no one student is allowed to dominate the discussion and that a pro-con sequence is maintained to assure balance.

The discussion is called to a close early enough to allow a representative from each side to make a brief (less than five minutes) summary presentation and to allow time to bring about closure for the class period. This closure includes a general summary and categorization of the new information presented, and provides an opportunity for students to relate the experience directly to an instructional objective.

Although a modified debate is useful for shifting the presentation of new information from the teacher to the student and allows individual talents to emerge, it is inefficient in terms of the amount of new material that can be presented. Its main intent, then, is to increase students' analytical and presentation skills.

Panel Discussions

Another instructional procedure in which the teacher plays a reduced role is the panel discussion. Panel discussions are useful for allowing a small group of students to delve deeply into an area of interest and then to act as a source of information for the rest of the class.

To arrange a panel discussion, a small group of students (six or fewer) is identified as participants on the panel, and one student acts as chairperson. If needed, assistance is provided in dividing up research responsibilities and setting up a time schedule. Responsibilities on the panel are assigned commensurate with the abilities of the students. For some students, providing specific references and sources may be necessary.

When the panel is ready to act as an authority, the chairperson or other moderator may follow several courses of action. One common approach is for the moderator or chairperson to explain briefly what the panel is prepared to discuss with the class, to introduce each of the panel members and identify his or her special area of interest, and begin accepting questions from the class.

An alternative approach uses the moderator or chairperson to introduce briefly the topic to be discussed and then to introduce each of the panel members, allowing each about five minutes to discuss or explain his or her particular area of interest. The moderator or chairperson then briefly summarizes the findings and opens the panel to questions and comments from the class. This procedure has the benefit of providing the rest of the students with information upon which to base questions.

In both approaches the moderator or chairperson insures that all panel members participate on an equal basis and that sufficient time is left for a final summation. Time is also allowed for the teacher to bring the panel discussion to a close near the end of the class period and establish the relationship of the discussion to the instructional objective.

Sociodramas

Sociodramas are useful for dramatizing particular social problems and for increasing student empathy for the feelings, viewpoints, and problems of other members of society. Teachers who use sociodramas successfully find they are most useful when working to help students achieve various affective domain objectives. Typical of such objectives might be the following:

The student will:

1. Identify and explain the cause for his reaction to the statement, "Homosexuality is normal." (Conforming/ Validating)
2. Add or eliminate at least one rationale used to defend his or her attitude about abortion. (Validating)

To conduct a sociodrama successfully the teacher makes certain that all students understand that participants will be acting out roles as they believe people would actually behave. Participants, therefore, theoretically do not act out their *own* feelings, but what they perceive the feelings of others to be. It is made clear that the sociodrama will be stopped if a student steps out of his or her role and begins to get too emotionally involved.

Once the ground rules are understood, the class proceeds to identify a situation in which two or more people interact and the specific roles and "positions" of the participants. After this is done students are encouraged to volunteer to play each of the roles. No one should be forced to participate.

Participants are allowed to confer briefly about how they intend to act out the situation (not to rehearse), and should then act it out. Usually two or three minutes is sufficient for students to decide how they intend to present the situation, and another ten minutes for the actual sociodrama.

Before any discussion of the sociodrama takes place, it is sometimes worthwhile to have a second set of students confer and act out the same situation. After the second sociodrama, students can compare and contrast pertinent points in the dramatizations. No effort is made to evaluate the performance level of students. The focus of the discussion after a sociodrama is on the differing perceptions of the roles by the participants and nonparticipants, on an attempt to understand the probable feelings and beliefs of the person(s) in the real situation, and on an examination of personal rationales for values held.

Guest Speakers

The chief purposes of inviting guest speakers into the classroom are to expose students to experts in particular fields, especially individuals who may have views different from those already explored in class, and to help motivate students. Taking advantage of such people in the classroom—a controlled situation—establishes a direct contact between the classroom and the real world.

To maximize the usefulness of guest speakers as an instructional experience, the teacher involves students in organizing to obtain and utilize the guest speaker. When the class identifies a need in a particular area in which a speaker can provide a unique contribution, a list of potential speakers is compiled. The names of the prospective speakers are then cleared through the principal or other appropriate administrator, and permission is obtained to invite them to speak to the class. On the list should be persons who can fit such a visit into their schedule. Administrators may be able to suggest individuals who are willing to speak to classes and who have been well received in the past.

It is a good learning experience for students when they can be used to contact the prospective speaker. Among the things the prospective speaker may wish to know will be the age and grade level of the students, the topic being studied, how much the students already know about the topic, what type of unique contribution he or she might make, and the specific time, date, and topic.

It requires effort to prepare students for a guest speaker. If the speaker is to discuss a relatively new topic, it is usually possible to have students read available relevant information and/or discuss the topic. This gives students a matrix in which to work, thereby increasing their interest and enabling them to ask more intelligent questions. Some speakers prefer to respond to questions written by students before the talk. The quality of such questions depends upon the students' having experience in the content area prior to the speaker's visit.

On the appointed day the speaker will appreciate a student escort, who can meet the speaker at the entrance to the school and guide him or her to the classroom. In the few moments before introducing the speaker, the teacher can determine the approach the speaker will take. It is proper to suggest that time be left for a question-and-answer period after the presentation. If the teacher wishes to make a tape recording of the presentation, the permission of the speaker must be obtained.

After the presentation is complete, the teacher. ties loose strands together and brings about a closure. Points may have been made that will require further study and aspects of the content presented may need to be related to previously learned material and to the instructional objective underlying the presentation. If students do not suggest a thank-you note, the teacher may wish to remind them and discuss a procedure for writing it.

Field Trips

The logical extension of bringing part of the world into the classroom is taking the class into the "real" world. Field trips are useful not only because they give students firsthand knowledge and enable them to see how a number of skills, processes, and so forth, blend into a whole, but also because they can be used to provide students with cultural experiences available in no other way. Many students, for example, would never get to see the printing of a newspaper from start to finish unless they saw it on a school field trip. Similarly, many students might never go to an art museum, concert, or professional play unless they were introduced to them on a field trip.

Field trips should be directly related to an ongoing unit of work. When possible, it is desirable to capitalize on a perceived student need for a field trip, but if the teacher knows that long-range planning is a necessity for a particular trip, he or she may take the initiative. Once it has been decided that a field trip is useful or desirable, specific objectives to be achieved by the trip can be shared with, or generated by, the class. Of course, the teacher will often have determined beforehand that such a trip is an instructional experience that can help achieve some of the objectives on the list handed out at the beginning of the term. In either case, the objectives can be used as a springboard to produce specific questions to be answered by students while they are on the field trip or upon their return. During a trip there will be many activities and new experiences competing for the students' attention, and the questions will help focus their attention on the most important activities and experiences.

Student involvement during each step of planning a field trip helps generate interest and makes the trips more worthwhile. For example, while some students are building questions that will focus attention on important aspects, others may gather information about the facilities at the site of the field trip. This latter group may wish to write for information on whether guided tours are available, admission costs, dates and times the facility is open, any specific clothing requirements, and the availability of eating facilities. Still another group may obtain information about transportation. Even though the teacher will be familiar with the bus use, it is instructive to students to discover for themselves whether school district regulations allow classes to use school buses for field trips and whether this use is dependent upon the buses' being returned before they are needed to transport students home from school at the end of the day; whether the distance is such that students will have to leave particularly early or get back after school hours; how to charter a bus if necessary; and the importance of school insurance policies that cover field trips, and their ramifications for the use of private automobiles.

If chartered transportation is needed it must be paid for, which may be an inhibiting factor. Depending on the student population, it may be unfair to expect parents to contribute enough money to cover both the incidental expenses of their children and transportation costs. If such is the case, the class may decide to raise the necessary money. Regardless of how the money is raised or collected, it is important to keep accurate and public records. The procedures adopted should coincide exactly with those advocated by the school.

Most schools require that the parents or guardians of students going on a field trip sign permission slips. These slips are not legal documents meant to protect a teacher from a lawsuit; they are simply devices to assure the school that parents know where the students will be going that day and approve of the trip. Teachers can extend the utility of permission slips by including on them details parents would wish to know, such as departure and arrival times, whether students are to bring food with them or purchase it, and special clothing requirements.

All of these considerations are influenced by board and administrative policies. Teachers must cooperate with the school administration to insure that policies are followed concerning absences from other classes, providing for students who are unwilling or unable to go, securing sufficient chaperonage, special cases such as financially or physically handicapped students or students with particular religious or dietary restrictions. There may also be regulations concerning taking along a first-aid kit or extra cash. Students, of course, should be asked to demonstrate that they know where the bus will be waiting for the group should they get separated, and what time it is scheduled to leave the field trip site.

Properly handled follow-up activities are particularly important with respect to field trips. Unlike other instructional activities, field trips involve staff members outside of the class. If, after disturbing the instructional plans of other teachers and perhaps keeping students from attending other classes, the field trip does not yield worthwhile results, the teacher may find it difficult to secure permission for other trips. This possibility, coupled with financial problems, has caused many boards of education to prohibit field trips completely. When the field trip has focused on specific objectives and students are given adequate preparation, follow-up discussions and evaluations do not prove difficult. General and ambiguous reactions to the trip, while perhaps of passing interest, are not the main concern. The experience should be evaluated primarily on the basis of how well the instructional objective was achieved, how well the newly acquired information was related to previously learned information, and how well the experience can serve as the basis for future instructional experiences.

School-community relations tend to improve as interaction between the two increases. Field trips and the use of outside speakers both provide interaction and thus help to improve school-community relations.

Small Group Activities

There are a number of instructional situations that will lead teachers to decide to use small group activities. Such activities are useful for increasing social interaction and thereby maximizing social development: They make efficient use of limited materials and resources; they allow complex problems and tasks to be divided into less complex components; they provide opportunities for peer-to-peer tutoring situations to arise; and they enable students to take more responsibility for planning and carrying out educational tasks.

Depending upon the situations, the teacher may choose any one of several procedures to determine group makeup. Simple random assignment or alphabetical arrangement is useful when no homogeneity is desired. Social development is maximized by such grouping since students will interact with other people with whom they may or may not have much in common.

Another procedure for the grouping of students is on the basis of friendship. When students are motivated, an advantage to this grouping pattern is that since the students are already on a friendly basis they tend to get to work more quickly. Digression, when not purposefully motivated, however, is a potential hazard.

Groups can also be formed on the basis of interest. The main advantage to this pattern is that productivity is usually high since students are intrinsically motivated and the motivation of each reinforces the motivation of the group.

A fourth grouping pattern is by achievement. In this pattern, no one individual overshadows all the rest and the work load can be divided equally. Progress is usually rapid because the group is not held back by one or two members who work at a different pace. This type of grouping is useful if there are a few slower students who seem to be on the fringe of the class activities. Grouping these students together and providing them with special help makes it possible for them to make a significant contribution to the class and to build up their own self-concepts.

Still another way to group students is heterogeneously. By deliberately putting students with varying abilities and interests in the same group the teacher can increase social interaction and development and provide opportunities for slower students to receive spontaneous help from brighter students. It is crucial, however, to consider very carefully the personalities of the students in the group, to be sure the slower students will be helped and not ridiculed.

Once the group is formed the teacher insures that the group realizes how their work will fit into the ongoing class activities. The teacher stresses that each of the four, five, or six members will have a specific job to do by prearranged deadlines if the class as a whole is to accomplish its task. The students may be encouraged to write out an operating plan.

When the small group activities are completed, the results are brought to the attention of the entire class. This not only enables the class to benefit from the work of the small groups, but it also provides the teacher with an opportunity to commend publicly the members of the groups for their efforts. Frequently panel discussions and/or modified debates provide appropriate vehicles for the dissemination of the results of such efforts.

Teachers should be aware of groups in which one or two members are being "carried" by the rest. Assisting in decisions about what each member is to do helps minimize this problem, but evaluation of individual contributions is still difficult, especially when students of differing abilities and interests are assigned to the same group.

Out-Of-Class Assignments

Among the possible instructional procedures available, the use of individual or whole-class "homework" assignments creates more than its share of controversy. The opponents of such assignments point out that many students have neither the time nor the environment to complete such assignments. They point out, too, that once the student leaves the classroom there is no assurance that he or she will be the one actually doing the assignment. A friend, relative, or parent may do the actual work and the student may then pass it in as his or her own. Finally, many question the justification of asking students to continue doing formal schoolwork on their own time.

Proponents of out-of-class assignments, on the other hand, point out that a student's chief responsibility should be schoolwork, that formal learning should not be restricted to particular school hours, and that many valuable instructional experiences cannot easily be engaged in within the four walls of a classroom or within the usual class meetings. For these reasons the proponents claim out-of-class assignments are absolutely necessary.

As with most controversial issues concerning education, there is no one right or wrong position that is valid for all situations. If the teacher attempts to minimize mundane out-of-class assignments, the probability of such assignments being completed and being completed properly increases. As with any other instructional procedure, overuse is counterproductive.

Some of the purposes appropriate for out-of-class assignments include

1. *Helping students acquire new information.* When teachers assign a section of a textbook to be read as a basis for a future discussion, or ask students to view a particular television program, or listen to a particular tape-slide sequence, they are asking students to acquire new information. This new data will be dealt with in class but it is to be acquired outside of class.

2. *Providing practice in particular skills.* Some skills, such as typing, solving mathematical problems, and so forth, can be polished by repeated practice. Since teachers are frequently reluctant to use class time for extended periods of such practice, they ask students to engage in such practice out of class.

3. *Giving students practice in long-term planning.* Some assignments, such as term papers and correspondence-type projects, require a good deal of student planning. The fact that students must allocate time to achieve the long-term objective is, in itself, a valuable experience that many teachers consider sufficient justification for such assignments. In this case the process and the product are of equal, or nearly equal, importance.

4. *Providing for student creativity and particular student needs.* In-class activities generally force students to be one of a group and leave little opportunity for them to demonstrate skills unique to them as individuals or to engage in instructional activities they feel are of particular interest to them personally. By working with individuals in planning out-of-class assignments, teachers can do much to make school relevant and interesting.

For whatever reasons teachers make out-of-class assignments, there are certain steps that help make those assignments more effective and valuable. If the assignment is one in which all students are going to engage, the teacher must insure that all students understand the exact nature of the assignment. Such assurance can be gained by writing the assignment on the board and/or duplicating it and handing it to each student. A verbal explanation may accompany the written directions, and questions concerning the assignment may be elicited from the students. If the assignment is one designed to help students acquire new information, guided questions may profitably be utilized. If the assignment is one in which a product is generated, students should have a clear idea of the qualities necessary for minimum acceptability of that product. If the assignment is long-term in nature, a final deadline should be determined and students should be encouraged to bring in drafts, partially completed work, and so forth for periodic appraisal. If the assignment is individualized, the teacher should make sure there is agreement on exactly what is to be done and what the final product is to be. Teachers can facilitate student accomplishment of out-of-class assignments by making sure that required instructional materials are available. Placing needed books, magazines, film strips and so forth on reserve in the library is one step in this direction, and providing worksheets is another.

If an assignment is worth making it is worthy of careful evaluation and student feedback. If students perceive that their work is being ignored or dealt with lightly, a large incentive for continuing such efforts will be lost. In addition the teacher loses an excellent opportunity to detect students' problems and determine the effectiveness of instruction.

One useful out-of-class assignment procedure is the self-instructional package. Self-instructional packages can be used for any of the purposes mentioned earlier and have a number of advantages. They are built around specific instructional objectives, all the information or sources the student needs to achieve the objective have been included or specified, preassessment and self-assessment instruments are included, and practice exercises are provided. Even more important, self-instructional packages can be self-paced and are designed with this goal in mind. This means that students receive the benefit of a carefully sequenced set of learning activities and are at the same time being given the freedom to learn at their own rates. Self-instructional packages make an ideal intermediary between whole-class, teacher-dominated experiences such as lectures and questioning, and experiences such as individual projects in which individual students design and carry out instructional projects reflecting their own needs and desires with guidance from the teacher only when perceived necessary by the student (see chapter 9).

SUMMARY

In this chapter a number of instructional procedures that teachers can use to improve the teaching-learning process have been surveyed. It is important to vary instructional experiences not only to stimulate and maintain interest and vitality but also to facilitate achievement of various types of objectives. Differing objectives require differing instructional experiences if they are to be achieved expeditiously, and the selection of an inappropriate instructional experience can prove frustrating to both the teacher and the students.

Some procedures, such as discussions and debates, require extensive preparation by students before their initial utilization. Other procedures require more extensive teacher preparation, but their benefits can counteract the extra preparation time necessary.

Procedures that allow active student participation will extract more student learning than those that require students to sit passively. Some procedures, such as lectures and demonstrations, minimize this participation while others such as brainstorming and exploratory discussions, maximize it.

All instructional procedures need evaluation. Some procedures (such as lectures, speakers, and field trips,) lend themselves to evaluation through the use of formal paper and pencil tests. Other procedures (such as exploratory discussion, brainstorming, and sociodramas) are more difficult to evaluate and teachers must rely on such factors as the extent of student participation, the degree of interest apparently generated by the experience, and the degree to which students expressed a desire for additional similar experiences.

Instructional procedures should be evaluated in terms of how well they helped students achieve specific objectives. Good procedures are usually more effective, when they provide analogous and/or equivalent practice. If practice was effective, students will be better able to perform the competence specified in the objectives. When teachers plan instructional procedures with regard to specific instructional objectives and are willing to use a variety of instructional experiences, they will provide environments that have the potential to maximize learning.

SELECTED READINGS

CALLAHAN, STERLING G., *Successful Teaching in Secondary Schools*. Glenview, Ill.: Scott, Foresman, 1971.

CLARK, LEONARD H., and IRVING S. STARR, *Secondary School Teaching Methods*, 2nd ed. New York: Macmillan, 1967.

GROSSIER, PHILIP, *How to Use the Fine Art of Questioning*. Englewood Cliffs, N.J.: Teachers Practical Press, 1964.

GULLEY, HALBERT E., *Discussion, Conference and Group Process*, 2nd ed. New York: Holt, Rinehart and Winston, 1968

HENSON, KENNETH T., *Secondary Education: A Personal Approach*. Itasca, Ill.: F. E. Peacock, 1974.

HYMAN, RONALD T., *Ways of Teaching*. New York: J. B. Lippincott, 1970.

JOYCE, BRUCE, and MARSHA WEIL, *Models of Teaching*. Englewood Cliffs, N.J.: Prentice-Hall, 1972.

MORINE, HAROLD, and GRETA MORINE, *Discovery: A Challenge to Teachers*. Englewood Cliffs, N.J.: Prentice-Hall, 1973.

POPHAM, W. JAMES, and EVA L. BAKER, *Planning an Instructional Sequence*, Englewood Cliffs, N.J.: Prentice-Hall, 1970.

7

Instructional Media And Materials

For many educators, it is somehow unsettling to realize that in a technologically advanced country such as ours, much instruction is still conducted in the same manner it was 2400 years ago. When Socrates, Plato, and Aristotle were helping students learn at about 400 B.C., they did it by asking questions, telling, and discussing. Most students today learn in school in the same way. While it is not the intention of the authors to downgrade the value of lectures or discussions, it is important that prospective teachers recognize the unique and valuable contributions to the teaching-learning process that can be made by alternative instructional forms.

There is an ancient proverb that says, "A picture is worth a thousand words." One wonders then what the "exchange rate" would be for a time-lapse motion picture that enables students to watch a rosebud as it unfolds into full bloom; or a motion picture that gives students an idea of the drama and mindless passions aroused by one of Hitler's torchlight parades. How does one calculate an "exchange rate" when a student makes a mistake in an auto simulator rather than in a real car? Without the use of mediated instruction, many valuable and interesting learning experiences would be either impossible or impractical, and the students' education would be that much poorer.

Since virtually all teachers find themselves using mediated instruction at one time or another (with varying degrees of effectiveness), this chapter will be devoted to familiarizing the reader with a variety of alternative instructional forms. Such a familiarity will increase the probability of alternatives being used intelligently to enhance and enrich the learning experiences of students.

OBJECTIVES

The student will:

1. List, in writing, three forms of mediated instruction. (Knowledge)
2. Given the names of three forms of mediated instruction, write at least one example of how each could be used to enhance learning in his or her own subject area. (Comprehension)
3. Given an example of one utilization of a mediated instruction form (such as an opaque or overhead projector), describe at least one other way the same device could be used to aid learning. (Application)
4. Given hypothetical situations calling for the use of mediated instruction and a list of mediated instruction forms, select the most appropriate form for each situation. (Analysis)
5. Write a lesson plan for a fifty-minute lesson in which the use of some form of mediated instruction plays a central part. (Synthesis)
6. Take a position for or against the use of mediated instruction by classroom teachers and defend that position by citing specific facts or examples in a paper of less than three pages. (Evaluation)

GENERAL UTILIZATION FACTORS

Mediated instruction, by definition, includes any instruction that makes use of some device (mechanical or otherwise) to facilitate learning.

Although there is tremendous variety in the forms of mediated instruction available to teachers, there are some utilization procedures that are applicable to many forms. Among these are the following:

1. *Select mediated instruction for specific instructional objectives.* To be of maximum effectiveness, mediated instruction should be an integral part of the instructional procedures; its use should not be an afterthought. Familiarity with a variety of forms of instruction enhances learning by enabling teachers to:

   a. Obtain an overview of the types of mediated instruction they intend to use and thus provide for greater variety;

b. Order materials well in advance;

c. Use material effectively.

When mediated instruction is used on a spur-of-the-moment basis without relationship to specific objectives, students will realize that it is being misused, probably as a time-filler or diversion. If the medium contains a message, do not let the message be, "I did not have anything else planned, so we will try this."

2. *Become familiar with the material or device prior to using it with students.* Depending on the form of mediated instruction being considered, teachers are wise to read it, view it, handle it, and otherwise use it prior to exposing students to it. This procedure not only provides assurance that the instructional aid is exactly what was expected, but it also enables the teacher to estimate how much time to allow for correct use and to pinpoint specific strengths and weaknesses and thus better prepare students. When mechanical devices are involved, the teacher will become more proficient in the operation of the device and thus avoid the potential loss of attention that accompanies the misuse of equipment.

3. *Prepare the students.* If students are to derive the full benefit of mediated instruction, they should be given some idea of its general content or purpose beforehand so they will know what to emphasize. Usually a brief description is sufficient to orient students, but some teachers find it useful to formulate a set of guide questions for students to answer. This helps further to focus student attention on important points.

4. *Use the mediated instruction correctly.* There is little value in attempting to use a form of mediated instruction if there is insufficient time for its proper use or if other conditions are not appropriate. While most forms of mediated instruction have utilization factors unique to them, common sense will dictate acceptable procedures. For example, if the device being used has a volume control, remember that it controls only the machine's volume, not students'. If students are noisy, raising the volume on the device will not necessarily cause them to quiet down; in fact it may have just the opposite effect. Establishing the proper motivational set is a function of preparation activities, and it is often difficult to use the mediated instruction itself for this purpose.

Among other common-sense considerations is the problem of light. In most classrooms there is sufficient light control for all activities, but many teachers find it difficult to get their rooms dark enough to use some forms of mediated instruction, particularly film projectors and opaque projectors. Light control should be checked before materials are ordered.

5. *Conduct follow-up activities.* Follow-up activities provide an opportunity to clarify confusing points, answer questions, discuss interesting

points, and integrate the new information with previous learning. The need for follow-up activities varies with the form of mediated instruction being used, but it is most crucial when aids such as films or broadcasts have been used. Since it is inconvenient or impossible to interrupt these types of aids while they are in use, students may misinterpret some point or miss subtle points altogether because of lack of teacher emphasis. Follow-up activities enable teachers to correct misconceptions and tie up loose ends. As with all instruction, follow-up activities should be planned in advance and insure student participation.

6. *Evaluate the mediated instruction.* After using any form of mediated instruction it is helpful to write a short evaluation of how effectively it helped students achieve the specified objectives. As these evaluations accumulate they can be used to assist the teacher to select the most appropriate and effective form of mediated instruction for each type of objective.

AIDS TO TEACHING

Materials That Are Read

Textbooks (Traditional)   Ever since the mid-1400s when Johann Gutenberg developed movable type, educators have made increasing use of books as instructional aids. Today books are by far the most common aid to instruction available to classroom teachers and, surprisingly, they can be one of the most powerful.

Textbooks have a number of sometimes forgotten advantages. Most people, for example, can read and comprehend at least twice as fast as they can listen and comprehend. Students without reading problems can acquire information from texts quickly and efficiently. Textbooks also provide students with a common body of information arranged in some logical order. It is possible to base discussions on commonly available data and to help students perceive cause-effect relationships. Most texts also include chapter summaries, questions to be answered, and associated learning activities that provide guides for studying the information. Considering that most textbooks can be used repeatedly and that many contain pictures, charts, graphs, and maps, they are relatively inexpensive. Finally, textbooks can be adapted to individualization and self-pacing if the teacher chooses to use them in this way.

As with any instructional aid, textbooks can be misused, and most of the disadvantages associated with them stem from such misuses. Perhaps the greatest single misuse of texts is teachers' allowing them to dictate what will be taught. While the author of a text might be a specialist in some field, he or she cannot be familiar with each teacher's particular group of students or each teacher's particular instructional objectives. In some cases, especially in those that involve older texts, the information may not be up-to-date.

Often teachers are guilty of using the "chapter a week" approach; sometimes teachers assume that because they are using a text they must teach the contents from cover to cover before the last day of school. If teachers adopt this approach they will tend to find the slower readers in the class falling further and further behind as the rest of the class lock-step their way through the material. This in itself will cause problems, but more important, more emphasis is being placed on how many pages are being turned than on how much is being learned. Such an approach also stifles the creativity of both teachers and students and can discourage full utilization of some of the text's built-in features.

The often-neglected first step in using a textbook is for the teacher to review it. While teachers may have a grasp of the material they intend to teach, the approach of the text may be unique. Each textbook author includes what he or she feels is important and excludes whatever he or she feels is less important. A careful perusal of the text will enable the teacher to capitalize on that author's particular insights.

The next step is to help students grasp an overview of the text. Many teachers have found that students at all levels can benefit from a short lesson on using the textbook. Good teachers will often include a survey of the table of contents with comments concerning what will and will not be emphasized, a discussion of the author's intent, an explanation of how the index is organized, and a survey of a representative chapter.

When surveying the representative chapter it is helpful to encourage students to convert the chapter title and headings to questions and then read to find answers. Encouraging students to look at the chapter summary and the questions at the end of the chapter *before* reading it is profitable. Perusing boldface type, italics, maps, charts, and so forth will help later in locating major points. Some teachers find it useful to teach students the skills of skimming, with particular emphasis on the importance of introductory and culminating sentences. Still others find it useful to encourage students to write out answers to teacher-posed questions pertaining to, and reinforcing, important points in the chapter.

Textbooks (Programmed) Programmed instruction began as an attempt to make learning more efficient by applying what was known about reinforcement and animal behavior to the teaching-learning process. Programmed instruction did not gain broad attention, however, until 1954, when B. F. Skinner published an article entitled "The Science of Learning and the Art of Teaching."[1] This article gave major impetus to the programmed learning movement.

---

[1] B.F. Skinner, "The Science of Learning and the Art of Teaching," *The Harvard Educational Review*, 24 (Spring 1954), pp. 86-97.

Programmed instruction presents information to students in a series of very carefully planned sequential steps. As the student moves from step to step, he or she receives immediate feedback concerning learning progress, and in some programs, is "branched" to review remedial or enrichment information depending on the response made to a given question. The active student participation in the learning process (students are forced to construct or select a response) makes up one of the major differences between programmed and traditional texts and instruction. A second difference is that the formation of misconceptions is reduced (or eliminated entirely) because the sequential nature of the program carefully relates each new piece of information to the one immediately preceding it.

There are two basic kinds of strategies for all programmed materials, whether they are presented through the use of programmed texts, teaching machines, or computer-assisted instruction. These are linear and nonlinear strategies.

Linear Programs   Linear programs are most closely associated with B. F. Skinner.[2] The following are some of the characteristics most closely associated with such programs:

1. Each student is required to go through *an identical sequence* of small steps.
2. Each student *constructs responses*, usually by writing a word or a number, from recalled information.
3. Via the *liberal use of cues* such as boldface type, italics, and underlining, an attempt is made to keep each student's performance as errorless as possible. Usually an error rate of less than 5 percent is sought by authors of programmed materials.
4. *No remedial steps are taken when a student makes an error.* Except with slightly modified, quasi-linear programs, the student simply sees the correct response and moves on.

Nonlinear Programs   Nonlinear (or branching, or intrinsic) programs are most closely associated with Norman Crowder.[3] The following are some of the characteristics most closely associated with such programs:

1. Each student is able to take a *unique route* through the material depending upon his or her particular responses to questions.
2. Each student *selects responses* to multiple-choice questions. The choice of response determines whether he or she goes to new material, review material, or enrichment material.
3. *Little, if any, use of cues is made* since errors are anticipated and remedial instruction is provided to deal with the specific weakness disclosed by the student's choice of response.

[2]B. F. Skinner, *The Technology of Teaching* (Englewood Cliffs, N.J.: Prentice-Hall, 1968).
[3]Norman A. Crowder, "Automatic Tutoring by Means of Instrinsic Programming," in *Automatic Teaching: The State of the Art*, ed. Eugene Gatanter (New York: John Wiley, 1959), pp. 109-10.

Another kind of "programming" has been advocated by Sidney L. Pressey.[4] It was Pressey's work in 1924 that served as a basis for the later development of sophisticated teaching machines, but although he himself was a strong advocate of programmed learning, he saw it as an adjunct to more traditional kinds of instruction. He felt that information should first be acquired in some traditional manner and then reinforced via programmed techniques. The term "adjunct programming" is therefore sometime used to label Pressey's view.

According to Briggs, et al., in 1954 W. S. Schramm surveyed thirty-six studies that compared programmed instruction with traditional instruction. One half (eighteen) of the studies showed no significant differences in students' achievement scores, but seventeen did show significant differences and the authors concluded that some student use of programmed materials was desirable.[5] These findings, and others like them, indicate that teachers may expect to find an increasing body of programmed materials available.

This does not mean, however, that students of the future will find themselves sitting at a teaching machine or following a programmed text as the exclusive learning mode. Most programmed material currently available deals with basic, concrete facts, and this situation is not likely to change in the near future. By its very nature programmed instruction virtually eliminates student creativity. All acceptable responses are already programmed and divergent thinking is, in terms of the program, incorrect thinking. There are many who believe that for very basic, sequential kinds of material, programmed materials will eventually replace traditional kinds of instruction and that it is in the integration and application of knowledge that human teachers are most needed and least adept.

Since the use of texts, programmed texts, and teaching machines require students to read, their use must be limited to students who exhibit this skill with a competence commensurate with the materials used. This limitation inhibits their use.

All of the forms of mediated instruction surveyed in the balance of this chapter are useful as adjuncts to more traditional kinds of instruction.

Audio Aids

Radios, Record Players, and Tape Recorders   Radios, record players, and audio tape recorders all utilize a single input sense, that of sound. With the advent of films, television, and videotapes, purely auditory devices are being used less frequently, but they still have their place.

---

[4]Sidney L. Pressey, "A Machine for Automatic Teaching of Drill Material," *School and Society*, 25, no. 645 (May 7, 1927), pp. 549-42.

[5]Leslie J. Briggs et al., *Instructional Media: A Procedure for the Design of Multi-Media Instruction, A Critical Review of Research, and Suggestions for Future Research* (Pittsburgh, Pa.: American Institutes for Research, 1967), p. 116.

Radios, for example, are still a convenient means for getting up-to-the-minute news reports for class analysis. Record players make it possible to listen conveniently to plays, operas, concerts, and speeches, while tape recorders make it possible to record broadcast material or live performances of guest speakers, class debates, and so forth for later use and analysis. These forms of mediated instruction are also extensively used as audio models for students, and the audio tape recorder provides an added dimension by enabling students to record and then listen to their own voices for diagnostic, developmental, or remedial purposes.

As young people have increased their leisure-time use of films and TV, they have become accustomed to having a visual point on which to focus their attention. When using audio aids, students may literally not know what to look at. Teachers may take the position that learning to use straight audio input is a skill that needs development, or that appropriate visual aids (pictures, maps, etc.) that relate to what the students are listening to and that can serve as visual focal points, should be supplied.

Research in the area of listening is enlightening. It is estimated, for example, that approximately 45 percent of the average adult's working day is spent listening, and that this figure rises to 60 percent for elementary school students, and to 90 percent for high school and college students.[6] Unfortunately, the research also shows that even if students are concentrating on what they hear, they will retain only about 50 percent and within two months will be able to recall less than half of that.[7] Obviously students can use additional practice in the frequently overlooked skill of effective listening, and radios, record players, and audio tape recorders can be used to provide that practice.

Telephones   Telephones represent yet another purely auditory form of mediated instruction. Although the telephone was invented in 1876 and the radio in 1895, the telephone's nineteen-year advantage has not been reflected in its significantly greater use by educators. This is unfortunate because the telephone companies have much to offer and they are generally quite willing to work with educators.

One unique application of telephone technology is the "teleinterview." Upon request, most telephone companies will rent to schools equipment that makes it possible to set up two-way communication between a whole class and a speaker at some distant point. The equipment is relatively inexpensive (especially when compared to the costs of bringing the speaker physically to the class), and yet it has many of the advantages of actually having the speaker there. All students can listen at the same time and can ask questions and receive answers.

[6]James W. Brown, Richard B. Lewis, and Fred F. Harcleroad, *AV Instruction—Media and Methods*, 3rd ed. (New York: McGraw-Hill, 1969), p. 327.
[7]Brown et al., *AV Instruction*, p. 327.

Although student preparation is important with all forms of mediated instruction, it is particularly important when teleinterviews are used, since the charges are calculated according to the time the telephone line is in use. Adequate preparation in this case would include preparing the speaker by involving him or her in the objectives of the telelecture. Preparation of the students should include the formulation of specific questions to ask the speaker.

In 1971 the American Telephone and Telegraph Company developed a device called a Variable Speech Control (VSC). The purpose of the VSC is to change the rate at which speech can be understood by omitting pauses and shortening vowel sounds. The practical applications of the device include enabling blind people to listen to, and comprehend, spoken words nearly as quickly as sighted people can read and comprehend written words, and enabling teachers and students to make greater use of taped materials by allowing them to listen to extensive recorded tapes in shorter periods of time.

Visual Aids

Pictures   Still pictures, whether in the form of paintings, magazine clippings, photographs, slides, or filmstrips, have unique properties that make them extremely valuable as instructional aids. Among these properties is their ability to convey abstractions powerfully without depending on verbal descriptions, their ability to focus attention on a characteristic situation or on a particular step in a process, and their ability to allow students to study a picture at length, to refer back to it conveniently, and to make side-by-side comparisons. The combination of these properties is not available in many other forms of mediated instruction.

Pictures, such as those available from magazines, travel bureaus, and commercial concerns, represent one of the easiest to acquire, and least expensive, forms of mediated instruction available to teachers. Teachers can increase the instructional value of pictures if common-sense principles are followed. For instance, teachers should be sure the picture selected is appropriate for the students who will see it. Very complex pictures, for example, are not well suited for younger students regardless of how attractive they may be otherwise. Colored pictures can usually attract and hold students' attention better than black and white pictures, and all pictures must be large enough to be seen easily. Insuring that the picture is relevant to what will be studied and that it does not present a biased view (unless such a view is intended) is important.

Opaque Projectors   It sometimes happens that a picture is of particular benefit but is too small to be seen by the entire class at one time. In such instances, the opaque projector may be useful. The "opaque" will project and enlarge any flat picture whether it is a single sheet or a page bound in a book. Furthermore, most opaque projectors come equipped with a built-in light arrow, which can be used to draw students' attention to particular points on the projected image. Many teachers have also found the "opaque" useful for projecting images on chalkboards so they can be traced.

Opaque projectors make use of a large and powerful bulb as a light source, and this bulb gets hot. Most "opaques," therefore, include a built-in, heat-absorbing glass plate between the bulb and the projection stage. In spite of this precaution, thin materials sometimes curl or scorch. Proper use would then include checking prior to using an "opaque" to make sure there is a heat-absorbing glass plate and checking material periodically during use.

Although opaque projectors generate a lot of heat, they do not project a lot of light. Opaque projectors use a reflected light source rather than a direct light source such as is found in film projectors. Less light reaches the screen than with other kinds of projectors, and unless the room is reasonably dark students may have difficulty seeing the projection. Check to see if the room can be darkened sufficiently before using the "opaque" with students. Because the room must be darkened, students may be unable to take notes. For this reason most teachers do not use opaque projectors for extended periods of time.

Slides and Filmstrips   Slides and filmstrips have all the advantages of pictures and the added advantage of increased realism. Because slides are actual photographs and are shown via a bright light source, the scenes they portray appear more "real" than printed pictures and the colors appear more brilliant. These factors appeal to students. In addition, it is much easier to store a set of slides than to store a set of large, mounted pictures.

A more significant advantage associated with slides is the opportunity they provide for teachers to create their own instructional aids. Many teachers make it a point to take along a camera and slide film (rather than print film) when encountering circumstances pertinent to their teaching area, and many have thus compiled an impressive set of slides that are useful in stimulating and maintaining students' interest. Many teachers have also initiated class projects wherein students organize a slide program complete with an accompanying tape recording. Such projects have the dual advantages of being useful, interesting learning activities and increasing the teacher's store of instructional aids.

A filmstrip is essentially a series of connected slides. Most filmstrips are commercially prepared and many have brief captions printed on each frame. A recent development is the sprocketless filmstrip projector, which should result in longer life for a filmstrip. As the filmstrip is advanced and each frame is discussed by the teacher, various procedures may be used to enrich the experience. Besides a basic approach, such as asking students to read the captions out loud, teachers have discovered that teacher and student comments and discussion are possible and profitable while the filmstrip is being shown as well as afterwards.

Bulletin Boards   Bulletin boards are ideally suited for the display of visual materials such as pictures, cartoons, postcards, newspaper clippings, outstanding papers, and student-made collages and montages. Common sense will dictate procedures for the use of bulletin boards. Teachers will find, for instance, that bulletin boards should concern a single idea or topic. They should also be neat and uncluttered, make use of bright colors and attention-getting materials such as colored yarn and plastics, and they should be pictorially rather than verbally oriented. The instructional value of bulletin boards can be further increased by building into the display participation devices, such as questions with the answers covered by flaps, or manipulative devices.

A bulletin board's instructional value lasts a relatively short time, in some cases not more than a few days. Once teachers go to the trouble to construct an exceptional bulletin board they may be reluctant to take it down. There is certainly no reason to take down a display that students still find useful, but once students stop paying attention to the display or the class moves on to some other topic, the bulletin board display needs replacement.

Teachers have found that some groups of students enjoy the responsibility for putting up new displays periodically throughout the year. This helps increase students' interest in the display and can lead to increased learning as groups find that research in the area will assist in developing an attractive and interesting display. Teachers can provide advice and assistance in the form of suggesting sources for materials and providing actual materials.

Maps and Globes, Charts and Graphs   Maps, globes, charts, and graphs are grouped together because each of these forms of mediated instruction may require increased student preparation. Students may have difficulty interpreting maps, globes, charts, and graphs unless teachers make a special effort to help them.

Maps and globes are used to show portions of the earth's surface in a less-than-life-size scale. Cartographers (map makers) have constructed maps and globes to emphasize political, geographic, and climatic divisions and have developed a number of different map projections. Teachers find it useful to draw students' attention to the particular kind of projection being used and to discuss the way it distorts the real size and shape of particular geographic features. Without an understanding of projection, students may have misconceptions about maps.

Efforts to draw students' attention to the legend of the map or globe will reap dividends. It is here that the cartographer explains the meanings of the symbols used on the map or globe, gives the scale to which features are drawn, and provides additional information such as the meanings of particular colors.

Teachers should study maps and globes before using them. Political divisions, particularly boundaries and names, change more often than is suspected, and it is not uncommon for a map or globe in a classroom to be out of date. If so, this fact should be made known to students and, if possible, transparencies and overlays should be used to emphasize the changes.

Charts differ from graphs and diagrams in that they may include a wider variety of pictorial forms. Graphs and diagrams generally have only simple lines or bars. The most common kinds of charts are flow charts (showing sequential steps), process charts (showing some process from start to finish), and time charts (showing developments over a period of time). The instructional value of charts is maximized when teachers take the time to make sure students can read and interpret the data presented. A special lesson devoted to reading all types of charts is time well invested.

Graphs are used primarily to condense and convey numerical data in visual form. The most common kinds are the circle graph (useful for showing the relationship of parts to the whole), bar graphs (useful for showing comparative data such as the changes in unemployment from year to year), and line graphs (useful for plotting profiles of patterns).

Although students should be given special instruction in the use of maps, globes, charts, and graphs, teachers should obtain the least complicated aid that will serve their immediate purpose. Trying to select an aid that can be used in a variety of lessons will be a false economy if students have difficulty interpreting the aid or are confused by it.

Chalkboards   Chalkboards are available in almost every classroom and most teachers use them frequently. Chalkboards are logically used by the teacher to display instructions, diagrams, examples, and other information that is subject to frequent change. Board work also gives students the chance to demonstrate their abilities and allows active student participation.

There are a number of ways teachers can utilize chalkboards to make them more valuable to students. One is not to talk to the board. Students may have difficulty hearing teachers who insist on trying to face the board and talk to students at the same time. Teachers who make frequent use of the board often construct, or invest in, templates to facilitate the drawing of frequently used shapes. This not only saves time, but allows more consistency. An inexpensive form of template can be made by simply tracing a design and punching holes along the traced lines. Brushing a dusty chalk eraser across the template while it is held to the board will create a dotted outline. As was mentioned earlier, pictures can also be traced on the board from projected images.

When using the chalkboard, teachers should avoid cluttering. Once an item written on the board has served its purpose, it is best to erase it so students will not be distracted by it. Certain types of colored chalk are intended for use on paper, not chalkboards. If the wrong kind of chalk is used it may stain the chalkboard permanently. Finally, lettering must be large enough to be seen easily. Usually letters that are about two and a half inches high can be seen easily from a distance up to thirty feet.

Overhead Projectors   Of the types of projectors available to teachers, overhead projectors are easily the most common. Overhead projectors can project any material that is drawn, written, or printed on transparent film. They are often used instead of the chalkboard because they allow the teacher to write and at the same time face the students. Enabling teachers to maintain eye contact with their students is one of the overhead's greatest advantages. Another advantage is to be able to use the machine without darkening the room, which facilitates note taking and, more important, student interaction.

The use of overlays with base transparencies is a particularly effective instructional tool. A typical overlay package might contain a base map of the United States, a transparency to go over the base outline to show major river systems, a third transparency to depict major cities and to show their relationship to rivers, and a fourth transparency to show railroad development.

To use an overhead projector as an "electric chalkboard" a teacher needs only a sheet of clear plastic (usually acetate, but cellophane or even a commercial plastic wrap will do) to protect the glass projection plate, and a grease pencil, china marker, crayon, or felt-tip pen. Grease pencils are usually filled with a wax-based material and generally project black lines. Some grease pencils may be purchased that will project colors, but if color is desired (and it does make the projections more attractive), felt-tip pens are less expensive and work just as well. Crayons and china markers will project black lines regardless of their color but have the advantage, along with the grease pencils, of being easily erased by light rubbing with a soft cloth or tissue. To remove transparent ink it is often necessary to use a cleaner or even a solvent, depending on the kind of ink in the pen. Some overheads come equipped with a roll of acetate. The instructor writes on the acetate and then simply rolls up the used surface to expose an unused portion, thus temporarily eliminating the need to erase.[8] Teachers may construct their own transparencies by simply drawing them, but if better quality or permanency is desired, one of a number of heat processes, or an ammonia process known as "diazo," may be used. Most school librarians will have

---

[8]Most overhead projectors have a thermostatically controlled switch that permits the fan to continue operating until the interior of the projector is cool. Do not be upset if the machine does not stop when it is turned off, and do not pull the plug. It will automatically stop when it has cooled down.

sources of information concerning these processes, or the audio-visual department in the school or a nearby college or university may offer assistance.

As they become experienced in the making of transparencies and overlays, teachers will find: that the use of color can add interest and emphasis, that printed (manuscript) characters are easier to form and read than are cursive characters, and that typing (especially when done with a primary typewriter) adds to the neatness and legibility of the finished product. Including too much on one transparency can inhibit optimum use by learners; about twenty lines seems to be optimum. Typewriters with pica or elite type are not commonly used for transparency work since the projected image is usually too small to be read easily.

It is often possible to acquire commercially prepared transparencies and overlays, made by experts with a wealth of materials to work with, and thus usually more polished than teacher-made materials. But they may also involve more expense.[9]

Realia   The term "realia" refers to any specimens, models, mock-ups, or artifacts that can be used to help students learn. Depending on what is being taught, teachers and students may display living animals, coin collections, insects or any of dozens of things. The list is as limitless and as varied as there are real things in the world that may be displayed without danger or great expense. Modified representations of real things, such as cut-away or "exploded" models are also helpful. In the latter, the whole is broken into segments and each segment is held apart from the others, while the pieces still maintain the same relative positions as in the unexploded model. Other good teaching tools are models that students can assemble and disassemble.[10]

Audio-Visual Combinations

Multimedia Kits   As an increasing number of schools adopt a systems approach to education, many educators are finding multimedia kits helpful. Multimedia kits are compilations of instructional materials that include a variety of mediated instruction forms designed to help students achieve a specific instructional objective by exposing them to different types of closely integrated educational experiences.

A typical multimedia kit may contain, for example, booklets, filmstrips, a loop film, audio tapes, and artifacts. All of the components are selected

[9]Among the many sources of commercially prepared transparencies are the following: Encyclopedia Britannica Films, Inc., 1150 Wilmette Ave., Wilmette, Ill. 60091; Instructo Products Company, 1635 N. 55th St., Philadelphia, Pa. 19131; and the 3M Company, Visual Products, 2501 Hudson Road, St. Paul, Minn. 55119.

[10]Although most realia are brought to the classroom from the collections of either the students or the teacher, there is a wealth of models, etc., available commercially. Just two of the many sources are: Models of Industry, 2804 Tenth St., Berkeley, Calif, 74710; and the W. M. Welch Scientific Co., 1515 Sedgwick St., Chicago, Ill. 60610.

with a single purpose in mind—to generate and maintain students' interest in a particular topic or subject while at the same time providing them with as much pertinent information as possible.

Multimedia kits can be used with excellent results for groups, but perhaps their greatest utilization is found when they are used as self-instructional devices for students to use at their own convenience and at their own rate. Like most other forms of mediated instruction, multimedia kits may be prepared by teachers themselves or can be purchased ready-made.[11]

Films and Television   Films and television provide students with more of a "you are there" feeling than most other forms of mediated instruction. They also enable students to view demonstrations (both scientific and social) experiments, natural phenomena, and other events that would be too difficult, dangerous, or even impossible to view otherwise (for instance, moon walks and erupting volcanoes).

Techniques such as time-lapse photography, micro-photography, long-range photography, animation, and slow-motion projection offer unique approaches for students' exploration. Students may watch as a flower gracefully unfolds into full bloom or as a single cell divides. They can see the earth as a spaceman would see it or gain an understanding of the phenomenon of nuclear fission. Infrared photography, "zoom-ins," and even X-ray photography are also possible through films and television.

Proper preparation of students and good planning in the use of films can enhance learning. One researcher has found that students who are well prepared for a film (by being given such things as questions to be answered, study guides, and explanations of new or difficult words) experience a learning gain 20 percent greater than students who are not so prepared.[12] Other researchers have found that periodically stopping a film to provide time for active student participation, or splicing into the film questions for discussion, can also increase student learning.[13]

Teachers are often pleasantly surprised at the ease with which films can be borrowed. Most universities and state departments of education maintain extensive film libraries, as do many businesses and public utilities. A check with the audio-visual department in any public school or with a school librarian can result in the acquisition of good sources of free or inexpensive films.[14]

[11]Two sources of multimedia kits are: the American Telephone and Telegraph Co., 195 Broadway, New York, N.Y. 10007; and the Westinghouse Electric Corp., P.O. Box J, Sea Cliff, N.Y. 11579. (See chapter 11.)

[12]Briggs et al., *Instructional Media*, p. 112.

[13]Briggs et al., *Instructional Media*, p. 114.

[14]Some very excellent sources include: the local telephone company; the American Iron and Steel Institute, 150 E. 42nd St., New York, N.Y. 10017; General Motors Corp., General Motors Building, Detroit, Mich. 48202; and Coronet Films, 65 E. South Water St., Chicago, Ill. 60601.

In addition to 16mm films, educators are also finding that 8mm, single-concept or single-skill continuous-loop films are very useful. Like the larger 16mm films, 8mm films can be used for large groups, but they are especially well suited for individual use and can thus play an important part in the individualization and self-pacing of instruction. Most 8mm loop films are silent, but that has not detracted from their popularity.

An advantage of television over film is that of immediacy. Via television, students can watch events as they are actually happening. In effect they are seeing for themselves, but the television camera can even improve on personal presence by providing each student with a clear, unobstructed, and close-up view.

Television has been used effectively in a variety of ways. The first, and most common, is the use of commercial programs. Although often thought of only in terms of its entertainment value, commercial television frequently broadcasts special programs and documentaries that have significant instructional value.

Another type of broadcast television is educational television or ETV. ETV broadcasts are primarily instructional in nature, but they are aimed at a broad, public audience and, therefore, attempt to meet a variety of needs. Typical ETV programs include discussions with industrial, political, and social leaders, "how-to-do-it" courses, and nonviolent children's programs. One of the most famous of the ETV children's programs is *Sesame Street*.[15]

A third type of broadcast television is instructional television, or ITV. The distinctions between ETV and ITV are considered to be both in programming intent and in program financing. ETV programs, such as *Sesame Street*, are not intended for specific and formal instruction; ITV programs generally are. ETV programs are frequently sponsored by commercial concerns, whereas ITV programs are most often financed by governmental grants, private foundations, individual school systems, and colleges and universities.

Closed-circuit television represents a fourth way to use the medium. In closed-circuit television, only television sets connected directly to a transmitter, or adapted to receive the 2500-mHz (megaHertz) wave length reserved for closed-circuit television, can receive the programs. Closed-circuit television is most often used on an "in-house" basis to televise meetings and debates, demonstrations and experiments, and even regular classes. Because it is an "in-house" operation students can participate in the actual program development and televising, thus adding yet another dimension to their educational experience.

---

[15]For further information concerning ETV, teachers can write to either the National Association of Educational Broadcasters, Washington, D.C., or NET Film Service, Indiana University, Bloomington, Indiana 47401. Nearby colleges and universities are also likely sources of information about ETV.

A fifth way to use television is via videotape recorders (VTR). Videotape recorders are directly analogous to audio tape recorders, with the obvious difference that the former provides a visual, as well as an audio, record. More and more schools are acquiring VTR equipment, not only to tape and save lectures, demonstrations, and theatrical presentations, but also for use in everyday teaching situations. As a way of enabling both teachers and students to see themselves as others see them, VTR equipment has found increasing use. Coaches, for instance have found VTR equipment invaluable in athletic programs for instant feedback of student psychomotor skills.

Computer-Assisted Instruction

Most early "teaching machines" did not do much more than control the actions of the learner. The machines kept the student from skipping ahead or going back to change answers. With the advent of computers, however, it became possible to design truly sophisticated teaching machines.

Computer-assisted instruction (CAI) is, without doubt, the single most complex and sophisticated form of mediated instruction yet developed. As the name implies, computer-assisted instruction makes use of a computer and a computer program to assist students in the acquisition of skills and information. Because CAI programs are written to react to student responses, it is possible to design exercises specifically for individual needs and ability levels and to present new information at a rate and degree of complexity compatible with the student's ability. CAI is also useful in providing students with practice in responding to lifelike situations without the hazards associated with the actual endeavor and in automatically keeping accurate records of students' performances in any or all of these activities. In addition, the computer does not get tired or short-tempered. It is willing and able to work twenty-four hours a day, has infinite patience, and when properly used, does not threaten students personally. It is not hard to see why some educators feel that extensive use of CAI can improve the teaching-learning process.

There are four principal kinds of CAI programs. Drill and practice programs are probably the most common. They are usually branching programs and can thus vary the complexity of the material to keep it commensurate with the proficiency demonstrated by the student. If students have difficulty with one level of problems, for example, CAI drill and practice programs can automatically shift them to less complex levels and then, as they become more proficient, automatically shift them back through successively more complex levels. To date, most drill and practice programs focus on mathematical or language skills.

A second type of CAI program is the tutorial program. Unlike drill and practice programs, tutorial programs present students with new information and then, on the basis of student responses to questions or problems, provide further new information, or supplemental information.

A third type of CAI programming is known as simulation or gaming. The function of simulations and games is usually to provide a "real-life" situation to which the student can react. Depending on the programming strategy used, simulated situations can change on the basis of sequentially or randomly occurring variables or solely on the basis of student input.

Simulation programs have been used at a number of medical schools. At one school, prospective doctors are presented, via a CAI terminal, with a patient and a set of symptoms. The student prescribes treatment via the terminal and the computer acts upon this input. After an appropriate length of time has elapsed (that length of time that would have elapsed in real life), the terminal prints out the patient's reaction to the treatment. Variables such as allergic reactions and unexpected complications can also be programmed to test the student's abilities further.

At another medical school a manikin called SIM ONE is used for the practice of endotracheal intubations.[16] The simulation enables the manikin to twitch and jerk as a real patient might and to "die" from drug overdoses or incorrect prescriptions. In this situation, as in the preceding one the "death" of the patient may be traumatic for the prospective doctor, but instantaneous reincarnation is possible by simply restarting the program.

The fourth kind of CAI programming is simple problem solving. Here the student can capitalize on the power of the computer to compute. Students can try out complex mathematical solutions without hours of stultifying work with a pencil and paper. They can make projections and change variables without regard to the difficulty of the computations. The computer is able to do it all virtually instantaneously.

One of the most ambitious CAI projects in the United States is the PLATO project at the University of Illinois. PLATO (an acronym for Programmed Logic for Automatic Teaching Operation) may eventually consist of thousands of CAI terminals connected to a single large computer. The speed of the computer will enable each of the users to receive "individual" attention, and the sophistication of the terminals will be such that students will be able to receive visual and auditory feedback, view data stored in microfiche, and, with some terminals, communicate with the computer simply by touching their fingers to the display panel.

Although CAI is very efficient for certain kinds of instruction, it is unlikely to become very common until the price of both hardware (computers, terminals, tape drives, etc.) and software (programs) is greatly reduced. The cost is slowly being reduced and this trend is augmented by the fact that CAI can potentially reduce the amount of time that human teachers must spend

---

[16]"The Versatile Computer Is A Patient," *American Education*, 3 (November 1967), p. 18.

in the classroom. As costs go down and programming sophistication increases, the probability of teachers and students having access to CAI terminals in their own classrooms is increased. The probability of schools undergoing a transformation, with students having CAI terminals in their homes or in small attendance centers, is becoming less remote.

Biofeedback and the Chemical Transfer of Knowledge

Since this chapter began with an examination of one of the oldest forms of instructional aids, it is fitting that it be concluded with a look at some forms possible in the future.

Biofeedback refers to the process whereby people may be made aware of body and mental processes that are normally unobservable and learn to control these processes to their own advantage. By using a device known as an electroencephalograph (EEG) scientists have been able to identify those brain-wave patters generated when people are relaxed (Alpha waves—8 to 12 cycles per second) and when they are concentrating (Theta waves—3 to 7 cycles per second. In one experiment involving the monitoring of radar screens, individuals given feedback concerning their brain-wave patterns were able to outperform individuals who were not given such feedback.[17] It is possible that further work in this area will result in students being able to monitor their own brain waves and thus increase their powers of concentration.

In an experiment conducted at the Stanford Research Institute, a subject was able to control the action of a computer by simply "thinking at it" and having it monitor, and react to, specific brain-wave patterns.[18] With such direct communication possible between human and electronic "brains," it may become possible to program computers simply by "thinking" the program at them, or conversely, to learn from computers by allowing them to "think" at people.

Chemists have not been idle either, and in one experiment rats trained to prefer a particular size of circle were killed and extracts of their brains were fed to a second group of rats. The second group of rats were trained to prefer circles of the same size in much less time than an "untreated" control group.[19] As further experimentation in the chemical transfer of learning is conducted it may become possible literally to bottle knowledge.

The possible ramifications of biofeedback and the chemical transfer of learning for the teaching-learning process boggle the imagination. Will

[17]Jackson Beatty et al., "Operant Control of Occipital Theta Rhythm Affects Performance in a Radar Monitoring Task," *Science*, 183, no. 4127 (March 1, 1974), p. 871.
[18]"Mind-Reading Computer," *Time*, July 1, 1974, p. 67.
[19]Lendell W. Braud and William G. Braud, "Biochemical Transfer of Relational Responding (Transposition)," *Science*, 176, no. 4037 (May 26, 1972), p. 942.

devices such as electroencephalographs or bottles of "knowledge" become the mediated instructional devices of tomorrow? Predictions are dangerous, but the possibility exists.

SUMMARY

Aids to instruction range from simple forms such as textbooks and radios to moderately complex forms such as films and TV, to very complex forms such as multimedia kits and computer-assisted instruction, and even to problematical forms such as electroencephalographs and chemicals. Mediated instructional aids in their many forms provide teachers with unique instructional tools and with alternatives to the common sit-and-listen-to-the-teacher instruction.

Regardless of the kind of mediated instruction considered, specific forms must be selected in relation to specific instructional objectives. To be of maximum effectiveness good teaching requires that the teacher be thoroughly familiar with the material or device before using it with students. Proper preparation of students for the mediated instruction is also crucial. Follow-up activities are important, particularly when a one-way communicator such as radio, television, or film has been used. A file of evaluations of the mediated instructional materials used will facilitate decisions regarding the inclusion or exclusion of the media in future learning activities.

Although this chapter has dealt with many of the forms of mediated instruction that most teachers will find commonly available, no attempt has been made to make the chapter all-inclusive. Other forms of mediated instruction (such as magazines, dioramas, and posters) are equally valid and useful. Master teachers strive to increase their familiarity with as many forms of mediated instruction as possible. The more variety teachers include in their instructional activities, the more their students will learn, and the more they will enjoy learning.

SELECTED READINGS

BRIGGS, LESLIE J., et al., *Instructional Media: A Procedure for the Design of Multi-Media Instruction, A Critical Review of Research, and Suggestions for Future Research.* Pittsburgh, Pa.: American Institutes for Research, 1967.

BROWN, JAMES W., RICHARD B. LEWIS, and FRED F. HARCLEROAD, *AV Instruction—Media and Methods.* 3rd ed. New York: McGraw-Hill, 1969.

BUSHNELL, DON D., and DWIGHT W. ALLEN, eds., *The Computer in American Education.* New York: John Wiley , Inc., 1967.

DALE, EDGAR, *Audio-Visual Methods in Teaching*, 3rd ed. New York: Holt, Rinehard & Winston, 1970.

GERLACH, VERNON S., and DONALD ELY, *Teaching and Media: A Systematic Approach*. Englewood Cliffs; N.J., Prentice-Hall, 1971.

GILLETT, MARGARET, *Educational Technology—Toward Demystification*. Scarborough, Ontario: Prentice-Hall of Canada, Ltd., 1973.

KEMP, JERROLD E., *Planning and Producing Audiovisual Materials*, 2nd ed. San Francisco: Chandler, 1968.

KINDER, JAMES S., *Using Instructional Media*. New York, N.Y.: D. Van Nostrand, 1973.

OETTINGER, ANTHONY G., and SEMA MARKS, *Run, Computer, Run.* Cambridge, Mass.: Harvard University Press, 1969.

SCHRAMM, WILBUR L., *Instructional Television: Promise and Opportunity*. Washington, D.C.: National Association of Educational Broadcasters, 1967.

SCHULTZ, MORTON J., *The Teacher and Overhead Projection*. Englewood Cliffs, N.J.: Prentice-Hall, 1965.

SCUROZO, HERBERT E., *The Practical Audio-Visual Handbook for Teachers*. Englewood Cliffs, N.J.: Prentice-Hall, 1967.

WITTICH, WALTER A., and CHARLES F. SCHULLER, *Audiovisual Materials: Their Nature and Use*, 4th ed. New York: Harper & Row, 1967.

8

Evaluation

This chapter is divided into four main sections. The first section deals with fundamental considerations for teachers as they plan evaluation procedures. The second section deals with paper and pencil tests and is divided into subsections dealing with teacher-made objective tests, teacher-made essay tests, and standardized tests. The third section deals with alternatives to formal paper and pencil tests for evaluating progress. The final section deals with calculating and reporting grades.

OBJECTIVES

The student will:

1. Explain in writing at least three basic considerations that should be dealt with when planning an evaluation procedure. (Comprehension)
2. Construct two types of objective tests (twenty items each) and two essay tests (three items each) that meet the standards described for such tests in this chapter. (Synthesis)

3. When given a series of test scores, assign grades to the scores using a systematic procedure, and explain the procedure used to arrive at the assigned grades along with a rationale for its use. (Synthesis)

4. Within the context of a subject area, build a rationale for the predominate use of either criterion-referenced grading or norm-referenced grading and, in less than four pages, defend that rationale by citing specific facts and examples. (Synthesis; Evaluation)

THE GRADING DICHOTOMY

The evaluation of a student's performance often poses painful problems for teachers. Most teachers recognize the need for precise and objective data for evaluation of students. Besides being a prerequisite for assigning grades, evaluations are often the basis for important decisions concerning educational and vocational plans. Inaccurate data can cause misdirection in those plans. In addition, data concerning students' performance also serve as a partial measure of teacher effectiveness. Accurate knowledge of what students can and cannot do, coupled with knowledge of the instructional intent, provides teachers with a sound basis for evaluating their own instructional strengths and weaknesses. (See chapter 14.)

On the other hand, most teachers are aware of ethical considerations often associated with grading students. Is one morally justified in applying any absolute standards to twenty or thirty human beings when one realizes that each of those individuals is unique in terms of background, aspirations, and degree of personal effort? Is it fair, for example, to reward a bright student who does well even though he or she is working at minimal effort, and at the same time to fail to reward a slower student who does not do well but exhibits maximum effort?

The need to provide accurate data concerning students' performance must be balanced against the fact that educators are dealing with human beings and not machined products. In efforts to acquire such data, care must be exercised not to trample the feelings and values of students—to do so might well impede or even destroy the potential love for learning within students. It would be a hollow victory to obtain accurate evaluation data only to find that the evaluation process itself has made students cynical and contemptuous of learning as a worthwhile activity.

Unfortunately, there is no single evaluation or grading technique that can simultaneously solve all the problems associated with the evaluation and grading of students. It is possible, however, to acquire a number of basic evaluation criteria and a variety of grading techniques that, when used in combination, may enable the teacher to synthesize evaluation and grading procedures with which he or she feels comfortable.

BASIC EVALUATION CONSIDERATIONS

Honesty

It is assumed that all teachers approach the evaluation of students with ethical intentions. Certainly, for example, no professional teacher would deliberately set out to fail a student or to punish a class by misgrading a test. It does happen, however, that evaluation problems arise because of unintentional acts by the teacher. These acts often take the form of misleading students concerning the basis upon which they will be graded, or of failing to state explicitly the objectives of the course. For example, students in a writing class may be told to concentrate upon developing clear and logical arguments only to find that their grades depend, to a large degree, upon the grammatical correctness of their papers.

In terms of being honest with students regarding evaluation criteria, there are few substitutes for properly written precise instructional objectives. If the teacher specifies exactly what is expected of students, and goes over those expectations so that everyone has the same interpretation of what they mean, a substantial portion of this criterion has been met. When the targets and standards are known, students are more able to focus their efforts on acquiring those skills without hesitation. When the teacher is consistent in evaluating students on the basis of stated objectives, the procedure will be deemed "honest" by students.

Variety

Currently, a high percentage of academic evaluation programs rely heavily upon paper and pencil tests. This phenomenon is not predominant by chance, but rather has evolved over the years as an expedient way to assess the achievements of large numbers of students. Many of the arguments that have been used successfully to defend paper and pencil tests are still valid and powerful. Among these arguments are the following:

1. Paper and pencil tests can be used to pose the same problems to all students under the same test conditions and can therefore provide a reasonable basis for comparison.
2. Paper and pencil tests generate products (student responses) that are easily stored and are therefore readily accessible for later analysis or review, if and when marking procedures are questioned.
3. Paper and pencil tests can be used equally well to sample a broad scope of a student's knowledge or to probe deeply into a single area.

These advantages have made many teachers reluctant to deviate from this form of evaluation, even when legitimate alternatives exist. It is true that paper and pencil tests can provide reliable and objective evaluation data. It is equally true, however, that teachers must attempt to evaluate a whole that is greater than the sum of a series of test scores.

Alternatives to paper and pencil tests include more frequent use of demonstrations and products. If teachers devise activities that call for the synthesis and application of a number of subsidiary skills, and if students can demonstrate those skills through the construction of a product, sound evidence has been produced to evaluate required objectives. In addition to skill-oriented classes—sewing, for instance, in which each student constructs a garment—academic classes offer unique opportunities for such efforts; for example, an economics class might offer an opportunity for students to build and minipulate their own hypothetical stock portfolio. Student development of tape-slide programs, booklets, instructional packages, school-to-school projects, community projects, models, and class presentations are other possibilities.

It is apparent that it is easier to use demonstrations and products to evaluate student efforts in some courses than it is in others. Remember, however, that demonstrations and products represent ways for students to begin to apply what they have learned. If teachers cannot suggest practical applications for many of the skills they expect students to master, then a reconsideration of those skills may be in order. No teacher wishes to be accused of teaching content and skills that are irrelevant.

Frequency

The optimum frequency for evaluation varies with specific circumstances. The reliability of grades is endangered if decisions are based on only one or two evaluations. Giving too many tests, however, has the effect of emphasizing the wrong aspect of the teaching-learning process. A balance between too few evaluations and too many is necessary. Using a variety of evaluation forms (paper and pencil tests, demonstrations, and products) helps provide students with the information they need to guide their learning and can also provide teachers with the information needed to plan future lessons without upsetting the balance.

When instructional objectives are used in individually paced programs, the emphasis is on having each student work at his or her own rate and demonstrate competencies as they are acquired, rather than on having all students progress at the same rate and be tested at the same time. The former process may imply more evaluation, since each objective is checked separately for each student. The frequency of evaluations can become a headache for both teachers and students, and therefore, variety in evaluations is even more crucial.

In addition to formal evaluations, it is important to provide students with informal evaluations (such as comments, corrected homework, and self-assessable activities) to provide feedback as often as possible. The more input students receive as they practice skills, the more able they are to correct errors. These informal evaluations can assist in the task of student assessment without alienating the student, especially if students are provided with positive reinforcement for good points in their work.

Purpose

One basic reason for evaluating students is to acquire accurate data concerning the skills and knowledge they have acquired and the proficiency with which they can demonstrate that skill and knowledge. Besides the teacher, students, parents, administrators, counselors, prospective employers, and admissions officers of colleges and universities may, at one time or another, need such data. If teachers bias that data for any reason whatsoever, it becomes invalid and discredits the whole evaluation program. The potential anger, frustration, and heartache that students might undergo because teachers failed to evaluate their achievements, or lack of achievements, accurately is cause enough to insist that evaluations be conducted with rigor and professionalism.

If a fundamental purpose of evaluation programs is to acquire accurate data concerning students' achievements, this implies not only scholastic achievements, but improvements (or regression) in other areas such as dependability, honesty, effort, and citizenship. An often-neglected point is the importance of evaluating each characteristic or achievement separately and not clouding the issue by allowing one variable to bias another. If teachers intend to evaluate achievement, then they should evaluate achievement; if the area of concern is effort or dependability, then the focus should be on those things. One judgment should not influence the other. Attempting to use any evaluation procedure for something other than what it was specifically designed for is a misuse of that procedure and will yield little, if any, useful information; it can, however, do a great deal of harm.

When dealing with the problem of how to reward the bright but lazy students or the slow but hard-working students, teachers must be completely honest with each student concerning his or her actual achievements. At the same time, however, teachers can be equally honest in conveying their perceptions of the amount of effort each put forth and the effect that attitude can have on future undertakings. If each student must be given an achievement grade, the grading should be done on the basis of demonstrated achievement alone, but teachers need not hesitate to supplement that grade with additional, relevant data concerning demonstrated effort and/or possibilities for profitable remedial instruction.

Throughout this chapter the term *evaluation* is meant to include not only the computation of a student's test scores but also more nebulous factors, such as effort, dependability, and so on. The crucial point to remember is that the grade must reflect *only* the student's demonstrated achievements; the other aspects (i.e., effort, dependability, etc.) that make up the total evaluation must be reported as the separate factors they are.

Review

When thinking about the evaluation and grading of students, the teacher would be wise to consider at least these four essentials:

1. *Honesty*. Both teachers and students should know, prior to the beginning of instruction, the exact basis upon which students will be evaluated. This knowledge will enable students to focus their efforts on the most important matters and will help keep extraneous factors from clouding evaluation data.
2. *Variety*. Students should be given the opportunity to demonstrate their achievements not only by means of paper and pencil tests, but by other means as well, particularly by the accomplishment of those culminating activities that synthesize subsidiary skills and knowledge.
3. *Frequency*. All students need formal feedback concerning their progress given at logical intervals as close to the practice period as possible. The more feedback students receive, the more likely they are to improve their skills and finally to succeed.
4. *Purpose*. All students have the right to receive accurate evaluation data concerning their achievements and equally accurate data concerning teachers' perceptions of other variables such as effort, dependability, and citizenship. Each variable, however, should be evaluated and reported as the separate and distinct entity it is.

These principles are most effective when the teacher is able to construct, administer, interpret, and report the results of evaluation instruments properly.

RELIABILITY AND VALIDITY

There are two terms with which the teacher must become familiar when dealing with evaluation: *reliability* and *validity*. They are referred to throughout this chapter with the specific definitions that follow in mind.

Reliability is an index of how consistently a device measures whatever it measures. Elaborate statistical procedures have been developed for determining the reliability of norm-referenced paper and pencil tests. It is useful to think of reliability as a measure of the probability that a student would achieve the same score if he or she were to repeat a particular test; or how close the two scores would be if the student took two equivalent forms of a test. Another way of viewing reliability is to think of test results for a class of students with the scores ordered from best to worst. If, after sometime elapsed, all the students were to retake the test and receive a score placing them in the same relative order, the test would be reliable. The key to reliability is how *consistently* students score on similar forms or repeated tests, or how consistently they score in relation to each other.

There are several types of validity. The validity with which classroom teachers are most concerned is *content validity*. This simply means that the evaluation instrument is valid when it measures what the teacher wishes it to measure, namely the amount of content or the proficiency of skills learned in class. Many extraneous factors can cloud the determination of content validity. For example, if the teacher has engaged in straight lecture and then asks the class to answer rigorous analytical questions on an essay test, the students may do poorly. Since there was no practice of analytical skill (only the giving of information during the lecture), the content validity of the test may be in question.[1]

Predictive validity is a measure of how well a student will do on a later task or on a test based upon his or her score on a preliminary measure. The higher the correlation between the two measures, the higher the predictive validity.

CRITERION- VS. NORM-REFERENCED TESTS

Evaluating students to determine their abilities relative to objectives involves comparing each student's performance with certain preset standards or criteria. This kind of evaluation is known as *criterion-referenced evaluation* and is an integral part of the use of precise instructional objectives. Because the purpose of this evaluation of students is to determine who can demonstrate specific competencies, precise instructional objectives are stated, and these objectives will include the evaluation criteria. The evaluation becomes a matter of observing who can and who cannot achieve the minimum acceptable standards.

Criterion-referenced evaluation usually does not provide *comparative* evaluation data, however, and this kind of data is often desired. Ours is largely a competitive society, and it is commonly asked not only what people can do, but also how well they can do it in comparison with other peo-

[1]See Walter Pierce and Howard Getz, "Relationships Among Teaching, Cognitive Levels, Testing and IQ," *Illinois School Research*, 6, no. 2 (Winter 1973), pp. 27-31.

ple. To get this kind of data each student's performance must be compared with the average performance of those students with whom he or she has certain similarities (such as age or grade level). This comparison group is known as a norming group and this type of evaluation is known as *norm-referenced evaluation*.

Much might be said about norm-referenced tests. Their reliability, for instance, tends to increase with the size and homogeneity of the norming group and with the generality of the skills and knowledge being evaluated. Norm-referenced and criterion-referenced tests may often seem to be almost identical. There is, however, a subtle difference. Norm-referenced tests are most powerful when there is a wide disparity among the test scores. To achieve this, norm-referenced tests contain items that range in difficulty from the nearly impossible to the very simple, and it often happens that the items at both extremes have little relationship to the original instructional intent. Many such items are included more to differentiate between students than to differentiate between those who can and cannot demonstrate specified competencies. In criterion-referenced tests there is no attempt to achieve a spread in the test scores, so items tend to be of equal difficulty and the focus is on validity so as to obtain an accurate reflection of the original instructional intent.

PAPER AND PENCIL TESTS

Teacher-Made Objective Tests

Perhaps the most popular form of teacher-made paper and pencil tests is the objective test. Multiple-choice, true-false, matching, and completion items are all varieties of a basic test form that requires students to select or construct a response from a given, or very limited, range of options.

One of the many reasons for the popularity of objective tests is their ability to sample a broad range of knowledge at one time. Rather than concentrating on just one or two questions (which might be the "wrong" questions for a particular student), objective tests ask a relatively large number of questions about a number of different aspects of any given topic. The larger the number of questions and the range of the information covered, the higher the chance to obtain reliable test scores. Proponents of objective tests also point out that they are relatively easy to score and minimize the number of value judgments teachers have to make when assigning grades.

There are also a number of disadvantages associated with objective tests. Some educators point out that objective tests can emphasize the memorization of bits and pieces of information. They claim that students often do very well on the basis of memorizing and recognizing these bits and pieces even though they may have no idea of the relationship of the parts to a larger whole. In addition, constructing items for objective tests is time-consuming, and even though the teacher may work hard to construct good items, it is not uncommon to find that some questions still confuse students.

Considering all the pros and cons, many teachers have concluded that their own objective tests meet some of their evaluation needs better than any other means, especially when they wish to sample students' general knowledge about some topic. Typical objectives for objective tests might include:

1. Each student will recall and apply information about the steel industry, from mining through smelting and product production, well enough to achieve a score of at least 80 percent on a multiple-choice test dealing with this information.

2. Each student will, given a wiring diagram containing numbered connections, place a check before the numbers of all incorrect or superfluous connections.

Important general rules can be followed that will help teachers build and administer valid and reliable objective tests.[2]

1. *Keep the language simple.* Unless the purpose of the test is to survey the extent of students' vocabularies, there is no point in using words that are unfamiliar to students, or in phrasing questions so they are difficult to understand. Students will be justifiably angry and frustrated if they get answers wrong because they could not understand what was being asked rather than because they did not know the right answer. Compare the following two examples:

A. The physical relationship between most petroleum products and most purely aqueous solutions is generally such that physical interaction and diffusion of the two is severly limited. (1) True (2) False.

B. As a general rule, oil and water do not mix. (1) True (2) False.

The only justifiable reason for using example A is if the teacher were attempting to check students' vocabulary. Ask questions as simply and concisely as possible to help insure valid and reliable test results.

2. *Ask students to apply, rather than simply recall information.* If students can apply the information they learned, it is a safe bet they have committed it to memory. It does not follow, however, that simply because students have memorized information they can also apply it. This being the

---

[2]Since evaluation techniques can be complex enough to warrant courses in their own right, a number of sources have been included at the end of the chapter to which the reader can turn if further exploration in this area is desired.

case, the teacher would be wise to aim questions at application rather than simple recall. Consider the following two examples:

    C. The area of a rectangle is found by multiplying the length by the width. (1) True, (2) False

    D. A rectangle 2' x 4' has an area of 8 square feet. (1) True, (2) False

The computation involved in example b is not difficult and yet it enables students to apply what they learned and thus emphasizes learning for the sake of practical application rather than learning for the sake of passing tests.

    3. *Make sure that each item is independent.* Check questions to be sure that one question does not provide a clue to some other question, or that the answer to one question is not crucial to the answer of another. Both situations decrease the reliability of the test results. For example

    E. The number of square feet in a room 9' x 12' is
       (1) 3, (2) 21, (3) 81, (4) 108, (5) 144.
    F. At $2 a square foot, what would it cost to carpet the room described in question E? (1) $6, (2) $42, (3) $162, (4) $216, (5) $288.

Given these two questions, any student who missed E would almost certainly miss F. Other than having the student miss two items instead of just one, nothing was gained by linking the questions. It would have been more advantageous if questions E and F had been combined, i.e., "How much would it cost to carpet a room 9' x 12' if carpeting costs $2 a square foot?" and the extra space used for a separate and distinct item.

    4. *Do not establish or follow a pattern for correct responses.* Regardless of how clever an answer pattern is, some student will eventually discover it and compromise the test results. The problems involved with detecting compromised tests and doing something about them are far greater than any possible advantage to patterning responses.

    5. *Do not include trick or trivial questions on tests.* Sometimes teachers are tempted to ask questions that require extended effort for correct interpretation or that deal with unimportant points. This temptation may stem from being unable to build items as quickly as one would like or from a desire to assure a wide spread among test scores. Trick or trivial questions not only reduce the validity and reliability of tests, they may have a powerful negative effect if they antagonize students.

    6. *Do not answer questions after the test has started unless it is done publicly.* Sometimes individual students will seek further clarification of a question as they work through the test. If additional information is provided

to that student the test results may be biased since that student will have had access to direct help when others did not. It is wise on the part of teachers to make a general announcement prior to each test concerning their reluctance to answer questions during a test. This, plus careful proofreading of tests prior to their administration, should forestall most questions. If it does become necessary to answer a question about some test item, assume that other students may be equally confused about it and call everyone's attention to the clarification. Remember, however, that interrupting students during a test destroys their train of thought and thus should be avoided whenever possible.

In addition to these few general rules, other considerations relevant to the construction of specific kinds of objective test items are presented below.

Multiple-Choice Items   Multiple-choice items are particularly useful because they can easily be used to sample cognitive skills ranging from simple recall through analysis. The following examples illustrate several levels of cognitive thought:

Recall Sample

G. Which should have the ultimate responsibility for adapting precise instructional objectives?
   (1) Curriculum specialists
   (2) Teachers
   (3) Principals
   (4) Textbook publishers
   (5) Student/administration committees

Application Sample

H. The scores on a test were 95, 90, 90, 85, 70, 60, 0. What is the mode?
   (1) 90
   (2) 85
   (3) 81.66
   (4) 70
   (5) 47.5

Analysis Sample

I. A teacher suspected a particular student of storing drugs in his locker. Staying late one day the teacher forced open the student's locker, found drugs, and turned them over to the principal. In a later trial, the case against the student was dismissed because the evidence (the drugs) had been acquired illegally. What *should* the teacher have done?
   (1) Gotten a key to open the student's locker.
   (2) Turned the drugs over to the police.
   (3) Searched the locker and then, if he found drugs, called the police immediately.

(4) Asked the principal, student, student's parents, and the police to be present when the locker was opened.

(5) Asked the principal and another teacher to be present when the locker was opened and photographed its contents immediately.

Principles for Building Multiple-Choice Items

1. *Put as much of the item as possible into the stem.* The "stem" of a multiple-choice question is that part which asks the question or states the problem. If the stem does its job properly it gives the student an idea of what is sought before reading the options. Consider the following two examples:

J. John Adams was:
   (1) the second president of the United States
   (2) the third president of the United States
   (3) the fourth president of the United States
   (4) none of the above
K. The second president of the United States was:
   (1) John Adams
   (2) Thomas Jefferson
   (3) James Madison
   (4) none of the above

In example J, the student does not know what is sought until he or she has read the options. Furthermore, because it is necessary to repeat the same words in each option, the student must spend more time reading. Both points make for inefficient testing.

In example K, the options are shorter than the stem (which is, in itself, a good guide), the stem clearly and concisely asks the question, and it provides sufficient data to help the student start thinking about the correct answer.

2. *Make options reasonable.* In norm-referenced tests, the teacher attempts to discriminate among students. This discrimination process is facilitated by insuring that all options seem reasonable to someone who is unsure of the exact information. Option 4 in examples J and K above for instance, may not be very useful since most students are aware that John Adams was one of our early presidents. Even though the student was not sure just which president Adams was, he or she could still eliminate option 4 and thus increase the chance of guessing correctly from among the remaining options. One way to construct good options is based on the type of error students are most likely to make. In the recall sample on page 152, for instance, the second option is the median, the third is the mean of the three middle scores, the fourth is the mean, and the fifth is the mean of the highest and lowest scores. To someone who was unclear about measures of central tendency, any of these options might seem reasonable. The advantage to this

tactic is that the student's *incorrect* response can be used to diagnose the source of difficulties.

3. *Make sure unintentional clues are not provided.* It sometimes happens that an option can be eliminated simply because it is grammatically incorrect. If, for example, the stem of an item is of the completion variety, and the last word is "an," students can safely ignore any option beginning with a consonant. Similarly, incorrect tenses or forms of words can provide clues, as can correct options that are consistently longer or shorter than the incorrect options. The use of "always" or "never" is frequently a giveaway, as is the use of "all of the above" or "none of the above" if they are used simply as fillers. Careful proofreading of each stem along with each of its options can eliminate many of these unintentional clues and help make tests more reliable. The following item is an example of a grammatical giveaway:

L. Factual recall is best checked through the use of an:
    (1) objective test.
    (2) short answer test.
    (3) matching text.
    (4) subjective test.

True-False Items   True-false items are often singled out as prime examples of the superficiality of objective testing, and often they stand justly accused. Because true-false items seem so easy to write, many teachers rely heavily upon them and forget that they are most appropriate for the lower-level cognitive skills. Under the best of circumstances, a student who has no idea of the correct answer still has a 50-50 chance of guessing correctly. Although true-false items are often misused, it is possible to excercise the needed care to construct true-false items that sample cognitive skills as high as the analysis level. Consider the following examples:

Recall Sample

M. In the United States, FORTRAN is one of the most common computer programming languages. (1) True (2) False

Application Sample

N. A man earning $250 a week would earn $13,000 a year if he worked each week. (1) True (2) False

Analysis Sample

O. If every school system were given its own computer, the most difficult problems currently limiting wider use of computer-assisted instruction would be solved. (1) True (2) False.

Even though it is possible to write true-false items at various levels of the cognitive domain, it is still questionable whether the time required to write such items is well spent considering that other kinds of items could sample the same cognitive levels without requiring as much preparation time. Here are a few points to keep in mind when writing true-false items.

1. *Be sure that every item is definitely true or definitely false.*
2. *Whenever possible, avoid terms such as "generally" and "usually."* These terms, while not as obvious giveaways as "always" and "never," are still open to varying interpretations.
3. *Be sure that items are not dependent upon insignificant facts.* Make sure each item asks something of importance and worth remembering.
4. *Be sure that correct items are not consistently longer or shorter than incorrect items.*
5. *Avoid the use of double negatives, but if you use any negative at all, call attention to it by underlining or capitalizing it.*

Matching Items   Matching items are most easily used to measure-low level cognitive skills such as recall and comprehension. A typical matching test might ask students to link people with events or dates. Variations include asking students to match terms with numbers on a diagram or to match labels for a chart, graph, or map in which such labels have been replaced by letters or numbers. Guidelines for the construction of matching items follow:

1. *Keep the number of items to be matched short.* If students are required to search through more than ten or so items as they respond to each question, they will spend valuable time just searching. Their time would be better spent responding to another series of items in another question.

2. *Make sure that all items concern one topic.* Unless all items are concerned with one topic, students can simply eliminate some options as being irrelevant to some questions. This reduces the reliability of the test.

3. *Include more possible answers than questions and/or stipulate that some answers can be used more than once.* These steps will also help prevent students from getting right answers purely by eliminating some options.

4. *Arrange the options in some logical order such as chronological or alphabetical.* This will make it easier for students to search through the options and will help avoid providing unintentional clues.

Completion Items   Completion items depend almost entirely upon the student's ability to recall a key word or phrase. Since most secondary teachers are after more than rote memorization, completion items are generally not used as frequently as other kinds of objective test items. Here are some points to keep in mind if completion items are written.

1. *Write items that can be completed with a single word or a short phrase.* There is a difference between a completion item and an essay exam.

When students are required to "fill in" more than a few words, the grading of the item is complicated and it ceases to be a completion item.

2. *Be sure that only one word or phrase can correctly complete the sentence.* In a phrase such as, "The First World War began in_____" either a date or the name of a country could correctly be used. Guard against this common error by trying different words or phrases to see if there are correct alternatives. Revise each item until only the one word or phrase sought can be used correctly.

3. *Put the blanks near the end of the sentence so the student is guided toward the correct response.*

4. *Make all the blanks the same length.* Sometimes unintentional clues are provided when teachers try to make the size of the blanks correspond to the size of word or phrase to be inserted. The items should be clear enough to make this kind of clue unnecessary.

5. *Do not put more than two blanks in any one item.* The more blanks in the item, the greater the chance the student will be unable to determine just what is sought.

Although there is considerable overlap, the following chart helps to illustrate the types of test items that are usually most appropriate with specific types of precise instructional objectives. Keep in mind that the overlap exists because different kinds of test items *can* be written to sample almost any behavior. The following chart is simply illustrative.

OBJECTIVE	POSSIBLE TEST ITEM
The student will:	
1. List, in writing, two distinguishing characteristics of a thigamagig. (Knowledge)	1. Two distinguishing characteristics of thigamagig are: (1)_____(2)_____ .
2. Given a graph and a series of statements relating to the data presented, label all the incorrect statements. (Comprehension)	2. According to graph A, the greatest production of thigamagigs occurred in 1783. (1) True, (2) False.
3. Given word problems involving the derivation of cost per yard, label the correct solution to at least 80 percent of the problems. (Application)	3. At $10 per square yard, how much will it cost to carpet a room 9' x 9'? (a) $810 (b) $90 (c) $890 (d) $270 (e) none of the above

OBJECTIVE	POSSIBLE TEST ITEM
4. Given a wiring diagram with various circuits showing specific colors, match the outcome of power input to any given circuit and its result. (Analysis)	4. Power input in this circuit (input column) will cause this output (output column).

Input	*Output*
red	ring bell
blue	blow horn
green	light bulb
yellow	turn on fan
	start motor

Objective Tests—A Final Word   This section has outlined procedures helpful in the construction of objective tests. Of particular importance is the fact that objective test items should be constructed so they are clearly and concisely stated. Item construction time tends to increase as items are designed to measure successively higher levels of cognitive skills.

Although they are called "objective" tests because of the objectivity inherent in their grading, it would be foolish to maintain that objective tests are as objective as the term implies. The teacher still makes important subjective decisions about what questions to ask and how to ask them, and unless those decisions are based on the originally stated instructional objectives, "objective" tests will not be very objective.

Teacher-Made Essay Tests

Essay tests represent a second kind of teacher-made evaluation device. The greatest single advantage of essay tests is that they require students to synthesize a response and, in so doing, to demonstrate not only their understanding of the relationships among bits and pieces of information but also their understanding of the body of information as a whole. Essays allow the teacher to call upon students to interpret, evaluate, and organize data, draw conclusions, make inferences, and express their thoughts coherently. This makes the essay test useful in assessing higher level cognitive skills such as synthesis and evaluation.

Offsetting these strong points are a number of disadvantages.

1. Teacher fatigue, subconscious biases and other extraneous varibles can affect students' grades.
2. Essay tests are inherently biased in favor of those students who can write quickly, neatly, and effectively;
3. Essay tests are often low in reliability and validity since only a few questions are asked and a student may, by chance, be asked questions about which he or she happens to know a great deal (or very little);
4. Essay tests take a longer time to grade than other types of evaluations.

Other problems, particularly those concerning reliable grading, can be avoided or minimized by following definite procedures in the construction and grading of the tests.

1. *Be definitive about what is expected from students.* As test items are formulated, keep in mind the types of thought processes in which students are to engage, and the types of points that should be included in their responses. Consider the following two examples:

P. Describe the "Water Cycle," including the cause-effect relationships among the various phases.

Q. Identify three problems associated with mandatory public education and explain how these problems might be eliminated or lessened.

Example P requires more precise information than does example Q, and may only be checking student comprehension. It may be more efficient to check student comprehension by an objective test.

In example Q, students are expected to demonstrate greater originality than in example P so this item is better suited for an essay test.

2. *Describe the task clearly.* Examples P and Q describe clearly what the student is to do. They provide sufficient direction so that if the student has the necessary information he or she would be able to formulate acceptable answers. Compare the two examples above with the two following examples:

R. Discuss the effects of World War II.

S. State your opinion concerning East-West detente.

Example R provides so little direction students would not be able to formulate precise answers. Some students might concentrate upon the military effects, others on the social effects, others on the technological effects. The structure of the question is too broad. Depending upon the teacher's intent, some students would find they had included some of the appropriate information while others would find they had not—even though all might have been able to formulate acceptable answers had they known more precisely what the teacher wished.

Example S presents a similar problem. Unless teachers specify prior to the test the exact grading criteria, they should give full credit for any given answer. How can it be argued, for example, that a student's answer did not represent an opinion? When teachers ask general questions they must be prepared to accept general answers.

3. *Make sure students have sufficient time and materials to do the job.* One strength of essay tests is the opportunity they provide to give students

the chance to analyze relationships among points within a topic or problem and then formulate responses by synthesizing the information they possess. This process is much more time-consuming than responding to objective test items, and students must have sufficient time to analyze the items, perhaps outline their answer, and then write it legibly. If students are unduly pressed for time, their responses may not be as true a reflection of their abilities as they might otherwise have been.

A practical way to estimate the amount of time to allow students for each item is for teachers to time themselves as they write an acceptable response and use this base to allow students additional time. This procedure not only provides a good estimate of how many items students can reasonably be expected to respond to, but also provides a model response against which student responses can be compared.

Many teachers find it easier to read responses that are written in ink on provided, lined paper. Other teachers prefer to have students write their answers on the same sheet containing the questions.

4. *Grade papers anonymously.* Sometimes, when evaluators know the author of a paper it can bias the evaluation. This possibility can be minimized by using procedures that make it possible to ignore the names on the papers. One such procedure is to use code numbers on papers rather than names. This factor, for conscientious teachers, may ultimately become difficult because teachers soon can identify many students from handwriting samples.

5. *Compare each response to a model or a list of crucial points.* There is a tendency, after having graded a few responses, to begin comparing those read later with those previously read, rather than comparing them to the model answer or to a list of important points. This tendency can be minimized by making continuous references to the model response or list of crucial points. This is essential when using the essay test as a criterion-referenced measure.

6. *When possible, use more than one evaluator and then average the grades.* Greater reliability can be achieved if more than one evaluator is used and the separate evaluations are averaged.

7. *Avoid mixing essay items and objective tests items on the same test.* The intellectual operations required to synthesize a response to an essay item are significantly different from those required to select a response to an objective test item, and to expect students to demonstrate both kinds of cognitive skills within a single class period may be expecting too much.

Quick Reference Guidelines—Teacher-Made Tests

Objective Tests

I. Advantages
   A. Provide a broad sampling of students' knowledge.
   B. Present the same problems and the same alternatives to each student.
   C. Minimize the chance of student bluffing.
   D. Can be scored quickly and with little, or no need for subjective decisions.
   E. Items can be improved on the basis of item analysis.
   F. Reliability can be increased through item improvement.

II. Disadvantages
   A. Difficult to assess some cognitive skills, such as synthesis and creativity.
   B. Increases the possibility of guessing.
   C. Items take a relatively long time to construct.

III. Utilization Factors
   A. Construction and administration
      1. Keep the language simple.
      2. Ask students to apply, rather than simply recall information.
      3. Make sure each item is independent.
      4. Do not establish or follow a pattern for correct responses.
      5. Do not include trick or trivial questions.
      6. Do not answer questions after the test has started unless you do so publicly.
   B. Multiple-choice items
      1. Put as much of the item as possible into the stem.
      2. Make all options reasonable.
      3. Do not provide unintentional clues.
      4. Avoid the use of all-inclusive or all-exclusive terms.
   C. True-false items
      1. Be sure that each item is definitely true or definitely false.
      2. Avoid the use of all-inclusive or all-exclusive terms.
      3. Be sure that items are not dependent upon insignificant facts.
      4. Be sure that true items are not consistently longer or shorter than false items.
      5. Avoid the use of double negatives and call attention to single negatives by underlining or capitalizing the negative word.
   D. Matching items
      1. Limit the number of items to be matched to ten or less.
      2. Make sure all items concern one topic.
      3. Have more answers than questions or stipulate that some answers can be used more than once.
      4. Arrage options in some logical order.
   E. Completion Items
      1. Write items that can be completed with a single word or a short phrase.

    2. Be sure that only one word or phrase can correctly complete the sentence.

    3. Put the blanks near the end of the sentences.

    4. Make all blanks the same length.

    5. Do not put more than two blanks in any one item.

Essay Tests

I. Advantages
   A. Emphasize high-level cognitive skills, such as synthesis and evaluation.
   B. Provide an in-depth sampling of students' knowledge of a specific topic.
   C. Allow for student creativity, analysis, and synthesis skill assessment.
   D. Easier to construct than objective tests.

II. Disadvantages
   A. Reliability and validity tend to be lower than on objective tests.
   B. Biased in favor of those students who write well.
   C. Grading is time-consuming.
   D. Increase the possibility of bluffing.

III. Utilization Factors
   A. Be definitive about what you expect from students.
   B. Make sure students have sufficient time and materials to do the job.
   C. Grade papers as anonymously as possible.
   D. Compare each response to a model response or to a list of crucial points.
   E. When possible, have tests checked by more than one evaluator and average the grades.
   F. Do not mix essay items and objective items on the same test.

Validity and Use of Teacher-Made Tests

Teacher-made essay and objective tests deserve emphasis because the teacher, better than anyone else, knows what the instructional objectives were and what kinds of questions need to be asked to determine whether the objectives have been achieved. Hence, the teacher determines whether content validity of the evaluation exists.

Both essay tests and objective tests can be used prior to instruction (to determine students existing abilities), during instruction (to check on progress and determine areas of strengths and weaknesses), and after instruction (to determine final achievement). Well-constructed teacher-made tests, if tailored to precise needs, can be a key tool to help improve the teaching-learning process.

STANDARDIZED TESTS

Standardized tests are usually constructed by commercial test producers. Each item that appears on a standardized test has generally been checked carefully to assure that it: (1) is appropriate in difficulty for a particular, described population; (2) has high discrimination power (spreads the scores), (3) has a high reliability index; and (4) has a good biserial correlation (students who score well on the test tend to get any given item correct, and students who score low tend to get any given item wrong). Standardized tests usually come with a detailed set of instructions for administration and can often be machine scored.

Appropriate "norms" are included to facilitate the interpretation of scores. Test "norms" are averages against which individual scores can be compared. In the case of most standardized tests these norms are derived by averaging the scores of a wide sampling of students all having in common some characteristic such as age or grade level. The large size of the norming group helps eliminate gross distortions caused by extreme scores, thus making the norms rather stable measures. Additional information relevant to the norms (such as the test's standard error, standard deviation, and standard scores) also help make score interpretation more valid.

In order for test manufacturer to stay in business they must produce tests that are not only reliable but also attractive to large numbers of prospective users. One characteristic of standardized tests that contributes to their reliability and attractiveness is their generality. Most standardized tests concern themselves with general kinds of skills and knowledge, thereby enabling measurement experts to construct items that provide a reliable survey of that skill or topic as a whole.

Since standardized tests are *general* measures they are often not appropriate for use in measuring achievement of specific instructional objectives. It is unlikely that a standardized test will emphasize the exact content a teacher is emphasizing, and therefore the test's content validity may be questioned. It would be foolish for teachers to assume that their efforts were wasted simply because their students did not do well on a standardized test. To determine whether students achieved stated objectives it is usually necessary to use teacher-made tests, not standardized tests. The former are specific measures, the latter general ones. When the purpose of the test is to compare the student to a large population in a broad content area, standardized tests may be in order.

Types of Standardized Tests

Standardized tests usually measure general intelligence, achievement, aptitude, or interest. A brief description of each follows.

Intelligence Tests   Intelligence is an ambiguous term often defined by phrases such as "mental abilities," "capacity to learn," and "the ability to cope successfully with new situations." Most intelligence tests require the person being tested to solve a series of previously unseen problems by manipulating factual information, perceiving relationships, making generalizations, and applying other cognitive skills.

Intelligence tests can be administered on either an individual or a group basis. Individual tests, such as the *Stanford-Binet Intelligence Scale* and the *Wechsler Intelligence Scales*, tend to be more reliable than the group tests, but because they require one test administrator for every person being tested, they also tend to be more expensive and more time-consuming.[3] Group tests, such as the *Otis Quick-Scoring Mental Ability Test* and the *Lorge-Thorndike Intelligence Tests*, while somewhat less reliable than the individual tests, still have good predictive validity and are much more commonly used.

When looking at an individual's IQ score it would be wise to remember that (1) "intelligence" has no precise definition and therefore cannot be precisely measured; (2) most intelligence tests are verbally oriented and culturally biased; and (3) they cannot be interpreted without understanding a statistic called a "standard error," included in score interpretation data. The standard error is intended to be used to construct an interval into which the student's "true" score would be likely to fall. For example, if a student's IQ score is 100 and the standard error is 10, it is commonly interpreted to mean that there are about two chances in three that the student's IQ is between 90 and 110. This is considerably different from stating that the IQ is exactly 100.

Achievement Tests Achievement tests are more narrowly focused than intelligence tests. Intelligence tests function by posing problems and giving the individual the freedom to integrate whatever skills and knowledge he has at his command in order to solve those problems. Little effort is made to test the individual's abilities in any specific subject area. The intention of the achievement test is somewhat different. Achievement tests specify particular subject areas (such as mathematics, reading, and language), and then test students' abilities in each of those areas by providing appropriate subtests.

Test manufacturers intend their tests to evaluate content achievement, but they are faced with the complex problem of attaining reliability, discrimination, and good biserial correlations and consequently are in a peculiar position. The more precise and detailed the questions that are asked, the further the test may get from a particular school's instructional objectives, the lower the content validity will become, and the less likely will be the purchase of the test by large numbers of schools. On the other hand, if the manufacturers use a minimum of detailed facts and depend upon those concepts that are common knowledge, they must depend more upon

[3]Further data on the instruments included in this section may be obtained by referring to Oscar Buros, ed., *Mental Measurement Yearbook, Seventh Edition* (Highland Park, N.J.: Gryphon Press, 1972).

analytical skills to achieve statistical goals. With this dilemma in mind, it is not hard to understand why the results of achievement tests and IQ tests will often correlate highly. Both tend to emphasize general data widely accepted as "important."

Although achievement tests deal with more specific areas than do intelligence tests, their scores are *not* necessarily more precise. Both kinds of scores are best thought of as estimates, both can be affected by variables such as student illness, tension, and distraction, and both need to be interpreted in light of specific students and objectives. Some educators have found that achievement test scores can be made more useful if they are compared to norms constructed for a specific school rather than to national norms. There is an inherent danger in using scores from any standardized test as the sole criterion for establishing expectations of individual students or for making decisions about them.

Some of the commonly used achievement tests include the *California Achievement Tests*, the *Metropolitan Achievement Tests*, and the *Iowa Tests of Educational Development*.

Aptitude Tests   Whereas achievement tests focus on what students have already achieved, aptitude tests focus on their potential for future development. Aptitude tests function by grouping into occupationally oriented categories those items designed to measure specific abilities. For example, one of the most commonly used aptitude tests, the *Differential Aptitude Test Battery*, includes items involving verbal reasoning, numerical ability, abstract reasoning, space relationships, mechanical reasoning, clerical speed and accuracy, and language usage. Another commonly used aptitude test, the *General Aptitude Test Battery*, includes items involving vocabulary skills, numerical ability, spatial relations, form perception, clerical perception, motor coordination, manual dexterity, and finger dexterity. By evaluating the results of such tests, guidance personnel are able to suggest vocational fields in which students are most likely to experience success. Some fields, such as music and art, require unique kinds of abilities for success, and specific aptitude tests have been developed that focus very narrowly on those abilities.

It should be noted that few aptitude tests are known for their high predictive validity. It is not uncommon for a student who has shown a low aptitude in some area later to become interested in that area and go on to become highly successful in it. The importance of the student's own goals should never be minimized.

Interest Inventories   Most interest inventories are similar to aptitude tests in that they are vocationally oriented. However, whereas most aptitude tests function by sampling specific kinds of skills, most interest inventories function by sampling student attitudes toward particular kinds of activities.

Since students' likes and dislikes are subject to more rapid changes than their abilities, interest inventories are generally regarded as less valid predictors than either achievement tests or aptitude tests.

The most commonly used interest inventories include the *Kuder Preference Records*, the *Strong Vocational Interest Blanks*, and the *Thurstone Interest Schedule*.

General Utilization Factors

When using standardized tests, two pertinent points should be kept in mind. The first is that all test administration directions must be followed explicitly. The generally high reliability of standardized tests stems partly from the fact that all students who take the test do so under conditions as nearly alike as possible. Every student is provided with the same materials and environment and is given the same amount of time in which to complete various sections of the test. As a general rule, students' scores will become less reliable to the degree that testing conditions are allowed to vary.

The second point is that although a good deal of time, money, and expert help were probably used to construct, refine, and norm any given standardized test, the score a student earns on that test still reflects only a sample of ability. In order to avoid making foolish, unfortunate, and even tragic decisions concerning any individual it is imperative to obtain as much and as varied data as possible. Standardized tests provide just one input.

ALTERNATE EVALUATION PROCEDURES

Once the teacher begins to use specific objectives and focuses on the ultimate skills students will be able to demonstrate, paper and pencil tests often receive less emphasis. There are few instances in which being able to pass a test is the ultimate reason for learning. Because the use of precise instructional objectives can increase the use of evaluation devices other than formal paper and pencil tests, and because these "alternative procedures" lend themselves so well to the evaluation of individual performance, the issue of how to make these alternate evaluation procedures valid and reliable needs examination. The following points can assist in building alternative evaluation procedures that will withstand critical scrutiny:

1. *Specify standards clearly.* Since clearly spelling out standards is so critical, it is reemphasized here. As an illustration, consider the following objectives. Each involves a student construction, but in each case the product is less important than the cognitive skills necessary for its construction.

A. The student will write a "mailable" one-page letter to a company or politician in which some problem is delineated, a desired course of action is outlined, and supporting rationales for that action are given. ("Mailable" is a
business term used to denote a letter that is free from errors in spelling,
grammar, punctuation, usage, etc., and ready for signature and mailing.)

B. The student will demonstrate his or her understanding of "power politics,"
in part, by assuming the role of leader of some small foreign government and
describing, in less than three pages; (1) why some commodity under his or
her control is critical; (2) why his or her current manipulation of that commodity (its price, availability, or use) is justified; and (3) how he or she plans
to resist pressures to stop such manipulations.

C. The student will construct a 2' x 3' poster designed to sway people's opinion
for or against some controversial issue and describe, in less than three pages,
how each element (color, message, design or figure placement) helps make
the poster a powerful communicator.

The elements included as part of the minimum acceptable standards for
these objectives partially spell out the criteria to be used in assessing
achievement, and in each case the "product," by itself, is clearly insufficient.
The objectives are designed to assess synthesis and evaluation level skills
and unless the student manifests those, he or she would not meet all the
criteria.

Suppose, however, the student wrote the following letter in response to
the first objective.

Dear Sir:

I recently purchased a new Doohicky and it does not work right. Neither the
store I purchased it from nor your factory representative accepted responsibility
for the Doohicky's malfunction and now I'm tired of fooling with it and want a
refund. Unless I get a refund within two weeks, I will turn the issue over to my
attorney.

Sincerely yours,

This letter contains all the elements suggested in the objective, and the
teacher may be pressed to give the student credit for achieving the objective.
On the other hand, the letter leaves room for improvement. What can be
done?

2. *Whenever possible, provide a model.* Models are helpful from a
number of standpoints. Students will find them helpful because they will
have an actual sample of the final product. Regardless of how explicitly
written criteria are, actually seeing an acceptable product will help sharpen
the student's mental picture of what is expected. The picture can be
strengthened further if both good and bad models are provided and explanations of why they are good and bad are included.

Through the use of audio tapes, videotapes, and actual samples, as well
as written models, teachers can provide models for virtually every kind of

behavior or product students are to manifest. The possibilities are limited only by the teacher's imagination.

3. *Provide a checklist.* A checklist is really an elaboration of the stated minimum acceptable standards. It will be impossible, in most cases, to specify all important steps or criteria in every objective, but in the case of those objectives calling for the construction of some product, regardless of whether the product is a paper or a paperweight, a checklist can help students. In the case of the previous letter, for example, students could have been given a checklist for writing letters to companies that included items such as, "Did you specify where and when you bought the product and did you explain exactly what your problem was?"

Checklists can function as both instructional and evaluative aids. As instructional aids, checklists provide students with a logical sequence of steps of points that, if followed or included, lead to the development of an acceptable product. As evaluative aids, checklists provide students (and evaluators) with a list of the specific points being sought in the final product, and since checklists can be much more detailed than the standards included in instructional objectives, they can be particularly helpful to students.

Checklists, like models, can be constructed to guide students toward the achievement of virtually every kind of expected behavior. If the checklists are clear enough, there is no reason why they, together with models, cannot be an aid in attaining a reliable grading system that enables teachers to differentiate between quality levels of students' work. The more the teacher relies on measures of student achievement other than formal paper and pencil tests, the more students will see a practical value in what they are learning. What is learned is seldom important in and of itself; its importance stems from how it can be used.

Individual "alternative" forms of evaluation can also be used in concert with one another and with "traditional" forms of evaluation in the formation of specific "contracts" with individual students. A student doing independent study might, for example, contract with a teacher to pass a test for a grade of "C," pass the test and do a report that meets set criteria for a grade of "B," and pass the test, do the report, and make a presentation for a grade of "A." Contracts are useful when teachers individualize the learning process, and alternative forms of evaluation can provide many appropriate possibilities for the formulation of these contracts.

CALCULATING GRADES

Grade Calculation Schemes

Preset Levels   Most students at some time experience an evaluation system wherein grading standards are preset. In many cases students are given standards such as A=90-100, B=80-89, C=70-79, D=60-69, and anything less than 60=F. In most of these cases those standards were arbitrarily set at some "traditional" level. Why do educators use such an arbitrary grading system? For one thing, the determination of grade levels for any objective test is, in the final analysis, a subjective decision, and opinions differ as to which, if any, is *the* best. For another, this particular method is advocated by proponents for two reasons: First, many students and teachers are familiar with having grades calculated on the basis of preset levels and feel comfortable with this system. Grading "on a curve" or by some other method gives the appearance of being less consistent than the preset level method, and is thus (in their minds) open to more suspicion. Second, once the grade levels are set, they can remain set. This means that by constructing tests of varying difficulty teachers may control grades. The preset level grading method does not contain any built-in mechanism to guarantee a somewhat normal distribution of scores and therefore there is no necessity for some percentage of the students to fail. By constructing easy tests, the teacher can guarantee success for every student.

The obvious disadvantage is that since so many people are familiar with this grading scheme they are prone to accept the grades at face value (i.e., an 85 is a B) and never bother to question what the B represents. As has been pointed out, the designation of some number as an A or a B, etc., is arbitrary; it has no relationship except to itself. Yet when it is used as a measure of student achievement great meaning is often attached to it. It seems to say more than it really does say.

The "Curve"   Another way of calculating grades is known as grading "on a curve." The curve referred to is the "normal curve" or the curve that results if the frequency of some characteristic normally distributed among a very large population is plotted on a graph. Statisticians use procedures in which the resulting graph is divided into areas through the use of standard deviations (SD's). These SD's theoretically remain constant with about 34 percent of the population falling between the mean (average) score and one SD above the mean, 34 percent falling between the mean and one SD below the mean, and most of the remaining scores divided between one SD's and two SD's above and below the mean.

Standard deviations and the normal curve are useful because they are based on the mean score rather than some arbitrarily fixed point. Thus, if the teacher administers a particularly difficult test containing 100 items and the mean score happens to be 23, the teacher can still assign A-F letter grades by calculating how far above or below the mean each score is and then applying the standard deviation cutoff points. If the teacher had previously decided that an A was going to be any score one and one-half standard deviations above the mean, it would not matter whether the mean was 23 or 83. One and one-half standard deviations would be calculated from that point and the grade assigned.

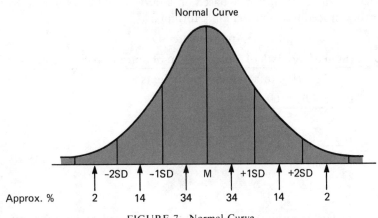

FIGURE 7 Normal Curve

There are a number of formulas by which approximations of the standard deviation can be calculated, but one often used because of its ease is the one suggested by W. L. Jenkins.[4] The steps to this procedure are as follow: (1) Arrange all the scores from high to low; (2) find the sums of the top one-sixth of the scores and the bottom one-sixth; (3) subtract the sum of the bottom one-sixth from the sum of the top one-sixth; and (4) divide the difference by one-half the total number of scores. In equation form the formula is

$$\text{Approximate Standard Deviation} = \frac{\text{Sum of top sixth} - \text{Sum of bottom sixth}}{\text{Half the number of students}}$$

Suppose a teacher had a class of twelve students and gave them a twenty-item test worth 100 points. After deducting five points for each incorrect response the scores were calculated to be: 95, 90, 85, 75, 75, 75, 70, 70, 65, 65, 60, and 40. Suppose further that the teacher had decided upon the following standard deviation cutoff points:

$$A = 1.25 \text{ SD's or greater}$$

$$B = .25 \text{ SD's to } 1.25 \text{ SD's}$$

$$C = -1.00 \text{ SD to } .25 \text{ SD's}$$

$$D = -2.00 \text{ SD's to } -1.00 \text{ SD}$$

$$F = \text{Less than } -2.00 \text{ SD's}$$

[4]Paul B. Diederich, "Short-Cut Statistics for Teacher-Made Tests," *Evaluation and Advisory Series*, no. 5 (Princeton, N.J.: Educational Testing Service, 1960), p. 23.

Grades for the class of twelve based on a curve could be estimated by the following procedure using Jenkin's formula:

$$\text{Approximate SD} =$$

$$\frac{(\text{Sum of top sixth of scores } - \text{ Sum of bottom sixth of scores }}{\text{Half total number of students}} =$$

$$\frac{(95 + 90) - (60 + 40)}{6} =$$

$$\frac{185 - 100}{6} =$$

$$\frac{85}{6} \approx 14$$

Next, calculate the point equivalents to the standard deviation cutoffs by adding the approximate SD to, and subtracting it from, the mean score.

$$\text{Mean} = \frac{\text{Sum of scores}}{\text{Number of scores}}$$

$$= \frac{(95 + 90 + 85 + 75 + 75 + 75 + 70 + 70 + 65 + 65 + 60 + 40)}{12}$$

$$= \frac{865}{12}$$

$$\approx 72$$

Since an A is any score 1.25 SD's or greater above the mean, the point equivalent can be found by multiplying 1.25 by 14 (the approximate SD) and adding the product (17.5) to the mean (72). The minimum A grade is therefore 17.50 + 72, or 89.5. Since the B range is .25 to 1.25 SD's above, its point equivalent can be found by multiplying .25 by 14 and adding the product (3.5) to the mean (72). The B range thus extends from 72 + 3.5, or 75.5, to 89.49. Similarly, the C range would be found by multiplying −1 by 14 and *subtracting* the product from the mean. The C range would extend from 72 − 14 or 58, to 75.49. The D range would extend from 72 − (2 x 14), or 44, to 57. The F range would be anything less than −2 SD's, or anything less than 44. The actual test scores might then be determined by using the following scale.

$$A = 89 \text{ or better}$$

$$B = 75 \text{ to } 88$$

$$C = 58 \text{ to } 74$$

$$D = 44 \text{ to } 57$$

$$F = 43 \text{ or lower}$$

The grade distribution for the scores given at the beginning of this problem would then be

95 = A	75 = C	65 = C
90 = A	75 = C	65 = C
85 = B	70 = C	60 = C
75 = C	70 = C	40 = F

Practice Problems for Assigning Marks Using a Curve Calculate the mean score and approximate standard deviation, to the nearest tenth, for the following 24 test scores using the Jenkins method and its equation space is provided below.

24, 22, 20, 19, 19, 18, 17, 17, 16, 16, 15, 15, 15, 14, 14, 13, 13, 13, 13, 12, 12, 12, 11, 11

First calculate the mean (average) of the scores (add all scores together and divide by the total number of scores).

Compare your calculated mean to the work below:

```
                        17
            13    15    18
   11       13    15    19
   11       13    15    19      58
   12       13    16    20      80
   12       14    16    22      94
  +12      +14   +17   +24    +139
   58  +    80 +  94 +  139  =  371
```

```
              15.45
        24 | 371.00
             24
             131        Mean = 15.45
             120
             110
              96
             140
```

Now calculate the approximate standard deviation. Compare your work with that shown below. Check any discrepancies. Determine the nature of any differences between your work and the answer provided.

$$11 \ 13 \ 15 \ 18$$
$$11 \ 13 \ 15 \ 19$$
$$12 \ 13 \ 16 \ 19$$
$$12 \ 14 \ 16 \ 20$$
$$12 \ 14 \ 17 \ 22$$
$$13 \ 15 \ 17 \ 24$$

sum of top ⅙ scores   = $24 + 22 + 20 + 19$ =   85

sum of bottom ⅙ scores   = $11 + 11 + 12 + 12$ =   46

$$SD = \frac{85-46}{12}$$

$$SD = \frac{39}{12}$$

$$SD = 3.25$$

Assume that the school district wishes you to assign marks on the curve using the standard deviation scale given below:

Mark   SD above or below the mean

A   = +1.5 SD or greater

B   = + .5 SD to + 1.49

C   = − .5 SD to +.49

D   = −1.75 SD to −.51

F   = Less than −1.76 SD

Assign the grades the students would receive using the scale given above to the scores provided.

Compare your grade assignment with the answers below, using

Mean = 15.45

SD = 3.3

Calculating A grades (scores 1.5 SD above mean and greater)

$$
\begin{array}{ll}
\begin{array}{r}
3.3 \text{ (SD)} \\
\times 1.5 \\
\hline
1.65 \\
3.3 \\
\hline
4.95 \text{ scores above mean}
\end{array}
&
\begin{array}{r}
15.45 \text{ (Mean)} \\
+ \ 4.95 \\
\hline
20.40
\end{array}
\end{array}
$$

Scores 20.4 and above get A's. There are two scores above 20.4.

Calculating B grades (scores between .5 and 1.49 SD above mean)

$$
\begin{array}{ll}
\begin{array}{r}
3.3 \text{ (SD)} \\
\times \ .5 \\
\hline
1.65
\end{array}
&
\begin{array}{r}
15.45 \text{ (Mean)} \\
+ \ 1.65 \\
\hline
17.10
\end{array}
\end{array}
$$

Scores from 17.1 to 20.4 get B's. This means the students with scores of 18, 19, and 20 would get B's. There are four scores in this range.

Calculating C grades (scores between .5 below the mean to .49 above the mean)

$$
\begin{array}{ll}
\begin{array}{r}
3.3 \text{ (SD)} \\
- \ .5 \\
\hline
-1.65
\end{array}
&
\begin{array}{r}
15.45 \text{ (Mean)} \\
- \ 1.65 \\
\hline
13.80
\end{array}
\end{array}
$$

Scores from 13.8 to 17.1 get C's. This means the students with scores of 14, 15, 16, and 17 would get C's. There are nine of these scores.

Calculating D grades (scores between 1.75 and .51 SD below the mean)

$$
\begin{array}{ll}
\begin{array}{r}
3.3 \text{ SD)} \\
\times 1.75 \\
\hline
1.65 \\
2.31 \\
3.3 \\
\hline
5.775
\end{array}
&
\begin{array}{r}
15.45 \text{ (Mean)} \\
- \ 5.78 \\
\hline
9.67
\end{array}
\end{array}
$$

Scores from 9.7 to 13.8 get D's. This means the students with scores of 11, 12, and 13 get D's. There are nine of these scores.

Calculating F grades (scores more than 1.76 SD below the mean)

$$
\begin{array}{ll}
\quad 3.3 \;(\text{SD}) & \quad 15.45 \;(\text{Mean}) \\
\times 1.76 & -\;\;\; 5.81 \\
\hline
.198 & \quad 9.64 \\
2.31 & \\
\underline{3.3} & \\
5.808 &
\end{array}
$$

This means that scores below 9.6 would receive "F's." There are no scores this low.

The assignment of grades would look like this:

A	24	C	17		14	13
	22		16		14	12
B	20		16	D	13	12
	19		15		13	12
	19		15		13	12
	18		15		13	11

Although estimating standard deviations and grading "on a curve" enables teachers to assign grades on the basis of statistical procedures, the procedure has rather serious disadvantages. Standard deviations originate from large samples in which the normal curve of percentages apply, i.e., 50 percent of all cases will always fall below the mean, approximately another 34 percent will fall between the mean and one SD above the mean, and approximately another 14 percent will fall between one and two SD's above the mean. With small samples, such as are found in classrooms, these percentages are much less exact. Once teachers decide upon a set of cutoff points, they are virtually guaranteeing that there will be inequities because of the sample size. For instance in the one example given, there are no D grades, in the other there are no F grades and only two A's.

Another closely related point concerns the fact that standard deviations are calculated with respect to mean scores. This means that in an advanced class a student might have to get a 95 to get an A while in a slower class, a student might need only a 65. Since an A is an A in the final records, many educators have reservations about grading "on a curve". The reservations are particularly great when grades are calculated "on a curve" in advanced classes in which students compete with each other for a handful of high grades, when such grades would have been assured had they been in a regular class.

Eyeballing Another method of calculating grades consists of simply tallying the scores on a scale, looking for natural divisions in the distribution, and assigning letter grades to these divisions. Although this "method" seems rather haphazard, it is often used in practice even though decisions are completely arbitrary.

It can be seen from looking at a tally of the scores in our first example that there are three natural divisions. A decision must be made as to the cutoff point for A's and B's, B's and C's, etc. There are no right or wrong answers here. Depending upon the teacher's assessment of how difficult the test was, how well he or she felt the teaching had gone, etc., the teacher may assign grades in a variety of patterns.

Scores	Frequency of Each Score
100	
95	1
90	1
85	
80	1
75	111
70	11
65	11
60	1
55	
50	
45	
40	1
35	
0	

Here are four possible eyeballing grading patterns for grade distribution:

Score	Freq	Grade	Score	Freq	Grade	Score	Freq	Grade	Score	Freq	Grade
100			100			100			100		A
95	1		95	1		95	1	A	95	1	
90	1	A	90	1	A	90	1		90	1	B
85			85			85		B	85		
80	1	B	80	1	B	80	1		80	1	
75	111		75	111		75	111		75	111	
70	11	C	70	11		70	11	C	70	11	C
65	11		65	11	C	65	11		65	11	
60	1	D	60	1		60	1		60	1	
55			55			55			55		
50			50		D	50		D	50		
45			45			45			45		D
40	1	F	40	1		40	1		40	1	
35			35		F	35		F	35		

Credit   When working with behavioral objectives and the Logical Instructional Model, it soon becomes obvious that the key to success for students is to attain the minimum acceptable standard described in the objective or in supplemental checklists or descriptions. Many educators who are using such a model have gone to a "credit" system. It is, perhaps, the simplest of all methods available.

At the outset of instruction all the competencies are delineated. They may be modified by student input, but a final decision is reached. Each of them has a minimum acceptable standard or criterion level (see chapter 3). As students demonstrate a competency, they are given credit and proceed to the next. When all competencies are completed for the course, the student is finished. Under individualized instruction, the "normal curve" now reflects *time* rather than *scores*. Instead of the majority of students receiving an average grade, they will finish about the same time. Instead of receiving a high mark, a brighter student will achieve the competencies sooner.

Many schools have attempted to blend grading schemes with such programs. This is usually done by assigning an average grade for the basic competency and then encouraging "quest" or "enrichment" activities for high grades.

Grading and Subjectivity

All the grading methods examined have had one point in common. In each instance the method depended upon some subjective decision. The preset level method required a subjective judgment concerning the placement of the levels; the "curve" method required a subjective judgment concerning the standard deviation cutoff points; the "eyeballing" method depended entirely upon subjective decisions; and even the "credit" procedure requires subjective judgments concerning the level of proficiency desired in order to receive credit.

Some educators argue that since all grading methods ultimately depend upon subjective decisions, none is any better or worse than any other. The advantages and disadvantages balance out. Without intending to add to the argument it can be said that any choice should be guided by at least two factors: (1) the circumstances in which the teacher finds himself or herself (for instance, a particular school may have a set policy concerning grading); and (2) the importance attached to the material included in the test (very definite standards may be kept in mind for crucial material and more flexibility allowed with other material).

REPORTING GRADES

Assuming one or another of the many available methods to arrive at grades has been adopted, the question of how most effectively to communicate information regarding student progress still remains.

Many school systems have adopted a policy, at least with respect to standardized tests, of not reporting the student's exact score at all. To minimize the misinterpretations associated with "exact" scores, many school systems convert these scores to *stanines*. Stanine is a term that stands for "standard nine," a structured distribution that consists of nine equal intervals. The nine intervals account for 100 percent of any given population with the intervals representing 4 percent, 7 percent, 12 percent, 17 percent, 20 percent, 17 percent, 12 percent, 7 percent, and 4 percent of that population respectively. Most standardized tests provide tables by which individual scores can be converted to stanines and thus placed in an appropriate interval. Because the intervals created by the stanine distribution are so large, teachers can be fairly certain that any given student's "true" score falls into the stanine interval indicated by the test score.

Stanines, like scores calculated by teachers, are best reported to parents and students in a conference. The teacher can more fully explain the implications of particular grades as well as how the grades were calculated. (This procedure is seldom used for the secondary level.) Teachers find it important to be able to substantiate any grade given or comment made, and they can minimize parental uncertainty or anger by initiating explanations about grading procedures and providing reasons for using whatever grading scheme was selected. Having an understanding of the mathematics involved in a particular grading method means very little, however, if grades do not reflect achievement or nonachievement of specific instructional objectives. Parents are not normally interested in how sophisticated a grading system may be; they are interested in how well the grades reflect what their child has accomplished.

Teachers who are concerned with the need to report evaluations, rather than just grades, will find that parent-teacher (or parent-teacher-student) conferences or telephone conferences yield better results than the one-way mailing of grades or comments. Conferences enable the teacher to relate factors such as effort and dependability to the student's actual achievement. Conferences are even more valid if the student is present and can provide additional input, provided the conference does not degenerate into an accusation/ defense match.

Given the fact that conferences are sometimes difficult to arrange, educators rely heavily on some other reporting device—usually a report card. Unfortunately, grades on a report card do not really reflect a student's specific abilities, even though a great deal of importance is frequently attached to report card grades. If the school depends solely upon report cards, the teacher should explore the possibility of including with each report card a list of the instructional objectives for the class or course with indications of those that the student achieved. Such a list will provide parents with a much clearer picture of what their son or daughter has actually accomplished.

SUMMARY

This chapter has surveyed important points concerning the evaluation of students' progress. It is suggested that evaluation be tied to specific instructional objectives; that those objectives be communicated to students prior to instruction; that students be evaluated in a variety of ways with an increasing emphasis on techniques other than formal paper and pencil tests; and that students be provided with frequent feedback concerning their learning progress either in the form of formal tests or informal comments and self-evaluation devices. Tests can be constructed either as criterion-referenced or norm-referenced instruments, and a chief difference between the two is that the goal of the latter is to achieve a spread in the scores whereas the former has as its goal discerning whether students can perform at a minimum proficiency level.

Objective tests are most useful for sampling the breadth of students' knowledge of some topic, whereas essay tests are most useful for sampling the depth of student's evaluating, creative, or synthesis skills. Even though the purposes are different, some similarities exist between objective and subjective tests. The items or problems on both types of tests need to be worded simply and precisely, and both types are most effective when they require students to apply, rather than simply to recall or repeat, information. Objective items and essay items should not be included on the same test, because they require different kinds of cognitive skills, and students waste time shifting from one cognitive orientation to the other.

Standardized tests are mainly used to measure general kinds of abilities such as intelligence, achievement, aptitude, and interest. Part of their reliability stems from their emphasis on general skills rather than specifics. The norms associated with standardized tests usually reflect the average performance of large numbers of students from a wide sample. The size of the sample contributes to the stability and utility of the norms.

The teacher would be wise to emphasize tasks that require the integration of many subskills and information. Such tasks not only emphasize the practicality of what is being learned, but they also decrease the need for formal paper and pencil tests. Students can be helped to succeed at these alternative tasks if the standards are specified as precisely as possible in the instructional objectives, if both good and bad models are provided for students to examine, and if checklists of important steps or points are included.

All grading methods ultimately depend upon some subjective judgments, and any one of several methods might be most appropriate depending upon the situation. These procedures, when used in conjunction with a provision for two-way communication with parents and students, will provide those most concerned with the information necessary to make intelligent decisions.

SELECTED READINGS

BROWN, DONALD J., *Appraisal Procedures in the Secondary Schools*. Englewood Cliffs, N.J.: Prentice-Hall, 1970.

DIEDERICH, PAUL B., "Short-cut Statistics for Teacher-Made Tests," *Evaluation and Advisory Series*, no. 5. Princeton, N.J.: Educational Testing Service, 1960.

EBEL, ROBERT L., *Essentials of Educational Measurements*. Englewood Cliffs, N.J.: Prentice-Hall, 1970.

GONLUND, NORMAN, *Constructing Achievement Tests*. Englewood Cliffs, N.J.: Prentice-Hall, 1968.

MAGER, ROBERT F., *Measuring Instructional Intent*. Belmont, Calif.: Lear Siegler, Fearon Publishers, 1973.

SCHOER, LOWELL A., *Test Construction: A Programmed Guide*. Boston: Allyn & Bacon, 1970.

STANLEY, JULIAN C., and KENNETH D. HOPKINS, *Educational and Psychological Measurement and Evaluation*, 5th ed. Englewood Cliffs, N.J.: Prentice-Hall, 1972.

"Setting Standards of Competence: The Minimum Pass Level," study by the Evaluation Unit, Center for the Study of Medical Education, University of Illinois College of Medicine, Chicago, 1972.

TERWILLIGER, JAMES S., *Assigning Grades to Students*. Glenview, Ill. Scott, Foresman & Co., 1971.

THORNDIKE, ROBERT L., and ELIZABETH HAGEN, *Measurement and Evaluation in Psychology and Education*, 3rd ed. New York: John Wiley, 1969.

9

Individualizing Instruction

Among the ideals continually advocated by educational theorists over the past twenty years has been the notion of individualized instruction. Educational psychologists point out that because every child is unique and has different curricular needs and readiness levels, ideal teaching should therefore "individualize." The term "individualization of instruction" has, however, come to stand for a variety of ideas such as (1) special individual lesson plans; (2) self-paced instruction; (3) self-selected curriculum; and (4) large-group instruction with individual help. This chapter explores possibilities for self-pacing through the use of self-instructional packages and for the use of self-instructional packages within a systems approach. It also contains the fundamental steps necessary for building a self-instructional package. Most of these ideas are presented in the form of model packages.

OBJECTIVES

The student will:

1. When given a specific set of material covering the background of self-instructional packages and the status of self-instructional packages and

systems, to recall and show comprehension of facts about the material by answering at least 75 percent of a series of questions correctly on an objective test. (Knowledge; Comprehension)

2. Following a model and a set of instructions, construct a self-instructional package in his or her content area, suitable for use by pupils and containing a minimum of five prescribed elements. These elements must exhibit the minimum qualitative criteria described in the "Evaluation" section of Model Package #2, found in this chapter. (Application; Analysis; Synthesis)

THE SYSTEMS APPROACH TO INDIVIDUALIZING

There are a variety of possible ways for a self-instructional package approach to achieve self-pacing. One procedure is to operate separate classrooms as self-contained units wherein each teacher decides how to achieve the objectives. Another approach is to combine several classrooms, departments, or the entire school under one larger system for instruction. Whatever the administrative procedure adopted, all the approaches are based on the construction of sets of self-paced instructional packages that have objectives encompassing a variety of domains and levels. Following is a description of a typical middle-school system's concept for self-instruction. It is not a description of any particular school but has elements of many that are in operation. Included are some of the processes necessary to engage in a changeover from a traditional school, although a more complete analysis is the province of texts on supervision or curricular development.

After achieving staff agreement (no easy chore in itself) that a thrust toward a self-paced systems program is desirable, the hypothetical school can initiate a first phase toward a gradual changeover. The recommended first step is an agreement among staff members of each department upon the objectives of that department. These objectives will undergo the critical examination described in chapters 3 and 4, including an analysis of terminal and en-route objectives, and identification of the necessary prerequisite skills for each objective identified.

After the identification of objectives, a procedure for building self-paced instructional packages and pilot testing is organized using small numbers of students. No attempt is made at this point to convert classrooms to a systems approach. The packages are offered as supplements to, or temporary replacements for, the regular instructional program. Built-in evaluation procedures for the constituent parts of the packages to be used by the student are included (for example, questions like, "What learning activity was helpful?" and "Did you understand the objective?"). In this way, the packages are polished and improved.

As a department increases its stock of proven self-instructional packages to the point where all objectives of a particular course are covered, that course may be put on a systems basis. Assume that there are three teachers of eighth-grade English during the third period each day. When self-instructional packages have been built for the entire course, the decision can be made to try the packages as a system that includes all three classes.

At this point the role of the teacher changes dramatically. Instead of fulfilling the traditional role, the teacher's new responsibilities will focus on four basic activities. First a teacher will have a responsibility to the system that replaces responsibility to a single class. For instance, instead of keeping track of grades for each student in the one class, a teacher may keep track of the packages completed by students in all three classes. In return, another teacher who previously kept track of materials for his own class may now keep track of materials for all three classes.

Second, the teacher will be expected to write new packages and to review old packages. Continual additions and improvements are necessary to keep a system viable. If there is a problem with a particular package, immediate alteration is required. The teacher most concerned with that particular package must be willing to modify it quickly to insure success of the system. This package building implies a growing need for proficiency in the production and selection of media. Most packages need a variety of learning modes to be successful. As new information and ideas appear in the content areas, the teachers should be alert to the possibilities of including good new ideas in the packages.

Third, the teacher should expect to serve on content-area committees that will continue to examine the selection and evaluation of objectives in terms of overall school goals and community changes. A perfectly good set of terminal objectives for last year's student population may become obsolete because of the influx of a new type of student population during the course of the year. The committees may also consider many other issues connected with the operation of the system, such as new package adoption or revision of old packages.

Finally, the teacher becomes an advisor and counselor in addition to a content-area specialist. The student-teacher contacts become more one-to-one as the teacher assists each student with particular concepts or procedural details.

The role of the student also changes as he or she works through part of a course using self-paced materials. Assuming that the required objectives of the course have become the objectives of learning packages, the student may consult the teacher about which package should be worked on next. A plan and appropriate materials may already have been individually prepared for the student, and he or she may only need to consult that plan; or the student may consult a routing sheet that all students are following. After determining which is the next learning package, the student may select that package from his or her personal set of materials, or may go to a central location and check out an individual package. Once the package is in the student's hands, the work can begin.

Packages take a wide variety of forms, but most contain a preliminary statement of the skills that will be demonstrated upon completion of the package. If the student does not fully understand the precise instructional objective as stated, he or she will need the assistance of one of the teachers. At this point (depending upon the sophistication of the package), the student may take a preassessment test that will enable him or her to determine (1) which learning activities need to be engaged in, (2) which learning activities may be omitted because of prior knowledge, or (3) whether he or she already has the competency and can go immediately to the final evaluation instrument. In some cases a preassessment may be set up under test conditions, and the student may demonstrate the competency directly after or during preassessment.

After determining the specific learning activities necessary to build the skill needed to demonstrate the competency, the student begins to work at these activities. It is at this point that many programs succeed or fail. The learning activities must be interesting. They need to include a variety of learning modes and should be based on sound learning principles. Films, filmstrips, records, multimedia kits, lab work, and visitations are just some of the learning modes that students can use to acquire skills and information. Reading is not the only option available in the self-instruction packages.

After completion of the learning activities, the student is ready for evaluation. Evaluation can take many forms. If it is to be a test, the student may acquire a copy of the examination from the teacher and go to a special area to take it, or he may be tested at a central test station in the school that has its own support staff. Results from this test should include feedback if the necessary minimum competency is not obtained so that the student can determine which learning activities need reemphasis or whether an alternate learning activity is more appropriate to specific needs.

The system for informing students of their progress and for keeping accurate records can range from individual record keeping by teachers to a computer-oriented surveillance of an entire school. The information is vital for continuous process adjustment.

By blending a combination of "required" packages with a variety of "self-choice" packages, the student can begin to have some control over curriculum content. While it is obvious that eighth-grade students need to continue to write to improve competency in written communication skills, the choice of content between science fiction and sports short stories, for instance, can be left to the student if both types of literature will help him or her attain the same skill competency.

THE STATUS OF SELF-INSTRUCTIONAL PACKAGES— MODEL PACKAGE 1

Part 1: Objectives for Model Package 1

Given a specific set of material covering the background of self-instructional packages and the status of self-instructional packages and systems, the student will be able to recall and show comprehension of facts about the material as demonstrated by correctly answering at least 75 percent of a series of questions on an objective test. (Knowledge; Comprehension)

Part 2: Self-Preassessment

The following questions will assist you in determining whether you already have the knowledge necessary to pass successfully the examination for the first objective; and, if not, which learning activities you should emphasize in order to demonstrate your ability to understand these facts. If you are sure you know the answers to all the following questions and can demonstrate all the required skills, you may want to move directly to Part 4, evaluation (page 203).

1. There are many institutionally and commercially produced sets of self-instructional packages. Most are known by their initials, which form acronyms. Name at least four. (Learning activity 2, B)
2. Most self-instructional packages have a minimum core of *at least* four sections. What are these? (Learning activity 2, A)
3. What proportion of a conventional high school unit is included in a self-instructional package? (Learning activity 2, D)
4. Upon what factors does the number of packages in a unit depend? (Learning activity 2, D)
5. What functions are performed by the behavioral objectives in a package? (Learning activity 2, A and C)
6. In what ways does the student's role in educational decision making in a traditional program differ from his or her role in a systems package program? (Learning activity 2, E)
7. List at least five alternate instructional modes available for learning activities package programs. (Learning activity 2, E)
8. A package may include several tests. What are the common types of these tests? What function does each of these types of tests perform? (Learning activity 2, F)
9. Name at least three types of evaluations that could be used to check a student's work in a package. (Learning activity 2, F)
10. What is meant by "enrichment activities"? (Learning activities 2, H)

11. What are two basic purposes of the movement toward self-instructional packages? (Learning activity 3, A)

12. Describe the changing role of the teacher when he or she moves from a traditional program to a systems self-instructional package approach. (Learning activities 1, B and 3, B)

13. Describe two separate ways in which packages may be utiized. (Learning activity 3, C, D, and E)

14. What are the implications for student scheduling and staffing patterns implied by a systems self-instructional approach? (Learning activity 1, B and C)

15. Give three common reasons for the failure of some self-instructional package programs. (Learning activities 1, B and 1, D)

16. There are several types of record-keeping systems being used in self-instructional package programs. Describe three. (Learning activity 1, E)

17. How can numbering systems for package programs show a sequence or nonsequence to a series of packages? (Learning activity 1, F)

18. Why is internal format consistency among packages within a school important? (Learning activities 1, G and 2, G)

19. What factors help determine the design and size of a self-instructional package? (Learning activities 1, G and 2, D)

20. Give at least two reasons why a complete evaluation of a student's work should be done. (Learning activity 1, H)

21. List at least four major differences between a traditional classroom and a classroom using self-instructional packages. (Learning activity 1, I)

22. Give at least one advantage and one disadvantage of using a central test center rather than the classroom for evaluation. (Learning activity 1, J)

23. Give one reason for, and one reason against, a complete conversion to package programs. (Learning activity 1, K)

Note that these items, because they are designed to help the student in a preassessment of his or her understanding of self-instructional packages, are content oriented, and each refers to a specific learning activity. In some instances the student may already know the answer to a question, in other instances the student will need to engage in the prescribed learning activity to gather the background information.

Part 3: Learning Activities

1. Read the article entitled "Procedures for Classroom Implementation of Self-Instructional Packages" found in this package; or, listen to the audio tape of the same name; or see the tape-slide presentation of the same name. As you read or go through the materials, determine answers to the questions in the preassessment section.

2. Read the article entitled "Self-Instructional Packages Described" found in this package; or listen to the audio tape of the same name; or see the tape-slide presentation of the same name. As you read or go through the materials, determine answers to the questions in the preassessment section.

3. Read the article entitled "The Effect of Self-Instructional Packages on Curriculum" found in this package; or listen to the audio tape of the same name; or see the tape-slide presentation of the same name. As you read or go through the materials, determine answers to the questions in the preassessment section.

4. Take the trial test and compare your answers with those provided.

Note that the student is offered an alternative learning mode for each learning activity. The articles referred to here are included in this package. When building packages for students, the teacher may use articles from periodicals, chapters from books, or material from other sources, or create his or her own material which the student may prefer. The learning activity may simply refer to those materials and their location. For instance, "Read pages 22 to 30 in the book entitled *Self-Instructional Packages* located in the Materials Center," may be the entire learning activity instruction for a package.

The audio tape may be simply a cassette covering the same content, and the same tape with accompanying visuals could make up the tape-slide presentation. The audio-visual aids mentioned in both packages are available at nominal cost by writing to PEP Educational Aids, 1108 East Grove, Bloomington, Illinois 61701.

Learning Activity 1:
Procedures for Classroom Implementation
Of Self-Instructional Packages

A. *Introduction*   Much of the criticism that has been leveled against self-instructional packages since they first began to have an impact on education can be traced to poorly planned implementation of the self-instructional package program. Teachers who view package programs as an automatic panacea will usually be disappointed. This approach, as with most educational endeavors, takes continued dedication and effort if it is to be successful.

Let us examine various aspects of self-instructional package programs to emphasize the importance of sound implementation in insuring a successful structure.

B. *The Changed Role of the Teacher*   Self-instructional package programs imply a changed role for the teacher. No longer a dispenser of knowledge and classroom authoritarian, the teacher assumes a role of advisor, counselor, and subject-matter consultant. This new role of instructional manager is one that threatens many teachers. Using a gradual introduction to the new program in the form of in-service work prior to the change, and a changeover of only one aspect of the program at a time, make it possible to ease the anxieties that are certain to appear.

It is important to remember that self-instructional packages are really nothing more than a change to a new system for transmission of knowledge and skills. The success of the program is, in large part, determined by the view of the program that the teachers involved hold. Nothing will destroy a self-instructional package program faster than having the very people who are responsible for it undermine its success. If the staff is not sold, the program cannot succeed.

C. *Student Schedules*   Is there an optimum administrative schedule system for packages? Package programs may be run in almost any time pattern. Flexible schedules lend themselves better to a systems approach, however. In this approach, schedules may vary and allow for more student freedom and less rigid time modules.

Successful package programs may be run on a very traditional six-period day or on a modular schedule. In most modular scheduling approaches there are various amounts of time when a student is not scheduled into a class and has time for any of a variety of activities. The schedules lend themselves to self-instructional package programs because the student may go to any of various learning centers and work on self-instructional packages of his or her choice.

D. *Learning Activity Variety*   One of the ways to make a package program deadly is to restrict the learning activities to a few instructional modes. The learning activities possible for packages span the full range of those that have been advocated in methods textbooks and practiced by master teachers for years. A self-instructional package program, once adopted, does not restrict the potential variety of learning activities.

When the learning activities in a self-instructional package are such that they can be carried out only by individuals on their own, then the package builder should make every effort to increase the variety of learning modes. The package builder creatively plans alternate routes to the objective using a wide range of audio-visual aids (see chapters 6 and 7).

E. *Keeping Accurate Student Records*   One of the common complaints heard about classrooms from elementary schools to graduate school is that pupils are not kept informed of how they are doing. The principle of adequate feedback as an important part of reinforcement principles is well documented.

The basic criteria for an adequate student record system are: (1) accuracy; (2) availability; (3) simplicity of understanding; and (4) ease of administration. The application of these criteria, of course, varies with the degree of school involvement in package programs. At the least involved level, students are in traditional classroom settings and become involved in packages only as supplemental, remedial, or enrichment activities. In these instances the teacher in the classroom simply notes which packages are completed in the grade book and awards the student grades according to whatever preconceived ratings he or she had imposed on, or agreed upon with the student. At the other end of the scale, entire schools using a self-instructional systems approach may be involved in a complex, computerized surveillance system. In this type of operation students usually fill out mark-sensing forms of some kind for each objective completed. These are "read" by a scanner, which records the data on computer tape or cards. The computer then sorts the data and periodically prints out information sheets listing the work completed by each student.

Between these two extremes, successful programs have utilized approaches from large wall charts organized by teachers that indicate each student's progress, to file cards maintained by teacher's aids, to loose-leaf notebooks for each student. Most of these devices contain spaces for all the required and optional packages, and a code is inserted by hand.

Whatever system for rewarding success is adopted for use by the school, the record-keeping system and its use in that reward system must be clearly understood by the students at the onset of instruction. One procedure is to weight each package with "merits" or "credits." An accumulation of appropriate amounts of merits then results in a corresponding mark or other reward system notation.

F. *Sequential Packages*   Because titles are cumbersome to a record-keeping system, numbers are often used to label each package. By judiciously utilizing coding systems, the self-instructional package program can avoid the problem of implied sequence when it is not intended. Often several packages will need to be done sequentially. When this is the case, these packages need to be grouped for easy identification. If the teacher uses five digits to number each package, students soon learn, for instance, that packages beginning with two zeros (00123) can be taken in any sequence. If, however, the package begins with two numbers other than zero (12043 or 25021), the students know that all the 1200 series needs to be taken in order; that is, 12001 is the first package in a sequence and must be completed before 12002 is begun. In sequential learning, the final evaluation of 12001 may also serve as the preassessment for 12002.

G. *Consistency Leads To Success*   Without a high degree of consistency within the format of each package and between disciplines and departments within the school, the student will encounter unnecessary difficulty. Students learn to adjust to total package programs more quickly if they can use the same approach each time. If they must take a new approach to each self-instructional package, their learning progress will be hampered.

The length of a package and the degree to which attempts are made to vary stimuli in learning activities is a function of the age and maturity of the student. In some instances it is best to make each objective a separate package. Package builders making this decision should take into account approximately how much time they wish the student to spend on a given package.

H. *Accurate Evaluation Of Student Work* In order to say with conviction that a particular student has obtained a given competence, an accurate assessment of his or her work must be undertaken. Being able to assure administrators and the public that students completing the program have acquired various skills is a large step toward achieving the implied goals of accountability so prevalent today.

When a complete assessment of a student's work has been accomplished, the proper feedback can be given in those instances of lack of success so the student may discern what part of a package's learning activities to review. When each learning activity is multimodal, the student has an opportunity to go through a different mode but still experience the same content. Through experience, the student will soon learn that he or she may learn better through one mode than another, for instance, through the use of audio materials rather than reading materials.

I. *Differences Between A Traditional Classroom And A Self-Instructional Package Program* If a school has undergone a major change toward self-instructional packages, then an observer is likely to experience some bewilderment at the motion and "looseness" with which the operation moves. Students on open modules may be moving from one learning area to another as they shift from content area to content area. Because some group work is encouraged, subsections of students may be engaged in work and discussion on the same package. They may or may not have organized into a formal group. Other clusters of students may have asked for and be receiving a special "help" session where activities more resemble those of the traditional classroom. Depending upon the number and kinds of audiovisual materials available, students may be operating at individual levels where they are in control of a tape-slide sequence, TV tape, or a cassette. Others may be getting procedural advice or individual content counseling from teachers. A few will be engaged in finding out results of evaluations from whatever feedback system has been evolved.

This independence of action is in stark contrast to the traditional classroom. One difference should be particularly stressed. It is likely that students will need both time and assistance in learning how to use self-instructional packages. Teachers may be reluctant, for example, to include answers to practice exercises and self-tests for fear that students will simply look at the answers and not bother to do the practice exercises or take the tests. Such misuse may occur, but it will quickly decrease as students learn for themselves that the exercises and self-tests actually help them demonstrate the final objectives and as they learn that there is no stigma attached to making mistakes in the practice exercises or on the self-tests. The idea of self-pacing and independent action is a new one to most students, and teachers should expect a period of transition, with its attendant problems, when packages are introduced.

J. *Testing* As a self-instructional package program expands, the possibility for incorporaing a central location for testing increases. If a test center is utilized, it will have certain advantages and disadvantages. One reason for its existence is so that the burden of testing does not fall on the individual teachers. The job of working with students on content, and providing advice, is demanding. Constant interruptions in this flow, to administer individual tests, inhibits continuity and makes the move toward a test center a desirable one. But, too many students could also flood the test center. Adequate help must be available or the test center cannot function properly. Usually this means hiring additional personnel or reassigning those already on staff.

A typical test center operation would proceed with students arriving on their own accord to take tests. On occasion a package may tell the student that he or she should check with the teacher to get a permit slip for certain tests. This type of package usually focuses on one or two important concepts that have been identified as troublesome for students. The teacher may pre-test the student orally in a sentence or two to see if going to the test center seems appropriate.

Upon arrival the student requests the test for the particular self-instructional package on which he or she has worked. It is best if there are several forms of the test so that the student can take a different form if the competence was not demonstrated on the first trial. The procedure to insure that the students take alternate forms on subsequent attempts is a clerical chore that may be deemed too tedious when large numbers are involved, and the student simply receives one of several forms at random.

One of the disadvantages of a test center versus classroom testing is that poor test instruments and items are spotted much more quickly by the classroom teacher and corrections are made more rapidly.

It is usually easier to speed up test corrections for faster feedback when a test center is used. The clerks in the center can often correct tests and give students results immediately. In some systems the papers are sorted and machine scored so that results are posted the following day. Speed is important because students have a tendency to wait for results of one package before proceeding to a new one.

K. *Total Systems Approach Versus a Blend of Self-Instructional Packages and the Traditional Setting*   Few self-instructional package programs have developed a staff with enough experience in handling the system and at the same time building packages so that the learning experiences contain enough variety to keep students motivated all the time. As with any endeavor, continuous evaluation of the program will reveal that new objectives may be viewed as "better," and that new packages must be built. Each package will undergo a trial and improvement stage, and during that stage it is easy to "turn off" students when they hit a package that needs improving. On the other hand, certain students blossom under a complete package program. They not only enjoy the success that they attain through this method, but are pleased to assume a role as special "feedback" students who operate at the leading edge in testing new packages. In this role they not only learn the material but have a sense of pride as they see their suggestions incorporated into package revisions. For such youngsters a complete conversion to packages is feasible.

The real answer, then, is to be able to offer the flexibility necessary to handle the differences among students. Having alternative learning activities geared to the learning style of each youngster is a dream that may never be completely attainable, but it is a goal worth striving for.

Learning Activity 2:
Self-Instructional Packages Described

A. *Common Characteristics of Self-Instructional Packages*   Self-instructional packages remind one of the old saying, "All men are like every other man, like some other men, and like no other man." There are certain characteristics that are essential to self-instructional packages if they are to fit into the Logical Instructional Model pattern.

The first prerequisite for an instructional package is a precise statement of what the student should be able to do after the self-instructional package is completed. The second element is a procedure for assessment of the skills students already possess along with some type of feedback to direct them to appropriate learning activities. The third element is a set of learning activities designed to help students accomplish the objective. The last element is an evaluation to insure that the objective was attained. Surrounding these four basic elements are a variety of embellishments that can assist the student toward the goal.

According to R. Herbert Ringis, there are six specific elements forming the basic structure of self-instructional packages:

1. Concept focus
2. Behaviorally-stated objectives

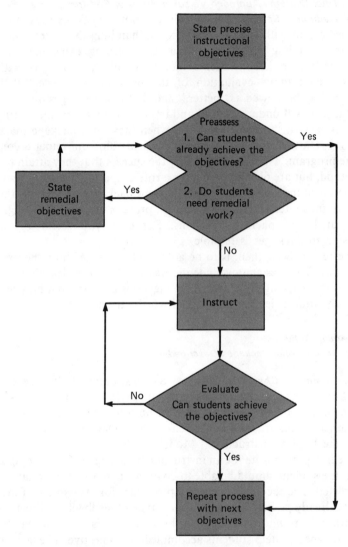

FIGURE 8 The Logical Instructional Model

3. Multiple activities and methodologies
4. Diversified learning resources
5. Evaluation instrumentation
6. Breadth and/or depth suggestions.[1]

[1]Herbert Ringis, "What Is a Self-Instructional Package?" *Journal of Secondary Education*, 46, no. 5 (May 1971), p. 201.

As you can see, there are some discrepancies between the elements of the Logical Instructional Model and those in Ringis's list. It is the purpose of this chapter to examine lists like these, and other ideas, and to arrive at a structure of a self-instructional package that is consistent with the Logical Instructional Model. Many different arrangements have been successful, and no one arrangement is necessarily best. It is up to the teacher and the school to select those parts that seem to fit their philosophical stance and the characteristics of the particular students of a particular school.

B. *Commercial Packages*   There are many self-instructional package programs on the market. Following are a few that are often cited.

Home Economic Learning Packages (HELP)
Home Economics Department
School of Education
University of Pittsburgh
Pittsburgh, Pennsylvania

Individually Prescribed Instruction (IPI)
Learning Research and Development Center
University of Pittsburgh
Pittsburgh, Pennsylvania

Learning Activity Package (LAP)
Nova Schools
Fort Lauderdale, Florida and
Hughson High School
Hughson, California

Learning Packages (LP)
Hartford City Schools
Hartford, Connecticut

Teaching-Learning Unit (TLU)
Westinghouse Learning Corporation
Project PLAN
2680 Hanover Street
Palo Alto, California

UNIPAC (not an acronym)
Teachers UNIPAC Exchange
1653 Forest Hills Drive
Salt Lake City, Utah

Each of these programs utilizes a different format, but they are all based on the concept of self-paced individualized instruction.

C. *What Should Be The First Step in a Package?*   Ringis defines, as his first step, "concept focus." Its function is to delineate the ideas in the package and their relationship to the total content in order to determine the suitability of that package for a learner. His definition could be described as a subject-matter oriented approach, for preassessment.

Since the focus of attention in a behaviorally-stated objective is on what students are going to be able to do after they are done with the package, it could be argued that a "concept focus" may distract from the necessary attention needed on the behavioral objective as the first step in a self-instructional package. This is countered with the position that seeing the relationship between a particular objective and the total picture combats "fragmenting."

Sometimes, instead of a concept focus, self-instructional package makers have chosen to make the first item in a package a rationale for the existence of the package. The rationale is an attempt to answer beforehand the question, often heard in secondary schools, "Why do I have to learn to do this?" If a satisfactory answer cannot be given to the question, then good reason for abandonment or modification of a package would seem to be in order.

Whatever the choice for the first step in a package, it is essential that the behaviorally-stated objective be close to the beginning (if not the first step) and be clearly understandable to the student, since it is upon this understanding that all subsequent effort will be based.

D. *Relating Self-Instructional Packages to Traditional Units*   Teachers and students are used to dealing with subject matter arranged in units. In teacher preparation, almost all colleges and universities require at some point a unit plan of their preservice teachers. Since self-instructional packages focus on from one to a few objectives in each package, the question of the relationship of a self-instructional package to units is raised.

There are no set rules for determining how many packages will make up a unit, and it is beyond the scope of this chapter to investigate in depth the various theories of arranging knowledge structures. Instead, the following set of steps that teachers may use to guide themselves when translating units into packages is proposed:

1. Remember that the number of packages depends on two factors: (a) the complexity of the subject (which implies that the more complex the content the smaller the content of each self-instructional package will be); and (b) the maturity of the student (which implies that the more mature the student, the more scope each package can cover).
2. Build the behavioral objectives implied by the unit.
3. Cluster these objectives into groups according to common characteristics.
4. Taking into consideration the first rule above, delineate packages for each cluster of objectives.
5. Build packages for each objective or set of objectives.

E. *Learning Activities*   Various procedures have been developed for inspiring teachers to create a variety of learning paths to accomplish the objectives of the self-instructional package. By focusing on multiple activities or multiple methodologies, opportunity is provided for more than one path to teach the competency required.If alternate paths are available for students, some students may be able to reach sound educational decisions on their own as to which path to follow. Others will need teacher guidance. It may be that one route to the objective is easier but takes longer than an alternate route. When this is the case, the teacher may encourage the bright, motivated student to select the shorter more difficult route, and counsel a less able youngster to take the easier route.

It is immediately apparent that some of the instructional modes teachers commonly use are still available in self-instructional packages: for instance, films, filmstrips, TV, magazines, monographs, books, teacher-produced articles, audio tapes, sound filmstrips, and small group sessions are still available in package programs. The continuous attempt to blend the personality of the learner with the content and mode is the elusive goal of all instruction and is no less viable in self-instructional packages than in any classroom. This formula for success can be stated as:

$$S =$$

$$C_1 + C_2 + M$$

or

Success in learning =

| Characteristics of Learner Defined | + | Content of Subject Arrangement | + | Proper Mode of Instruction |

In instructional situations using self-instructional packages, the teacher must assess the learner's personality and direct the student to the proper path. The blend of mode and content may theoretically be assembled in any of several appropriate ways.

F. *Tests in Self-Instructional Packages* A package may contain a number of possible tests. These may include

1. A pre-test to assess the starting point of the student. The results tell the student as to whether or not she already possesses the competency asked for in the objective and which learning activities would be most helpful.
2. A self-administered trial test so that the student can determine if he or she is ready for the final test. More than one of these trial tests may be included in self-instructional packages, reflecting various sections of the material. They provide immediate information to students, telling them how they are doing.
3. The final test serves to check the student for total competency of the objective.

The final evaluation need not be a paper and pencil test. Just as the activities may take in a wide range of possibilities, so may the final evaluation, but the final evaluation must specifically check on the behavior described in the objective. Ringis puts it most succinctly:[2]

> The *posttest* does not necessarily have to be a paper and pencil examination. If the nature of the concept, and the performance objectives written for it called for a construction, an oral performance, or for completion of a laboratory project, then examination of such a product would constitute the posttest. Some packages require the learner to use accumulative experiences wherein the total sum of the learner's efforts throughout the package are examined at the conclusion. In those cases, the objectives would have called for the end product to be a diary, an experimental log, or such other device which recorded all his efforts for the time spent on the package. Perhaps the most important aspect of the posttest is that it provides closure for the learner: he experiences a sense of personal accomplishment. The learner knew what his objectives were, has worked through the learning activities and has been exposed to various learning resources, and now the posttest has shown him he has achieved the specified performance called for in the objectives.

Last of all, the final evaluation should provide a procedure to tell the student where to review if the competency was not demonstrated.

G. *Internal Consistency and Elimination of Irrelevancies* Making sure that the objective preassessment tools, learning activities, and evaluation are all designed to accomplish the same thing is a must. It is easy to digress to material that is not directly related to the objective; thus, constant evaluation of all aspects of the package for pertinence to the objectve is urged.

H. *Enrichment Activities* Many self-instructional package builders include a section at the end of self-instructional packages to inspire the student who has taken an interest to go beyond the competency level described in the objective. Suggested activities have such labels as "Breadth and/or Depth," "Quest," "Enrichment," "Bonus Work," and "Self-Selection".

The purpose of such a section is to encourage students to continue their self-directed learning, going beyond the required level. Normally, the student submits a small design based on the Logical Instructional Model. That is, the student submits to the teacher what he or she wants to be able to do as a result of the enrichment, how the student proposes to get there, and how he or she will evaluate whether the objective was accomplished. The teacher attempts to counsel the student to get the project in manageable form, and works out the credit possibilities before the student undertakes the task.

[2]Ringis, "What Is a Self-Instructional Package?" p. 205.

Learning Activity 3:
The Effect of Self-Instructional Packages
On the Curriculum

A. *The Purpose of Package Programs* The most persuasive reason for the increased popularity of self-instructional package programs is its potential for individualizing instruction. Although educators' implementation of this long-advocated position on individualization is, unfortunately, far from complete, self-instructional packages provide an effective start in the right direction.

A second reason for the implementation of self-instructional package programs is the opportunity they afford for rigorous curricular examination. When the question is asked, "What is the student going to be able to do after completing the self-instructional package," the reply necessitates examination of a behavioral objective, and the result may be a clean-up of outdated curricular inclusions.

A third reason for self-instructional package programs is that they eliminate duplication of material and insure inclusion of important material. It is well known that when course guides are displayed for classes in the secondary school, they often do not reflect the actual teaching. Teachers may neglect certain content areas and overemphasize or re-teach other areas. Self-instructional package programs eliminate this problem since once a student can demonstrate a competency, he or she need not rehash the old material again.

B. *The Teacher as Advisor* When a self-instructional package program is underway, the teacher assumes a new set of responsibilities. Without describing in detail the extent of this change, it is worthwhile here to point out a new phenomenon in the relationship between student and teacher generated by a self-instructional package systems approach.

Under a traditional education system, the student's perception of the teacher-student role often approaches an adversary concept. The instructor assigns the work, teaches the class, administers tests, and hands out grades. The student competes with other students for attention and grades and learns that the teacher is the most powerful element in the process. Oftentimes learning is inhibited by the threat of competition with peers, the possibility of alienation of the teacher, fear of the subject content, or previous unsuccessful experiences.

In a self-instructional package program the student is not competing with peers but striving to achieve a predetermined competency level. The teacher in this situation has the opportunity to work *with* the student to reach this mutual goal. The student's success becomes the teacher's success, and together they can take mutual pride as competency in each area is proven.

Teachers taking full advantage of this role possibility will find a more relaxed interchange building up between themselves and the students, leading to more profitable personal relationships.

C. *Packages as Enrichment Activities*   One of the problems faced by all teachers handling large classrooms is how to accommodate the bright student who has conquered the current material. One common technique utilized by textbooks and teachers is to provide a set of topics and encourage the students to generate a project of their own. There are several disadvantages to this approach if a complete independent study program is not in effect. The first is that independent study projects can be a time-consuming enterprise for the teacher. Four or five active "independent scholars" in addition to a room full of other students can increase the workload beyond feasibility. A second disadvantage is that without structure, the topic limits and approach of the projects can easily get out of hand. A third problem is that just about the time the bright student gets rolling on the project, the class has caught up and is starting work in a new area. The bright student must stop the project (generated from an interest in the last topic) and shift gears into the new area. Students may have lost interest when they have time to return to the old project.

Having a series of supplemental self-instructional packages for each topic can offer relief for several of these problems. The student may pick among them according to interest and, because of their calculated length, complete as many as time permits before the next unit.

Things don't alway go in practice exactly as in theory, so there will be occasions when there won't be enough packages and more will have to be built, and other occasions when the student will attest that none of the possible packages are interesting. But a self-instructional package program can certainly assist teachers in providing enrichment for many bright youngsters.

D. *Remedial Use of Packages*   When it has been discerned that there is no point in having a student continue in a classroom topic because he or she has fallen too far behind in the regular classroom situation, it is possible to shift to a self-instructional package program on an individual basis. This technique is applicable in those instances where the course is broken down into discrete topics. In these instances, the student need not continue in frustration in that unit, but can move to a series of slightly less difficult objectives in a self-instructional package program where he or she can experience success. When a new topic is started, the student can be shifted back to the classroom with a "fresh start" in that topic.

When the class content builds throughout the year and each new piece of information depends upon mastery of the previous information, the student may be shifted to a self-instructional package program at the point where learning from class presentations is no longer profitable. That is, enough new terminology and concepts are being used in the course of instruction that the student does not benefit from the presentations. The student may or may not be on a package program for the rest of the course. In some instances, the self-instructional package program may allow him or her to catch up with the class. Even then, however, the student often prefers to stay in the package program because of the success experienced.

E. *Extended Absence* In some instances when self-instructional package programs are available as a counterpart to the traditional classroom situation, the student who is absent because of illness or other extenuating circumstances can keep pace with the class by undertaking self-instructional package programs at home. One possible drawback, of course, is that packages are often not self-contained and refer the student to other material, which must be obtained from the school, or the public library, or other sources. In addition, when the packages have several possible learning modes, students may be faced with the problem that the best learning modes for them are available only at school. In spite of these obstacles, many students have been able to keep up with their school work while physically away from school through the use of self-instructional packages.

F. *Partial Package Programs* In some classrooms teachers are blending packages with regular classroom instruction. In one popular approach to partial programs the students are involved in topics related to the content of the regular class during time opened specifically just for self-instructional packages. Students might be doing traditional classwork on Monday, Wednesday, and Friday; on Tuesday and Thursday, however, they work on any of the several available self-instructional packages. During this time they operate independently and are given credit for competencies gained.

A second approach has the self-instructional packages built more closely into the curricular content of the traditional class. There may be less of a variety of self-instructional packages, sometimes as few as three or four, and they are reproduced in enough quantity so that the class may be broken into groups by interest areas or ability.

Each group area works on the related self-instructional packages for a portion of the time. In some cases students can start the self-instructional packages with some group work and then branch to individual work. In other instances a subgroup of students with the same self-instructional package can be brought together during the work period for a particular learning activity and then returned to individual work.

G. *Modified Systems Programs*   Some programs combine aspects of a traditional classroom with a total systems approach. Various procedures are used but only one is examined here.

Students are broken into three groups and each individual starts on the self-instructional package assigned to that group. The time allotted for completion of the package is enough so that about two-thirds of each group will have demonstrated the competency by a specified date. During work periods occasional compulsory traditional-type classes are held as part of the learning activities described in this package. At the end of the allotted period, the two-thirds who demonstrated the competency move to the next set of self-instructional packages. The one-third who did not demonstrate the competency may be recycled through the classroom activities along with the students who are moving into the same package from one of the completed self-instructional package groups. In this fashion a student will have three "cycles" to complete a self-instructional package in which some of the learning activity is based on traditional classroom-type instruction. After a particular package is repeated three times, other forms of instruction are substituted for the classroom part of the learning activities.

H. *Full Self-Instructional Package Systems*   The full self-instructional package systems available have been described elsewhere in more detail (see Learning Activity 1). However, a brief description of characteristics often encountered in a systems approach to self-instructional packages follows:

1. The teacher's role changes from instructor to advisor, counselor, content helper, package builder, and systems worker.
2. Evaluations are given when the *student* is ready, often at a central location.
3. The student moves at his or her own pace.
4. The student usually has some self-instructional packages that are required work, and some that are his or her own choice.
5. A wider variety of instructional modes are used than in traditional classrooms.
6. The competency approach lends itself to a credit-no-credit marking system.
7. Self-instructional packages may be self-contained, or may refer the student to a materials center to obtain much of the content through outside sources.
8. Instructional sessions are usually at the request of a student or group of students to supplement the learning activities prescribed in the self-instructional packages.
9. Evaluations may take a wide variety of forms.
10. Self-instructional packages are built on the components of the Logical Instruction Model.
11. Personnel are usually arranged into differentiated staffing and/or teams.

Learning Activity 4:
Trial Test

The accompanying trial test is intended as a sample trial test in its simplest form to help the students quickly check their comprehension of the material in this Self-Instructional Package. The notation after the question refers the student back to the proper learning activity for review if necessary.

True-False   *Proficiency Level 24*

_____ 1. IPI, UNIPAC, LAP, are initials standing for different types of commercially or institutionally produced self-instructional packages. (Learning activity 2, B)

_____ 2. In order to be classified as a "self-instructional package," any such set of material must have certain characteristics which are readily discernible. (Learning activity 2, A)

_____ 3. It would be possible to build a self-instructional package acceptable to the authors of the material you have studied that would not include behaviorally stated objectives. (Learning activity 2, A and C)

_____ 4. There is general agreement that the first step in a self-instructional package should be a statement of rationale explaining why the package is important. (Learning activity 2, C)

_____ 5. Objectives in a package give the learner the "means" to his or her learning without specifying the "ends." (Learning activity 2, A and C)

_____ 6. Learners should be encouraged to work alone, since group work would destroy the individualized nature of a self-instructional package. (Learning activities 2, E and 1, D)

_____ 7. Ideally, a package should offer more than one learning mode for each learning activity. (Learning activity 2, E)

_____ 8. Evaluations within each package are made up of two types: (1) pre-test; and (2) post-test. (Learning activity 2, F)

_____ 9. One important aspect of the post-test is to provide a means of telling the learner which learning activities to review in case of failure to demonstrate the competency. (Learning activity 2, F)

_____10. In some cases inconsistencies between objectives, learning activities and evaluation are tolerable. (Learning activity 2, G)

_____11. In spite of the verbalization paid to individualized instruction, teachers as a whole have failed to implement comprehensive individualized procedures. (Learning activity 3, A)

_____12. Learning packages may be sequenced in a logical order for continuous program learning or particular packages may be prescribed to help individual youngsters with individual problems. (Learning activity 3, D)

_____13. Although there are some changes, the role of the teacher in a self-instructional package system is essentially the same as under a traditional type program. (Learning activity 3, B)

___14. In a self-instructional package program the wise teacher will use competition among students to complete packages as a primary motivating force. (Learning activity 3, **B**)

___15. A self-instructional program can be effective even though each student is not allowed to proceed through the system at a rate chosen by himself or herself. (Learning activity 3, F and G)

___16. Schools that have gone to package systems have found that staffing patterns modified to team teaching or differentiated staffing serve the students better than self-contained classrooms. (Learning activities 3, H and 1, C)

___17. Regardless of how carefully individual learning packages are planned and prepared, other administrative considerations must be made to insure their success with students. (Learning activity 1, **A**)

___18. In order for a self-instructional package program to be successful, a modular schedule is necessary. (Learning activity 1, **C**)

___19. An advantage of a self-instructional package system is that it can "run itself," thus overcoming the objections of staff members who are less than enthusiastic about the program. (Learning activity 1, **B**)

___20. Limiting learning styles (activities) has considerable negative effect on the motivational success of the program. (Learning activity 1, **D**)

___21. Simplicity is of primary importance in designing and implementing a record-keeping system. (Learning activity 1, **E**)

___22. It is possible to design a numbering system for labeling self-instructional packages that tells the student whether working in sequential order to complete packages is important. (Learning activity 1, **F**)

___23. When an entire school goes to a self-instructional package program, the student should learn to adjust to a variety of formats and package designs because of the differences in nature of the various academic departments. (Learning activity 1, **G**)

___24. With the current emphasis on accountability, it becomes more important for complete evaluation of students' work accomplished in packages. (Learning activity 1, **H**)

___25. In self-instructional package programs, a central test center is a prerequisite for a successful operation. (Learning activity 1, **J**)

___26. Because of higher motivation, individualized classrooms will usually have a noise level of less volume than most traditional classrooms. (Learning activity 1, **I**)

___27. One-hundred-percent individualized classrooms may have motivational problems unless the packages are very interesting. (Learning activity 1, **K**)

___28. In complete self-instructional package systems, a computerized surveillance system for record keeping is almost imperative. (Learning activity 1, **E**)

___29. In building the learning activities for a package, a primary consideration is the age and maturity of the student. (Learning activities 2, D and E)

___30. When a test center is used in a self-instructional package program, building several forms of each test is encouraged. (Learning activity 1, **J**)

Correct your trial test, using the answers below. If you answered 24 or more correctly, you can feel prepared for the final test. If you scored between 20 and 24, a review of the learning activities indicated by the question should be undertaken. If you scored less than 20, shift to an alternate learning mode, use the questions in the self-preassessment section (page 184) as a worksheet, and go through learning activities 1, 2, and 3 of the package.

1. T	7. T	13. F	19. F	25. F
2. T	8. F	14. F	20. T	26. F
3. F	9. T	15. T	21. T	27. T
4. F	10. F	16. T	22. T	28. F
5. F	11. T	17. T	23. F	29. T
6. F	12. T	18: F	24. T	30. T

Part 4: Evaluation Procedures

When you have completed the learning activities you deemed necessary in order to answer the questions in the preassessment section, you may take the sample test covering this section. The criterion level for this test is 75 percent correct.

The following paper and pencil test is submitted as a sample final evaluation instrument for the accomplishment of the same self-instructional package. Instructors may choose to use this as a guide to build their own set of final evaluation questions, as a second trial test, or as equivalent practice for their own test.

Sample Final Evaluation for Learning Package 1

True-False   *Proficiency Level 24*

_____ 1. Discrepancies between the Logical Instrumental Model and the formats of various self-instructional packages may be attributed to their application and method of use in different educational programs. (Learning activity 2, A)

_____ 2. In its simplest form a package could be considered as a "lesson plan" for an individual learner. (Learning activity 2, A)

_____ 3. Most packages are designed to deal with a variety of objectives. (Learning activity 2, D)

_____ 4. The number of packages for any one unit or course of study depends on the subject matter, the complexity of that particular aspect of the curriculum, and the maturity of the student. (Learning activity 2, D)

_____ 5. Objectives for a package should not have much meaning for the student until he or she begins the learning activities. (Learning activity 2, C)

_____ 6. In a properly constructed package the learner is directed through the learning activities in such a way as to relieve him or her of any decision making. (Learning activity 2, E)

_____ 7. If at all possible, it is best to use a variety of media in a package. (Learning activity 2, E)

_____ 8. Evaluation possibilities within a self-instructional package are of two types: (1) self-test; and (2) final evaluation. (Learning activity 2, F)

_____ 9. A post-test should be in the form of a paper and pencil test for ease in grading. (Learning activity 2, F)

_____10. Enrichment activities at the end of a package would ideally be initiated by the learner. (Learning activity 2, H)

_____11. A basic goal of self-instructional packages is to individualize instruction. (Learning activity 3, A)

_____12. Teachers using self-instructional packages are recast as instructional managers who prescribe learning experiences, manage the learning process, and evaluate results. (Learning activities 3, B and 1B)

_____13. In a classroom using self-instructional packages, if the materials have been appropriately designed, the majority of the teacher's time is free for evaluation. (Learning activities 3, B and 1, B)

_____14. When a school is not on a full package program, self-instructional packages can be useful as enrichment activities for bright students. (Learning activity 3, C)

_____15. An individualized instructional system using learning packages leads to a smaller amount of organizational flexibility within a total school program. (Learning activity 1, C)

_____16. In order to insure accurate record keeping, it is often necessary to sacrifice simplicity and ease of administration. (Learning activity 1, E)

_____17. The failure of package systems often lies not in the packages, but in the management of the program. (Learning activity 1, A)

_____18. A modular schedule is a basic requirement for a package systems approach to instruction. (Learning activity 1, C)

_____19. Because of the nature of self-instructional packages, there is a decrease in the variety of student activities as compared to a traditional program. (Learning activity 1, I)

_____20. Package builders should try to avoid a numbering system for packages because it makes students think that all packages must be taken in a particular order. (Learning activity 1, F)

_____21. Record keeping for a package system must be flexible enough to allow students to enter the program and exit at any time without a complete reorganization. (Learning activity 1, E)

_____22. In some package systems, packages may be completed without regard to order. (Learning activity 1, F)

_____23. It is not important to have a consistent package format between departments in a school when more than one department is using self-instructional packages. (Learning activity 1, G)

_____24. In a systems approach, instructional sessions composed of one teacher and a group of students are often held at the request of students as a supplementary activity, rather than as a regularly scheduled activity. (Learning activity 3, H)

_____25. One effect that conversion to a self-instructional package program will have is to force a penetrating look at the curriculum. (Learning activity 3, A)

_____26. The test center has definitely been shown to be superior to classroom evaluations. (Learning activity 1, J)

_____27. Students helping other students is a common practice in individualized classrooms. (Learning activity 1, I)

____28. Package programs have the advantage of eliminating the unnecessary duplication of material that can be experienced from class to class. (Learning activity 3, A)

____29. Self-instructional packages used for remedial activities for students who are behind have the disadvantage of precluding the possibility of the student's joining the class again. (Learning activity 3, D)

____30. Self-instructional packages have been unsuccessful with students at home because of extended illness because of access to materials referred to in the learning activities within the packages. (Learning activity 3, E)

Answers for Sample Final Evaluation

1. T	7. T	13. F	19. F	25. T
2. T	8. F	14. T	20. F	26. F
3. F	9. F	15. F	21. T	27. T
4. T	10. T	16. F	22. T	28. T
5. F	11. T	17. T	23. F	29. F
6. F	12. F	18. F	24. T	30. F

BUILDING A SELF-INSTRUCTIONAL PACKAGE—MODEL PACKAGE 2

Part 1: Objective for Model Package 2   Following a model and a set of instructions, the student will be able to construct a self-instructional package in his or her content area suitable for use by pupils, and containing a minimum of five prescribed elements listed in this package. These elements must exhibit the minimum qualitative criteria described in the evaluation section of this package. (Analysis; Application; Synthesis)

This objective calls for the development of a new product. In order to accomplish this objective you should understand the principles in the preceding package, and analyze the similarities and differences between this model and your own package as you proceed to construct it. As you gather ideas from your content area and the model package, you will be able to synthesize them in building your own package.

Part 2: Self-Preassessment   If you have already built one or more self-instructional packages, you may compare them with the criteria in the evaluation sections to see if they meet that criteria. If so, they may be submitted to your instructor for evaluation. Since you were not working with the instructor on the project, be prepared to answer technical questions about it in order to demonstrate clearly that it is your own work. Even if you have already built an instructional package, you may wish to build another to satisfy this competence, because (1) the more times you work at this skill the better you will become, and (2) no teacher ever has enough self-instructional packages to satisfy all the needs of students.

Part 3:   Learning Activities

1. The student should have demonstrated competency in the preceding self-instructional package.
2. Study the section "Constructing Self-Instructional Packages" found in this package, or view the tape-slide presentation of the same name.[3]
3. As you study either the section or the tape-slide presentation "Constructing Self-Instructional Packages," attempt to see the similarities and differences between this article and the article "Self-Instructional Packages Described" that you studied for the preceding self-instructional package.
4. After this preparation, you are ready to begin construction of your package. Follow the steps described in the section "Constructing Self-Instructional Packages" and in the evaluation section of this package (page 215).
5. Use the "Checklist for Building Self-Instructional Packages" to check each component of your package.
6. Schedule a help session with your instructor if you feel it is necessary.

Learning Activity 2:
Constructing Self-Instructional Packages
(this section is the reading for Learning Activity 2 listed above)

This self-instructional package on self-instructional packages will serve as our model to guide you step by step in the contruction of your own self-instructional package. You will want to prepare your own with care so that you can use it in your work.

We shall build each of the four basic divisions in the self-instructional package separately, always being careful that each step focuses exactly on the objective. Before we are done, your self-instructional package should at least include:

1. A clear, understandable, description of the *behavioral objective* of the self-instructional package.
2. A procedure for students to use to *preassess* their ability in the subject area and guide themselves to appropriate activities.
3. An interesting set of *learning activities* that will build the student's ability as described in the behavioral objective.
4. An *evaluation process* that will assess whether or not the student has acquired the competency described in the behavioral objective.

In addition to these four basic sections, your self-instructional package may include other elements, such as

1. A list of materials that the student will need to complete the package.
2. An enrichment section to guide the student to additional activities in the same content area.

[3]This tape-slide presentation is available at nominal cost by writing to PEP Educational Aids, 1108 E. Grove, Bloomington, Illinois 61701.

3. A discussion of the approximate time needed to complete the entire package or parts of the package.

4. A rationale explaining why it is important for the student to acquire the skills or information described in the objective.

5. Optional learning activities to help students attain the objective, not necessary if the student engages adequately in the required learning activities.

6. Self-evaluation prior to the final evaluation, to provide feedback of competency before actual attempts are made at final evaluation.

7. A section early in the package warning the student to schedule certain items in advance, for instance when any learning experiences involve scheduling a room, special material, or group session.

8. Any other sections that may seem appropriate because of the unique nature of the content of a particular package.

Evolving the Package   In theory, a package could evolve from mutual student and staff recognition of a curricular need. For instance, it could become apparent in a home economics class that students lacked ability in personal money management. If enough students felt frustrated because of personal money mismanagement, a self-instructional package on that topic would evolve.

In practice, however, a self-instructional package usually evolves from a teacher's own body of content. Unfortunately, this process also lends itself to our situation here, because the reader may not have had contact with students in whom unfulfilled needs were apparent. If you have, then you should by all means make such needs the subject of your self-instructional package; if not, then follow along as we go to step one.

STEP 1   From a school library, obtain a typical text in your content area that might be used in a high school. Locate in that text a topic you find interesting. If you choose, you may utilize sources of content material other than a textbook.

STEP 2   Translate this content into precise instructional objectives. At this point you may need to review chapters 3 and 4 in order to write good instructional objectives. You should include more than just lower-level cognitive objectives. In the objectives for this and the preceding model packages, there are both knowledge-comprehension objectives and higher-level objectives. You may particularly wish to review the part of chapter 3 dealing with the taxonomic levels in the cognitive domain before proceeding.

Suppose you are an industrial arts teacher and you have chosen to develop your self-instructional package somewhere in the area of metalwork. The text you have chosen is *Metalwork Technology and Practice* by Oswald A. Ludwig and Willard J. McCarthy.[4]

[4]Oswald Ludwig and Willard McCarthy, *Metalwork, Technology and Practice* (Bloomington, Ill.: McKnight and McKnight, 1969), p. 53.

In looking through chapter 6 on "Layout Tools," you decide that a self-instructional package could be built on the use of inside calipers. There seems logically to be two levels to a self-instructional package on this topic: first, we wish the student to comprehend information *about* calipers; and second, we wish him or her to be able to *use* calipers. After some thought, objectives such as the following are generated:

1. After studying specific material on the care and use of inside calipers, the student will be able to demonstrate comprehension of that material by answering correctly nine out of ten written completion-type questions.
2. When presented with a set of inside calipers, a steel rule, and a piece of iron with five holes drilled in it, the student will be able to use the calipers to measure the inside diameter of four of the five holes to within 1/64 of an inch.

The first objective is at a skill level lower in the cognitive domain than that required in the second objective. The second objective is a combination of the cognitive skill application (Level 3), and psychomotor skills.

This procedure of delineating what you wish your student to be able to do after the instruction should cause you some real thought and introspection. Don't be satisfied with an objective because it was easy to build. Try hard to analyze what it is that you really wish the student to be able to do and translate that into words that communicate powerfully. The student should be able to understand immediately from the objective what competency will have to be demonstrated. If some of the words used in the objective are complicated and are only later defined in the material in the learning activities, it is absurd to assume the objective will perform its intended function.

STEP 3   Although the order of the self-instructional package as used by the student has the preassessment section next, the package writer is generally better off arranging the rest of his self-instructional package first, and then returning to build the preassessment. This enables him to set the link-ups to the corresponding learning activities from each part of the preassessment activity.

Let us return to our example. We ask ourselves, "How can I transmit the necessary background information about the use and care of inside calipers most easily to the student?", and "What alternative learning procedures for this objective can be made?" Some of the possible ways to transmit this information are by having the student

1. Read material from a text.
2. Read articles on the subject from trade magazines.
3. Read specially produced material prepared by the teacher (usually the material most precisely tuned to your objectives).

4. Listen to commercially produced audio tapes on the subject.
5. Listen to audio tapes produced by the teacher.
6. Modify numbers 4 and 5 of this list by listening to the tape while viewing accompanying handouts.
7. View a filmstrip made either commercially or locally.
8. View and listen to a tape-slide presentation—either commercially or teacher produced.
9. Refer the learner to a student who already has the competency. The "tutor" uses a special guide to make sure all the points required are covered and receives some credit for successful demonstration of the competency by the "pupil."
10. Arrange small help sessions during lulls in the class for the students who have signed up on a special sheet.
11. View and listen to a filmstrip on the subject while filling out an accompanying worksheet that emphasizes the important points in the filmstrip.
12. Engage in a single linear "programmed learning" sequence covering the material.
13. Engage in a more complex, branched program using a computer terminal.
14. Engage in any other learning activity deemed appropriate.

After the package writer decides upon instructional modes for the learning activity, the material that will make the learning activities "come alive" must be built. For the first objective, in which the student is learning about the care and use of calipers, let us assume that the learning activity chosen is a teacher-prepared sound filmstrip. All the content material is gathered and arranged into a script. The script is then recorded on a tape cassette. It is found that the entire taped content runs twelve minutes. Simple photographs are then taken of the main points emphasized in the script, and the student is told in the script when to move to the next slide. A good way to focus on the important points would be to have an accompanying worksheet, which the student could fill out as the tape-slide sequence is viewed and from which he or she could later study.

Some teachers are concerned about making the quality of their work look professional. It certainly does not hurt for the slides to look as though they came out of a magazine and for the voice on the script to sound like Richard Burton, but it is not *necessary* to have perfection in order to have a high degree of learning take place. In fact, students identify with everyday photos of other students used in the slides and respond to the voice on the tape when it is someone they know. Using a tape cassette, a set of slides clearly numbered from 1 to 30, and a simple hand-held slide viewer can be as effective as a slick professional treatment. If alternate learning activities are desired, the script may become reading material generously illustrated with the prints and made available as check-outs from the materials center.

For purposes of learning to *use* the inside calipers, it is obvious that the student should engage in the equivalent practice necessary to gain the proficiency. For this, the second objective clearly points to the self-instructional learning activity required. A series of various size holes are drilled into pieces of metal and identified with a key. The student simply engages in the necessary amount of practice until he or she is measuring the inside diameter of the holes correctly. (Our example objective's criterion level is probably too low, since after one gets the "feel" and some practice with inside calipers and micrometers, measurements accurate to within .005 of an inch should be possible.)

This objective happens to align itself well with the equivalent practice providing immediate feedback to the student as he or she practices. Other learning activities, like this self-instructional package on building self-instructional packages, may not be so easy to design. For instance, if you are using this book independently, the only way you can check the behavioral objectives you design for your package is to compare them with the objectives in this package, the objectives at the beginning of many of the other chapters, and the samples in chapters 3 and 4. If you are using this book in conjunction with an instructor, he or she should also be able to give you advice as to the appropriateness of your objectives and the rest of your self-instructional package as you build it.

You should now try your hand at building your instructional learning activities. It may be that your objective leads you to a particular activity. You may want to ask yourself the following questions to guide your choice and work:

1. Are the materials necessary for building the activity available?
2. Is the importance of the objective large enough to warrant multimodal activities?
3. Is the target population of students who will use the package confined to a particular level, thereby restricting the range of the possible learning activities?
4. What restrictions does the content of the objective place upon learning activity development?
5. What do I know about learning activities that have been used for this content area in the classroom that will be effective for a self-instructional package?

After building the learning activities, it may be possible, even though the entire package is not complete, to explain the objectives to a small sample population and obtain suggestions improving the learning activities. A small "trial run" can often save a lot of headaches. It can be especially helpful to insure the alignment of the objective with the learning activities. You may also be able to get ideas from your peers or your instructor at this point to help polish these activities.

STEP 4 Without forgetting that we will return to build our preassessment section, the next step is to design the evaluation for our self-instructional packages.

Whatever the skills we described in our objective, they will be checked to insure that the student can now successfully demonstrate the described competency at the minimum criterion level. The first objective in our example leaves little doubt about our check. We wanted the student to show comprehension of facts about the care and use of inside calipers and we were willing to accept as a demonstration of that competency "correctly answering nine out of ten written completion-type questions." We have left out of the objective other conditions surrounding the demonstration of the competency, so the first thing our evaluation section should do is communicate any and all conditions. Let us assume that there is a test center in this school, so the instruction may be something like, "When you have completed the learning activities and filled out your worksheet, and feel that you understand the material, report to the test center for the short completion exam on this material. If it is the first time that you have taken the exam, ask for Test #0034 on *Calipers*—Form I. If you have taken the test before, ask for Form II. You will be expected to complete nine out of ten completion questions correctly on this test."

If we had decided to include a trial test, then the instruction above would be modified to encourage the student to take this self-administered trial test and check his or her work against provided model answers. In this circumstance the trial-test answers would direct the student to the approximate part of the worksheet for review in case of missed answers.

A simple sample item of the form described in the objective might be, "An inside caliper is a two-legged, steel instrument with its_____bent outward." (See learning activity II, slide 4, or learning activity III, page 5 for review.) Answer: Legs.

The second objective also leads us to an obvious evaluation. It implies the use of inside calipers, a rule, and a piece of metal with holes drilled in it. The operation of the typical test center may or may not preclude the student from using these materials there. Let us assume that we cannot use the test center. Then our instructions might read: "When you have completed the learning activities in this self-instructional package, and you feel that you can successfully use inside calipers to measure the inside diameter of holes drilled in metal, ask your instructor for the steel bar for testing and the test answer sheet for this objective. Bring a 6-inch steel rule and an inside calipers with you at this time. You will need to measure four out of five holes to within 1/64 of an inch to successfully demonstrate this competency."

If you know that you will be involved in a self-instructional package program with certain restrictions, build them into your instructions. For instance, you may know that you will be evaluating only on Tuesdays and Fridays. Then say so in your evaluation section.

A much less satisfactory procedure for this objective would be to describe and illustrate a series of inside caliper measures on a straight written test administered in the test center. In this instance the student would answer questions about the descriptions and pictures. We could assume that if the student could honestly answer such questions, he or she could find the inside diameter of drilled holes. Such assumptions are risky and should be avoided, although analagous situations can be found throughout school systems.

You should now build your evaluations for your self-instructional package. The trial test is a sound procedure and should be used if possible. Make sure test items are straightforward and clear. At this point you may wish to refer to the section in chapter 8 on evaluation in this text (page 212) for guidance in the construction of criterion-referenced test items.

It is often hard to determine initially how well the student must perform on a new test instrument on untried learning activities. Fortunately as your skill as a package writer increases, your intuitive notions about the proper criterion level will rapidly increase. A flat 80 percent proficiency level for all tests in a system is unrealistic. It is obvious that for this purpose alone conducting trial runs is worth the effort.

STEP 5   We are now ready to return to the preassessment section. We have postponed it until now because, even though the behavioral objectives in your package tell you exactly what the students are going to be able to do at the end of instruction that they could not do before, they do not consider the instructional approach to be used. Building the learning activities and the evaluation section has structured an approach to help the student achieve the objectives, and this approach can now provide a basis for sequencing and referencing preassessment questions.

There are many facets to the problem of preassessment. Chapter 5 in this text covers several approaches to rapid assessment of the readiness of individuals for learning. For our purpose we are interested in giving students a procedure to judge their own knowledge and skills in relation to the knowledge and skills presented in the package. Two procedures are exemplified in these two model self-instructional packages. In the first package a series of questions about the content are asked in the preassessment section, and student can go through the questions carefully and attempt to answer them. Whenever students hit a question they cannot answer, they can refer to the appropriate section in the accompanying articles. If a student finds that he or she cannot answer very many questions, then it is definitely best simply to start with the learning activities and go through them. If a student knows that he or she learns best from an alternative mode to reading, the slide filmstrips and audio tapes that accompany those learning activities can be used. If a student knows most of the answers and chooses to use the preassessment to figure out which portions of the material he or she needs to go through, the slide filmstrip and the audio tapes are more difficult to shuffle through to find various parts. Therefore it would probably be best for the student to start at the beginning, review all the material, and *emphasize* the parts that the questions have referred him or her to.

A second type of preassessment is described for the second model self-instructional package. In this case, the evaluation will be of a product—a self-instructional package. Either the student has completed a self-instructional package in the past or not. If he or she has, and it meets the qualitative criteria listed in the evaluation section, the student may immediately submit it to the instructor for demonstration of the competency.

A wide variety of procedures are acceptable for preassessment purposes. In some packages primarily concerned with a very specific set of facts, the preassessment, trial test, and final test may be virtually the same instrument. For instance, in the case of a set of precise safety rules for the chemistry lab, when the rules are specific enough and 100 percent competency is mandated, the three test instruments may be changed only enough to insure comprehension and to avoid the rote memorization of a list of correct answers.

Going back to our example of the inside calipers, let us describe a third alternative. For purposes of illustration, let us assume that the shop teacher has a senior student who has majored in metalwork and is now a student assistant. For our preassessment we ask the students who believe they can use inside calipers to see the student assistant to demonstrate their ability. The assistant has a short checklist, and the pupils who feel that they already have the proficiency simply demonstrate each skill on the list. If they reach a certain level on the checklist they need not engage in the package.

If this package is one of many covering the use of hand tool skills, the preassessment process could be the same for all of the packages. If that is clearly understood by all students, then there need not any mention of preassessment in each of the separate packages. Instead, the condition can be announced generally and posted. On the other hand, it is always a good idea to repeat any uniform instruction in each package, so that nothing is left to chance and the instructor is protected.

At this point you should build your preassessment procedure and any instruments for that procedure. You will then have the four basic parts to your package completed and again, a trial run to check the complete flow is encouraged.

STEP 6 From the trial runs and self-analysis you may now have the feeling that other embellishments are needed to make the package complete. You may want to go back to the introduction of this article on "Constructing a Self-Instructional Package" and review some of the additions that are often helpful to self-instructional packages. For instance, this model package has a checklist to use when constructing your own package.

In our running example of the inside calipers, the student may be warned in a separate early section of the self-instructional package to schedule his or her final evaluation to demonstrate the ability to use the inside calipers a day in advance of the day the demonstration is to take place. This will enable the evaluator to schedule a mutually convenient time and to be sure all needed materials are on hand.

STEP 7 Before turning in your self-instructional package for final evaluation, use the in Learning Activity 5 checklist to make sure you have included all the minimum requirements for a successful package, and that they make good sense in light of the above discussion.

Learning Activity 5:
Checklist For Building
a Self-Instructional Package

1. Does your self-instructional package contain the *minimum* requirements of (a) behavioral objective; (b) preassessment; (c) learning activities; and (d) evaluation?
2. Do the objectives contain
   a. An observable terminal behavior that tells the student what he or she should be able to do after completing the package?
   b. A minimum acceptable standard that explains how well he or she must be able to accomplish the objective?
   c. The conditions that describe the circumstances under which he or she will demonstrate the competence described in the objective?
3. Is the objective a valid one for the field?
4. Can the objective be evaluated in precise terms?
5. Does the preassessment section describe a procedure that will give the student the necessary information to determine his or her background in relation to the anticipated outcomes?
6. Is the procedure described in the preassessment section workable and not cumbersome?
7. Are there a variety of learning activities available in the learning activities section?
8. Can the student locate the cited material easily?
9. Do the learning activities concentrate on preparing the student to be able to accomplish the objective with a minimum of digression?
10. Are the learning activities designed at a level the student can understand?

11. Are the learning activities lively and interesting?
12. Does the evaluation truly check the competency described in the objective?
13. Will the evaluation tell the student and the teacher where the breakdown in learning occurred when the competency described in the objective is not demonstrated?
14. Are the instructions for the evaluation clearly stated so that there is no question in the mind of the student as to how to proceed?
15. Are all the additional sections you have included necessary?
16. Would additional sections be helpful?

Part 4: Evaluation

The evaluation of this objective is a judgment as to whether or not a package constructed by you meets the following minimum qualitative criteria:

1. One or more behavioral objectives that contain an observable behavior, conditions under which the behavior will be exhibited, and the criteria upon which it will be judged.
2. A preassessment of the competence already possessed by the student in the area described in the objectives. The preassessment should guide the student to the appropriate learning activities.
3. Precise learning activities (at least two), explained so that students clearly know what they are to do in order to acquire the competency. These learning activities will preferably have more than one instructional mode so that the students may select instructional procedures they like or learn from best.
4. An evaluation description, with precise directions as to exactly how the student will be evaluated, including where to go, whom to see, and to whom to submit products.
5. Evaluation instruments. If the evaluation is to be a test, then that test must be prepared. If the evaluation is to be the assessment of a skill, then a checklist to guide assessment should be prepared. If the evaluation is to be the construction of a product, then a model and qualitative criteria need to be provided.
6. Internal consistency. The objectives, preassessment, learning activities, and evaluation should all zero in on the same competency. Material extraneous to that goal, and subtle differences in the thrust from one section to another, must be eliminated.
7. Any or all of the supplemental parts of packages that are mentioned in the article "Constructing Self-Instructional Packages," such as work sheets, checklists, and self-tests, may be included.
8. Compliance with the "Checklist for Building a Self-Instructional Package" found in this package.

When you are done with your package, make sure you have gone through numbers 1 through 8 of this list of qualitative criteria and see that you have complied with all of them. If appropriate, turn in your package to your instructor for final evaluation.

SUMMARY

The phrase *individualizing instruction* has come to mean a variety of educational procedures. For purposes of this chapter it is used to cover self-paced instruction using learning packages.

Self-paced learning packages are often used in conjunction with a systems approach. The initiation and move to such an approach can be difficult if not carefully thought out. Included in this chapter are two self-instructional learning packages. The first model package covers the present status of systems approaches currently in use in the United States. It can help the student in procedures for implementing a self-instructional program, and in understanding the characteristics of package programs and the effect of learning packages on the curriculum. The second model package can assist the student in learning to build self-instructional packages.

SELECTED READINGS

Association for Supervision and Curriculum Development, *Individualizing Instruction*. Washington, D.C.: National Education Association, 1964.

DAVIES, IVOR K., *Competency Based Learning: Technology, Management, and Design*. New York: McGraw-Hill, 1973.

DeCARLO, JULIA E., and CONSTANT A. MADON, *Innovations in Education for the Seventies: Selected Reading*. New York: Behavioral Publications, 1973.

Designs for Individualizing, The Administrator's Approach, A Multi-Media Kit. New York: Westinghouse Learning Corporation, 1975.

ESPICH, JAMES E., and BILL WILLIAMS, *Developing Programmed Instructional Materials: A Handbook for Program Writers*. Palo Alto, Calif.: Fearon Publishers, 1967.

JACOBS, Paul I., MILTON MAIER, and LAWRENCE STABUROW, *A Guide to Evaluating Self-Instructional Programs*. New York: Holt, Rinehart, & Winston, 1966.

KAUFMAN, ROGER A. *Educational Systems Planning*. Englewood Cliffs, N.J.: Prentice-Hall, 1972.

JOHNSON, RITA B, and STUART R. JOHNSON, *Toward Individualized Learning, A Developer's Guide to Self-Instruction*. Reading, Mass.: Addison-Wesley Publishing Co., 1975.

POPHAM, JAMES, and EVA BAKER, *Classroom Instructional Tactics*. Englewood Cliffs, N.J.: Prentice-Hall, 1973.

10

Unit Planning

How should a teacher go about deciding upon instructional procedures for a semester or an entire year? Should he or she begin by writing down objectives as they come to mind? How about insuring a variety of instructional experiences during the year—is long-range planning necessary? Planning seems to be warranted, but its accomplishment seems formidable. Fortunately there are ways to organize planning so it can become efficient and manageable. One of the most often used procedures is unit planning.

This chapter concerns itself with explaining the functions, construction, and utilization of unit plans. It deals with such things as using the unit plan format for organizing instructional objectives and instructional experiences, and procedures for continually upgrading unit plans. Proper use of this information can facilitate instructional planning and result in more effective teaching and learning.

OBJECTIVES

The student will:

1. Explain, in writing, the functions of at least three unit plan components. (Comprehension)

2. Construct an outline of a unit plan and describe, in less than two pages, which instructional experiences will be included and why. (Analysis; Synthesis)

3. Construct a unit plan for a given length of time in his or her major area, including a rationale, precise instructional objectives, suitable content and instructional experiences, optional instructional experiences, and an evaluation instrument. (Synthesis)

PLANNING UNITS

The task of generating a list of precise instructional objectives for an extended period and deciding how to help students achieve those objectives seems, at first glance, to be extremely complex. If approached haphazardly, its complexity is multiplied and made even more difficult. Few teachers, of course, wish to approach any task in a disoriented fashion, so they make an effort at organization. In the case of large blocks of time, the structure often takes the form of dividing the possible course content into broad categories to facilitate the achievement of specific objectives. These categories can be the basis of units of work.

What Is a Unit Plan?

A unit plan is a compilation of precise instructional objectives, content appropriate to the achievement of those objectives, instructional experiences appropriate to both the objectives and the content, optional experiences, and needed materials. The plan often begins with a rationale and ends with an evaluation instrument. A unit plan represents the teacher's most complete conceptualization of what students will accomplish in a given block of time (usually from three to six weeks), and how they will go about working to insure success. A unit plan is a teacher's plan of action and his or her overall strategy.

Generating Appropriate Objectives

Many teachers begin the process of selecting precise instructional objectives used in unit plans by listing the major skills and information students should acquire. A home economics teacher, for example, may decide that students should demonstrate competencies such as the following:

1. Given the food intake (kind and quantity) of a "typical" undernourished individual, list in writing the specific nutrients missing and the probable effects (diseases or symptoms) of such a lack. (Analysis)

2. Plan menus for seven days for a family of four (one pregnant adult, one very active male adult, one typical ten-year-old, and one infant) that meet the minimal needs of each family member. (Synthesis)

3. Given four one-day menus, decide which is best for him or her, and in less than two pages defend that choice by citing specific facts and examples. (Evaluation)

Once these and other major objectives are written, many teachers find it useful to write subsidiary or enabling objectives for the major objectives that are particularly complex. Enabling objectives facilitate daily lesson planning by breaking the major objective into subskills that may be achieved within a single class period. Possible enabling objectives for the first of the preceding examples might include the following:

1. List, in writing, at least three foods in each of the Basic Four categories. (Knowledge; comprehension)
2. List, in writing, the specific deficiencies known to cause pellagra, rickets, and beriberi. (Knowledge)
3. Given the specific geographic location of a described underdeveloped country, identify, in writing, particular diet deficiencies that might exist and explain why. (Analysis)

If teachers take the extra time to attach to each objective the proper taxonomic domain and level, it becomes relatively easy to scan the objectives to see if emphasis is being placed on too few levels. It often happens, for example, that too many low-level cognitive skills are emphasized at the expense of the higher-level cognitive skills. If such a disparity becomes obvious, steps should be taken to shift the emphasis.

Teachers usually find that the time required for the preceding activity is worth the effort. Since all other components of unit plans reflect the objectives, it is essential that the objectives state the most important skills and information inherent in the content. If there is misdirection built into the objectives the entire unit plan can be misdirected.

Writing a Rationale

Having decided upon objectives, there is usually no question in the mind of the teacher concerning the importance and utility of the skills and content to be learned. Nevertheless, it is not uncommon for students to ask, "Why do we have to learn this?" or for an entire class of students to sit with expressions on their faces that indicate they cannot see the relevance of the content to their own lives.

Unless the teacher has given some serious thought to questions concerning the importance and utility for students of the information or skills to be learned, he or she may be forced to answer with responses that will be deemed superficial by students. Students do not usually accept rationales such as, "You need this for the college entrance exam," "Because I said so," or "Most people think this is important." The most effective rationales are those that indicate to the students how the new information or skills can be of immediate personal use.

Less effective rationales may include arguments that the acquisition of certain skills may improve academic performance in a number of related subject areas or contribute directly to specific vocational plans. Although teacher and student views are frequently parallel, rationales written with the students' point of view in mind are more effective.

Sample Rationales

1. *For a short unit on compiling reports ethically and legally.* Whenever factual reports such as term papers, theses, dissertations, and business reports are compiled, it is often necessary to refer to material written by someone else. These references make it possible to capitalize on research and reports that bear on the report being written. However, because they were written by someone else, recognition must be given to the author(s) to give credit where it is due and to avoid charges of plagiarism. This unit is designed to show the student how to record various bibliographical materials in a logical and concise manner.

2. *The Metric System*   Any modern industrial nation depends on its ability to measure a quantity accurately and to state that measurement in written form. This act of communication is found everywhere in our daily lives, and we all use units of measure to purchase, create, and relax. Who can avoid pounds, ounces, cups, inches, miles, gallons, and degrees fahrenheit in food and clothing purchases, automobile use, or weather reports? The answer is the approximately 90 percent of the world's population who use grams, centimeters, kilometers, liters, and degrees centigrade. They use the metric system of measuring rather than the "English" system.

The United States is the only major industrial country that does not use the metric system of measurement, and there is considerable effort being expended to assist us in converting, also. Our current system of measurement is confusing, redundant, and often difficult to use for scientific work. People who believe they are on firm ground using "our" system are invited to test their acquaintance with the following questions:

   a. How many cubic inches in a gallon?
   b. How many feet in a fathom?
   c. How many square feet in a square mile?
   d. Which is larger, a dry quart or a liquid quart?
   e. How many pounds in a "long" hundred weight?
   f. How many feet longer is a nautical mile than a land mile?

This unit is intended to provide you with an understanding of the metric system and to provide you with practice in using metric units of measurement and in converting our current measurement units to metric units. The information is timely since many food products already carry both our current measurement units and the metric equivalents, and many highway signs specify kilometers as well as miles. The switch has begun and this unit can help you prepare for it.

Specifying Content

Even before the unit is put into use the precise instructional objectives begin to prove their value. The objectives suggest to teachers the specific content to which the students will need to be exposed if they are to achieve the objectives. Since unit plans are generally made well in advance of the time they are used, teachers have sufficient time to sift through a great deal of material concerning, and related to, the chosen topic. As teachers select the most important and/or interesting content for inclusion in the unit, they frequently discover relationships among facts and concepts that previously eluded them. The skills described in the objective may be acquired more easily by using one particular item rather than another.

Taking the time to acquire content from a number of different sources has advantages. A variety of sources act as an internal accuracy check assuring that information is correct, the examples appropriate, and the anecdotes relevant. This kind of preparation tends to increase a teacher's self-confidence. This self-confidence, in turn, tells students that the teacher is well prepared, knows what he or she is doing, and is convinced the material is worth learning.

There are many sources to which teachers can turn for supplemental content for unit plans. Among the obvious sources are the teacher's own college tests and notes, personal experiences, and the school library. Many of the sources in the library have low reading levels, and teachers can scan them relatively quickly and extract relevant information with a minimum of effort. The librarian may have suggestions for other possible aids.

One of the best sources of information for unit plans are compilations called *resource units*. Many public schools, state departments of education, and university instructional materials centers maintain resource units on a wide variety of topics. These compilations often contain such items as lists of possible instructional objectives, rationales, subject-matter outlines, suggested instructional experiences, optional experiences, instructional aids, bibliographies, and even sample tests. The wealth of material available in most resource units can tempt teachers to build their own units solely from this material, but resource unit material should be supplemented not only with the most current material available but also with whatever other material the teacher feels is needed to meet the specific objectives and instructional needs of his or her particular students.

The subject-matter outline for the unit should cover all the information students will need to achieve the objectives. The outline should be complete enough to be used without the need for supplemental sources (which may not be available when needed) or "remembered" material (which may be forgotten when needed). A helpful rule to follow is that if the content is important to students (or if it will help students learn or remember something) it should be written into the outline, including not only facts, figures, definitions, diagrams, and explanations but also supplemental information, such as examples and anecdotes.

The primary advantage to building a comprehensive subject-matter outline is the elimination of last-minute research or attempts to find appropriate examples. Everything perceived as needed should be built into the unit while the teacher has the time and the resources to be selective and thorough. A secondary advantage is that the teacher will become familiar with the "big picture." If the teacher knows the exact nature of the material to be presented in the future, he or she can refer to points yet to be made (thus cueing the students) and can more readily refer to points previously made (thus appropriately reinforcing prior learning.)

Collecting Mediated Instructional Aids

When some part of a particular unit will be learned through the use of mediated instruction, unit planning allows for long-range planning. The long-range view made possible by good unit planning enables teachers to order films, books, videotapes, models, and other instructional aids early enough to assure delivery when needed. Early delivery will insure sufficient time to preview material, test equipment, and still make alternate plans if either the material or the equipment is unavailable or unsuitable.

To get information about films and filmstrips teachers often find it helpful to survey film and filmstrip catalogs available in the school library, the audiovisual department, or the film and filmstrip libraries maintained by nearby colleges and universities. Additional sources include the state department of education, many public utilities, the local telephone company, large corporations, and national organizations. (See chapter 7 concerning mediated instruction for specific addresses.)

The following types of information concerning films and filmstrips are helpful if included in the unit plan:

1. The exact title of the film or filmstrip.
2. The name of the company that produced the aid (sometimes needed in ordering).

3. The length of the aid in minutes or frames. (Make sure there is time in available time modules to use the aid effectively.)
4. Whether color or black and white.
5. The address from which the aid can be obtained.
6. The cost.
7. Rental or loan conditions. Of particular importance are the deadline for ordering to insure delivery when needed (two weeks in advance, six months in advance, etc.), and the length of time the aid can be retained.

In addition to films and filmstrips, teachers should take advantage of other forms of mediated instruction. As a general rule, the more variety in instructional experiences, the more chance students will become genuinely involved in the material.

Selecting Instructional Experiences

Each instructional experience, like each portion of content and each use of mediated instruction, should be selected on the basis of how well it will help students achieve the precise instructional objectives. The objectives themselves will suggest appropriate instructional experiences. For example, a low-level cognitive objective such as, "Each student will list, in writing, at least two characteristics of carbohydrates and two characteristics of lipids," could easily be facilitated by a teacher presentation or a film. A higher-level cognitive objective such as, "Given a series of facts and fallacies concerning diet and nutrition, each student will underline each of the facts," might be better achieved in a guided practice session accompanied by student discussion.

When selecting instructional experiences, effective teachers consider the types of analogous (practice of skills similar to, but not the same as, the final skill) and equivalent practice (practice of a skill virtually identical to the final skill called for) that students will need as preparation for the demonstration of the instructional objective. For the objective cited earlier concerning dietary facts and fallacies, a teacher may wish to plan one lesson that would provide analogous practice (such as listing fallacies on the board and briefly discussing why they are fallacies) and another lesson that would provide equivalent practice (such as examining articles containing both facts and fallacies about diet and nutrition and identifying the specific facts and fallacies.)

ORGANIZING THE PARTS OF A UNIT:
AN ABBREVIATED MODEL

The preceding unit plan components can be arranged in many ways. A simple outline form is one way, as exemplified in the abbreviated model below. A full model is included as Appendix B.

I. *Rationale*
   The information in this unit will help students plan balanced diets which, in turn, will help prevent serious illness and assist in minimizing other physical problems such as hidden malnutrition, obesity, and acne.
II. *Objectives*
   The student will:
   1. Write an explanation of the function of each of the following: amino acid, protein, basal metabolism, calorie, lipids, and hemoglobin. (Comprehension)
   2. Given a list of foods, correctly classify at least 80 percent of them into carbohydrate, protein, or fat categories. (Knowledge)
III. *Subject Matter*
   A. Functions of food.
      1. Supplies energy for maintaining life and carrying out daily activities.
         a. Nutrients required for these functions.
            (1) Proteins
            (2) Fats
            (3) Carbohydrates
         b. Energy demand must be satisfied before the body uses food for other functions such as growth.
      2. Builds new cells and repairs those that are worn out every day.
         a. Nutrients required for these functions.
            (1) Proteins
            (2) Minerals
            (3) Vitamins
      3. Regulates complex body processes.
         a. Nutrients required for these functions.
            (1) Proteins
            (2) Minerals
            (3) Water
            (4) Fats
         b. Examples of body processes.
            (1) Movement of fluids
            (2) Activation of enzymes (a protein secreted by living cells)
            (3) Coagulation of blood
IV. *Materials and Experiences*
   A. Functions of foods.
      1. Materials
         a. Overhead projector, grease pencil, and acetate
         b. Nutrition Chart
         c. Mimeographed handout listing functions and sample foods
      2. Experiences
         a. Present information via teacher presentation
         b. Use overhead to list functions and nutrients as they are presented
         c. Use mimeographed handout as basis for further discussion

Another procedure for organizing unit plans is to write out separate lesson plans for each of the objectives. Since the objectives, subject matter, materials, and instructional experiences have already been selected (or, in the case of instructional experiences, at least seriously considered), the writing of separate lesson plans is greatly facilitated. The advantage to such an organizational pattern is that extremely little preparation is needed once the unit is under way. The disadvantage is that the lesson plans may impose too rigid a structure on the progress of the class, thus discouraging deviations from the plans even when such deviations would be worthwhile.

Still another way of organizing unit plans is by subject matter and experiences that are to be used. A teacher may decide, for example, to use certain subject matter or certain instructional experiences to stimulate interest in the unit. Other blocks of subject matter and other experiences may be designated for use in developing understandings and general instruction, while still others may be earmarked for concluding kinds of activities such as summarizations and reinforcement. If teachers organize their unit plans according to introductory, developmental, and concluding categories they can, of course, use such a pattern in conjunction with either of the patterns described earlier.

DECIDING ON OPTIONAL ACTIVITIES

There are two major categories of optional activities teachers may consider for unit plan inclusion. The first category includes any that students may be interested in. For example, activities such as constructing a bulletin board, model, or diorama, participating as a panel member in a panel discussion, or engaging in an independent study project, have the potential appeal for a wide variety of students.

A second category includes those designed for exceptional students. Perhaps the most common experience found in this category is a carefully selected special reading opportunity. As teachers gather and select content for units, they encounter numerous sources of information written at differing difficulty levels and representing various points of view. If the teacher builds a file of short, annotated bibliography cards on such sources, he or she has a ready-made pool of sources to which students with varying abilities can be directed. In this way slower students can be given material written at a lower level so they do not fall behind, while brighter students can be directed to more challenging material, such as special readings, reports, interviewing. The key is to gear optional activities to the specific abilities of the students in the class.

The optional activities section is an excellent place for the teacher to place experimental experiences. Since most teachers will generate some innovative and creative instructional possibilities while planning units, these untried experiences may be listed in the optional activities section and attempted on a voluntary basis by students. If the activities prove fruitful, they may become part of the regular instructional activities.

PLANNING FOR EVALUATION AND FUTURE USE

The final step in planning a unit is to construct the instrument(s) needed to determine whether the objectives have been achieved. The objectives of the unit dictate the types of evaluation instruments needed. At the same time that the evaluations are constructed, the teacher may wish to construct answer keys or appropriate models. If skill tests are to be used, appropriate checklists need to be constructed.

The master teacher will have written objectives that require students to synthesize a number of subsidiary skills in the process of demonstrating competence in the objective. Such objectives enable teachers to develop evaluation procedures that communicate to students the applicability of the content more clearly than traditional evaluation procedures. Objective and essay tests have important roles but it is desirable to supplement them with other forms of evaluation whenever possible. (See chapter 8 for other suggestions for evaluation.)

After the unit plan has been constructed and the components are in polished form and suitably organized, teachers find it useful to make an expanded title page, which includes the title of the unit, the name of the course for which the unit was written (such as American History, or Home Economics I, etc.), the type of student and grade level for which the unit was designed (such as general—freshmen, college preparatory—juniors, etc.), a brief overview of the unit (four or five lines describing the main points covered), a brief statement describing the unit preceding or following the unit (to help place the unit in a logical sequence), and a close estimation of the time frame needed for the unit.

This information will save the teacher time when instructional programs are being planned for future classes and the use of a previously written unit is being considered. Such concise data also facilitates the sharing of unit plans among teachers if such arrangements can be made.

SUMMARY

A unit plan is a compilation of precise instructional objectives, subject matter, instructional materials and experiences, optional experiences, and appropriate evaluation instruments, all of which are concerned with a central theme or topic.

A major advantage to unit planning is that such planning usually takes place when teachers have the time and the energy to construct realistic and taxonomically balanced objectives; to sift through a large amount of subject matter and extract that which is most appropriate; to plan for varied instructional experiences; to preview films and filmstrips; to create innovative optional experiences; and to build appropriate evaluation instruments.

The following outline shows the components that may be included in a completed unit plan.

Unit Plan Components

I. *Title Page*
   A. Title of unit
   B. Name of the course for which the unit was designed
   C. Academic and grade level of students for which the unit was designed
   D. Brief overview of the unit
   E. Statement describing preceding and/or following the unit(s)
   F. A close time estimation

II. *Objectives*
   A. Should be stated in terms of observable and measurable outcomes
   B. Should be balanced so that there is not too much emphasis on any particular level (although there should be more higher-level cognitive objectives than any other kind)

III. *Subject Matter*
   A. Should contain *all* the information (facts, definitions, examples, explanations, anecdotes, etc.) students will need to achieve the objectives
   B. Should be gleaned from a variety of sources

IV. *Materials and Activities*
   A. Should include appropriate ordering information for mediated instructional aids
   B. May be organized as a general outline, as separate lesson plans, or in broad categories such as introductory, developmental, and concluding
   C. Should contain an annotated bibliography of sources (both used and possible)

V. *Optional Activities*
   A. Should contain optional and enrichment activities open to all students, with another section designed for exceptional students
   B. Can serve as a proving ground for innovative ideas.

VI. *Evaluation Instrument(s)*
   A. Must reflect objectives
   B. Must have answer keys, and/or models, and/or checklists
   C. Greater utilization of evaluation forms other than formal paper and pencil tests recommended

SELECTED READINGS

ALCORN, MARVIN S., JAMES D. KINDER, and JIM SCHUNERT, *Better Teaching in Secondary Schools*, 3rd ed. New York: Holt, Rinehart and Winston, 1970.

BLOUNT, NATHAN S., and HERBERT J. KLAUSMEIR, *Teaching in the Secondary School*, 3rd ed. New York: Harper & Row, 1968.

CALLAHAN, STERLING, *Successful Teaching in Secondary Schools*, rev. ed. Glenview, Ill.: Scott, Foresman, 1971.

CLARK, LEONARD H., and IRVING S. STARR, *Secondary School Teaching Methods*, 2nd ed. New York: Macmillan, 1967.

HOOVER, KENNETH H., *Learning and Teaching in the Secondary School*, 2nd ed. Boston: Allyn & Bacon, 1964.

INLOW, GAIL M., *Maturity In High School Teaching*, 2nd ed. Englewood Cliffs N.J.: Prentice-Hall, 1970

11

Lesson Plans

This chapter is divided into five main parts: (1) objectives suitable for the chapter; (2) a brief perusal of some of the pros and cons of lesson planning; (3) a description of some of the common components teachers build into lesson plans; (4) a work section in which a step-by-step procedure for writing a lesson plan is described; and (5) models of lesson plans.

OBJECTIVES

The student will:

1. List, in writing, at least three components of a lesson plan. (Knowledge)
2. In a paper of no more than two pages, explain at least two possible advantages and two possible disadvantages associated with lesson plans. (Comprehension)
3. Given a precise instructional objective, describe, in writing, at least two possible teaching-learning activities that are logical outgrowths of the objective, and explain how these activities will help students achieve the stated objective. (Application)

4. Observe a peer-taught, fifteen-minute lesson and, using a copy of the plan for that lesson, write down all instances of differences between the lesson as planned and the lesson as taught. (Analysis)

5. Construct a one-page lesson plan so the instructional objective, the content, and the teaching-learning activities are directly related to one another in such a way that if the plan were followed exactly, it would be logical to expect students to achieve the stated objective. (Synthesis)

6. Given a sample lesson plan for a hypothetical teaching situation, judge whether it is a good or bad lesson plan, writing at least five reasons for that judgment. (Evaluation)

PROS AND CONS OF LESSON PLANNING

Teachers have been debating the pros and cons of lesson planning for years. The main reason no agreement has been reached is that both sides are able to support their positions with convincing arguments. Those teachers who favor lesson plans, for example, include the following points among their arguments:

1. Lesson plans specify the instructional objective of the lesson and thus help keep the main purpose of the lesson clearly in focus.

2. By containing all of the important content, lesson plans help assure that no crucial points will be inadvertently omitted;

3. Lesson plans include teaching-learning activities that were determined to be most likely to help students achieve the instructional objective(s), thus eliminating, or at least decreasing, the need for improvisation.

4. Lesson plans provide a basis for determining how effective particular teaching-learning activities were in helping students achieve particular objectives, and thus provide a basis for modifying instructional methods.

5. Lesson plans facilitate long-range planning by providing a record of what was taught during each lesson, thus assisting in maintaining continuity.

6. Lesson plans are essential if a substitute teacher is to do more than conduct a supervised study period in the teacher's absence.

Opponents of lesson plans have an arsenal of arguments to support their position, including:

1. Lesson plans are largely unnecessary since most teachers already know what and how they are going to teach.

2. Once teachers go to the trouble to write a lesson plan they may tend to follow that plan as closely as possible, rather than feel free to capitalize upon immediate student interests.

3. Planning lessons takes an inordinate amount of time, and this time could be better spent doing content-area research or gathering instructional material.

4. The presence of a lesson plan can cause complications when a teacher chooses to deviate from the plan and an administrator expects the plan to be followed.

5. Once a series of lesson plans are written, if any lesson goes much faster or slower than was anticipated, subsequent plans must be modified or scrapped, thus wasting time and effort.

Obviously, both sides have some sound arguments. There are, however, three other points that teachers should keep in mind. The first is that since it is generally not possible to individualize all instruction, some group instruction will be necessary. Second there is little doubt that lesson plans help beginning teachers to feel more at ease and confident in the classroom, and therefore help them to be more effective. Third, many school systems and individual principals require their teachers to prepare written lesson plans, and some go so far as to require that those plans be approved before they are implemented.

LESSON PLAN COMPONENTS

Objectives

Teachers write lesson plans primarily to increase their effectiveness in helping students to learn, or, to be more precise, to increase their effectiveness in helping students achieve specific instructional objectives. It therefore follows that a crucial component of a lesson plan is the instructional objective. It is the objective that states exactly what students will do at the end of the lesson.

The prime source of objectives for lesson plans is the master list of objectives the teacher and students generated for the course or unit. If, when these original objectives were written, the teachers wrote them so they could be achieved within single class periods, no difficulty is encountered when transferring objectives from the master list to the lesson plans. Certainly low-level cognitive objectives such as; "The student will be able to list, in writing, at least three components of a lesson plan," are amenable to such transfer since students can achieve them within a single class period; but unit and course objectives frequently reflect final behaviors and thus must be broken down into subobjectives before they can be used in daily lesson plans. It may be possible for the teacher to use the complex objectives as they are and have the lessons carry over to another day; but more likely the teacher will divide the complex objectives into a number of less complex, enabling or en-route objectives, each of which becomes an objective for an individual lesson plan.

There are at least three reasons teachers should try to avoid carrying a lesson over to a second day. The first is that the longer the wait between the use of particular teaching-learning activities and the assessment of student performance resulting from those activities, the less sure the teacher can be that his or her teaching resulted in student learning. Waiting even one day, for example, can enable numerous variables to affect student performance. Without accurate information concerning the effectiveness of instructional methods, teachers are less able to modify, and thus to improve, those methods.

The second reason is that stopping properly in mid-lesson is easier said than done. Under ideal circumstances lesson closure includes summarization, review, student demonstrations of competence, and a report to students concerning their progress. This kind of closure provides students with a feeling of accomplishment and serves as an impetus to further learning. Some elements of the ideal closure will have to be omitted or at least modified if the lesson is carried over to a second day. The degree to which students achieve a feeling of accomplishment and are able to continue the lesson on the following day depends greatly upon what kind of closure the teacher provides. If the teacher anticipated the problem and built into the lesson plan a series of possible stopping points (which is tantamount to writing a series of mini lesson plans), and if the teacher has kept track of the time, he or she can provide for a summarization and review and can lay the groundwork for the next day's lesson. Teachers who do not plan for this contingency may find themselves trying to make one last point after the class should be over and half the students are out the door. In this case the value of the time and effort committed to the lesson may be in jeopardy.

The third reason concerns effective time utilization. When a lesson is carried over to a second day it is difficult to determine how much time will be needed to complete the old lesson and how much time will be available for new work. If teachers continually find themselves with awkward blocks of time left at the end of class periods and are unable to improvise or plan activities for those blocks (for example, by giving individual help to students), they will have to deal with growing student boredom and its attendant problems. (Interestingly, the problems of excess time and student boredom sometimes result from the use of instructional objectives that are too simple or too easily achieved.) It is best to avoid carrying lessons over to a second day and instead to break complex objectives into less complex enabling or en-route objectives. One example of such a subdivision is provided below.

Suppose the teacher and students saw value in developing the ability to analyze lessons on the basis of what actually took place in comparison with what the teacher had *intended* to take place. An objective reflecting this ability might be, "The student will observe a one-hour lesson and, using a copy of the plan for that lesson, write an in-class paper that cites each instance of difference between the lesson as taught and the lesson as planned."

While this objective may seem reasonable at first glance, a second look reveals that if students are to observe carefully what is going on in the class and compare that with the plan for that lesson, they will miss some differences while they write down their observations. The problem could be avoided by dividing the original objective into two subobjectives:

1. The student will observe a lesson taught within a single class period and take sufficient notes to enable him or her to compare the observed lesson with the plan for that lesson with respect to objective, content, and teaching-learning activities; and
2. The student will, using any notes, write a paper of no more than four pages comparing the observed lesson with the plan for that lesson citing specific instances of differences between what was observed and what was planned with respect to objectives, content, and teaching-learning activities.

These two enabling objectives provide sufficient time for students to demonstrate the desired competencies and are therefore suitable (at least in that respect) for use on individual lesson plans.

One source for objectives for impromptu lesson plans is unexpected events. Although the vast majority of lessons will be planned before they are taught, events sometimes occur that should rightfully pre-empt planned lessons. When these events occur it is the teacher's responsibility to devise and share instructional objectives so that the efforts of the class to capitalize upon the learning potential of the interrupting event are focused on some clearly understood goal. Teachers proficient in this skill can make the difference between an unexpected event causing confusion in the classroom and the same event becoming the basis of an interesting and profitable learning experience.

Content

The content of a lesson plan is dictated by the objective, and consists of the actual information (the facts, definitions, explanations, etc.) that students will need to achieve competency. Teachers should not try to write into the content every single thing that will be covered, nor should they try to rely on the content portions of a lesson plan for information with which they are not familiar. The functions of the content component are to help assure that in the midst of a hectic or complex lesson the teacher does not unintentionally omit crucial points, and to provide a means of insuring the relevancy of the content with respect to the objective.

The *form* of the plan will depend upon the teaching-learning activities selected. A lecture, for example, is most facilitated by a word or phrase outline of factual information. A discussion moves most smoothly if the plan consists of key statements, examples, and pivotal questions with possible answers. Activities such as demonstrations or experiments can progress according to plan with a content component consisting of procedural steps and descriptions, while art lessons might require limited verbal, but extensive visual content, such as slides or pictures. Regardless of the form of the content, it should still contain the minimum data students will need to achieve the objective.

Some instructional objectives require that students demonstrate a skill that is not dependent upon specific content. Once the basic information concerning that skill has been conveyed, other lessons may provide students with practice in that skill although the "content" for these lessons may have little or nothing to do with the original objective. For example, examine the following objective: "The student will write a computer program that will use at least two nested do-loops, will run in less than two minutes, and will result in an accurate printout." Aside from the technical information necessary, the content on the printout could consist of anything from information about a company's payroll requirements to an airline's flight schedule. Trying to concoct hypothetical content on the spur of the moment as a vehicle to develop a skill can be a nerve-wracking experience, and because this procedure is prone to error, it can seriously weaken an otherwise strong lesson. Depending upon the objective, either or both kinds of content may be needed.

Teaching-Learning Activities

The teaching-learning activities are those in which the teacher and students will engage during a particular lesson to facilitate achievement of the lesson plan's objective. Often teaching-learning activities will be implied by the instructional objective. In most instances the teacher will want to select activities that will provide students with either analogous practice or equivalent practice, or both.

For example, if an instructional objective was, "The student will describe, in one paragraph each, at least four ways information can be fed into a computer," appropriate activities might include a short demonstration or filmstrip concerning input modes (to provide basic information), a discussion during which students could suggest examples, a review period to allow students to review main points orally (analogous practice), a time during which students would actually write short explanations of input modes (demonstration of the stated competence), and a short session in which students receive feedback through a discussion of selected student responses.

Five separate teaching-learning activities were included in this single lesson. By selecting a variety of activities the teacher provides for a "change of pace," thereby reducing the possibility of students becoming bored. Of course, in the hands of the master teacher one activity may be used consistently without boredom and in the hands of a poor teacher all the activities described may become deadly. It is a good idea, however, to look back periodically through lesson plans to see if there has been too much reliance on just one or two types of activities.

Materials

Occasionally the teacher will wish to use instructional materials that are not readily available in classrooms. A delineation of these items (such as films, projectors, models, collections, etc.) in the lesson plan, serves to remind the teacher to make sure the required materials are available when they are needed. Since not all lessons will require special materials or equipment, it is not necessary to include this component in every lesson.

Evaluation

In the description of teaching-learning activities above, one of the activities listed was student demonstration of the stated competence. Since the point of the lesson plan is to help students achieve a particular competence, it is obvious that it is essential to have planned the demonstration of that competence as the basis for evaluating the lesson. Ideally, this demonstration should be a part of the lesson on that day, but it may take place at a later time.

The evaluation component may contain space for the teacher to write comments relative to student achievement of the objective, the reaction of the class to particular teaching-learning activities, and possible ways in which the lesson could have been improved.

Time

Since the teacher will be operating within certain time limitations, he or she may want to assign approximate lengths of time to each of the planned activities. This procedure is particularly helpful for beginning teachers since they often have a great many details requiring their attention and sometimes lose track of time. It can be a shock to hear the dimissal bell ring or to be informed by a student that the time is gone and realize that the lesson is only partially completed.

Miscellaneous Components

Since lesson plans reflect the needs of the particular teachers who write them, not all plans have the same components. Most lesson plans provide for an instructional objective, content, and teaching-learning activities, and many contain sections for materials, evaluation, and time estimations. Other components are often included, however, that are not as common. Because they are largely self-explanatory, they are listed here with no discussion: homework assignments; date; title of course and/or subject; grade level; title of the unit; and special announcements; preassessments;

preliminary tasks. Additional components may be added at the teacher's discretion.

WRITING A LESSON PLAN

As an example of beginning to write a lesson plan, it will be assumed that a teacher has a master list of objectives for an elementary computer science course and has decided to write a plan for an objective that states, "The student will describe, in one paragraph each, at least four ways information can be fed into a computer."

Having selected the objective, the teacher next surveys a variety of sources, both to make sure that what is remembered about the topic is accurate and to find out if any new data concerning the topic has been added since the last academic contact. The research indicates that there are at least ten ways to feed information to a computer, and it is decided to condense the findings in a short outline. For example:

Input Devices and Modes

1. *Punched cards.* Either beam of light activating a photoelectric cell, or a metal brush, is used to detect the presence or absence of a hole at each predetermined spot on a card. This data is then converted to an electrical impulse and "read."

2. *Punched paper tape.* Analogous to a continuous punched card; however, the metal brush cannot be used for reading because of the inherent weakness of the material.

3. *Magnetic tape.* Spaces on a strip of magnetic tape are magnetized or demagnetized. These spaces are then "read" by a device sensitive to magnetic fields.

4. *Light pens.* A light-sensitive pen-like device is held against a cathode ray tube and used to indicate certain areas to the computer. Light pens are often used in conjunction with more conventional terminals.

5. *Terminals.* Typewriter-like devices that can be used to code data directly into a computer via either direct electrical hook-ups or indirect hook-ups such as acoustic-couplers.

6. *Consoles.* Analogous to terminals but usually connected directly to the central processing unit.

7. *Electron pens.* Analogous to light pens, but utilizing a stream of electrons on either a CRT display or an electric table. Specific spots are activated by the electron stream.

8. *Magnetic ink.* A magnetically sensitive device compares configurations of characters printed in ink containing a ferro-magnetic substance with a series of precoded configurations. When a match occurs the computer "recognizes" the character and converts its value into a series of electrical impulses. Magnetic ink is used extensively on checks.

9. *Optical scanners.* Marks made in pencil at small but specific spots on a sheet of paper are "read" via reflected light and converted to a series of electrical impulses. Optial scanners are used extensively to machine score tests.

10. *Profile scanners.* Still in the experimental stage, but will use a TV-like device to convey images to a computer for comparison against a series of precoded images. When matches occur the data is acted upon. Has been used to enable robots to move about freely, and for crude personnel identification.

In order to select appropriate teaching-learning activities, the next step is to preassess the students' knowledge concerning input devices. To accomplish this the teacher might decide to make the first teaching-learning activity an exploratory discussion during which students would be asked to list and, if possible, explain input devices with which they are familiar. Student responses could be listed on the board by a student or on an overhead projector, which would enable the teacher to maintain eye contact with the students. Of course, the teacher may have predetermined that this content will be new to the students and may therefore be able to eliminate preassessment procedures.

Assuming the students would provide relatively little of the information, the teacher might decide to make the next teaching-learning activity the presentation of material to provide the remaining data. The form of this presentation could be any that the teacher deems effective using whatever means are available. It would be logical to follow the presentation with any of the possibilities for student-centered analogous practice and to follow this practice with a period during which students could attempt the objective. By selecting at random two or three student responses, and going over them orally, a final review could be provided and students could also receive evaluations of their progress.

Having done all the thinking, gathering, organizing, and condensing, the teacher can now write out the lesson plan in its final form. Generally speaking, the teacher will find that the plan will be most useful if it is on a minimum number of sheets of paper. The final form of this lesson might very well look like the plan in Figure 10 (c) on page 242. There are, however, a great number of possible formats from which the teacher can choose. A small sampling is included in Figure 10 (a-h). Rather than adapting any of these formats exactly, the reader may find it easier simply to arrange the components so they reflect personal preference. Once this is done, the teacher can duplicate a number of blank lesson plan forms.

For practice the reader may wish to write a one-page lesson plan to help students achieve the following objective: "The student will be able to list, in writing, at least three components of a lesson plan and at least one example of each." These efforts can be compared to those shown in Figure 10 a-c.

SUMMARY

There is varying agreement among educators concerning the need for experienced teachers to write lesson plans. Advocates of lesson plans claim that plans are needed to focus attention on the lesson's objective; as a basis for improvement of instructional methods; as a record of what was taught and what students accomplished; and for utilization by substitute teachers. Opponents of lesson plans claim that written plans are superfluous for experienced teachers, inhibit teacher freedom, and are rendered useless if a preceding lesson does not go according to plan. Even in the midst of this disagreement, however, there are few educators who argue that beginning teachers do not benefit from written lesson plans, and none who can deny that many school systems require their teachers to write such plan.

Success in learning depends to a large degree upon the skill of a teacher in bringing together objectives, content, and teaching-learning activities, all of which are appropriate for a given group of students. The compilation of these elements into a lesson plan enables a teacher to ascertain the legitimacy and logic of their interrelationships and to add, delete, or modify elements to achieve greater coherency.

The most common components of a lesson plan include the following:

1. *Instructional objective.* States what students will be to able do at the end of the lesson.
2. *Content.* Consists of the basic information the student will need to achieve the objective or serves as a vehicle for the accomplishment of the objective. Often takes the form of a word or phrase outline.
3. *Teaching-learning activities.* Briefly describes the specific activities in which the teacher and students will engage during a particular lesson. Sometimes divided into student activities and teacher activities.
4. *Materials.* A listing of those aids needed for a lesson but not usually found in the classroom.
5. *Evaluation.* A space for comments concerning procedures for assessing student achievement of the stated objective and informal assessments of the effectiveness of particular teaching-learning activities, particularly with an eye toward future improvement.
6. *Time.* Approximate lengths of time allocated for each activity.
7. *Assignments.* Descriptions of out-of-class learning activities.
8. *Preassessment.* Determination of whether students need the planned instruction. (Usually takes the form of either a pre-test, an informal assessment of student standing, or a student attempt at the final objective.)
9. *Special announcements.* Usually administrative in nature.
10. *Preliminary or routine tasks.* Taking attendance, etc.

Other components might include the date; the title of the course, subject, and unit; and the grade level.

Experience has shown that some or all of these components can be combined in one- or two-page lesson plans and that such plans can increase the probability of one's success as a teacher by increasing the probability that students will learn.

After deciding which components best fit particular needs and deciding upon a convenient lesson plan format, the teacher would be wise to duplicate a number of blank lesson plan forms. Their use will make writing lesson plans easier and will help assure that important components are not omitted. All of these preparations will help teachers do a better job in the classroom and help make the teaching-learning process more enjoyable and valuable.

CLASS: Secondary Education   GRADE LEVEL: Junior

DATE: 10/3

UNIT: Instructional Planning

PRELIMINARIES: Take attendance, make announcements

ANNOUNCEMENTS: Evaluation of records for graduation begins next Monday.

OBJECTIVE: The student will list, in writing, at least three components of a lesson plan and at least one example of each. (Comprehension)

PREASSESSMENT: Ask students to demonstrate objective. If they can do so, go on to next lesson.

CONTENT: Lesson Plan Components
1. A precise instructional objective (tells what students will be able to do).
2. Content (the information to be dealt with).
3. Teaching-learning activities (*how* the lesson will be taught).
4. Materials (unusual instructional aids needed).
5. Evaluation (answers question: Was the objective achieved?).
6. Time allotments (approximate lengths of time for each activity).
7. Preassessment (answers question: Do students need the instruction?)
8. Date; course; grade level; unit; announcements; assignments.

Examples of Components: Use this plan as a source of examples.

Component Priorities
1. What would be the minimum components you would need for a viable lesson plan? (Probably an objective, content, and activities.)
2. When would other components be useful? (For use by substitute teacher or principal.)

ACTIVITIES AND TIME: Present components via tape-slide sequence (10 min.); short discussion concerning priorities and examples (10 min.); review components via recitation and write components on chalk board as students list them (5 min.); have students write components and examples (10 min.); discuss points made in randomly selected papers (10 min.).

ASSIGNMENTS: Have students construct a one-page lesson plan for a lesson of their choice for tomorrow's class.

EVALUATION: (Have students turn in lists of components. Check to see how many students achieved the objective. Evaluation of lesson procedures.) Students were able to accomplish the objective, but the use of an overhead projector to record student suggestions for components would have helped.

FIGURE 10(a)   Model for Lesson on Lesson Plans Utilizing All Components

DATE: 10/3

OBJECTIVE: The student will list, in writing, at least three components of a lesson plan and at least one example of each.

CONTENT: Components

1. Precise instructional objective (what students will be able to do).
2. Content (information to be covered).
3. Teaching-learning activities (how the lesson will be taught).
4. Materials (what will be needed).
5. Evaluation (assessment of success).
6. Time allocations (how long for each activity).
7. Preassessment (are students already competent?)
8. Date; course; grade level; unit; announcements; assignments.

ACTIVITIES:

1. Begin by asking students what would be the very least they would need to know, as substitute teachers, in order to teach a lesson.
2. List responses using an overhead.
3. Order the responses given from most important to least important and add from the component list any that were missed.
4. Agree upon at least three basic components (probably objectives, content, and activities).
5. Have students demonstrate objective.
6. Discuss points made in randomly selected papers.

FIGURE 10(b)   Model for Lesson on Lesson Plans Utilizing a Minimum
Number of Components

CLASS: Secondary Education   UNIT: Instructional Planning   DATE: 10/3

ANNOUNCEMENTS: Identification cards may be picked up at the gym beginning today.

OBJECTIVE: The student will list, in writing, at least three components of a lesson plan and supply at least one example of each. (Comprehension)

CONTENT	ACTIVITIES	TIME	MATERIALS
1. Differences between complete and incomplete lesson plans	1. Examine and discuss examples of a complete, typed lesson plan and a "scratch-paper notes" lesson plan.	1. 4 min	1. Dittoed lesson plans
2. Objective for lesson	2. Explanation and questions	2. 2 min	2. None
3. Usefulness of complete and incomplete lesson plans	3. Discussion	3. 3 min	3. None
4. (a) Precise instructional objective (b) Content (c) Teaching-learning activities (d) Materials (e) Evaluation (f) Time allotments (g) Preassessment (h) Date, course, grade level, unit (i) Announcements (j) Assignments	4. Listing of student suggested components of lesson plans	4. 7 min	4. Overhead
5. Rearrangement of order of suggested components	5. Discussion	5. 6 min	5. Chalkboard
6. Examples of each component	6. Discussion	6. 5 min	6. None
7. Demonstration of objective	7. Have students list components of lesson plans and supply at least three examples of each one listed.	7. 10 min	7. None
8. Feedback to check answers	8. Student papers selected at random and discussed	8. 6 min	8. None

ASSIGNMENTS: Ask students to construct a one-page lesson plan for tomorrow.

EVALUATION: (Evaluate procedures)

FIGURE 10(c)   Model for Lesson on Lesson Plans Utilizing a Horizontal Format

CLASS: Elementary Computer Science   UNIT: I/O Devices   DATE: 10/3

OBJECTIVE: The student will describe, in one paragraph each, the ways in which at least four devices can be used to feed information into a computer. (Comprehension)

CONTENT: Input devices and modes include at least the following:

1. *Punched cards.* Metal brushes or photoelectric cells detect holes.

2. *Paper tape.* Analogous to punch cards.

3. *Magnetic tape.* Spots are magnetized or demagnetized on a strip of plastic tape coated with a ferro-magnetic substance, and their state is "read" by the computer.

4. *Terminals.* Typewriter-like devices used to code data directly or indirectly into a computer.

5. *Consoles.* Analogous to terminals but usually linked directly to the CPU.

6. *Electron pens.* Pen-like devices that "write" with a stream of electrons. Used with CRT displays and electric tables.

7. *Magnetic ink.* Character configurations written in magnetic ink are matched against precoded configurations. Used on most checks.

8. *Optical scanners.* Uses light reflected from pencil marks made at specific locations on a sheet of paper to "read" data.

9. *Profile scanners.* Still experimental but will use a TV-like device to convey images to a CPU for comparison with precoded images.

TEACHING-LEARNING ACTIVITIES:

1. Begin by engaging students in a discussion of how information can be fed into a computer. List points on the overhead projector. (5 min.)
   Possible questions:
   a. What are those strange figures at the bottom of most checks? (*Numbers written in magnetic ink.*)
   b. What happens to machine scored tests after you finish coding in your answers? (*They are run through a device that senses—via a beam of reflected light—exactly where your marks are, and this data is then fed into a computer via electrical impulses.*)

2. Presentation over the remaining points using the overhead projector. (15 min.)

3. Turn the projector off and review the main points via questions and answers. (10 min.)

4. Hand out paper and have students attempt the objective. (10 min.)

5. Collect the papers and go over two or three (at random) to provide feedback to students. (5 min.)

MATERIALS: Overhead Projector

EVALUATION: The papers will be checked by the teacher. (The teacher adds comments about the effectiveness of the lesson.)

FIGURE 10(d)   Model for Lesson on Computer Input Methods Utilizing Suggested Components

DATE: 10/3

OBJECTIVE: Each student will describe, in writing, at least two ways computers are affecting man's vocational and avocational activities. (Comprehension)

CONTENT:
1. Nature of jobs is changing
   a. Computers are taking over unskilled jobs.
   b. More complex jobs call for better educated workers.
   c. More industrial, in-house training programs are being started.
   d. More technical and vocational teachers are needed.
2. Nature of workers is changing
   a. More highly educated workers demand more autonomy.
   b. Nature of work enables workers to take better advantage of free time.
   c. Interest is growing in recreation and adult education.
   d. New needs of workers are creating new jobs.

ACTIVITIES:
1. Begin by asking, "What kind of work do computers do?"
2. Discuss various answers and build discussion around points included in the content section.
3. Have a student list on the board ways of using leisure time that are increasing in popularity.
4. When all points have been discussed, erase board and review main points by asking students direct questions.
5. Allow students about five minutes to demonstrate the objective, then collect and go over orally three or four anonymous responses at random to reemphasize main points and provide immediate feedback.

MATERIALS: Posters showing computerized machinery and recreational activities.

EVALUATION: At end of period pass out lined paper and ask students to describe, in about one paragraph each, at least two ways computers are affecting man's vocational and avocational activities.

FIGURE 10(e)   Model for Lesson on Effects of Computers on Vocational and Avocational Activities, Utilizing Suggested Components.

DATE: 10/3

OBJECTIVE: Each student will explain, in writing, at least six characteristics of Romanticism. (Comprehension)

CONTENT:
1. Definition: Romanticism is a way of looking at life and at oneself with a state of mind centered around emotions.
2. Major characteristics of Romanticism
   a. A return to "nature"
   b. Sympathy for the rural life and its activities
   c. Sentimental contemplation
   d. Predominance of imagination over reason
   e. Idealization of the past
   f. Concern for all that is aesthetically beautiful in the ideal sense
   g. Praising of childhood
   h. Idealization of women
   i. A wish to explore the personal inner world of dreams and desires (soul searching)

LEARNING ACTIVITIES:
1. Show students pictures of a jackhammer and a sunset and ask what thoughts each brings to mind.
2. Explain, and discuss briefly the term *Romanticism*.
3. Divide the class in groups of four or five and have half the groups act out a three-minute skit portraying people as they normally are, and the other half act out three-minute skits portraying machine-like, unemotional people (after the fashion of *Star Trek's* Dr. Spock).
4. Lead discussion of students' skits emphasizing the value of emotions. Introduce the various points listed in the content section if they are not introduced by students. List the points on the overhead as they are made.
5. When all points have been discussed, erase board and, via direct questions, review main characteristics of Romanticism.
6. Have students demonstrate objective, then use overhead to allow students to check their responses against the previously constructed list of characteristics.

MATERIALS:
1. Pictures of a jackhammer and a beautiful sunset.
2. Overhead projector, transparencies, and grease pencil.

EVALUATION: At the end of the period pass out lined paper and ask students to explain at least six characteristics of Romanticism. Provide immediate feedback concerning achievement of the objective by allowing students to grade their own papers. Use overhead to project complete list of characteristics.

FIGURE 10(f) Model for Lesson on Characteristics of Romanticism (Comprehension Level) Utilizing Suggested Components

DATE: 10/3

   OBJECTIVE: When given short poems that are typical of either the Romantic or Victorian period in literature, the student will place an "X" before those of the Romantic period. (Analysis)

CONTENT:

   1. What are some ideas characteristic of Romantic literature?
   2. What are some ideas characteristic of Victorian literature?
   3. How do the two differ: In involvement with the natural world around them? In looking inward to the self? In perspective with society? In regard to the pasts?

LEARNING ACTIVITIES:

   1. Begin by asking students what characteristics they would expect to find in a group of poems entitled, "Songs of Innocence."
   2. Define characteristics of the Romantic and Victorian ages. Use overhead projector to illustrate these characteristics.
   3. Engage class in a guided discussion regarding the third question in the content section. This discussion should give the teacher an indication of how the students understand the ideas.
   4. Give students short poems characteristic of one literary movement or the other and ask them to identify the movement.

MATERIALS: Overhead projector and overlay.

EVALUATION: Students will be given six short poems that are either romantic or Victorian in sentiment. Each student will place an "X" before those that are characteristic of the Romanticism.

   FIGURE 10(g)   Model for Lesson on Characteristics of Romanticism Analysis
                  Level Utilizing Suggested Components

DATE: 10/3

OBJECTIVE: Given a description of a hypothetical society, students will use that description to formulate a list of characteristics, values, attitudes, and behaviors for that society that are consistent with the characteristics of Romanticism. (Synthesis)

CONTENT: Possible seed materials.

1. What would the government in this society do about pollution and environment?
2. What would this society do about urban crowding and use of open space?
3. What would be the role of religion and use of churches?
4. What would be the status of historians, politicans, and scientists in this hypothetical society?
5. What would be the status of women in this society?
6. Would drugs be condoned in a society dominated by Romantics?

LEARNING ACTIVITIES:

1. Ask students to conceive of a society in which all or most members subscribe to or believe in the values implicit in the major characteristics of Romanticism.
2. Engage the students in a discussion of what a society would be like if it implemented laws, mores, etc., consistent with the values implicit in Romanticism. If students do not initiate an appropriate discussion, ask questions from content section.
3. Ask probing questions to lead students to relate their initial responses in learning activity 2, above, to a rationale for their responses based on the various characteristics of Romanticism.
4. Give examples to the class when discussion lags. Note which students do not respond, and call on them with specific questions.
5. For equivalent practice, give the students a description of a second hypothetical society and have them formulate a list of characteristics, values, attitudes, and behaviors for that society which are consistent with the ideals of Romanticism.

MATERIALS: List of major characteristics of Romanticism in a handout.

EVALUATION: Give students a description of a hypothetical society which is unfamiliar to them and have them formulate a list of characteristics, values, attitudes and behaviors for that society which are consistent with the characteristics of Romanticism.

Explain to the students that their list should be consistent with the characteristics of Romanticism and yet reflect the special problems of the hypothetical society. Explain also that they should produce as unique a list as they are able.

FIGURE 10(h)   Model for Lesson on Characteristics of Romanticism (Synthesis Level) Utilizing Suggested Components

SELECTED READINGS

BLOUNT, NATHAN S., and HERBERT J. KLAUSMEIER, *Teaching in the Secondary School*, 3rd ed. New York: Harper & Row, 1968.

CALLAHAN, STERLING G., *Successful Teaching in Secondary Schools*. Glenview, Ill.: Scott, Foresman, 1971.

CHRISTINE, CHARLES T., and DOROTHY W. CHRISTINE, *Practical Guide to Curriculum and Instruction*. West Nyack, N.Y.: Parker, 1971.

CLARK, LEONARD H., and IRVING S. STARR, *Secondary School Teaching Methods*, 2nd ed. New York: Macmillan , 1967.

DAVIES, IVOR KEVIN, *The Management of Learning*. New York: McGraw-Hill, 1971.

GRAMBS, JEAN D., JOHN C. CARR, and ROBERT M. RITCH, *Modern Methods in Secondary Education*, 3rd ed. New York: Holt, Rinehart & Winston, 1970.

HOOVER, KENNETH H., *Learning and Teaching in the Secondary Schools*, 2nd ed. Boston: Allyn & Bacon, 1968.

INLOW, GAIL M., *Maturity in High School Teaching*, 2nd ed. Englewood Cliffs, N.J.: Prentice-Hall, 1970.

12

Discipline

One of the greatest concerns of beginning teachers is whether they will be able to establish and maintain a classroom atmosphere conductive to effective teaching and learning. To put it more succinctly, they are worried about discipline. In this chapter some of the basic causes of discipline problems are explored, first from the standpoint of basic human needs, and then from the standpoint of specific teacher actions that will lead to fewer and less severe problems. Also described are various behavioral change procedures including operant conditioning, reality therapy, and chemotherapy, and a number of often discussed classroom control measures. In addition, a discipline procedure involving the school disciplinarian is explained.

OBJECTIVES

The student will:

1. Describe, in writing, at least one example of how each of the basic human needs might be manifested in a classroom. (Comprehension)

2. Describe, in writing, at least eight guidelines that can be used to help preclude discipline problems. (Comprehension)

3. Write a defense (substantiated by specific facts and examples) of his or her decision to use operant conditioning, reality therapy, or neither, in the classroom. (Evaluation)

4. Describe, in writing, a situation in which a teacher disregarded student needs and thus initiated an inappropriate disciplinary action, and then identify the need that was ignored and describe more appropriate actions. (Analysis; Synthesis)

5. When given a series of hypothetical disciplinary incidents, select a remedial procedure of his or her choice, and defend that choice with logical or empirical rationales. (Evaluation)

FOUR POSITIONS CONCERNING DISCIPLINE

Whenever educators discuss discipline problems it is generally possible to delineate at least four philosophical positions. One position is that discipline problems, per se, simply do not exist. Advocates of this position maintain that student behaviors usually labeled "discipline problems" are really nothing more than insignificant differences in normal human behavior. They claim these relatively minor differences would quickly pass by if teachers did not seize upon them, blow them out of proportion, and thus make them into bona fide problems.

A second, and somewhat related position, is that the teacher is the source of virtually all discipline problems. Advocates of this position maintain that it is only when teachers fail to make adequate plans, fail to keep students well occupied, or fail to act with sensitivity and humaneness, that problems arise. They claim that if teachers made, and carried out, adequate plans and were sufficiently perceptive of students' needs, discipline problems would not exist.

A third position is that students are the obvious source of virtually all discipline problems. Advocates of this position maintain that students are, in fact, young people who must learn to live in an adult world, and should therefore learn to follow established rules and be made to bear the consequences of infractions of those rules. They claim that the way to reduce discipline problems is to punish each and every rule violation quickly, fairly, and surely.

The fourth position is that all people, students included, tend to do those things that bring the greatest pleasure. Advocates of this position maintain that students rarely cause trouble deliberately since to do so would generally result in unpleasant consequences. They point out, however, that sometimes the pleasure gained from an act outweighs the consequence suffered. A student might engage in "inappropriate" behavior, for example, in order to retaliate for a perceived injustice; the pleasure of "getting even" might outweigh the probable consequence. They also point out that some "inappropriate" acts (such as falling asleep in class) may be beyond the student's control. In both cases the act would seem "inappropriate" only in the eyes of the teacher.

Advocates of this position, assuming that people do not intentionally seek out conflict and trouble, claim that most discipline problems are the direct result of specific causes and are susceptible to logical solutions. They do not claim that any specific problem always has the same cause or that a solution that works in one instance will work in all similar instances, but they do claim that solutions to discipline problems can be found by looking for the causes of the problems and that students are both willing and able to help find appropriate solutions. This position rejects the premise that human nature is basically perverse and accepts the premise that people are basically good.

MASLOW'S HIERARCHY

In 1943, A. H. Maslow described a theoretical hierarchy of human needs beginning with physiological needs and extending through needs for safety, love, esteem, and self-actualization.[1] It was Maslow's theory that people would devote their attention to the satisfaction of their most basic needs before they would divert their efforts to the satisfaction of less basic needs. He pointed out that full satisfaction of all needs is generally impossible and therefore most people are willing to accept a partial fulfillment of their most basic needs in order to achieve at least minimal fulfillment of their remaining needs. Thus a starving person may share some highly desired food in order to partially satisfy needs for both food and esteem. Maslow qualified the priorities within the hierarchy by suggesting that some shifting might occur if the hierarchy was used to account for the behavior of specific individuals in specific situations. Martyrs, for example, place more importance on love, esteem, and self-actualization than on life itself.

Physiological needs

According to Maslow's theory, the most basic needs are physiological needs such as air, water, food, elimination, sleep, and sexual release. Although there are other physiological needs, each of these six as it relates to classroom behavior is examined below.

[1] A. H., Maslow, "A Theory of Human Motivation," *Psychological Review*, 50, 1943, pp. 370-396.

Air   Few people like to be in a room that is hot, stuffy, or malodorous. If a classroom is overheated, lacks adequate air circulation, or smells bad, students (and eventually the teacher) will, depending on the severity of the problem, begin paying more attention to the problem than to the work at hand. The resulting inattention to academic concerns can hardly be considered a discipline problem per se, but if the teacher attempts to force students to be attentive instead of trying to eliminate the problem by opening a window or notifying the maintenance staff, real discipline problems can arise. Although it seems exceptionally elementary, simply assuring fresh air in the classroom can eliminate one potential source of discipline problems.

Water   The need for water does not generally constitute a major problem in most schools, particularly when it is remembered that Maslow was referring to such a need with respect to actual survival. Nevertheless, if students claim they are thirsty, not to allow them to drink will only focus more attention on such requests and make the teacher appear unreasonable. Of course, unusually frequent requests for water should alert teachers to the probable abuse of the drink request or a possible medical problem.

Food   Unlike thirst, hunger is a major problem in some schools. Since the passage of the National School Lunch Act in 1946, the federal government has been providing free or inexpensive lunches to indigent students. In 1954 a school milk program providing inexpensive milk was instituted, and in the early 1970's some breakfast programs were begun as part of some early childhood programs.

If a teacher suspects that a student is irritable or inattentive because of hunger, he or she should first discuss the problem with the student. It may happen that the problem is one the student can solve with just minimal guidance. If the problem is beyond the student's control, or if it persists, the school administrators should be alerted. They may be able to provide food for the student via one or another school program, or they may arrange to have a social worker visit the home and try to solve the problem by working directly with the parents.

As a general rule teachers should expect students to be somewhat less attentive toward the end of the period immediately preceding lunch. Being aware of the fact that hungry students would rather contemplate hamburgers than algebraic equations may help increase teacher tolerance of student inattention.

Elimination   The need to eliminate bodily wastes, like the needs for air, water, and food, is not open to negotiation or discussion, and a student who really has to go to the bathroom is going to go with or without the teacher's permission. This need like the need for water, can be used merely as an excuse to leave the room. While it is unwise for a teacher to deny a student permission to go the bathroom, if a particular student has the same need at the same time every day it would be wise to suggest that he or she see the school nurse and, if the problem persists, to make an appointment with the nurse for the student.

Sleep   If a student falls asleep in class the teacher should follow a similar procedure. First discuss the problem with the student. If the problem is beyond the student's control, or if it persists, alert the school administration or counseling department. If the sleepiness is due to some form of ill health the school nurse may be able to provide some help, or if the problem is caused because the student must work nights to supplement family income, the administration may be able to arrange alternative employment hours.

As with any of the preceding problems, it is best to talk with the students involved out of class rather than during class. This is particularly true with a student who has fallen asleep. It would be foolish to awaken him or her simply to make a public issue of sleeping in class. It is usually possible for a teacher to indicate, through nonverbal cues, that a nearby student should quietly awaken a sleeping student. If it is done discretely, and if the sleepy student is then drawn into the class activities by being asked to answer not-too-specific questions or to offer an opinion during a discussion, the student may be saved the embarrassment of total class attention being drawn to the problem.

Sexual Release   Given the trend toward increased premarital sexual relations, it is obvious that teenagers are neither immune to the need for sexual release nor ignorant of ways of satisfying that need. While the problem is not generally one that manifests itself overtly, teachers should be aware that teenagers are sometimes preoccupied with sex and that the preoccupation can easily become a major problem if it is made a public issue. Private discussions with the student(s) concerned can help them understand the need to separate their physical concerns from academic concerns, and since the issue is usually a sensitive one for most students, one conference will usually be enough. If the preoccupation seems particularly deepseated, of if it persists, referrals to apprppriate school staff may be in order. Since teenage students have just undergone pubescence they are naturally curious about their body, its functions, and its attractiveness to the opposite sex. Some concern about physical development and some flirtatious behavior is to be expected.

Safetv Needs

Maslow theorized that after the basic physiological needs had been fully or at least partially satisfied, the need for physical safety and well-being would begin to make itself felt.

At first glance it might seem as though modern-day students have little to fear concerning their physical safety, yet such is not the case. For one thing, modern-day students have good reason to fear bodily harm from their peers. During the 1971-72 school year, for example, Los Angeles reported 280 assaults with deadly weapons on school grounds, and 17 of those involved the use of guns.[2] In an attempt to curb this violence, the Los Angeles City School District found it necessary to divert over $2 million of badly needed school funds just to hire security agents.[3] Unfortunately, Los Angeles is not an isolated example; similar statistics can be found in almost any large school system. A U.S. Senate Subcommittee on Juvenile Delinquency has found, for example, that reported instances of student attacks on teachers increased from 25 in 1964 to 1801 in 1968.[4] With statistics such as these there is no doubt students have just cause to fear for their physical safety, and there is also no doubt that such fears substantially interfere with the teaching-learning process.

The practice of corporal punishment can constitute another threat to the physical safety of students. Despite years of controversy, corporal punishment is still practiced in many schools. In one survey, 64 percent of the teachers and 61 percent of the administrators contacted agreed that "corporal punishment, properly used, is an effective way to make students behave in school."[5] In the same survey it was revealed that 55 percent of the teachers and 80 percent of the administrators contacted agreed that "regardless of other available options, the option of using corporal punishment should be granted."[6]

In the face of these statistics there are other educators who claim that corporal punishment is not only barbaric, but that its very nature, a dependence on force as opposed to reason, contradicts the intent of the educational process. They claim that while corporal punishment may be expedient and may provide some satisfaction to the teacher, it actually teaches the student very little other than not to get caught. It appears reasonable to assume that if educators are unable to explain the rationale for or against a particular act with sufficient clarity to convince a student, a session with a paddle will not do the job either. Further, if students are paddled they may come to view educators as bullies and will eventually dislike learning since it will be associated with threats, pain, and humiliation.

Still another source of concern over physical safety is posed by classes in which students are expected to engage in activities they feel might cause

[2] Senator Alan Cranston, "The Congressional Campaign Against Crime in the Schools," *Intellect*, 102, no. 2351 (October 1973), p. 28.
[3] Ibid.
[4] Ibid.
[5] Jerry L. Patterson, "How Popular Is the Paddle?" *Phi Delta Kappan*, 55, no. 10 (June 1974), p. 707.
[6] Ibid

them harm. Prime examples include physical education classes in which students are expected to climb to the top of a high rope or to dive off a high diving board, home economics classes in which students are expected to work at hot stoves and ovens, and shop classes where students are expected to work with power and welding equipment. While the refusal of students to engage in such activities may be perceived by the teacher as a discipline problem, such may not be the case. If the issue is not forced and the student given more background information and more analogous practice, the problem will have a chance to work itself out.

Maslow's comment that young children prefer routines to unplanned activities may have some bearing on reducing students' anxiety over safety in high school classrooms.[7] If teachers consistently conduct well-planned lessons that minimize or eliminate unplanned time during the class period, students will be more likely to understand that time is valuable in that class and it is not to be wasted in extraneous activities or concerns. This businesslike environment is more likely to foster a sense of security than one in which there is unplanned time.

Love Needs

Maslow's description of love needs centers primarily on the love that usually exists between sweethearts, spouses, and parents and children. The need for this love has only an indirect relationship to classroom discipline because it is not the teacher's role either to provide or to withhold such love. Teachers can, however, be aware that students who are deprived of love at home may be less stable and more easily depressed than their more typical peers. Such awareness should prompt teachers to be more tolerant of the moods of such students and to make special efforts not to amplify the problem.

A second aspect of the need for love is the need to be accepted as one is. By moving to satisfy this human need teachers can help all students including those who are deprived of love at home. Teachers should make it clear, by words and actions, that their first and greatest concern is for each student as a fellow human being. Teachers who convey this feeling to students tend to have fewer discipline problems because their students do not feel they are regarded as inferior. If a student misbehaves he or she knows the teacher will not regard him or her as inherently "bad," but simply as a person who has made a mistake. Such feelings help increase amicable relations and help minimize the student-teacher adversary relationship that often springs up to interfere with the teaching-learning process.

[7]Maslow, "Theory of Human Motivation," p. 337

Esteem Needs

The need for esteem is the need for a sense of worthiness both in the eyes of oneself and in the eyes of others. Although this need is less basic than the preceding needs, it is more directly related to classroom discipline and is more amenable to teacher manipulation.

A student's self-esteem is, at least partially, an outgrowth of his or her perceptions of personal abilities and of how others view those abilities. This being the case, teachers can help students build self-esteem by helping them suceed. For example, if students are having difficulty learning, the teacher can help them help themselves rather than simply supplying answers or expressing disapproval. If the problem facing a student is broken into smaller components and the student is encouraged to work independently on each component with minimal assistance from the teacher, he or she will eventually be able to overcome the larger problem. This procedure requires careful monitoring of each student's progress, and it helps students perceive their true abilities and helps increase their sense of worthiness as they see their abilities increase via personal effort. Because this process helps students satisfy their need for self-esteem, it fosters favorable attitudes toward school and the teacher. Students are unlikely to jeopardize such a source of need fulfillment by causing discipline problems.

Peer esteem is often acquired (1) by those students who excel at something deemed important by their peers, or (2) by those students who successfully exercise their independence by defying "the establishment." Successful teachers capitalize on the first situation by identifying the most highly esteemed students and enlisting their cooperation in providing positive models of both behavior and work. If the enlisting is done tactfully (via appropriate praise and rewards), the teacher can acquire a powerful ally. If the enlisting is done crudely (via unearned praise, bribes, or threats), the student may hold the teacher in contempt and can become an opponent rather than an ally.

The second process for student acquisition of peer esteem presents a more challenging problem. If a teacher builds a rigid classroom environment complete with a multitude of rules and regulations, and assumes the role of dictator-in-residence, he or she may become the target of continual challenges. Many students will seek confrontations with such a teacher simply to gain the peer esteem that may result from "winning." From the student's standpoint, winning is measured by the degree to which one can get away with some rule infraction, publicly prove some rule is outdated or inconsistent, cause the teacher to lose patience, or use up class time that would otherwise be spent in activities perceived as meaningless. Regardless of how powerful the teacher's arguments are or how dire the threats, the teacher will find himself or herself losing more and more confrontations. In turn, more students will seek confrontations in order to acquire peer esteem and the teacher's life will become a cycle of discipline problems.

One obvious way to minimize such situations is to cut down the numbers of rules and regulations students can violate. Since students generally do not violate rules directly affecting their own safety or rules they make themselves, other rules and regulations should be examined with a critical eye. Outdated rules and rules that are inconsistent with accepted practice should, of course, be eliminated, and rules made purely for administrative convenience (and many are) should have their worth balanced against the probability of their being used as a point of challenge by students. Fewer rules and regulations will help reduce the probability of student-teacher or student-administration confrontations and thus help reduce one source of discipline problems.

Another way to minimize confrontations is to deal on a one-to-one basis with students engaging in such actions. Rather than "having it out" with a student during a class, it should be possible to arrange to see the student out of class. This procedure will deprive the student of the chance publicly to win a confrontation, thus minimizing any expected peer esteem, but more important, it will provide a cooling-off period and increase the possibility that both the student and the teacher will be able to discuss the problem calmly and rationally.

Teachers also need to be careful not to attack, consciously or unconsciously, students' esteem by using sarcasm, ridicule, or humiliation as control devices. Belittling students will cause them to lose esteem in the eyes of their peers, and teachers will cause themselves to be viewed as cruel and unfair. Such approaches by teachers will prompt students to retaliate in kind. Teachers need to make it a point to protect students' sense of esteem whenever possible by treating students as they themselves would like to be treated.

Looking at the need for esteem from a positive standpoint, teachers can provide partial fulfillment of the need by publicly acknowledging students' successes, communicating to parents and administrators things that students do well, and providing public, positive reinforcement whenever appropriate. However, while it is true that earned praise and recognition can contribute to students' fulfillment of esteem needs, unearned praise can do just the opposite. If teachers praise students indiscriminately (as in efforts to win their friendship, support, or good behavior), the value of the praise as a source of need fulfillment will decline. Furthermore, users of unearned praise will appear to be patronizing, insincere or untrustworthy. This, in turn, will cause students to be suspicious and unaccepting of praise even when it has been justly earned.

Self-Actualization Needs

The last explicit need described by Maslow is the need for self-actualization, or the need to develop as fully as possible. As Maslow put it, "What a man *can* be, he *must* be."[8]

The need for self-actualization is directly related to classroom discipline. As students move through the education process they are continually exposed to new and different avenues of physical, social, and intellectual development. If students believe that a particular teacher is keeping them from continuing the kind of development they consider most important, or if they believe they are wasting their time and efforts in meaningless and irrelevant activities, discipline problems can increase.

Teachers can help students meet their need for self-actualization in a number of ways. First and foremost, teachers can involve students in the planning of instructional objectives and activities. Student participation will help assure that objectives and activities are relevant to student goals and are perceived as such by students. Teachers can also take the time to build and communicate convincing rationales for the planned content and activities. Even if students participate in the initial planning, it is helpful for teachers to frequently remind them of the relationship(s) between the ongoing instruction and their continued development. The more immediate the applicability of the new information and skills, the more easily students will see the relationship between the instruction and their development.

In some cases individual students may not see a relationship between their personal goals and the work the class is doing. In such cases the potential for discipline problems increases, since few students are willing to sit quietly and "waste" their time. Teachers may need to make a special effort to discover and explain any possible relationships that do exist but that may have been overlooked by such students. If, in fact, no relationships do exist, the teacher has a limited number of options. Keeping in mind that students have a need for self-actualization, the teacher can allow them to plan and carry out independent student projects that are mutually agreed upon and that have some relationship to the on-going work of the class. For some students another option is to explain how achievement of the minimal course objectives can contribute to the student's eventual acquisition of a high school diploma which, in turn, can open many doors to further development. On occasion the teacher can discuss with the student whether taking a

---

[8]Maslow, "Theory of Human Motivation," p. 382.

different course might be of more immediate use, or whether retaking the course at a later time would be of benefit.

It is important for teachers to communicate to all students (not just the ones that are particularly troublesome) that they are aware of the need for self-actualization and are working specifically toward its fulfillment. Students who feel a teacher is helping them grow physically, socially, or intellectually are less likely to jeopardize that growth by causing discipline problems.

In review, it has been pointed out how teachers can minimize discipline problems by being cognizant of the relationship of many such problems to some very basic human needs. By consciously helping students satisfy their needs teachers will also be eliminating the causes of many discipline problems.

HELPFUL GUIDELINES FOR PRECLUDING DISCIPLINE PROBLEMS

Using the background information on human needs, along with other psychological principles and common sense, the following set of ten guidelines can be helpful in organizing to preclude discipline problems.

Eliminate physical distractions. As has been pointed out, students who are concerned about their physical well-being are likely to pay less attention to class work at hand. Simple steps, such as assuring a continual flow of fresh air through the room, maintaining a comfortable temperature, eliminating glare on the chalkboard, and establishing a reasonable policy concerning leaving the room for drinks or trips to the restroom, can help eliminate the causes of many "discipline problems."

Treat students with respect. Remember that students are fellow human beings and deserve to be treated with the same degree of respect and courtesy that adults extend to any of their peers. Remember that students are likely to treat teachers the same way they are treated by those teachers.

Elicit student help in planning. One of the most frequently cited causes of student discontent is the feeling that the content they are asked to learn or the activities they are asked to engage in are irrelevant. If students are allowed to participate in the planning and modification of instructional objectives and activities, and if the teacher takes the time to communicate sound rationales for those objectives, the problem of irrelevancy will decrease. Further, if students are involved in planning the instructional objectives and activities, they will be more likely to accept part of the responsibility for the achievement of those objectives and the success of those activities. Teachers who insist on doing all the planning themselves implicitly accept full responsibility for the success of those plans.

Maintain reasonable expectations. It usually does not take long for teachers to discover that mild student frustrations can be used to increase learning. The mildly uncomfortable feeling on the part of students, which continues until they achieve a goal, assists in speeding up the learning process. If teachers expect too little from students this sense of frustration will be lacking, the work will be viewed as busy work, and the final sense of achievement students could otherwise have experienced will be minimized. At the same time, unattainable goals or artificial barriers to goal achievement must be eliminated or students will become overly frustrated, and this frustration can be manifested in the form of discipline problems.

Use a variety of instructional experiences. An admitted cause of discipline problems is often student boredom. Teachers can combat this boredom by building into their lessons a variety of different learning experiences. It is unlikely that every student will be equally interested in each experience, but by having a number of different experiences in each lesson, teachers increase the probability of gaining and holding the interest of students more of the time. Interested students are less likely to cause discipline problems.

Provide prompt feedback. Students are generally extremely interested in finding out "how they did" on any given task. If a report is not forthcoming soon after the task is completed students are apt to think the teacher did not regard the task as very important and are therefore likely to feel they wasted their efforts. This feeling will continue to grow as such instances multiply, with the eventual result that students will feel that whatever they do in that particular class is of little value. Such an environment is open to the generation of discipline problems.

Provide positive reinforcement. When evaluating students' work, many teachers concentrate upon the identification and correction of errors. If teachers continually emphasize what students do incorrectly without recognizing those things they have done well, students will become discouraged and resentful. Their needs for esteem and self-actualization will go unsatisfied and they may seek other, undesirable sources of satisfaction. Teachers should point out sections of students' work that are well done and should encourage students to use those sections as models for the less well done portions. Sincere, positive reinforcement can go a long way toward making corrections more palatable and toward satisfying student needs.

Be consistent. If students perceive inconsistencies in a teacher's reactions to problems, or if they believe he or she is being unfair, their respect for that teacher will decrease. Once a teacher loses the respect of his or her class, discipline problems will begin to increase.

Peer approval can aid in the maintenance of discipline. As was pointed out earlier, peer approval or disapproval is an important element in the life of most adolescents. At times this force may motivate students more than any other single element. Teachers who gain the respect and approval of the majority of their students can tap this force and use it to help maintain an environment conductive to learning. Students who are "with" a teacher can assist, in many subtle ways, in controlling their peers.

It must be pointed out that although teachers can accept most forms of student support and can allow most forms of peer pressure to bear on students causing discipline problems, the tool cannot be used indiscriminately. Manifestations of peer pressure such as physical reprisals, ridicule, sarcasm, and humiliation cannot be tolerated. If teachers condone the use of such measures, the very student respect that generated the support in the first place will be lost.

Avoid punitive action. This principle is one of the most difficult for beginning teachers to follow. Many people have become accustomed to an eye for an eye philosophy, and when a teacher is inconvenienced by a student, his or her first inclination is often to inconvenience that student at least as much. There is little evidence, however, to support the idea that punitive action will have any lasting effect on deviant student behavior.

The selection of appropriate punitive action is not easy, nor is the prediction of consequent student reaction certain. An examination of common punitive actions follows:

1. *Detention.* This option punishes teachers as much as students since someone must supervise the detention. Often the student is bussed to and from school or has an afterschool job, and the hardship caused makes the punishment excessive. In other cases the student may be involved in sports or some afterschool club and the detention may therefore deprive him or her of one of the few school experiences that are keeping the student from dropping out.

2. *Extra schoolwork.* There seems to be no evidence supporting the idea that assigning extra schoolwork is helpful in eliminating discipline problems. In fact, it is likely that the assignment of such work will cause students to associate all schoolwork with unpleasant experiences and thus cause more harm than good.

3. *Repetitive sentences, and the like.* The use of repetitive sentences and similar busy work assignments has found widespread and long-term use among teachers for years. There must be teachers somewhere who have found this device effective in maintaining good discipline, but locating such a teacher proves to be difficult. Such tasks are likely to cause students to equate school work with busy work and to dislike both.

4. *Special seating assignments.* Special seating assignments usually take one of two forms. In the first form a seat is isolated from the rest of the class and students are assigned to it essentially as objects of ridicule. Ridicule is not effective as a discipline device.

Another form of special seating is to attempt to separate friends or arrange seats in a way that will minimize student interaction. This procedure is less satisfactory than using friendships in a positive way to foster intrinsic motivation. Further, separated students will still find ways to communicate despite the teacher's efforts.

5. *Physical Labor or Exercise.* The use of physical work or exercise is fraught with danger. A student who is asked by a teacher to do as little as move a desk and who is hurt in the process is in a position to bring suit against the teacher. In some states physical labor assigned to students is specifically forbidden.

Exercises, such as running the track, push-ups, and so on, are often used in physical education classes as punitive action. The same reservations apply here that applied in the assignment of schoolwork as punishment. How are students going to build an intrinsic desire for more exercise if it is deemed so distasteful by the teacher that it is used as punishment?

Occasionally a teacher in a classroom will use push-ups or some other physical action as punishment. Unlike the physical education teacher, who at least knows whether or not the student is physically able to do the assigned exercise, the classroom teacher may make an unjustified assumption about a student's physical abilities. It is possible that a student would rather injure himself or herself attempting the assigned exercise than lose face with peers; and it is unlikely that parents would lose the legal battle that could follow.

6. *Lowering of Grades.* In some school districts there are policies that condone the lowering of an academic grade for disciplinary reasons. This practice is analogous to withholding a diploma as punitive action when all necessary requirements have been met. **In this case the courts have ruled** that the diploma must be awarded.[9] In the case of grades, however, teachers can cloud the criteria for grading to the point where a grade could be lowered consciously or unconsciously because of discipline problems. This procedure cannot be logically defended, since once a student has achieved an objective and demonstrated a competence it is senseless to deny the accomplishment. Teachers who engage in this practice will be deemed unfair by their students and will quickly lose a large measure of student respect.

7. *Banishment from the classroom.* Along with lowering grades are the procedures that can cause students to earn lower grades, for instance, ac-

[9]Anne Flowers and Edward C. Bolmeier, *Law and Pupil Control* (Cincinnati: W. H. Anderson., 1964).

tions that deny the student access to on-going instruction. Insisting that the student stand outside the classroom may solve a problem for the moment, but the teacher will eventually need to spend extra time teaching the material to the student if academic achievement is considered important. Further, teachers are legally responsible for their students while class is in session. By banishing a student from the room the teacher removes that student from direct supervision and can therefore be held liable if the student is injured or gets into additional trouble.

BEHAVIOR MODIFICATION: OPERANT CONDITIONING

Operant conditioning is the formal name given to the process of encouraging people to behave in particular ways by systematically rewarding desired behaviors. Obvious examples of operant conditioning techniques include the planned use of praise to encourage the completion of homework and the use of prizes to motivate students to do well in school.

As a process, operant conditioning is not concerned with root causes of undesired behaviors. Instead, attention is focused on discovering and capitalizing on particular rewards that will help individuals to modify their behavior. This emphasis on rewards rather than causes seems superficial to many educators and has caused many to express reservations about using operant conditioning techniques.

Among arguments used by opponents of operant conditioning techniques is the opinion that they may cause as many problems as they solve. When teachers use operant conditioning techniques, the basic process is to identify the specific behaviors they wish to increase and reward the student when the desired behavior is demonstrated. Some educators maintain that it is not long until other students observe that one way to get extra attention or rewards from the teacher is to misbehave and then behave properly on cue. These educators also insist that operant conditioning techniques can be unfair to those students who behave properly.

Still another concern of many educators is that operant conditioning techniques imply that appropriate behavior should be demonstrated only because such behavior will generate an extrinsic reward such as praise, candy, money, or free time. They maintain that the use of rewards for appropriate behavior obscures the fact that such behavior has its own intrinsic rewards and will not, in fact, bring extrinsic rewards in the "real" world. They claim, therefore, that operant conditioning techniques mislead students by giving them a false impression of reality.

A further criticism leveled at operant conditioning practitioners questions the right of the behavior manipulator to make judgments as to what other people's behaviors should be. Operant conditioning practitioners must decide which behaviors are "good" and which are "bad," and use rewards to cause students to modify their behavior without necessarily making the students aware of the process. Such decisions, however, must be made daily by teachers in order to maintain an atmosphere conducive to the teaching-learning process. It is interesting to note that in one survey concerning behavior modification, 406 educators were questioned and 85 percent agreed that it was ethical to "manage behavior regardless of the techniques employed."[10] If nothing else, the finding speaks eloquently of the importance educators attach to "good" behavior on the part of students.

Many of the attacks on operant conditioning have been prompted by aversion to its abuses by individual teachers who use it indiscriminately and without regard for its ramifications. When used properly the rewards often pertain to student fulfillment of basic needs, such as the needs for esteem and self-actualization. Further, when teachers fully understand the ramifications of the technique, they are quick to point out to students the intrinsic rewards of the desired behavior and thus lead students away from continued extrinsic rewards.

Proper utilization of operant conditioning can minimize many of the problems associated with the technique and can thus provide teachers with an effective classroom control tool. Proper utilization of operant conditioning requires a careful and systematic series of steps designed to isolate and modify the undesirable behavior being manifested by a particular student.

Let us suppose, for example, that a student periodically disturbs the class and that the teacher has decided to try to modify the student's behavior via operant conditioning. Steps that would be appropriate follow:

Identify the specific behavior to be changed. What is it *exactly* that the student is doing to disturb the class? There is a tendency to generalize about a student's misbehavior, and to label a series of different actions as general misbehavior. If operant conditioning is to be effective however, it must focus on one specific behavior. In this case, the undesirable behavior is identified as a tendency to whisper to neighbors.

Determine what generally triggers the student's misbehavior. Does the student begin whispering when a particular stimulus is presented (i.e., when discussion of assigned homework is initiated), or when a stimulus is withdrawn (i.e., when the teacher shifts attention away from the student)? Although it may seem as though the student in question is always misbehaving, a careful analysis (after observation) will usually reveal the triggering stimulus. In this case it is determined that the student begins whispering when the class starts to discuss the previous night's homework assignment.

Determine What Generally Happens Each Time the Student Misbehaves. When the student begins whispering, what is the teacher's reaction? What is

[10]Sherman H. Frey, "Teachers and Behavior Modification," *Phi Delta Kappan*, 55, no. 9 (May 1974), p. 635

the reaction of the other students? This analysis of what happens immediately after the student misbehaves is important and it can be highly revealing. In this circumstance the analysis shows that as soon as the student begins whispering the teacher stops whatever he or she is doing and forcefully tells him to stop. Further, immediately following the chastisement, other students giggle and snicker, and the student usually responds with some wisecrack.

Devise and Try Countermeasures. At this point the analysis has begun to point the way toward the solution of the problem. The teacher knows, for example, that the student's disruption of the class usually begins with whispering to neighbors, which, in turn, is triggered by a teacher announcement that the class will begin discussing the homework assignment. Further, the disruption intensifies after a chastisement for whispering.

A number of countermeasures are available. One option is to ignore the student's whispering, thus depriving him of reinforcement from the attention focused on him. While this option may work, it may be undesirable because other students may misinterpret the lack of action, particularly if the student is a leader. A second option would be to move the student to a different seat where neighbors would be unlikely to whisper back. This option might work, but it may be less desirable than other possibilities because it is unlikely to bring about a lasting modification in the student's behavior. A third option could emerge. For example, it may be that there is a cause-effect relationship between the student's whispering and impending discussions of homework. It might be determined that the student rarely does his homework and that his whispering is an attempt to acquire survival data prior to the discussion.

An operant conditioning could be initiated by waiting for a time when the student is able to participate in a discussion of homework and then praising him for his good work and valuable contributions. If the praise (or other reward) was forthcoming each time the student contributed to the discussion without whispering beforehand, the whispering might soon cease, because the student would recognize that it was no longer necessary. This procedure, while effective, depends upon waiting until the student does his homework, and could turn out to be a long-term approach.

A fourth option to speed up the reinforcement process could be initiated. Keeping in mind that the class disruption is caused in part by the student's whispering and in part by teacher reaction to that whispering, the teacher might find the following steps effective:

1. Make specific homework assignments for each student.
2. Privately encourage the student to do the assignment.
3. Call on some students to discuss their homework, but call on the student the first day only if he or she has done his homework, and ignore whispering if it occurs.

4. Again make specific assignments and privately encourage the student to do hers or his.

5. As soon as the student has made an effort to do the assignment, even if it came only as the result of heavy prompting, call on him or her during the discussion and praise his or her contribution. Again ignore his or her whispering if it occurs.

6. The teacher repeats steps 4 and 5 each day, praising contributions by the student and ignoring whispering. The whispering should decrease and disappear within a few days. If it does not, the analysis must be reexamined for alternative explanations for the behavior.

The point of the operant conditioning process is to focus attention on desired behavior and to provide an incentive for the student to engage in that behavior. The incentive may be praise, points, or any other reward valued by the student, and the expectation is that the desired behavior will soon become self-reinforcing and will replace the undesirable behavior, which is never reinforced.

Keep in mind that sometimes the removal or withholding of a stimulus (for example, the denying of an opportunity to receive attention and reinforcement from peers) is as effective as the presentation of a stimulus (for example, the giving of praise or rewards). Once the right stimulus is found for any individual, a procedure is established to help bring about lasting behavioral changes via operant conditioning.

BEHAVIOR MODIFICATION: REALITY THERAPY

Reality therapy is another behavior modification tool that utilizes student needs, but its philosophical orientation is significantly different from that of operant conditioning. In operant conditioning, the individual undergoing the conditioning is generally unaware that his or her behavior is being manipulated. No attempt is made to treat the individual as a responsible person, to make him or her a partner in a joint effort to modify behavior, or to help him or her see the cause-effect relationships between the behavior and its short-term and long-term consequences.

Reality therapy, on the other hand, makes individuals the prime movers in the modification of their own behavior. Reality therapy is predicated on the idea that people engage in those behaviors they believe will bring them relatedness and respect (i.e., which will satisfy one or more perceived or unperceived needs), but that some individuals have either a distorted idea of what their goals are or a distorted idea of how to achieve them. Reality therapists see their role as a "perception sharpener"—one who attempts to help the individual perceive the reality of the situation.

Reality therapy begins with the current situation. Although reality therapists are well aware that many problems have roots in past events, they are not willing to allow those past events to become excuses for present actions. The individual's attention is focused on the behavior to be modified, not on the root causes of that behavior, and the individual is helped to see the consequences of continuing the undesirable behavior as well as the consequences of modified behavior. For example how would a teacher who chose to use reality therapy have dealt with the student who whispered? The following step-by-step procedure is illustrative.

Help the student identify the undesirable behavior. In this case the teacher may arrange to see the student privately. In the process of discussing the "problem" the teacher elicits the identification of the problem from the student. It is important that the student identify it, because then he or she is taking the first step towards its solution. If the teacher makes the identification, the student is likely to look to the teacher for the solution to the problem rather than to seek that solution for himself or herself.

Care is excercised not to ask the student why he is engaging in the undesired behavior (whispering). To do so would provide the student with an opportunity to offer an excuse for the actions and to focus attention on the excuse rather than the action. Again, the reality therapist does not deny that there may be legitimate reasons for inappropriate behavior—he or she simply insists on beginning with the inappropriate behavior rather than with a series of antecedent events. After discussion the student should identify whispering as an inappropriate behavior.

Help the student identify the consequences of undesirable behavior. It is important that the consequences identified be real and logical. If the environment is manipulated so the consequences of a particular action are unreasonably harsh or slight, the situation becomes contrived and unreal. In such a situation reality therapy is less effective. In this case, for example, telling the student that he or she will be suspended from school if whispering continues is unreasonable. Similarly, it would be unreasonable to tell him that inappropriate behavior will have no consequences. It is appropriate, however, to point out that consequences are often cumulative and tend to get more and more severe.

Through discussion it is determined that the student's whispering disturbs other students and that part of a teacher's responsibility is to maintain an atmosphere that is quiet and conducive to concentration. In keeping with that responsibility, the student should conclude that continued whispering will logically result in some form of exclusion from the group, which, in turn, will adversely affect progress.

Help the student make a value judgment about the inappropriate behavior and its consequences. The purpose of this step is to help the student see that the inappropriate behavior is contributing more to eventual unhappiness than to immediate or long-range happiness. The student is likely to have inaccurate perceptions about the effects of the behavior and may need help in making a value judgment about its desirability or undesirability. If the student does have difficulty making a value judgment about the behavior itself, then the focus is directed at making a judgment about the consequences of that behavior. In any event, the student is helped to conclude that the inappropriate behavior is undesirable or that it will bring more unhappiness than happiness. In the example, the student who whispers admits that whispering can bother other students and that one student should not interfere with the right of other students to learn.

Have the student formulate a plan for changing the behavior. Once the student has concluded that the behavior is not, in fact, in his or her own best interests, the next step is for the student to suggest alternatives to that behavior. If possible the student is encouraged to propose an alternative behavior, for example the student:

1. Will simply stop whispering.
2. Will admit to not knowing an answer or not doing his homework rather than try to acquire last-minute information via whispering.
3. Will tell the teacher before class when he or she is not prepared and then will not be called upon to answer questions.

Of these three alternatives, the last is the least acceptable, and should be rejected by the teacher if the student does not see its inappropriateness, because it forces the teacher to share responsibility for the student's action when, in fact, that responsibility belongs to the student. It is important that the student recognize, (1) that the current situation is a result of his or her own behavior, and (2) that he or she can be extracted from the situation by engaging in behaviors that are both socially acceptable and conducive to achievement of personal and other people's success and happiness.

Have the student select, and implement, a specific alternative. After alternatives have been suggested by the student (and perhaps by the teacher), the student should decide which alternative to utilize. At this point the teacher's role is to monitor carefully to determine how well the student is following the plan and to offer supportive praise.

As was pointed out earlier, the differences between the operant conditioning approach to behavior modification and the reality therapy approach are many and significant. It is unlikely that both approaches will appeal to all prospective teachers or that all prospective teachers will be able to use both with equal effectiveness. It is suggested, therefore, that before either approach is decided upon, the prospective user carefully assess his or her own philosophical position concerning classroom control and behavior modification. Haphazard or indiscriminate use of either or both of these procedures can not only be frustrating and futile, it can also harm the teachers' rapport with students. Properly used, however, these procedures can enable teachers to bring about lasting behavioral changes.

A DISCIPLINE PROCEDURE INVOLVING
THE SCHOOL DISCIPLINARIAN

Regardless of how carefully teachers plan and how skillfully their lessons are conducted, there will still be numerous minor disruptions of the ongoing class work that can develop into major discipline problems. In the mind of every teacher is a conceptual model of an "ideal" teaching-learning environment. Each teacher's model varies from those of most other teachers, and some teachers are willing to tolerate a much broader range of deviant student behaviors than are others. All teachers will find, however, that their typical classes will deviate, in one degree or another, from the ideal model, and that there will be some points at which the degree of deviation approaches unacceptable levels.

When teachers feel that some overt action on their part is necessary in order to maintain a reasonable teaching-learning environment, they must decide whether that action will cause more of a disruption than the continuation of the deviant behavior. Jacob S. Kounin reports that teacher-initiated disciplinary acts (which he and his associates labeled "desists") can have significant effects on the other students in the class who are not the target of discipline. These effects have been labeled "ripple effects." In one study it was found that teachers who use angry or punitive desists often cause other students in the room to refocus their attention from the work at hand to the disturbance and the teacher's reaction to it. Simple reprimands, on the other hand, to have much less of a negative ripple effect.[11] Kounin also reported that interviews with high school students indicate that if a teacher is viewed as fair and is generally liked by the students, his or her desist actions are less likely to cause ripple effects destructive to the teaching-learning environment.[12] One could conclude, therefore, that to deal successfully with most discipline problems, teachers should establish good rapport with their students and should use simple reprimands to deal with occasional deviant behavior. Mild desists can include actions such as moving toward disruptive students, standing by them, glancing at them, and directing questions at them, as well as direct reprimands. Further, reprimands should be in the form of direct statements rather than questions. "Would you please stop talking?" is less desirable than "Please stop talking," because it does not invite a verbal student response.

[11] Jacob S. Kounin, *Discipline and Group Management in Classrooms* (New York: Holt, Rinehart & Winston, 1970) p. 49.
[12] Kounin, *Discipline*, p. 142.

If the mild desists used by the teacher are not effective and the previously discussed preventive measures are being used, or if reality therapy or
operant conditioning techniques have failed, the teacher must have a plan of
action. In some schools, teachers are told exactly what disciplinary
procedure to use. If such a policy exists, it should be followed precisely. If
no complete policy exists, teachers should develop their own based on
whatever policies do exist. The following procedure is predicated on the possibility that the student may need to be referred to the school disciplinarian.

The Six Steps in a Model Discipline Procedure
Involving the School Disciplinarian

1. *Each time a violation of proper classroom decorum is observed, tell
the offender to desist.* As pointed out previously, if the teacher is respected
and utilizes a mild reprimand, the danger of negative ripple effects will be
minimal.

2. *Initiate, if it is deemed appropriate, a reality therapy or operant conditioning approach.* Note such efforts on an anecdotal record card.

3. *If the deviant behavior persists tell the student to remain in the room
after the class is dismissed.* If the class precedes a lunch break or the end of
the school day, the subsequent conference can be more leisurely. If the student is scheduled for another class immediately, the teacher should keep the
conference as brief as possible and should write a note to the teacher of the
student's next class explaining the tardiness. In either case the purpose of the
conference should be to explain to the student that violations of proper
classroom behavior have occurred and to attempt to obtain a commitment
from the student that such misbehavior will not reoccur. (Note the
difference between this tactic and its counterpart in reality therapy.) The
conference should be brief, businesslike, and to the point. It should be
recorded on an anecdotal record card with a specific explanation of the
offense and date. The student should sign the card and the teacher should retain it.

4. *If the offending student continues the disruptive behavior, schedule a
mutually convenient time for a longer conference with the student.* The reason
for assuring that the time for the meeting is mutually agreeable is that students will find reasons why they cannot meet at teacher-decided times. The
teacher should be willing to meet before, after, or at an appropriate time
during the school day. Make sure the student understands the commitment
to meet. If there is any doubt about the student's showing up, make two
copies of the time and place and mutually initial each copy.

It should be made clear to the student that such a conference is not synonymous with detention. The purpose of this conference is to review the student's offenses and to outline the consequences of future offenses. The teacher should explain why the offenses cannot be tolerated (because they disrupt the teaching-learning process and keep other students from learning). The tone of the conference should be that of identifying and eliminating the misbehavior. A record of the conference, offense, date, and so forth, should be added to the anecdotal record card and the student should again sign the card.

At this point the student may feel that the procedure and conferences are a bother (or even a little painful) but will also realize that the teacher means business. Notice that no punitive action has been taken. The emphasis is on changing the behavior of the student. The student should be told at this point that further misbehavior will result in his or her parents' being contacted.

If the misbehavior persists, enlist the aid of the student's parents. Since the student was appraised, as part of step 4, of the consequences of continued misbehavior, he or she should not be surprised at the initation of this step if the misbehavior persists. At the next offense, remind the student as he or she leaves the room that the parents will be contacted and their support enlisted. Once this step is announced it is important that the contact with parents be made as soon as possible, preferably before the end of the school day. If this is not done there is the possibility that the student will arrive home before the teacher calls and set a stage that is difficult or impossible to cope with. Once the contact is made the teacher should go through the anecdotal record explaining the actions taken and enlisting support. A record of the home contact should be made on the anecdotal record card.

6. *If the problem persists, the student is referred to the school disciplinarian.* Before making this referral, contact the disciplinarian and discuss with him or her the anecdotal record with the list of offenses and corrective efforts. This is important because the disciplinarian must understand that the teacher has already had a minimum of two conferences with the student and has contacted the parents. Once the disciplinarian understands that the problem is not superficial, he or she can try working with the student. If the disciplinarian decides upon some punitive action, the choice will be his or hers and not the teacher's.

7. *Steps 4, 5, and 6 are repeated.* Before referring the student to the office again, another conference should be held and another contact with parents made. This cycle should continue until (a) the student's behavior changes as home, class, and office pressures mount; (b) The disciplinarian

removes the student from the class; (c) the school term ends; or (d) the student removes himself or herself from the class.

Obviously the teacher will be most satisfied if the student modifies the behavior voluntarily, but the teacher's primary responsibility is the education of the entire class, and if one student is thwarting that education and refuses to modify his or her behavior, the teacher is obligated to take all reasonable measures to fulfill the educational commitment to the rest of the class.

POTENTIALLY DANGEROUS PROBLEMS

It is probable that most teachers will eventually encounter what can be labeled a "potentially dangerous problem," for instance, fighting, verbal or physical abuse of staff members, drinking, drugs, overt defiance, sexual assault, or malicious destruction of property. In such a situation it is almost always too late to attempt remedial action. Because of the legal ramifications, such problems are best handled by experienced administrators. Unfortunately, it is not easy to decide the best course of action in these volatile situations. In some cases the student will be rational enough to proceed directly to the office alone. In other cases the teacher may need to accompany the student to the office. If the teacher must leave a class in order to escort a student to the office, he or she should ask a nearby teacher to monitor the class. In many schools, classroom-office communication is possible and the teacher is able to summon help without leaving the room. The immediate goal is to keep the student from causing harm to himself or herself or harm to others.

HYPERACTIVITY AND CHEMOTHERAPY

Sometimes when teachers see a student who is continually restless, given to sudden outbursts, or unable to concentrate on the work at hand, they attribute it to hyperactivity. Hyperactivity is generally thought to be caused by the inability of an individual to assign priorities to the many sensory inputs constantly bombarding the brain. Most teachers are simply not qualified to diagnose such problems, but many try to do so anyway. What occasionally happens is that a teacher mistakes lapses of attention, restlessness, or even the normal exuberance of youth, for hyperactivity. Having "diagnosed" the problem, the uninformed teacher may call the student's parents (or have the school nurse call them) and suggest they take the student to a physician and, "have the doctor give him something to control hyperactivity."

Unfortunately, some physicians will, after only a cursory examination, accept the teacher's "diagnosis" and prescribe a treatment on that basis. The typical treatment for hyperactivity is the prescription of amphetamines such as Ritalin and Dexedrine. Although these drugs act as stimulants for adults, they act as depressants for children. It is difficult to predict accurately the exact effect of any specific drug on any specific child, and a growing number of children are being adversely affected by such chemotherapy. Even worse, because of the increasing instances in which drugs are prescribed for students on the basis of inadequate diagnoses, many students are exposed to drugs who do not need to be. In the spring of 1974 one researcher, Dr. Herbert E. Rie, reported to the American Medical Association that, "about twice as many children are being given drugs for hyperactivity as should be."[13] Teachers must accept at least part of the blame.

If teachers suspect that a student may be hyperactive, their initial step should be to double-check the basis for the suspicion. The procedures include keeping a written record of the frequency of each "hyperactive" act, checking with teachers to see if the student is demonstrating similar behavior in other classes, and engaging in discussions with the school nurse and guidance personnel to see if they have been told of any specific problems the student may be having.

If the suspected behaviors are persistent and not just isolated examples, the collected data should be discussed with the guidance department and nurse. If the results of this conference indicate that an examination by a physician is in order, then the parents should be involved in a separate conference in which such an examination is recommended. At this conference the parents are provided the list of incidents without suggestions that the student is hyperactive or that he or she needs drugs. The *doctor alone* should diagnose the problem and prescribe any treatment.

Assuming the teacher is informed of subsequent treatment, it is then his or her responsibility to continue to monitor the student's behavior. In this way the effectiveness of the treatment can be determined and its eventual elimination hastened. The ultimate goal, of course, is to help the student control his or her own behavior without the use of chemicals.

SUMMARY

In attempting to prevent discipline problems it should be kept in mind that students are human beings with all the needs common to human beings. A.

[13]Herbert E. Rie, address to the American Medical Association at their annual meeting in Chicago on June 25, 1974. Reported in *The Daily Pantagraph*, Bloomington-Normal, Ill., June 26, 1974, p. C-10.

H. Maslow has described five of those needs (physiological, safety, love, esteem, and self-actualization), and each has ramifications for prevention of discipline problems. Most important, if students' basic needs are not satisfied, or if students believe that school is standing in the way of need gratification, discipline problems are likely to develop.

In light of student needs and psychological principles, ten guidelines are suggested to assist teachers in precluding discipline problems. If discipline problems emerge, two techniques that can be used to modify student's behavior by capitalizing on their needs are operant conditioning and reality therapy. Operant conditioning is a technique whereby the conditioner brings about modifications in an individual's behavior by presenting stimuli valued by that individual. The technique is usually employed without the knowledge of the person whose behavior is being manipulated and for this reason, along with the fact that the individual may become dependent on the stimuli, many educators are reluctant to use it as a classroom control measure.

Reality therapy is another behavior modification technique, but it differs significantly from operant conditioning in that it helps the individual become the prime mover in the modification of his or her own behavior. Previous events are not accepted as excuses for current behavior, and attention is focused on the real consequences of continued inappropriate behavior as opposed to the consequences of behavior modified to become socially acceptable.

Unfortunately, these measures are not always effective with all students and at times the teacher must rely on a set plan of action to deal with persistent behavior problems. One such plan is described and discussed in the chapter, but at its foundation is the philosophy that the ideal way to handle discipline problems is to help the offending student change his or her behavior by helping the student realize the intrinsic benefit of conforming to acceptable standards of behavior, rather than to force the student to adjust through the use of punitive measures.

Another technique seeing more use in controlling some discipline problems is chemotherapy. This technique is usually restricted to students labeled "hyperactive," but because the term is interpreted loosely and the real problem is poorly diagnosed, many students are compelled to take drugs who should not be doing so. Chemotherapy is intended to solve medical problems, not discipline problems.

SELECTED READINGS

BLAKHAM, GARTH J., *The Deviant Child in the Classroom.* Belmont, Calif.: Wadsworth, Inc., 1967.

BRADBURN, NORMAN M., *The Structure of Psychological Well-Being*. Chicago: Aldine, 1969.

GNAGEY, WILLIAM J., *The Psychology of Discipline in the Classroom*. New York: Macmillan, 1968.

———,*Maintaining Discipline in Classroom Instruction*. New York: Macmillan, 1975

GRAMBS, JEAN DRESDEN, JOHN C. CARR, and ROBERT M. FITCH, *Modern Methods in Secondary Education*, 3rd ed. New York: Holt, Rinehart & Winston, 1970.

INLOW, GAIL M., *Maturity in High School Teaching*, 2nd ed. Englewood Cliffs, N.J.: Prentice-Hall, 1970.

JESSUP, MICHAEL H., and MARGARET A. KELLY, *Discipline: Positive Attitudes for Learning*. Englewood Cliffs, N.J.: Prentice-Hall, 1971.

LADD, EDWARD T., and WILLIAM C. SAYRES, *Social Aspects of Education: A Casebook*. Englewood Cliffs, N.J.: Prentice-Hall, 1962.

LARSON, KNUTE G., and MELVIN R. KARPAS, *Effective Secondary School Discipline*. Englewood Cliffs, N.J.: Prentice-Hall, 1963.

WOODY, ROBERT H., *Behavioral Problem Children in the Schools*. Englewood Cliffs, N.J.: Prentice-Hall 1969.

13

Examining Innovations In Education

The Logical Instructional Model is a sound strategy that can and will help teachers increase effectiveness. The LIM is, however, *only* a strategy and its success or failure depends upon the total instructional environment in which it operates and the learning activities chosen. In the process of working continually to upgrade education, the practitioner must be aware of new and unique procedures and formats that hold promise for instructional gains.

Some innovations, for example, modular scheduling, have been made possible by recent technological advances such as the computer. Others are reincarnations of ideas that originated hundreds and even thousands of years ago. Regardless of their origin, many of these innovations are now being seriously considered or used by educators across the country, and any or all of them could see large-scale implementation. It is only by being familiar with the process of change and with the advantages and disadvantages of the various innovations that teachers will be able to discuss them intelligently and have a sound basis for working for or against their implementation. This chapter is intended to provide such familiarity.

OBJECTIVES

The student will:

1. Describe in writing at least two arguments for and two arguments against each of three proposed educational innovations. (Comprehension)
2. Given a proposed innovation, describe, in less than three pages, at least two implications it would have for teacher preparation programs and teacher certification standards. (Analysis)
3. Given a hypothetical teaching-learning situation and a proposed innovation for implementation for that situation, take a position for or against the use of the innovation and defend that position, citing at least four logical rationales. (Evaluation)

THE PROCESS OF CHANGE

Public education is often thought of as a huge and ponderous monolith that goes its own way unmindful of attempts by individuals and groups to change its direction. The view is, of course, incorrect. Public education is a huge institution, involving millions of people, but it is far from being a monolith. Corporations such as Exxon and General Motors are also huge, as are institutions such as the army and navy, but unlike such establishments, public education has no single head. There is no admiral or corporation president of public education who can send out a directive for universal change. Each individual public school system has a high degree of autonomy that it guards jealously, and any changes in public education can come about only when significant numbers of these school systems (and individual teachers within them) wish it to happen.

Changes in public education come about slowly. For a proposed change to have any significant impact, large numbers of individuals must be made aware of the proposal, be convinced of its workability and desirability, and help implement it. Simply to communicate with so many people, even through mass communication methods, is an immense and complex task.

Few innovations are implemented in their original form. The process of changing public education usually begins when a few individuals become enthusiastic about an idea and begin enlisting supporters. As more and more people are made aware of the proposed change an opposition group usually develops. Members of this group, either because they are satisfied with the teaching-learning process as it is or because they are reluctant to change for other reasons, begin pointing out weaknesses and dangers in the proposed change. Eventually, as views are exchanged, the original idea is modified and ultimately school systems and individual teachers adapt their own versions of the modified innovation for particular uses.

The reader should keep in mind that most of the proposed innovations presented in this chapter have been discussed by educators for at least two or three years (and in some cases, for much longer), that all are still open to modification, and that many are inextricably entwined. Several of the ideas that are currently receiving the greatest attention are now examined.

CURRENT EDUCATIONAL EMPHASES

Accountability

Accountability for educators is not new. In 399 B.C. Socrates was forced to commit suicide because the ideas he promulgated angered the leaders of his day. A little more than four hundred years later another educator, Jesus Christ, was killed for much the same reason. While few people today propose holding educators accountable with their lives for what they do or fail to do, the idea of accountability is clearly as old and established as education itself.

Although it has always been present, the idea of accountability did not become a salient issue until the late 1950s. During the early 1900s large numbers of young people did not go to school, and most of those who did were satisfied with learning how to read and write and do simple calculations. People who had even this limited education found themselves with a tremendous advantage over the large numbers of immigrants then flooding the country, since many of the immigrants could neither read nor write English. Later, as the country grew, attending school was still considered a privilege and few thoughts were given to holding the poorly paid teachers strictly accountable for what went on in the classrooms. As more and more people attended school and the level of education rose, significant numbers of people began voicing their discontent with public education.

With the launching of Sputnik in 1957 the issue of accountability become paramount. Many critics of public education feel the schools are at least partly to blame for the fact that the Russians beat the United States into space in 1957, that the hippie movement began and flourished, and that violence in the United States is increasing. They feel that if educators had "done their jobs" these things might not have happened and, right or wrong, their feelings undoubtedly reflect the feelings of many other taxpayers.

The critics point out that public education is the only major "industry" exempt from both significant internal and external regulation and from the pressures of the marketplace that would normally cause inferior services to be replaced by more satisfactory ones. In contrast to public education, it is pointed out, private schools and institutions of higher learning quickly find themselves facing declining enrollments and eventual bankruptcy if they fail to satisy their students. Public education is seen as insensitive to the needs and desires of those it is meant to serve.

By way of defense, some educators have pointed out that their "products" are people and not machined tools, that variables beyond their control affect the teaching-learning process and, perhaps most important of all, that their task has never been precisely defined. These arguments, taken separately or together, are incontestable. Even so, they are not strong enough to allow teachers to be completely unaccountable for their actions. The real question is not *whether* educators should be accountable, but rather, *who* should be accountable *to whom* and *for what*? Many of the following suggestions for innovation address themselves directly to these points.

Precise Instructional Objectives   Using precise instructional objectives as a way of stating instructional intent is an innovation in and of itself. The utilization of precise instructional objectives is one way to increase accountability. Teachers, schools, and school systems that adopt sets of precise instructional objectives, in effect, adopt sets of job descriptions. These job descriptions spell out, in measurable terms, what the instructional intent is, and they make it possible for observers to determine how successful students were with respect to that intent. What these objectives do not do is account for such things as varying abilities among students, varying degrees of motivation, and varying facilities and instructional aids available to teachers. Nevertheless, they do help define the teaching task.

Thousands of school systems across the country are in the process of developing sets of precise instructional objectives, but one example will perhaps serve to illustrate the trend. In the Deer Creek-Mackinaw School System (a consolidated system just west of Bloomington, Illinois), a committee of teachers representing grades K-8 cooperatively developed a set of objectives for the broad area of communications. These objectives are divided into the subareas of reading, writing, speaking, and listening, and the continuity of skill development in each of these subareas can be traced from kindergarten through eighth grade. The objectives developed by the Deer Creek-Mackinaw teachers comprise their job description with respect to the teaching of communication skills. Although the objectives may change from year to year as more performance data is gathered and as people provide ideas, a basis for accountability has been established.

It should be noted that the major teachers' organizations (the National Education Association and the American Federation of Teachers) have taken a cautious stance with regard to precise instructional objectives. The professional organizations are concerned that administrators or citizen groups will misuse precise instructional objectives and regard them as absolute standards. If this should occur, teachers might be judged incompetent if all of their students did not achieve the same objectives regardless of beginning abilities, motivation, or any of the other variables beyond the teacher's control.

One way to minimize the misuse of precise instructional objectives as an accountability tool is to develop the objectives in conjunction with the administration and the entire teaching staff of the school system. In this way not only are the objectives exposed to a good deal of constructive criticism but their intent is publicized and is thus less likely to be misinterpreted.

Performance Contracts   Another component of accountability is performance contracting. A performance contract is an agreement between a school system and either a private business or some other group, such as a local teacher's association, to the effect that the contractor will take the financial responsibility for educating a specified group of students and will forfeit part of the fee for every student who fails to meet or exceed an agreed-upon level of performance. The performance level is usually expressed in terms of a set score on an achievement test.

Private businesses are interested in performance contracting because they expect to make a profit. It is their belief that by using their own methods, their own materials, and in some cases, their own personnel, they can meet their contractual obligations for less than they are being paid. To the extent they are correct they will make profits or withstand losses.

A number of school systems have tried performance contracting but the results have not been entirely satisfactory. One of the earliest experiments was conducted in Texarkana, Arkansas, and it ended in a flurry of charges that the company involved had essentially "taught for the test" and neglected those aspects of education not specifically covered by contract clauses. A number of perplexing questions arose from the Texarkana experiment. Who, for example, should monitor student achievement? Who is in control of the school system during the period of the contract, the contractor or the school officials? What about the use of unapproved materials, methods, and personnel: Is it legal? Many of these questions have not yet been answered.

In another experiment, the Gary, Indiana, school board turned over responsibility for an elementary school, for a period of four years ending in 1974, to a private contractor. The Gary Teachers Union objected to the contract clause calling for the guaranteed transfer from the target school of any teacher specified by the contractor. The Indiana School Board ruled that the degree of control wielded by the chief company agent was illegal and that full control of the school had to be exercised through a state-certified school administrator.[1] While the long-range results and ramifications of the Gary

[1] James A. Mecklenburger and John A. Wilson, "The Performance Contract in Gary," *Phi Delta Kappan*, 52, no. 7 (March 1971), pp. 406-410.

experiment cannot fully be assessed for a number of years, at least three things are certain. First, the profits expected by the contractor did not fully materialize. Second, the opposition from professional teacher organizations was much greater than expected. To the degree contractors try to displace certified teachers, they can expect vigorous and expensive court battles. Third, because the experiment was disruptive to the operation of the school system, it is unlikely that any similar experiments will be conducted in Gary in the near future.

Taking a somewhat different approach, the Stockton, California, and Mesa, Arizona, school systems signed performance contracts with their own local teacher organizations. Under the terms of the contracts, participating teachers, in addition to their regular salaries, were to be eligible for bonuses depending upon how many of their students improved at least one grade level in math and reading. It was hoped that the incentive pay would bring about an increase in student learning that would prove the system's own teachers could, without recourse to the expensive teaching machines and "experts" frequently employed by commercial contractors, meet contractual obligations.[2] Unfortunately, neither of these experiments was fully implemented as originally planned, and neither was deemed successful enough to be continued.

Perhaps the main issue in performance contracting is whether such an approach emphasizes the wrong aspect of the teaching-learning process. Many people feel that if there is a profit in having students achieve a particular score on a particular test, teachers (whether they be public or private) will simply teach for the test. They claim further that any test simply *samples* the information acquired by the students and does not touch upon the many insights and understandings that have undoubtedly been acquired by listening to, and participating in, numerous class discussions and other activities. It is feared that these "extraneous" activities will be curtailed since they may not contribute directly to achievement of the desired test scores. Others feel that if students can achieve the specified scores, teachers will have done all that can reasonably be expected of them.

Another concern is whether performance contractors will feel any obligation to help slow learners. There undoubtedly comes a point in the education of some students at which the money expended in helping them learn exceeds the money budgeted for their education. It is as yet uncertain whether commercial contractors will sacrifice part of their profits in attempts to help these slow learners, or whether they will simply give up the attempt when the costs threaten their profits. This issue, along with the many legal questions yet unanswered, will be pursued with new vigor if the move toward performance contracting begins to gain appreciable momentum.

[2] "Teachers' Organizations Try Performance Contracting," *Phi Delta Kappan*, 52, no. 4, (December 1970), p. 250.

Educational Vouchers   Still another approach to increasing educational accountability is the use of educational vouchers. Under one proposed voucher system, parents of students would be given payment vouchers sufficient to cover the cost of educating their children. After choosing the particular school (either public or private) they wanted their children to attend, parents could pay the school with the vouchers, which the school would then redeem to cover its operating costs. It is assumed that parents would be able to choose precisely the kind of school they wanted for their children (tight or loose discipline, traditional or progressive methods, etc.), and that those schools that failed to satisfy parents would eventually find themselves with no students, no vouchers, and no money.

The difficulties inherent in the system are obvious. What happens when a particular school builds such a reputation that applicants outstrip available spaces? It is hoped that the school would either expand or would give rise to sufficient imitators to accommodate all those who desired that kind of education. Until either of those alternatives materialized, the school would simply fill its vacancies by lot with those not admitted seeking admittance to second, third, or even fourth choices.

It is assumed that most parents would choose to send their children to nearby schools, thus minimizing transportation problems. But what if those schools were already filled? The whole concept of the neighborhood school, which enables students to share both in-school and out-of-school activities, seems threatened. What effect this would have on the establishment and maintenance of childhood friendships, which depend to large degree on physical proximity, is uncertain, and although there are numerous safeguards proposed to prevent discrimination, one wonders how effective they would be.

The voucher system is designed to make public education more responsive to the same law of supply and demand that operates in the marketplace, but in order for it to function properly, the consumers involved must take the time to become familiar with the "products." There is some doubt as to whether parents will inform themselves sufficiently to make wise choices, or even whether large numbers of parents care to do so.

Alternative Schools

The term *alternative school* is used here to cover a wide variety of traditional and innovative educational formats. Some alternative schools are more innovative than others; some have been developed by professional educators and are implemented within the public school structure, while others have been developed by nonprofessionals and are implemented outside the public school structure. There is no single kind of alternative school, and teachers should be sure of just what kind an "alternative" school is before praising or condeming any specific one.

Although alternative schools differ extensively in kind and purpose, they often have at least two points in common. First, they often have very low student-teacher ratios, sometimes as low as 10 to 1. With so few students, teachers in alternative schools are usually able to devote more time and attention to each student and are thus more able to individualize their instruction. Teachers in traditional classrooms would also like to individualize instruction for their students, but with thirty or more students it is often impossible. This point should be kept in mind when discussions turn to why the alternative is not the usual. Public education has never been known for low student-teacher ratios, or, consequently, for its ability to individualize instruction.

The second point most alternative schools have in common is that they are often designed to meet the needs of specific kinds of students, for example, drop-outs or potential drop-outs, discipline problems, slow learners, or gifted students. Designed to meet the needs of a rather uniform group of students, alternative schools are able to develop unique instructional patterns and plans that fit the needs of their particular kind of students, but that might not be appropriate for a more heterogeneous group (such as is found in traditional classrooms). This point, like the first point, is not meant to detract from the very real contributions of alternative schools, but prospective teachers should know that a large part of the success of some alternative schools is due to factors other than superior teachers or procedures.

Probably the oldest kind of "alternative" school is the private prep school or academy. This kind of school offers, for a price, small class size, more individual attention, and a host of extracurricular activities ranging from polo, to sailing, to close order drill, but because the cost of these private schools is high, few but the very wealthy can afford them. Private schools are not what most people are referring to when they speak of "alternative schools," but private schools *are* alternatives to typical public schools and have been for many years.

Perhaps the most widely known alternative school, is Philadelphia's Parkway program, or as it has come to be known, "The School Without Walls." Parkway is a four-year high school program in which students combine classroom instruction with out-of-class study. While the school may not sound unique, many things about the program make Parkway one of the most cited and copied alternative schools in the country.[3] Students elect to be in the program on their own and plan their own instructional programs (in conjunction with teachers, parents, and counselors); receive instruction from certified teachers and *qualified laymen* on a regular basis; are free to utilize, as study points, numerous businesses, factories, and institutions within the community; and work closely with teachers in evaluating their own learning progress.

[3]Robert Hutchins, "School Options in Philadelphia: Their Present and Future," *Educational Leadership*, 32, no. 2 (November 1974), p. 89.

In another type of alternative school, ALPHA (Alternative Learning Program for the High School Age), students can fulfill regular diploma requirements by a combination of volunteer work, work experiences, regular classes, independent study via student-teacher contracts (see chapter 6), and a regularly scheduled and required workshop in which communication and interpersonal skills are stressed.[4]

Still another example of an alternative school plan is the "Executive High School Internships" program in operation in twenty-seven cities in sixteen states. In this program high school juniors and seniors are able to earn a full semester's credit by working with a sponsor at professional-level tasks, attending weekly seminars on administration, and preparing logs and records of their activities.[5]

These examples by no means exhaust the numerous kinds of alternative programs in existence, nor do they explore the curricula of any of the alternative schools that have been established outside the public school structure. The important point to keep in mind is that most alternative schools have the students' best interests at heart and are dedicated to helping them learn as much as possible. Although alternative schools share with traditional schools the goal of maximizing student learning, to the extent that they are less bound by logistical, financial, or bureaucratic restraints than traditional schools, they are sometimes more able to achieve their goals.

Community Education

Perhaps as a direct offshoot of public schools' moving into the community and capitalizing on community resources, the community, in turn, is increasing its utilization of the schools and their resources. Many communities are initiating or expanding instructional programs for adults. In Bloomington, Illinois, for example, the public schools are continuing to expand an evening and weekend adult education program that began in 1948 and are currently offering upwards of 180 courses ranging from algebra to French, from auto mechanics to upholstering, and from swimming to bridge. Some of these courses are taught by certified teachers, but many are taught by lay persons who have acquired a great deal of expertise by virtue of their occupations.

Community education reaches beyond the secondary level. Many communities have a community college (usually a two-year institution specializing in business skills, vocational training, or general education), and many have two or more. The important point to keep in mind with respect to com-

---

[4]Dennis Sparks, "A Personal view of 'Alpha'," *Educational Leadership*, 32, no. 2, (November 1974), p. 131.
[5]Sharlene P. Hirsh, "Starting at the Top: Executive High School Internships," *Educational Leadership*, 32, No. 2 (November 1974), p. 112.

munity education is that teachers can expect to be called upon, at one time or another, to teach adults. Education is no longer seen simply as an activity for the young. More and more adults are continuing their educations, and teachers should seek to prepare themselves with that fact in mind.

Educational Parks

The concept of educational parks is directly analogous to industrial parks. By grouping together a number of different schools, such as elementary schools, junior high schools, and high schools, in a single geographic area, a school system may benefit in a number of ways. The schools, for example, can share a central and convenient warehouse, make more efficient use of centralized facilities such as libraries and athletic fields. and most important, take maximum advantage of the wealth of expertise that is available in such a large gathering of teachers.

Probably the best known of the educational parks now in existence is the Nova Educational Complex near Fort Lauderdale, Florida. The Nova Complex includes two elementary schools, a high school, a junior college, and a technological university. The Nova pattern is being followed in numerous cities, not only for the reasons already cited but also because such parks facilitate integration, and because they facilitate the building of a unified curriculum that has strong continuity from grade level to grade level and from school to school. Still further, educational parks make it possible for huge school systems to decentralize control by shifting authority and responsibility to smaller geographic areas—the areas served by the individual parks.

Schools-Within-a-School

At the same time that educators are considering increasing the size of schools and grouping them into educational parks, they are also considering ways of lessening the impersonalization that frequently accompanies bigness. One of the ways being used is the concept of *school-within-a-school*.

The schools-within-a-school idea is relatively simple. Each large school is divided into a number of sub-units frequently called "houses." Students are assigned to a particular house within a school and remain in that house throughout their stay at that school. The advantage to this plan is that even though a school might have thousands of students, those students would be divided into distinct groups, would frequently keep the same homerooms while they were in the school, and would be taught by a smaller cadre of teachers who would be more likely to know each student. In addition each house would have its own administration and record-keeping system.

The schools-within-a-school plan is being used in many school systems across the country with varying degrees of success. The Newton, Massachusetts, high school has used the system since 1959. In Newton each house has its own academic departments, with the exception of the science department, which is located entirely in one house to avoid duplicating expensive equipment.[6] The system seems to work well in Newton, and its teachers feel that the smaller size of the schools-within-a-school enables them to get to know students better and to meet their educational needs more effectively.

In the Bloomington, Illinois, school system, a junior high school of approximately eleven hundred students was divided into eight mini-schools in 1972. Most of the teachers in the school feel that the four seventh-grade and four eighth-grade mini-schools have enhanced the educational opportunities available at the school, and there are no immediate plans to go back to the more traditional organization.

The one major drawback to schools-within-a-school is that the plan does not necessarily cause teachers to vary the ways in which classes are conducted. Even though the school as a whole may undergo a significant reorganization, many teachers, rather than capitalizing on the reorganization by instituting new instructional patterns, find it just as convenient to conduct business as usual within their own rooms. To the extent that only the administration of the school is reorganized, the innovation's effectiveness is decreased.

Differentiated Staffing

In most school systems the function of all teachers is essentially the same (except for variations in grade level and subject area), and salaries are based on years of service and amount of education. Differentiated staffing operates so that the functions of teachers (and their compensation) are divided into four or five hierarchical categories, each level of which has a higher degree of responsibility than the preceding level.

Typical of differentiated staffing organizations is the one described by Dwight W. Allen.[7] This organization has four divisions beginning with associate teachers, and moving through staff teachers, senior teachers, to professors. The task of the associate teacher is primarily to engage in didactic instruction planned by the staff and senior teachers. The staff teachers are required to have academic credits beyond a bachelor's degree. They have a larger hand in planning for instruction and build upon the foundation es-

---

[6]Glenys G. Unruh and William M. Alexander, *Innovations in Secondary Education* (New York: Holt, Rinehart & Winston, 1970), p. 100.

[7]Dwight W. Allen, "A Differentiated Teaching Staff," in *Innovations in Education for the Seventies: Selected Readings*, ed. by Julia E. DeCarlo and Constant A. Madon (New York: Behavioral Publications, 1973), pp. 99-107.

tablished by the associate teachers. Because less of their time has to be spent teaching basic information, they can bring their higher degree of preparation to bear on the task of showing students subtle but important interrelationships among facts, and developing skills such as synthesis and evaluation. Because their planning responsibilities are greater than those of the associate teachers, their compensation is greater. Senior teachers have at least a master's degree, are responsible for developing self-instructional packages and other kinds of instructional materials, and have input concerning the concepts to be taught. The highest level of this particular system is occupied by the most highly prepared individuals, usually those with doctorates. It is their task to oversee the instructional program and to make long-range plans. They, like the senior teachers, conduct seminars and other instructional activities.

There are, of course, many other possible organizational schemes. Some of these schemes include student teachers and interns, and still others include teacher aids and other paraprofessionals. In all of the schemes, however, the intent is to divide the instructional tasks so that those individuals having the greatest responsibilities are also those individuals with the greatest academic preparation. Compensation is tied directly to responsibility and education.

While differentiated staffing holds much promise, it also contains problems. Most current teacher preparation programs, for example, do not prepare teachers for differentiated staffing. Even more important are problems such as precisely defining the specific responsibilities of staff members in each category and establishing a working relationship among all staff so a pecking order syndrome does not interfere with cooperative efforts.

Modular Scheduling

Modular scheduling is one of those innovations that are largely dependent on modern technology for successful implementation. Teachers have long known that having all class periods the same length is far from ideal. Lectures and discussions do not always take the same amounts of time, and science classes need a different length of time for discussing theories than for working in the laboratory. Recognizing the problem and being able to solve it economically, however, are two different things; but when computer technology was applied to the task of school scheduling, modular scheduling became practical.

When a school adopts a modular schedule, instead of dividing the school day into longer periods of equal length, it is divided into small blocks, or modules, that can be grouped to create time periods of varying lengths. Some classes may be thirty minutes long while others may be ninety minutes, and the same class might easily meet for different lengths of time on various days to facilitate various kinds of instructional activities.

The complexity of trying to arrange workable class schedules for hundreds of students within a modular scheduling framework is obvious, and without computer technology the task is usually too time-consuming to be practical. With the aid of computers, however, modular scheduling not only becomes practical, it may be highly desirable because it allows educators to use available time to maximum advantage.

Self-Paced Instruction

Few innovations have received as much attention as individualized instruction. Unfortunately, the term "individualized instruction" is something of a misnomer, because the kind of instruction referred to is seldom planned on the basis of careful diagnosis of the specific instructional needs of specific individuals, and it is seldom subject to continual modification on the basis of the individual's changing abilities. In fact, the tutorial approach implied by the term individualized instruction is almost totally at odds with the whole concept of mass education. What is usually meant by the term "individualized instruction" could more accurately be conveyed using the term "self-paced instruction."

Self-paced instruction is instruction in which all students go through essentially the same material to achieve the same objectives but do so at their own rates. Instead of having a whole class moving at the same pace (which is too slow for some and too fast for others), brighter students can move ahead more quickly and explore additional areas while the slower students can take the time they need to master the basic material.

Few people are opposed to the idea of individualized or self-paced instruction, but many are concerned that the problems involved with such approaches will be prohibitive. There are a number of ways to implement self-paced instructional programs, and some are discussed in more detail in chapter 9.

The use of self-instructional packages is rapidly growing as a means of implementing self-paced programs because teachers themselves can build them to help students achieve the particular objectives that will be emphasized in class. In chapter 7 multimedia instruction and computer-assisted instruction are discussed along with programmed instruction. All are ways to enable students to self-pace their learning, and all can become, with further development, ways to individualize instruction.

The "Systems" Approach

The "systems" approach is a way of looking at all or part of the instructional process in order to determine the best way to utilize all resources (personnel, time, facilities, materials, money, etc.) to achieve specific goals. The first step in the systems approach is specifying precise instructional objectives and ordering those objectives into a hierarchy of importance; the second step usually is deciding what portion of the available resources should be allocated to the achievement of each of the objectives; and the final step is deciding what methods and materials teachers will use to help students achieve the specified objectives. The key to the systems approach is the high degree of precision with which each step is spelled out and the willingness of the school system to bring to bear all available resources to achieve the desired ends. This contrasts strongly with more traditional approaches, in which individual teachers or small groups of teachers try to achieve less precisely defined objectives using much more limited resources (see chapter 9).

Many school systems that implement a systems approach in whole or in part often choose to implement one or more other innovative ideas at the same time. It is not unusual, for example, for a school to implement a modular schedule, differentiated staffing, or any of the other ideas already discussed, as part of their new approach. The point of using the systems approach is to focus all the resources of the school system on the achievement of specific objectives, and to use those resources most effectively and in concert.

An example of using the systems approach to solve a specific problem is the learning disabilities program in operation at Lincoln Community High School in Lincoln, Illinois. The educators at Lincoln found that a number of their students suffered from various learning disabilities such as perceptual handicaps and dyslexia. It was determined that these disabilities manifested themselves, at least in part, through poor reading skills, which, in turn, negatively affected the abilities of these students to learn English, math, social sciences, or any of the other academic subjects usually taught via textbooks. A systems approach was taken to solve the problem.

The Lincoln school system applied for and received Title III, ESEA funding for a multisensory approach to learning disabilities. The primary objective of the project was to "present the content of English, mathematics, and science to the secondary level learning disabled student through a variety of audio, visual, and kinesthetic instructional modalities that would bypass the students, reading deficits."[8]

Having established an overall goal, the teachers at Lincoln developed sets of precise instructional objectives for each of the subject areas to be taught. Utilizing all available resources in the school system and supplementing them with additional resources made possible by the Title III funding, the staff developed a series of self-instructional packages that used

[8]John Landis, Robert W. Jones, and Larry D. Kennedy, "Teaching the Learning Disabled Student: A Strategy for Learning at the Secondary Level," *Illinois Principal*, 5, no. 2 (December 1973), p. 14.

a wide variety of materials and media. Students were then guided in the use of the new materials and were allowed to move through the materials at their own pace. Frequent diagnostic, formative, and summative tests enabled staff members to monitor closely the progress of each student, and if and when a student overcame his or her difficulties he or she was returned to regular classes.

The systems approach at Lincoln was not a system-wide innovation for all students, but it did focus the resources of a whole school system on a particular problem, worked effectively toward the solution of that problem, and achieved a high degree of success.

Another example of the systems approach has been in operation since 1970 at Illinois State University. Called the "Professional Sequence," it is a program for preparing secondary school teachers. The Professional Sequence is one of the largest self-paced, competency-based teacher preparation programs in the country. During any given semester there are approximately twelve hundred students actively working in the program.

The decision to take a systems approach to teacher preparation rather than to continue with the traditional course offerings was made because both students and faculty were growing increasingly unhappy with the rigid structure of the courses and questioned their effectiveness. It was decided to build a new program that would (1) enable each student to learn at his or her own rate; (2) assure that each student would, in fact, demonstrate each required competence; (3) provide each student with accurate and continuous information concerning his or her learning progress; (4) avoid the duplication or omission of important content; (5) provide well-thought-out, unbiased evaluations; and (6) provide for more one-to-one interaction between faculty and students.

The system established to achieve the desired goals is centered around a series of self-instructional packages. This mode of instruction was selected because such packages seemed to provide the greatest potential for both self-pacing and self-determination of learning style. The format of the packages used in the Professional Sequence is very similar to the format described in chapter 9, and each is based on one or more precise instructional objectives.

Students are free to move through the Professional Sequence as quickly or as slowly as they wish. As they complete the suggested learning activities in each package, they demonstrate their competency by examination or by producing a product, teaching a lesson, or engaging in any other behavior specified in the objective(s). Successful completion of each package is monitored by a computerized record-keeping system, and students receive daily results on tests and papers and weekly accountings, through computer printout, of all work done up to that point.

For maximum efficiency any systems approach must be monitored continually, and the relationships between its various parts must be analyzed continually. In a program as large as the Professional Sequence, such monitoring and analysis would be difficult or impossible without the computer. In addition to grading objective tests and continually updating students' records, the computer is used to determine the success-to-recycling ratios of each of the packages, to keep track of student evaluations of each of the learning activities in the packages, to determine how many students earn how much credit in the program, to calculate and report grades automatically, and finally, to arrive at cost-effectiveness figures. In short, the computer helps the staff look at the program as a whole and determine how to modify it to make it more effective.

SUMMARY

This chapter has concerned itself with a number of innovative proposals that are currently being seriously considered and attempted by educators from coast to coast. Many of the innovations, such as precise instructional objectives, performance contracting, and educational vouchers, bear on the issue of making educators more accountable for their actions. Other ideas, such as alternative schools, community schools, schools-within-schools, differentiated staffing, and modular scheduling, relate to ways of using space, time, staff, and facilities. Still others, such as self-paced instruction and the systems approach, combine a number of innovations in an attempt to restructure basic educational patterns.

All of the proposals discussed in this chapter have been implemented, at least on a limited basis, and many are likely to be implemented on a large-scale basis in many schools throughout the country. While innovations are not put into large-scale use overnight or even over a year, it is to the advantage of teachers to be aware of the effect they will have on the teaching-learning process. Teachers who are aware of the strengths and weaknesses of proposed innovations will be able to discuss them intelligently and will be more able to adapt them to their own needs. Teachers who choose to remain uninformed may find themselves overwhelmed by the changes brought about when such proposals are implemented.

SELECTED READINGS

BEGGS, DAVID W., III, and EDWARD G. BUFFIE, eds., *Non-graded Schools in Action: Bold New Venture*. Bloomington, Ind.: Indiana University Press, 1967.

BREMER, JOHN, and MICHAEL VON MOSCHZISKER, *The School Without Walls.* New York: Holt, Rinehart, & Winston, 1971.

DeCARLO, JULIA E., and CONSTANT H. MADON, *Innovations in Education for the Seventies: Selected Readings.* New York: Behavioral Publications, 1973.

DEMPSEY, RICHARD A., *Differentiated Staffing.* Englewood Cliffs, N.J.: Prentice-Hall, 1972.

FABUN, DON, *The Dynamics of Change.* Englewood Cliffs, N.J.: Prentice-Hall, 1967.

FRYMIER, JACK, *Fostering Educational Change.* Columbus, Ohio: Charles E. Merrill, 1969.

GLATTHORN, ALLAN A., *Alternatives In Education.* New York: Dodd, Mead 1975.

GOODLAD, JOHN I., JOHN F. O'TOOLE, Jr., and LOUISE L. TYLER, *Computers and Information Systems in Education.* New York: Harcourt, Brace and World, 1966.

HUSSAIN, KHATEEB M., *Development of Information Systems for Education.* Englewood Cliffs, N.J.: Prentice-Hall, 1973.

JOYCE, BRUCE R., *Man, Media, and Machines: The Teacher and His Staff.* Washington, D.C.: National Education Association, 1967.

WITTROCK, M. C., ed., *Changing Education: Alternatives From Educational Research.* Englewood Cliffs, N.J.: Prentice-Hall, 1973.

14

Improving Continuously as a Teacher

student learning as a criterion
for good teaching

This chapter examines the use of the Logical Instructional Model as a procedure for aiding in continuous self-improvement as a teacher. One of the problems that have confounded educators over the past century has been the difficulty of defining a good teacher. In terms of the measurement specialist, the problem is one of predictive or statistical validity. It seems at first glance that if precise characteristics of a good teacher could be developed, then measures could also be built that would correlate highly with those characteristics. In this way it could be predicted who would be a good teacher and who would not. Carrying this premise to its logical conclusion, it should be possible to sort teacher applicants so that only those with a high probability of becoming successful teachers would be admitted to teacher training.

Why is it so difficult to predict teacher success? Because it has never been determined what qualities are necessary in the makeup of an ideal teacher. All students have had teachers they considered especially good or bad. Often students will have a teacher they do not like but from whom they learn a lot. In other instances students may have a lot of fun in a class and like a teacher a good deal but know deep down that they haven't learned much.

Some teachers use very few teaching procedures but use them with tremendous polish and skill and achieve excellent results. For instance, it is not uncommon for students to feel constantly uncomfortable in certain teachers' classes because the teacher uses higher-order probing questions within a discussion format; in such a setting no student feels safe from the continuous barrage of questions. Only one technique is being used, but it can be a mind-bending experience. The amount of learning that can occur is maximized, and this type of teacher usually commands *respect*. In a vote by students this type of instructor may rank low in popularity, but students' perception of the amount they have learned may be high. This example, however, is an exception to the general rule. For the most part students learn best from teachers they like. It is a well-known fact that teachers who are enthusiastic about their subject are often able to generate more learning. When asked what subject they liked best, students often link their answers to a class in which they enjoyed the teacher.

Where does this lead in the search for criteria by which to judge a good teacher? The considerations that currently receive the most attention cannot be deemed all-inclusive. It is perfectly appropriate to expect the teacher to fulfill an obligation to the operation of the school. How teachers handle such responsibilities as turning in reports on time, taking a turn at noon patrol duty, keeping the room ventilated and papers off the floor, attending PTA meetings, and maintaining a professional appearance, must be taken into account when judging the teacher. Certainly an examination of teaching methods used is also important. But in the view of many people, the most crucial consideration is *whether the teacher can teach as demonstrated by the performance of his or her students*.

In today's schools the move toward accountability is placing increasing pressure upon educators to provide proof that the teacher can teach, as judged by student performance. A study by James Popham lends credence to the supposition that educators have assumed teachers can be held accountable for students' progress without being able to show that those teachers were able to demonstrably increase their students' abilities.

Popham first recalls the research of Morsh and Wilder[1] in 1954, which indicated that no single teaching act had been discovered that was invariably associated with learner achievement, and then goes on to point out that as educators:

> We should have first focused our efforts on identifying teachers who could produce superior growth in learners, leaving aside for the moment the question of how such improvements were brought about. If one can identify satisfactory

---

[1] Joseph Morsh and Eleanor Wilder, "Identifying the Effective Instructor: A Review of the Quantitative Studies, 1900-1952," Research Bulletin AFPTRC-T-54-44.

measures of pupil attainment, then the next step is to identify the complicated procedures by which such achievements are attained. It is important to emphasize the complexity of this task, for the undoubted reason that such reviewers as Morsh find few descriptions of 'good teaching procedures' is that effective instruction represents a series of subtle interactions among a given teacher, his particular students, the instructional goals he is attempting to achieve, and the instructional environment.[2]

Popham attempted to validate performance tests of teaching skills in the fields of social science, auto mechanics, and electronics, in which the quality of the teacher could be judged by

his ability to bring about prespecified behavior changes in learners. In each case, the performance of experienced, certified teachers was contrasted with the performance of individuals who were not trained to be teachers or who possessed no prior teaching experience. *In none of the three contrasts did teachers significantly out-perform nonteachers.*[3] [Emphasis our own.]

This study means, of course, that the experienced, certified teachers were not able to out-teach a group of inexperienced, uncertified lay people as judged by student performance measured in numbers that were statistically significant. Yet the certified teachers were hired and retained after being judged competent. How is this possible? Because their competence was judged according to factors *other than the actual learning of students.*

How can a teacher be assured that he or she can teach so that students will learn and so that his or her own teaching ability will continually be improving? One answer may be found in using the Logical Instructional Model as a device to check teaching ability and to validate new techniques and teaching tools for an expanding repertoire of teaching skills.

OBJECTIVES

The student will:

1. When asked a series of eight oral questions about the application of the Logical Instructional Model to improve teaching as judged by student learning, answer at least seven correctly. (Knowledge; Comprehension)
2. Using a self-constructed lesson plan and the principles delineated in this chapter, teach a lesson and ascertain if the techniques used were acceptable or not as judged by student learning. (Application)
3. When provided with three peer evaluations of the lesson taught, cite, in writing, at least three similarities and three differences between those evaluations, and link those commonalities with the lesson, so as to suggest

[2]James W. Popham, "Performance Tests of Teaching Proficiency: Rationale, Development and Validation," *American Educational Research Journal*, 8 (January 1971), p. 106.
[3]Popham, "Performance Tests," p. v.

at least three modifications in the lesson that could increase student learning. (Analysis)

4. After review of all materials gathered in conjunction with the self-improvement lesson, synthesize and teach a second lesson on the same topic to a second set of youngsters or peers on a similar topic incorporating the changes delineated in his or her analysis. (Synthesis)

5. After teaching the second lesson and considering the amount of student learning resulting from that lesson, judge whether the techniques utilized in that lesson were effective or ineffective for his or her teaching personality, and give four rationales for this judgment. (Evaluation)

CRITERIA FOR JUDGING A SELF-IMPROVEMENT MODEL

If a model for continuous self-improvement is to be presented and learned, then it would seem appropriate that the model meet certain criteria. Criteria that would be applicable to such a model are given here.

1. The model must be practical enough to be used by teachers during the course of their work without a large amount of troublesome manipulation.
2. There must be sound philosophical and empirical evidence to support the ideas delineated in the model.
3. The details and complexity of the model must be such that it can be learned and practiced with a minimum of effort.
4. The model should be compatible with any analysis techniques for the teaching-learning act available to the teacher.

After presentation of the model, these criteria will be examined to assess how the model meets them.

THE STEPS OF THE SELF-IMPROVEMENT MODEL

This approach is based on the Logical Instructional Model applied to a short-term situation. That is, the steps of the Logical Instructional Model are used within a short time period to minimize extraneous variables that would keep the teacher from inferring that teaching efforts are the cause of student learning.

Step 1: Objectives

The initial step in this procedure involves the identification of a portion of a class unit that can be taught in one class period or less. For this piece of content, one or two behaviorally stated objectives are constructed. The objectives will be based on the principles discussed in chapter 3 and should contain (1) a precise terminal behavior, (2) the conditions under which that behavior will be demonstrated, and (3) a minimum acceptable standard for that behavior.

An eighth-grade general mathematics class studying the topic of the area of circles is used here to illustrate the model. The teacher has determined that the students should not only be able to apply the formula $A = \pi r^2$, but also understand why the formula, when used, yields the area of a circle. The behavioral objectives constructed for this purpose result in these statements:

> Given a circle drawn on a piece of paper and a ruler, the student will be able to find its radius and use it in the formula $A = \pi r^2$ to determine, in writing, the area of the circle within .5 square inches.

> Under test conditions, the student will be able to write an explanation in mathematical symbols and in his or her own words that logically shows why a proper application of the formula $A = \pi r^2$ yields the area of a circle.

Behavioral objectives for the self-improvement lesson have now been constructed and the second step is in order.

Step 2: Preassessment

If a teacher is to determine whether a particular teaching technique being checked in this lesson is effective, it will be useless to teach the lesson to a class that already possesses the skills and concepts. Nothing about teaching ability would be discerned. Similarly, it would be impossible to ascertain teaching skills if the students in class did not have the necessary prerequisite abilities to understand the lesson.

In terms of our example, if during the prior year the students received excellent instruction in finding the area of circles and the basis for the formula $A = \pi r^2$, and if they have retained that knowledge, the teacher would be deluded about his or her teaching ability because all that would be taught would be a review lesson. If, on the other hand, the students have not yet grasped the concept of area measure as differentiated from linear measure, preliminary material must be taught before the lesson can be continued. Therefore, the teacher must preassess the students. It would be possible, for instance, to ask the students to perform the tasks called for in the objectives on the day before the self-improvement lesson. This straightforward approach is often the most economical and convenient. The teacher could also delineate all the *prerequisite abilities* necessary for achieving the objective and conduct a preassessment over only those abilities, if the teacher already knows in some way that none of the students can perform the terminal behavior.

It may be, on occasion, that the material and objectives in the lesson are new or obscure enough for the teacher to feel certain that the new topic is fresh material. For instance, in a mathematics class, the teacher may know that the concepts behind the formula $A = \pi r^2$ are all new because the prerequisites taught in prior lessons were new. Or, in a U.S. history class studying the lifestyles of certain Midwestern Indian tribes is likely to be a big enough change from the normal curriculum that the teacher could take a chance on its acceptability for a self-improvement lesson. In its purest form, a lesson intended for self-improvement purposes should be an artificial lesson that needs no preassessment.

To reiterate, the teacher must make sure in some way that the students to whom the lesson is going to be taught (1) have the necessary ability to comprehend the lesson, and (2) cannot already demonstrate the competence in the objective.

In our example the teacher could administer what will become the final evaluation for the self-improvement lesson the day before the actual lesson. From this check it is determined that two students out of the class of thirty already have the necessary abilities, and four students lack certain prerequisites. Tutorial lessons for these remedial students could then be designed for use in a corner of the room. The students who already have the skills could tutor the students who do not have the prerequisites, while the self-improvement lesson is going on. If this arrangement is not satisfactory for some reason, then an alternate administrative procedure could be constructed. Perhaps the advanced students can be dispatched to the library for some meaningful activity, and the remedial students given self-instructional packages on the prerequisite skills. Or, all the students could be included in the lesson, but not all evaluations would be included for self-improvement purposes. There are many possibilities available, not the least of which is an appeal for help to school administrators who are usually receptive to creative ideas for improvement in teaching.

In some fashion, then, the teacher should be able to arrange to teach only those students who qualify for the self-improvement lesson after preassessment and sorting.

Step 3: Learning Activities

The next step is the actual teaching. It is assumed that at this point the teacher is attempting to try out a new teaching technique to see if it is effective. Or it may be that an old technique is going to be reexamined, perhaps because videotaping equipment is available for self-analysis. If peers are willing to attend a class session, observe, and tell what they felt were good or bad points in the lesson, this possibility may inspire the use of the self-improvement model.

It is, of course, in light of a successful or unsuccessful lesson (as defined by the degree to which students achieve the objective) that the use of techniques for analyzing teacher behavior make the most sense. Several teacher-student interaction analysis techniques provide useful feedback to teachers using a self-improvement model. Once the lesson has been determined to have been effective or ineffective, it becomes meaningful to analyze the behavior of the teacher in terms of the lesson. Probably the best-known analysis technique for studying styles of student-teacher interaction is the approach of Edmund I. Amidon and Ned A. Flanders.[4] A teacher may wish to use their categories for analyzing and adjusting teacher classroom behavior. When coupled with knowledge as to whether the pupils' learning resulted from the behavior, the analysis becomes much more powerful.

Another approach to analyzing teacher behavior was developed at Hofstra University and later at California State College at Hayward. Greta Morine, Robert Spaulding, and Selma Greenberg have produced a self-instructional book that teachers can use to learn their system. Answers follow practice excercises "so that the student gets rapid feedback as to the accuracy of his responses while learning the category system. Sample lessons are transcripts of actual dialogues recorded in lessons taught by student teachers and master teachers. They include lessons at both the elementary and secondary levels."[5]

There are other analysis techniques available, but the analysis is best evaluated after determining if the student can achieve the objectives of the lesson.

It would seem redundant at this point to review the countless possibilities and techniques for building lessons. The reader is referred to previous chapters for ideas and procedures to augment existing skills. It is hoped that the strategies employed to maximize learning during self-improvement sessions will creatively encompass a wide range of teaching techniques and procedural possibilities. It is only after extensive checking, improvement, and rejection that teachers will begin to approach their potential.

The instructional intent of this example self-improvement lesson was to move the student to the point where he or she would be able to compute the area of a circle within .5 square inches when supplied with a ruler, and to explain why a proper application of the formula $A = \pi r^2$ yields the area of a circle. Perhaps the technique that the teacher wishes to investigate is an interaction approach whereby the teacher is going to lead the students through the lesson utilizing an overhead projector and a series of questions and cues. This would seem to be an appropriate teaching procedure to check out if the primary mode of instruction had, in the past, been a chalkboard

[4]Edmund J. Amidon and Ned A. Flanders, *The Role of the Teacher in the Classroom* (Minneapolis, Minn: Association for Productive Teaching, 1967).
[5]Greta Morine, Robert Spaulding, and Selma Greenberg, *Discovering New Dimensions in the Teaching Process* (Scranton: International Testbook, 1971), p. vi.

demonstration for each new math lesson. This lesson can be based on intuitive notions about the relationships of triangles and circles and the number of diameters that could be placed around the circumference of a circle.

It might be determined that this lesson could be augmented through the use of realia. String and round objects can be used by the students to help establish the relationship between diameter and circumference. References to the problems of determining exact values can be brought into the discussion. In planning, the teacher can prepare an extensive list of the types of questions that would be most useful during the lesson.

After various ideas are "discovered" by the class, short periods of equivalent and analogous practice can be built into the lesson. Students could work at the chalkboard during practice sessions. Whatever process is chosen, the lesson should be carefully planned and the teacher should attempt to maximize learning using the new approaches he or she has worked out.

Step 4: Evaluation

The final step in the self-improvement model is to determine immediately whether or not the lesson's objectives were achieved. In this case the argument that one can not assess what the teacher has accomplished in terms of student learning because of outside influences and other variables too hard to control must be obviated by speed. Since there has been a preassessment of the students' knowledge, there has been a control for prior learning; but the evaluation should not be delayed because of the possibility of biased results due to extraneous variables.

The evaluation must accurately reflect the objectives. If there are discrepancies between the skill as described in the objective, taught in the lesson, and checked in the evaluation, the teacher will be making assumptions about his or her teaching based on erroneous data. If the lesson was a concept lesson in which the students were to remember and relate information as demonstrated by passing a twenty-point completion test, then the test must be administered. If the objective was to be able to set a table in a certain way in home economics, then the students must set that table. If the students were to be able to distinguish fact from opinion in editorials, then they must be provided with an editorial and do such distinguishing.

An additional variable that will effect self-improvement strategies is student ability. One of the important attributes of professional teachers is their ability to assess the existing learning characteristics of students. Just as important as subject-matter skill is the skill of being able to "read" the range of students' speed and pacing as lessons are taught. If the students are above or below average in ability, this fact, of course, is of paramount importance in the choice of style and approach in planning. In addition, this information relates to the evaluation process in self-improvement lessons. The teacher must use professional judgment in deciding on a class criterion level; that is, teacher should ask himself or herself the question, "What percent of the class must be able to demonstrate successfully the minimum standard in the evaluation before I will be satisfied?" In order to set this standard—by which the teacher will judge whether the lesson was acceptable or unacceptable—the ability of the students and the degree of lesson difficulty should be taken into consideration.

The teacher must be realistic as well as rigorous in this estimate, and as the teaching skill improves, the standards should be raised. Initially the teacher may be disappointed, but he or she must not let this disappointment dissuade him or her from use of the model.

For our sample lesson, the evaluation became apparent as soon as the objective had been clearly formulated. At the completion of the lesson, the students will need a sheet of paper with one or more circles on it, a ruler, and paper to compute the area of the circles and to explain why the formula yields the area of a circle. No other evaluation would be entirely acceptable. True, it would be possible to check student understanding by developing a list of multiple-choice questions that cover the content area comprehensively; and it could then be assumed that if these questions were correctly answered, the student could explain the desired content. No matter how much time this saves in teacher correction, if it is not an exact check of the behavior asked for in the objective, it is a step away from preciseness and adds an element of danger in the teacher's intention to improve.

For purposes of the model lesson, the teacher carefully analyzes the lesson and class abilities, and decides that for this initial lesson he or she will be satisfied if eighteen out of the twenty-four students who participate in the lesson can demonstrate minimum competency. (Of the thirty original students, two have prior ability and four need to accomplish prerequisite tasks.) This class criterion level is a product of thought and is, in the teacher's opinion, realistic and attainable, but will be challenging. If attained, it should yield some sense of pride of accomplishment. If not, it will point the way for analysis and attempts to improve and modify techniques.

Evaluating the Model

At the outset of this chapter certain criteria were structured that could be used to judge whether the model for self-improvement had value. We will repeat them here in essence.

1. The model should be practical enough to be used by teachers in their ongoing programs without much change in their regular work.

2. There must be sound philosophical and empirical evidence to support the ideas delineated in the model.
3. The degree of complexity and difficulty of the model must be such that the model can easily be understood and implemented.
4. If the teacher has access to any teacher analysis techniques, the model must be able to accommodate them.

First, is the·model practical enough to be used by the teacher without much disruption to classes? The planning of objectives, preassessment, learning activities, and evaluation are all activities that take place in classrooms routinely. None should disrupt the normal flow of classroom activities. The model insists that there be a preassessment to determine whether the students already have the skills necessary to perform the objective. It is after preassessment, when the teacher must sort out those students who already possess the skills in the objective or who are not ready for the objective, that there may be some administrative difficulty.

The logistical problem of sorting may be solved in a number of ways, some of which have been alluded to earlier. The easiest way, of course, is simply to include in the lesson students who are not ready for it, and hope something rubs off; and students who already possess the skills, and hope the boredom is tolerable. Even though it is common knowledge that this kind of teaching goes on in classrooms all over the country every day, once preassessment has been used, this attitude grates on one's professional integrity.

A process that avoids the preassessment problem entirely is to use only those lessons for self-improvement that the teacher has determined will be completely unfamiliar to all students, and at the same time require little prior skill in en-route objectives. Such lessons may be difficult to find for some classes (mathematics), but can be found easily for others (geography).

Another way to avoid having to preassess the class is to design and teach artificial lessons. These are lessons, designed by the teacher, that do not fit into the regular ongoing curriculum content and include facts, materials, or work that either is very obscure or has been created by the teacher. These short lessons, which can be conducted in a game-like atmosphere, have been proven effective. One such lesson, entitled "Ancient Classification Systems," is presented in Appendix C, as an example. This type of lesson fits best after the conclusion of one topic or unit and before the beginning of another, so as not to destroy the continuity of the content normally presented in class.

If it is determined that the students should be sorted before the self-improvement lesson, then the teacher should find a device that best fits his or her needs. Among previously mentioned procedures are the assignment of special projects in the library and tutoring sessions in which students who already possess the skills help students who need to review prerequisite tasks. Often it is possible to teach a small group while the rest of the students are engaged in a different activity. For instance, a film may be used to cover certain prerequisite skills for some students while the majority of the class is being taught the self-improvement lesson. Similarly, part of the class can cover advanced or prerequisite skills using self-instructional packages.

If the teacher is in a school that is using a modular schedule that includes student free time, it may be possible to obtain volunteer students for short self-improvement sessions. During mutually open teacher and student time, students may be trained not only to learn the content so that the model is viable but also to offer helpful ideas about the lesson.

If the teacher can work with several peers toward the goal of self-improvement, the building administrator will often be ready to assist in manipulating circumstances so that a team of teachers can work together to help each other through analysis, feedback, covering each other's classes, and working out other organizational details.

Examination of the first criterion presented, in relation to the self-improvement model, makes it apparent that it would be possible to use self-improvement lessons in a way that would cause a minimum of disruption. However, the potential of the model and professional commitment could lead to a wide variety of manipulative steps in order to maximize self-improvement even if those steps were somewhat disruptive to the ongoing program. The ultimate improvement in teaching must be weighed against this potential disruption to achieve a tolerable balance.

The second criterion asserts that a proposed self-improvement model must be based on a sound theoretical, philosophical, and empirical base. Although this criterion seems to invite it, the temptation is resisted here to review the extensive research that has gone on and is going on about a competency-based teaching approach. That there is a continual increase in the quality and quantity of research in this area is supported by the many papers and reports published in the professional journals over the past several years as part of a continued dialogue.

There is also evidence to support the notion that when teachers work to improve their own skills using analysis techniques, their behavior is more easily modified. It seems logical to assume that if those modifications are painted against a backdrop of success as demonstrated by pupil achievement, modifications that will serve the teacher best will be adopted.

It also seems apparent that teachers who for one reason or another reject the notions of behavioral objectives as a part of their ongoing programs could accept the idea for purposes of self-improvement. That is, if the commonly raised objections to the use of behavioral objectives seem to be persuasive to the teacher, there is still no reason why the teacher cannot use the Logical Instructional Model for self-improvement purposes. Of course, the authors feel that once the Logical Instructional Model is used for this purpose, the teacher may see its benefits and incorporate more of its notions into his or her regular program.

The third criterion is that the self-improvement model must be simple enough to be understood and used by teachers without extensive training. The Logical Instructional Model is easily understood, as are the basic psychological principles upon which it stands and also generates. The skills necessary to construct solid, precisely written objectives, however, are not developed without the expense of study and effort. The payoff is most definitely worth the effort, but it must be admitted, candidly, that there is no overnight solution to producing outstanding precise instructional objective writers.

For those teachers who can successfully write precise instructional objectives, there is no reason that the self-improvement instructional model cannot be utilized immediately. The procedures and practice excercises in chapter 3 can be used to polish the ability to write objectives to the point where the teacher could successfully generate the necessary objectives to use the model package.

Those individuals who do not yet possess the skills necessary to build precise instructional objectives are encouraged to build such skills. If it happens, however, that an active use of the self-instructional model is inhibited by a teacher's own inability to generate behavioral objectives, alternate procedures are suggested. First, in most school districts there are staff members who possess the skills needed to construct viable precise instructional objectives for self-improvement purposes. Teachers without this skill should be able to avail themselves of these staff members' services. In many larger districts there are curriculum specialists who are more than willing to engage in this type of help. A second possibility is to build a lesson around a precise instructional objective that has been selected from preconstructed lists. Sources for some of these lists are included in Appendix A. These objectives are usually in the form of terminal behaviors and leave the criterion level and conditions to the teacher; therefore they still take some work on the part of the teacher.

It is the authors' opinion, then, that the third criterion, when applied to the self-improvement model, reveals the weakness of being dependent for success upon the teacher's skill in writing precise instructional objectives. The other factors in the model, such as building learning activities, evaluation construction, are a usual part of the typical teacher's skills. Suggestions to make the model work in spite of this problem might therefore include seeking help to write the objectives, or using pre-prepared terminal behaviors. Analysis of the criteria so far as they apply to the model has revealed a problem, but not an insurmountable one.

The last criterion applied to the model for self-improvement insists that the model allow the teacher to use any already acquired analysis techniques.

In prior discussion it has been pointed out that this criterion is one of the strengths of the model. Any analysis techniques are appropriate. Knowing whether the lesson was a success or not in terms of student learning amplifies and clarifies any analysis.

SUMMARY

The steps necessary to make the model work are reviewed here.

1. The teacher first builds one or two precise instructional objectives that can be attained by students within a single class period or less. It is best if the content and objectives for the lesson are some relatively simple concepts or analysis skills, although a low-cognitive-level fact-oriented lesson, or a high-cognitive-level synthesis- or evaluation-oriented lesson will also work.

2. A preassessment is essential. The model is worthless if it has not been predetermined whether or not the students already possess the skills to be taught in the lesson. The teacher must either use devices to sort the students, or the evaluations of the students who already had the skill and those who did not possess the necessary prerequisites must be ignored.

3. The teacher will have some specific teaching skill or technique that he or she wishes to examine for its ability to inspire student learning. Here is the heart of the teaching strategy. There is no point in setting up the procedure to run through a technique in which the teacher is already highly proficient.

4. The teacher uses professional judgment to set a minimum level for acceptable class performance. The minimum satisfactory number of students who can perform the skill after the lesson must be established. The lesson is then taught by the teacher using whatever strategies and skills he or she has developed for the lesson.

5. Immediately upon completion of the lesson the students are evaluated. This evaluation is a direct reflection of the objectives and it checks the students' newly acquired skill level.

6. Against the background of success as measured by student learning, any analysis techniques can now be used that focus on teacher behavior. This freedom in the selection of analysis techniques is especially meaningful over several lessons as similarities in teacher behaviors used during successful lessons unerringly point to the techniques that are most successful for a particular teaching personality. Similarly, unsuccessful lessons can be analyzed for teacher behaviors that differed from behaviors in successful lessons. Even unskilled observers can take note of such things as a teacher's unconsciously allowing variances in the amount of time for different students to answer, calling on only a few students or failing to provide reinforcement for correct student responses.

The idea that all teachers are highly motivated to improve their effectiveness may or may not be true. There is little doubt, however, that teachers who utilize a self-improvement model are doing more than paying lip-service to the idea of improvement—they are taking concrete steps to become better teachers.

SELECTED READINGS

ALLEN, PAUL, et al., *Teacher Self-Appraisal, A Way of Looking Over Your Own Shoulder*. Worthington, Ohio: Charles A. Jones, 1970.

AMIDON, EDMUND J., and NED A. FLANDERS, *The Role of the Teacher in the Classroom*. Minneapolis, Minn.: Association for Productive Teaching, 1967.

AMIDON, EDMUND J., and JOHN B. HOUGH, *Interaction Analysis: Theory, Research, and Application*. Reading, Mass.: Addison-Wesley, 1967.

AMIDON, EDMUND J., and ELIZABETH HUNDER, *Improving Teaching: The Analysis of Classroom Verbal Interaction*. New York: Holt, Rinehart, & Winston, 1966.

CHRISTINE, CHARLES T., and DOROTHY W. CHRISTINE, *Practical Guide to Curriculum and Instruction*. West Nyack, N.Y.: Parker, 1971.

EMMER, EDMUND T., and Gregg Millett, *Improving Teaching Through Experimentation—A Laboratory Approach*. Englewood Cliffs, N.J.: Prentice-Hall, 1970.

MORINE, GRETA, ROBERT SPAULDING, and SELMA GREENBERG, *Discovering New Dimensions in the Teaching Process*. Scranton, Pa.: International Textbook, 1971.

POPHAM, JAMES W., and EVA L. BAKER, *Evaluating Instruction*. Englewood Cliffs, N.J.: Prentice-Hall, 1973.

Appendix A

Sources for Precise
Instructional Objectives

The CO-OP Center of Educational Research
University of Massachusetts
Amherst, Mass. 01002

Deer Creek-Mackinaw District 701
Mr. Virgil M. Jacobs, Superintendent
Mackinaw, Ill. 61755

Florida Center for (Competency-Based) Teacher Training Materials
William Spino, Director
College of Education
University of Miami
Miami, Fla. 33100

Institute for Educational Research
1400 W. Maple Ave.
Downers Grove, Ill. 60515

Instructional Objectives Exchange
Box 24095
Los Angeles, Calif. 90024

IPPES
Jackson Public Schools
1400 W. Monroe
Jackson, Mich. 49202

National Evaluation System, Inc.
P.O. Box 226-p
Amherst, Mass. 01002

Oakleaf Elementary School
Mathematics Continuum (and)
Behavioral Objectives for Reading
Baldwin-Whitehall School District
Pittsburgh, Penn. 15200

Professional Sequence
Pre-Service Secondary Teacher Education
Department of Curriculum and Instruction
Illinois State University
Normal, Ill. 61761

Project Spoke
Mr. John A. Stefani
37 W. Main St.
Norton, Mass. 02766

VAE Pre-Certification Teacher Education Program:
Competencies and Performance Objectives
Department of Vocational and Applied Arts Education
College of Education
Wayne State University
Detroit, Mich. 48202

Also available:

John Flanagan, William Shanner, and Robert Mager, *Behavioral Objectives*, vols. I,
II, III, and IV (Palo Alto, Calif.: Westinghouse Learning Press, 1971)

Appendix B

Sample Unit Plan

I. Introduction

  A. *Course*: Home Economics

  B. *Target Population*: 11th Grade—Average Students

  C. *Title*: Housing and Home Furnishings—Color and Design

  D. *Overview*: "Color and Design" is intended to prepare students with terminology, concepts, and principles involving color and design as used in furnishing a home. This unit will be preceded by "Buying, Building, Renting," a unit concerned with the living, working, and storage space considerations crucial to decisions about buying, building, or renting shelter; and it will be followed by "Furniture Styles and Accessories," a unit that concerns fabrics, textures, color harmonies, wall arrangements, furniture styles, accessories, and floor coverings.

  E. *Length of Time:* About two weeks

*This unit plan was conceived by Linda Kruger.

II. Unit Objectives

At the completion of this unit each student will:

A. Write the definition of, and cite an example of, each of the following terms and phrases: *the four elements of design; hue; value; tint; shade; intensity; warm and cool colors; primary, secondary, and intermediate colors; Prang and Munsell Color Charts; structural and decorative design; five principles of design; monochromatic; analogous; contrasting; complementary; split-complementary; triad; and accented-neutral harmonies.*

B. Given three pictures of completely furnished rooms, identify the line direction in each room and state, in writing, the mood that the line direction suggests.

C. Given five colored pictures of furnished rooms, label, in writing, the color scheme as being predominantly warm or cool; identify the hues, value, and intensity of the main color being used; and classify the color as being a primary, secondary, or intermediate color.

D. Given two color charts, label each, in writing, as being either a Prang or a Munsell chart, and cite at least one reason for your choice.

E. Given a colored picture of a furnished room, list, in writing, examples of each of the four elements of design (line, form, color, texture), and cite one factor that helped you decide which element it represented.

F. Given two pictures of the same room with identical furniture but different arrangements, identify the picture with the best arrangement using rhythm, proportion, and balance and guides, and write four reasons why the other picture exemplifies a less desirable arrangement.

G. Given a list of colors (black, red, yellow, white, blue, green, gray, brown, and purple), list, in writing, at least two symbolic meanings and/or ideas associated with each color.

H. Given diagrams of seven different types of color harmonies, correctly label each diagram as to type.

III. Content

A. Introduction: Beauty of Design (lecture) (transparencies)

1. Satisfaction in the home
2. Reactions to surroundings
3. Causes of good or bad impressions
   a. Elements of design
   b. Room planned as whole

4. Good taste
   Harmony of color and design
(Materials and procedure: Using pictorial examples mounted on construction paper, show examples of the above items, along with examples of different types of rooms to introduce the topic color and design. Show different room arrangements, color schemes, and moods of rooms.)

B. Elements of design (lecture) (transparencies)
   1. The live-basic element of beauty
      a. Psychological effects
         vertical—carries eyes upward; masculine in effect; severe, strong; creates feeling of height (for example, doorways, draperies, etc.)
         horizontal—solidity, repose, tranquility; breaks effect of vertical lines (for example, cornices, bookcases, baseboards, low tables)
         diagonal—action, forward push (for example, staircases, diagonal line in fabrics or wallpaper)
         curved—feminine in effect; graceful, subtle, gay (for example, tied back curtains, arches, curves in furniture)
         zig zag—movement-excitement
(Materials and procedure: After correlating pictorial examples with the lecture, show the different psychological effects that line can create. Use a self-prepared transparency. Discuss.)
   2. Form (shape)
      a. Created by three dimensions
      b. Line that encloses space
         curved—oval; dome; circular; rounded
         straight—square; rectangle; oblong shapes
   3. Texture
      a. Suggests fabric
         roughness vs. smoothness
         shininess vs. dullness
         softness vs. stiffness
      b. Wall finish; rugs; woodwork; wood in furniture
      c. Must go with style and use of object
(Materials and procedure: Show examples of upholstery fabrics to clarify texture. Discuss)
   4. Color and qualities of color
      a. *Hue*—name of color, family name
      b. *Value*, or amount of lightness or darkness in a color

> *tint*—light or high values (good wall colors)
> *shade*—dark or low values (good rug colors)

c. *Intensity*—brightness or dullness of color
d. Properties of temperature and force
   warm colors—convey feeling of warmth; seem to advance; make room appear smaller (yellow, red orange)
   cool colors—convey feeling of coolness; seem to recede; create illusion of space (blue, green)
e. classifications of color
   primary colors—cannot be broken down into other colors, and no combination of other colors can produce them (red, yellow, blue)
   secondary colors—mix two primary colors (orange, violet, green)
   intermediate colors—mix primary color with adjacent secondary color (yellow-green, blue-green, etc.)
f. Color charts
   Prang—traditional; three primary colors: red, yellow, blue
   Munsell—five principal colors: red, yellow, blue, green, purple

(Materials and procedure: Devise a flash card game using words and phrases involved with color terminology. This can be used for review as well as for evaluations. The students will seat themselves in a semicircle. Stand in the middle with the flash cards. When the teacher holds the cards up, the first student to raise his or her hand answers the questions involved. The answer appears on the reverse side of the card; it may, therefore, also be used for individual review. The students will bring into class three examples of rooms furnished with cool colors. From these pictures the class will choose the best examples of warm and cool colors used in room decorating and create a bulletin board.

Before proceeding to new material, the students will be involved in a group discussion. The students will form into small groups. Each group will be appointed a specific element of design for which they will find pictorial examples to best describe that element. One member from each group will present the groups' element and explain how and why they chose that picture to represent their element. Discuss.)

C. Classification of Design (lecture) (transparencies)

   1. *Structural*—good line, form, texture, and color as a result of the way something is made; functionalism—design concentrating on a function; keynote for modern furniture

   2. *Decorative*—starts where structural ends. Styles are:
      naturalistic—something in nature
      conventional—stenciled design on wallpaper, fabrics, and rugs
      abstract—plaids, dots, stripes, checks, or geometric patterns

(Materials and procedure: Use pictorial examples of above to correlate with lecture to clarify further. Students will choose, out of five pictures, the furniture that is structural and the furniture that is decorative. Give the factors that enabled them to classify them structural or decorative. After discussion and clarification, ask the students to bring in an example of each for the next class period. Discuss.)

D. Principles of Design (lecture) (transparencies)

1. *Proportion*—space divisions pleasingly related to each other and the whole

2. *Balance*—even: formal or symmetric; equal distance uneven: informal or asymmetric; one closer to center to balance one heavy and one light object

3. *Rhythm*—movement of eye as it follows line
   repetition: repeating shapes, sizes, lines, or colors
   gradation: progression in sizes
   opposition: lines come together at right angles
   transition: carries eye gradually from one place to another

4. *Emphasis*—eliminating competition creates center of attention

5. *Unity*—harmony: elements brought together as connected whole; sizes, shapes, textures, colors, and ideas related

(Materials and procedures: After a lecture correlated with pictorial examples, attention will be focused on the bulletin board. There will be a separate heading for proportion, balance, rhythm, emphasis, and unity on the bulletin board. Working individually the class will analyze pictures brought into class. Then as one group the class will decide on the three best examples of each principle. The students will then arrange the pictures on the bulletin board in an attractive manner for display under the correct heading. Discussion will follow explaining why the class picked the pictures they did to represent each principle.

Picking one of three pictures, each student will write an evaluation of that picture. The evaluation should consist of a list of the good and poor elements and principles of design found in the picture, and should give reasons why they are considered good or poor.

For review of the elements and principles of design, refer to the bulletin board that has been prepared from the mounted pictorial examples used with the lectures. Have the students discuss the pictures pointing out the elements and principles of design used in each. Then see if the students can pick out the primary, secondary, and intermediate colors used in the color scheme. After thorough discussion of the bulletin board, have the students divide into two teams. Go through the examples of the elements, color terminology, and principles of design one by one. The students will take turns, individually, on each team, and the teams will alternate with each picture. Each correct answer is a point for the team. A wrong answer enables the next member on the opposite team a chance to answer the questions. This procedure will continue until a correct answer is given. After both teams have gone through the stack of examples, the team with the most points wins.)

E. Color Associations (lecture) (transparencies)
   1. Emotional appeal
      a. Black—first color recognized by man; used for mourning since sixteenth century; symbolic of evil, old age, silence; strong and sophisticated; used in decoration for small quantitites of accent
      b. Red—second color recognized by man; associated with blood and life, fire and danger; symbol of love, vigor, action, danger; bright reds are forceful and are used in small areas as accent; light values make warm background colors
      c. Yellow—symbol of power; associated with deceit, cowardice, and jealousy, as well as wisdom, gaiety, and warmth
      d. White—Symbolic of purity, innocence, faith, peace, and surrender; off-white used extensively in home decoration
      e. Blue—not identified as separate color at first; thought of as a form of black; blue rarest color in nature hence the origin of terms "true blue" and "blueblood"; symbol of happiness, hope, truth, honor, repose, and distance
      f. Green—symbol of life and vigor; associated with luck; denotes life, spring, hope, and envy; cool enough to be restful, yet warm enough to be friendly
      g. Purple—symbol of royalty; associated with the spiritual, mystery, humility, penitence, and wisdom; a dignified color used in elegant rooms
      h. Brown—designated for peasants during Middle Ages, and thus associated with humility; reminiscent of autumn, harvest, and decay; ranges from yellow to red in cast; wood used in most traditional furniture is brown
      i. Gray—somber color; associated with retirement, sadness, modesty, and indifference; may have warm or cool cast; good background color in decorating
   2. Color preferences
      a. Tans, greens, browns popular rug colors
      b. Black, blue, gray, and green popular car colors
      c. Men prefer blue; women prefer red

(Materials and procedure: After the lecture, discuss and analyze three pictures listing the emotions that are expressed through the use of a particular color or color scheme.)

F. Principles of Design Applied to Color (lecture)
   1. Balance
      a. Colors must be balanced to give feeling of rest
      b. Light, dark, and dull colors used in largest areas
      c. Intense or bright colors in smallest areas
   2. Rhythm—Use of color can make a gradual transition from one room to the other
   3. Emphasis
      a. As people enter a room they should be conscious of one color, with other colors subordinated to it
      b. Blue family adds emphasis to rich dark woods

G. Standard Color Harmonies (lecture) (transparencies)
   1. Similar or related harmonies—restful but sometimes monotonous; produced from colors that lie near each other on color wheel
      a. Monochromatic harmony—one-color harmony; several values of one hue; hues must match, but value must contrast; example: light bluish purple should not be used with a dark reddish purple
      b. Analogous harmony—combination of neighboring hues that have one hue in common
      c. Contrasting harmonies—produced by combining colors that are far apart on the color wheel; should differ in value and intensity
      d. Complementary harmony—use two colors opposite each other on the color wheel
      e. Split-complementary harmony—combine one color, such as yellow, and the colors on each side of its complement
      f. Triad harmony—combination of any three colors that form an equilateral triangle on the color wheel
      g. Accented-neutral harmony—harmony in which the largest areas of a room are neutral with small areas of bright color used for accent

(Materials and procedures: Using colored construction paper, create an example of each of the harmonies listed above and mount them. Hand in at end of class period.)

H. Guides in Planning Color Harmonies
   1. Cool background—use picture or other accessories with warm colors
   2. Figured drapery fabric as central idea for color scheme in room, and other colors keyed to those in fabric

    3. Wall and floor covering should be appropriate background colors

I. Influences on Choice of Colors (lecture)
1. Family tastes
    a. Family room should not have colors that are predominantly female or male
    b. Individual rooms offer chance for expressing individual tastes
2. Physical characteristics of room
    a. Warm colors best on wall for rooms with north or northwest exposure
    b. Cool colors for rooms with south or southeast exposure
    c. Room with high ceiling will seem more cozy and less high if ceiling is painted slightly darker than wall
    d. Room will appear shorter by painting one end wall a warm color
3. Color of furnishings already on hand
4. Effect of lighting—artificial light changes effect of color
5. Texture—colors good in homespun textures often appear too strong in smooth or glossy textures
6. Manner of living

(Materials and Procedure: For review of the unit on color and design: Bring to class actual samples or pictures of wallpaper, paint, floor covering, furniture, draperies, and accessories. During two class periods use basic information concerning elements and principles of design, including color schemes and **textures,** to decorate and furnish one room of your choice. Discuss final products.)

Housing and Home Furnishings

11th Grade

Unit Test: Color and Design

Name —————————————————————————————

Matching: Identify by letter the word in the right hand column that suggests a mood of the word in the left column.

	Mood		Line
<u>D</u>	1. Gracefulness	A.	Vertical
<u>B</u>	2. Repose	B.	Horizontal
<u>C</u>	3. Push	C.	Diagonal
<u>A</u>	4. Masculinity	D.	Curved
<u>D</u>	5. Femininity	E.	Zig-zag
<u>C</u>	6. Action		
<u>C</u>	7. Pull		
<u>A</u>	8. Dignity		
<u>E</u>	9. Movement		
<u>E</u>	10. Excitement		

Multiple Choice: Fill in the letter of the correct answer.

<u>B</u> 1. The basic element of design is
 A. texture.
 B. line.
 C. color.
 D. form.
 E. balance.

<u>D</u> 2. Lines have an effect on an observer. This effect is
 A. architectural.
 B. physiological.
 C. functional.
 D. psychological.
 E. structural.

<u>D</u> 3. Form is
 A. solid.
 B. three-dimensional.
 C. shape.
 D. all of these.
 E. none of these.

C 4. _____ is the rarest color in nature.
  A. Black
  B. Purple
  C. Blue
  D. Gray
  E. Brown

D 5. Proportion is
  A. spacing of windows in a house
  B. arranging furniture in a room.
  C. hanging pictures over a fireplace.
  D. all of these.
  E. only A and C.

B 6. Which of the following represents *poor* balance?
  A. Two chairs, one on either side of a fireplace.
  B. Five windows on one side of a door and two on the other.
  C. Combination of heavy and light furniture throughout a room.
  D. None of these.
  E. Symmetrical arrangement on either side of a central point

A 7. How does rhythm help produce beauty in design?
  A. Suggests connected movement.
  B. Provides several directions of movement.
  C. Prevents eye from following smooth line.
  D. Enables eye to jerk from one side of room to another.
  E. Creates feeling of a musical atmosphere.

D 8. Emphasis is the principle of design that creates
  A. three-dimensional effect.
  B. competing centers of interest.
  C. confusion in figured rug and floral draperies.
  D. interest on most important item.
  E. all of these.

B 9. The color light blue is classified as
  A. a hue.
  B. a value.
  C. an intensity.
  D. complementary.
  E. split-complementary.

D 10. Considerations that influence choice of color in the home are
  A. amount of light in room.
  B. furniture already in room.
  C. family members who use room.
  D. all of these.
  E. none of these.

Define the following words or phrases and give an example of each.

1. Structural design (Good line, form, texture, and color as the result of the way something made—designed to concentrate on function—like a plain, straight-backed chair.)
2. Asymmetric balance (Informal or uneven balance—an arrangement with heavier object placed nearer center than light one.)
3. Character of home (Surroundings of home—impression one is left with—relates to family members' personalities.)
4. Hue (Name of color—family name—blue, red, green, etc.)
5. Tint (Light or high values—good wall colors—sky blue, etc.)
6. Shade (Dark or low values—good rug colors—forest green, etc.)
7. Primary color (Cannot be broken down into other colors—no combination can produce primary color—red, yellow, blue)
8. Intermediate color (Mix primary color with adjacent secondary color—yellow-green, blue-green, etc.)
9. Intensity (Brightness or dullness of color—bright Kelly green or dull moss green.)
10. Warm colors (Convey feeling of warmth—seem to advance and make room appear smaller—yellow, red, orange.)

Label and define each of the following color harmony diagrams.

1. (Monochromatic)

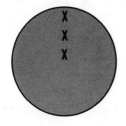

2. (Analogous)

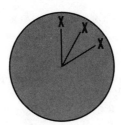

define: (several values of one hue)

define: (combination of neighboring hue with one hue in common)

3. (Complementary)   4. (Accented-Neutral)

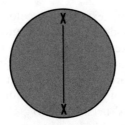   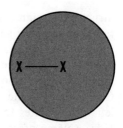

define: (2 colors opposite on color   define: (harmony in which large
wheel)   areas of room neutral with small
                                         areas of bright color for accent)

What is the name of the color chart on the blackboard? (Prang) or Munsell
Explain the difference between the two.
  (Prang—3 primary colors, red, yellow, blue)
  (Munsell—5 principal colors, red, yellow, blue, green, purple)

Choose one of the three pictures on the blackboard and evaluate it. List at
least five things about the picture that show use of color, elements, and principles of design, and explain the good and/or bad points of each of the five
things you listed. (Depends on what three pictures are used)

TEACHER-STUDENT BIBLIOGRAPHY

  Books

CRAIG, HAZEL, and OLA RUSH, *Homes With Character*. Boston: D.C. Heath ,
    1962

GREER CARLOTTA, and ELLEN GIBBS, *Your Home and You*. Boston: Allyn &
    Bacon, 1965.

LEWIS, KORA, JEAN BURNS, and ESTHER SEGNER, *Housing and Home
    Management*. (Macmillan Family Life Series) New York: Macmillan, 1969.

*PEPIS, BETTY, *Interior Decoration A to Z*. Garden City, N.Y.: Doubleday and
    Company, Inc.,

STARR, MARY CATHERINE, *Management for Better Living*. Boston: D.C.
    Heath, 1963.

Encyclopedias

The American Woman's New Encyclopedia of Home Decorating. Chicago: Book Production Industries, 1964.
The Practical Encyclopedia of Good Decorating and Home Improvement, volumes I and II. New York: Greystone Press, 1970.

*Teacher bibliography only
No star—student references

Appendix C

Sample Lessons
for Self-Improvement

I. *Contextual Framework:* The use of metaphor in poetry.
II. *Behavioral Objectives*
  A. *Terminal Objective:* (overall class goal): Given any poem, the student will be able to identify each instance of metaphor and write an explanation of the author's communication intent. (To further set the stage for this self-improvement lesson beyond the contextual framework, the teacher's terminal behavior objective is given above for this course in literature.)
  B. *Objective for the Teacher Self-Improvement Lesson:* Given Robert Frost's poem "Fire and Ice," the student will be able to identify a metaphor used by Frost and write an explanation of the author's communication intent. This explanation must agree with one of the

*This sample lesson first appeared in the January 1973 issue of *Contemporary Education*, pp.186-87.

usual suggested communication intentions proposed by experts and students. (This en-route objective is the first of a series of class examples by which the teacher wishes to induce the skills necessary to accomplish the terminal behavior. While it is only one of the en-route objectives of the program, it is sufficient for the teacher to determine his or her effectiveness in the use of a particular skill or method.)

III. *Identification of Students—Preassessment:* The objective is the first of a series of similar objectives. In order to determine which of the students already recognize metaphors, a pre-test must be given that will identify those students who already can accomplish this task. In order to maintain a valid assessment of the teaching skills being measured, these students must be eliminated from the lesson. Possibilities include sending them to the library; splitting the class through administrative devices; using aides; exchanging students with other teachers for the time of the lesson, etc.

IV. *Transmission Techniques—Strategy*

A. The attention of the class will be caught by lighting a match and then dropping it in a glass of water.

B. During the ensuing discussion a copy of the poem will be passed out, and the poem will be projected on the screen through the use of the overhead.

C. Through the use of probing questions, . . . (Since the transmission techniques and the methods the teacher chooses to use are a function of the particular skills the teacher possesses or is attempting to acquire or polish, they will vary widely; therefore, an entire transmission procedure is not included here. If, for example, the teacher were trained in the *Stanford Psychological Teaching Behaviors*, as used in micro-teaching, that model for development of skills might call A, above, the "establishing of set." B could be thought of as part of "stimulus variation." How the strategy is conceived is contingent upon the background and present skill level of the teacher.

V. *Evaluation*

The students will be asked to identify metaphors in "Fire and Ice," a poem not discussed in class, and to submit, in writing, an explanation of the author's communication intent immediately following the lesson.

The teacher anticipates that 85 percent of the class will be able to accomplish this task.

(Notice the evaluation is a direct reflection of the objective of the lesson. The teacher has submitted a class criterion level with which he or she will be satisfied. The check of the evaluation papers will tell immediately whether he or she taught up to expectations.)

SAMPLE LESSON 2: ANCIENT CLASSIFICATION SYSTEMS

The model lesson that follows is designed to overcome the problem of prior learning on the part of the student. Lessons of this type, for purposes of self-improvement, preclude the need for preassessment. In exchange for this advantage, however, teachers run the risk of disruption of the on-going program. The same structure that avoids the problem of preassessment also keeps the teachers from relating the lesson vividly to anything going on in class. For this reason, it fits best between units or topics. The entire lesson is based on an imaginary premise and is best taught in a game-like atmosphere.

Objective

After completion of a 15-minute lesson, given a series of thirty-five sentences, each of which contains an underlined word, the student will be able to classify thirty of the underlined words into one of five labeled categories.

Content of the Lesson

There are five "Ancient Classification" categories. Each has its own name, and a word with certain characteristics falls into a particular category. The only words to be classified are the ones *underlined* in the sentences below. The names of the five categories are: BRUSK, KRIF, DROTE, STRIN, and MERID.

Characteristics of BRUSK Words   A word that comes at the end of a sentence is always a BRUSK word.

Characteristics of KRIF Words   A word that begins a sentence and begins with a vowel is always a KRIF word.

Characteristics of DROTE Words   A word that does not begin or end a sentence and begins with a vowel is always a DROTE word.

Characteristics of STRIN Words   A word that begins a sentence and begins with a consonant is always a STRIN word.

Characteristics of MERID Words   A word that does not begin or end a sentence and begins with a consonant is always a MERID word.

Three sample test items are also included.

Sample Test Items

Directions: In each sentence one word is underlined. Classify the underlined word into one of five categories.

(1) BRUSK
(2) DROTE
(3) MERID
(4) KRIF
(5) STRIN

Mark the number of your choice for each item on the separate answer sheet.

1. <u>Madrigal</u> music is from the seventeenth century.

Answer: 5—STRIN The word starts a sentence and its first letter is a consonant.

2. Jim is my <u>friend</u>.

Answer: 1—BRUSK. The word is at the end of the sentence.

3. It is too <u>early</u> in the morning.

Answer: 2—DROTE. The word does not begin or end a sentence and its first letter is a vowel.

The entire test to be administered to the students follows. This test has been field-tested and should take *precisely this form*. There are only five items on each page and the order of the categories has been randomly changed each time so that the student must rethink the categories on each page. There are approximately the same number from each category in each set of answers, and the categories have been randomly arranged throughout the test by the use of a table of random numbers.

TEST
ANCIENT CLASSIFICATION SYSTEMS

DIRECTIONS: Each of the following 7 pages contains 5 sentences. In each sentence a single word is underlined. For each sentence classify the underlined word into one of the following categories:

1. BRUSK
2. DROTE
3. MERID
4. KRIF
5. STRIN

After you select your answer, mark the number of your choice for that item in the appropriate place on the separate answer sheet. You will have 10 minutes to complete this test.

NOTE: ONCE YOU HAVE COMPLETED A PAGE AND TURNED TO THE NEXT ONE, YOU ARE NOT TO TURN BACK. The above categories will be repeated for you on each page. Be careful, though, because they will be given in a different order each time.

DO NOT MAKE ANY MARKS ON YOUR ANSWER SHEET EXCEPT YOUR ANSWER. DO NOT MAKE ANY MARKS ON THIS TEST.

DO NOT TURN THIS PAGE UNTIL YOU ARE TOLD TO DO SO.

CLASSIFY THE UNDERLINED WORD IN EACH SENTENCE INTO ONE OF THE
FOLLOWING CATEGORIES:

1. KRIF
2. BRUSK
3. DROTE
4. STRIN
5. MERID

1. The hot lunch program is <u>in</u> operation.
2. <u>Direct</u> the marchers down 5th Avenue.
3. Students are encouraged to carry out a special <u>project</u>.
4. <u>Instead</u> of being frightened, she found herself exhilarated.
5. They painted different amounts of <u>area</u>.

GO ON TO THE NEXT PAGE

CLASSIFY THE UNDERLINED WORD IN EACH SENTENCE INTO ONE OF THE FOLLOWING CATEGORIES:

1. STRIN
2. DROTE
3. BRUSK
4. MERID
5. KRIF

6. <u>Music</u> has charms.
7. The <u>president</u> of the club is in charge of the meeting.
8. The laboratory has 30 <u>stations</u>.
9. He is <u>under</u> the bleachers.
10. Tickets for the <u>game</u> cost $1.

GO ON TO THE NEXT PAGE

CLASSIFY THE UNDERLINED WORD IN EACH SENTENCE INTO ONE OF THE FOLLOWING CATEGORIES:

1. DROTE
2. STRIN
3. KRIF
4. MERID
5. BRUSK

11. Although he graduated from college, he still likes <u>to</u> read comics.
12. <u>If</u> we go now we can see the entire show.
13. <u>Usually</u> he arrives at work at 8:10 a.m.
14. <u>Chapter 7</u> in the book is the most interesting.
15. The director of the band <u>wears</u> a wig.

GO ON TO THE NEXT PAGE

329

CLASSIFY THE UNDERLINED WORD IN EACH SENTENCE INTO ONE OF THE FOLLOWING CATEGORIES:

1. BRUSK
2. KRIF
3. DROTE
4. MERID
5. STRIN

16. Anyone caught cheating will be <u>asked</u> to leave.
17. Real <u>estate</u> taxes are going up.
18. Which is <u>bigger</u>, the volcano or the mountain?
19. University High School is a laboratory <u>school</u>.
20. <u>Unless</u> we hear from you soon, we will give the position to someone else.

GO ON TO THE NEXT PAGE

CLASSIFY THE UNDERLINED WORD IN EACH SENTENCE INTO ONE OF THE FOLLOWING CATEGORIES:

1. KRIF
2. MERID
3. STRIN
4. DROTE
5. BRUSK

21. <u>Members</u> of the club get discount rates at the movies.
22. There <u>has</u> been very little snow this winter.
23. <u>Sponsors</u> of the Little League teams are giving a dance.
24. <u>Five</u> of the group will dine early.
25. <u>Enough</u> people are already getting welfare checks.

GO ON TO THE NEXT PAGE

CLASSIFY THE UNDERLINED WORD IN EACH SENTENCE INTO ONE OF THE FOLLOWING CATEGORIES:

1. KRIF
2. BRUSK
3. MERID
4. DROTE
5. STRIN

26. Five people received awards for <u>their</u> work.
27. He is an <u>unwilling</u> participant.
28. Some high school graduates do not go to <u>college</u>.
29. There is a utility tax in Normal, <u>Illinois</u>.
30. The development of the new program is <u>completed</u>.

GO ON TO THE NEXT PAGE

CLASSIFY THE UNDERLINED WORD IN EACH SENTENCE INTO ONE OF THE
FOLLOWING CATEGORIES:

1. MERID
2. STRIN
3. DROTE
4. KRIF
5. BRUSK

31. There is no <u>other</u> way.
32. <u>Only</u> the basketball players can ride the bus.
33. <u>Varsity</u> players will have their banquet next week.
34. There will be an <u>angry</u> debate over the new dress code.
35. Another reason that insurance <u>costs</u> more is the rising crime rate.

CLOSE THE TEST BOOKLET

Answer Key

1. 3	10. 4	19. 1	28. 2
2. 4	11. 4	20. 2	29. 2
3. 2	12. 3	21. 3	30. 2
4. 1	13. 3	22. 2	31. 3
5. 2	14. 2	23. 3	32. 4
6. 1	15. 4	24. 3	33. 2
7. 4	16. 3	25. 1	34. 3
8. 3	17. 3	26. 3	35. 1
9. 2	18. 4	27. 4	

Class Criterion Levels

The teacher must professionally assess his or her class and the difficulty of the tasks of this lesson. When the test is administered to individuals who have not received instruction of any kind on the material, the scores reflect a chance distribution.

In field tests with 428 high school students using 42 instructors, all teacher trainees, the overall mean score was 28.4, the standard deviation was 8.8, and the Kuder-Richardson reliability (formula 20) was .93. The distribution was highly skewed to the left, with 50 percent of the students marking no more than one answer incorrectly. This indicates that although a large proportion of students learned the concepts in their entirety, there was considerable variability in the amount of learning that occurred, and this learning was able to be reliably measured. The test would seem to be an acceptable measure for criterion-referenced instruction.

Translating into an easier yardstick, it would appear that if the class to which the lesson is taught contains an average group of tenth-grade students, a good lesson will result in 75 to 80 percent the youngsters reaching minimum criterion level described in the objective.

Index